Race, Culture and Psychothe

D0143231

Race, Culture and Psychotherapy provides a thorough critical examination of contemporary multiculturalism and culturalism, including discussion of the full range of issues, debates and controversies that are emerging in the field of multicultural psychotherapy.

Beginning with a general critique of race, culture and ethnicity, the book explores issues such as the notion of interiority and exteriority in psychotherapy, racism in the clinical room, race and countertransference conflicts, spirituality and traditional healing issues. Contributors from the United States, Britain and Canada draw on their professional experience to provide comprehensive and balanced coverage of the following subjects:

* Critical perspectives in race and culture in psychotherapy
* Governing race in the transference
* Racism, ethnicity and countertransference
* Intersecting gender, race, class and sexuality
* Spirituality, cultural healing and psychotherapy
* Future directions

Race, Culture and Psychotherapy will be of interest not only to practising psychotherapists, but also to students and researchers in the field of mental health and anyone interested in gaining a better understanding of psychotherapy in a multicultural society.

Roy Moodley, Ph.D, is Associate Professor of Counselling Psychology at the Ontario Institute for Studies in Education, University of Toronto, Canada.

Stephen Palmer, Ph.D, is Honorary Professor of Psychology at City University, London and Director of the Centre for Stress Management, London, UK.

Contributors: Neil Altman, Dinesh Bhugra, Kamaldeep Bhui, John Chambers Christopher, Farhad Dalal, Nathan Field, Jacquelyn Gardner, Beverly Greene, Dorothy Evans Holmes, Jerald Kay, Narendra Keval, Deborah Y. Liggan, Ruth M. Lijtmaer, Judith Mishne, Roy Moodley, Stephen Palmer, Shumona Ray, Adina J. Smith, Ursula Streit, Richard Tan, Nadine M. Tang, Rinaldo Walcott, Carmen Braun Williams, Kris Y. Yi.

Race, Culture and Psychotherapy

Critical perspectives in multicultural practice

Edited by Roy Moodley & Stephen Palmer

Routledge
Taylor & Francis Group

LONDON AND NEW YORK

First published 2006 by Routledge
27 Church Road, Hove, East Sussex, BN3 2FA

Simultaneously published in the USA and Canada
by Routledge
270 Madison Avenue, New York, NY 10016

Routledge is an imprint of the Taylor & Francis Group

Typeset in Times by Garfield Morgan, Rhayader, Powys, UK
Printed and bound in Great Britain by MPG Books Ltd, Bodmin, Cornwall
Paperback cover design by Sandra Heath

British Library Cataloguing in Publication Data
A catalogue record for this book is available from the British Library

Library of Congress Cataloging in Publication Data
Race, culture and psychotherapy : critical perspectives in multicultural
practice / edited by Roy Moodley & Stephen Palmer.
        p. cm.
    Includes bibliographical references and index.
    ISBN 1-58391-849-3 (hbk) – ISBN 1-58391-850-7 (pbk) 1. Psychotherapy–
Cross-cultural studies. 2. Psychoanalysis–Cross-cultural studies.
3. Psychiatry, Transcultural. I. Moodley, Roy. II. Palmer, Stephen.
    RC455.4.E8R33 2006
    616.89'14–dc22
                                                                2005017762

ISBN10: 1-58391-849-3 hbk
ISBN10: 1-58391-850-7 pbk

ISBN13: 9-78-1-58391-849-3 hbk
ISBN13: 9-78-1-58391-850-7 pbk

Dedications

Dr. William (Bill) Hall, executive member of the British Association for Counselling (BAC) in the 1980s, and a pioneer of the RACE Group which used to be a subdivision of the now renamed British Association for Counselling and Psychotherapy (BACP). He was also instrumental in setting up the Association of Black Counsellors in the UK, and was its first chair.

Josna Pankhania, who in 1983 held the first Black Caucus meeting with the BAC leadership to put race issues on the agenda, leading to the setting up of the RACE group. She is now in Australia working as a counsellor and academic.

Shukla Dhingra, counsellor and therapist at Nottingham Trent University and one of the pioneers of the RACE Group.

In memory of RACE (Race Awareness in Counselling Education; subdivision of BACP; started in 1983, to be terminated soon), and all its members over 21 years.

Contents

Contributors

The Editors

Roy Moodley, Ph.D, is Associate Professor of Counselling Psychology at the Ontario Institute for Studies in Education at the University of Toronto. Research and publication interests include traditional and cultural healing; multicultural and diversity counselling; race, culture, and ethnicity in psychotherapy; and masculinities. Roy co-edited *Transforming Managers: Gendering Change in the Public Sector* (UCL Press/ Taylor and Francis, 1999); *Carl Rogers Counsels a Black Client: Race and Culture in Person-Centred Counselling* (PCCS Books, 2004); and *Integrating Traditional Healing Practices into Counseling and Psychotherapy* (Sage, 2005).

Stephen Palmer, Ph.D, is Honorary Professor of Psychology at City University, London, and Director of the Centre for Stress Management, London, UK. He supervises DPsych students at City University on a number of subjects. He is an award-winning counselling psychologist and psychotherapist. He has written or edited over twenty-five books including *Counselling in a Multicultural Society* (with P. Laungani; Sage, 1999), and *Multicultural Counselling: A Reader* (Sage, 2002). He is Honorary President of the Association for Coaching, and Honorary Vice President of both the Institute of Health Promotion and Education, and the International Stress Management Association (UK). In 2005 he was Chair of the British Psychological Society Special Group in Coaching Psychology. He is editor of the *International Journal of Health Promotion and Education* and *The Rational Emotive Behaviour Therapist*.

The Contributors

Neil Altman, Ph.D, is Associate Clinical Professor in the Postdoctoral Program in Psychotherapy and Psychoanalysis at New York University. He is co-editor of *Psychoanalytic Dialogues: A Journal of Relational*

Perspectives. He is author of *The Analyst in the Inner City: Race, Class, and Culture through a Psychoanalytic Lens* and co-author of *Relational Child Psychotherapy.*

Dinesh Bhugra, Ph.D, is Senior Lecturer, Honorary Consultant and Reader in Cultural Psychiatry at the Institute of Psychiatry, London, UK. He was appointed to the Chair of Mental Health and Cultural Diversity in 2002 and is Dean of the Royal College of Psychiatrists. Research and publication interests include psychosexual medicine, cross-cultural psychiatry, schizophrenia, pathways into psychiatric care, deliberate self-harm and primary care.

Kamaldeep Bhui is Professor of Cultural Psychiatry and Epidemiology, at Barts and the London School of Medicine, University of London and Consultant Psychiatrist at East London and City Mental Health Trust. He is Director of the MSc Transcultural Mental Healthcare programme at Queen Mary College, University of London, Associate Member of the British Association of Psychotherapists, Chair of the Transcultural Special Interest Group of the Royal College of Psychiatrists, and has researched and written extensively on cultural and mental health.

John Chambers Christopher, Ph.D, is a professor of counselling at Montana State University and a senior staff psychologist at MSU's Counseling Center. He has also taught at the University of Guam. He is the recipient of the Sigmund Koch Early Career Award from the APA's Society of Theoretical and Philosophical Psychology.

Farhad Dalal, Ph.D, is a supervisor and training group analyst for the Institute of Group Analysis, London, UK. He is an associate fellow at the University of Hertfordshire's Business School. He works with organizations and also has a supervision and psychotherapy practice in London and Devon. Publications include the books *Taking the Group Seriously* (Jessica Kingsley Publishers, 1998) and *Race, Colour and the Processes of Racialization: New Perspectives from Group Analysis, Psychoanalysis and Sociology* (Brunner-Routledge, 2002).

Nathan Field trained as a Jungian analyst with the British Association of Psychotherapists in the 1960s. After forty years in private practice, he retired in 2002. In 2004 he founded The Scribble Society (www. scribblesociety.com) for psychotherapists who aspire to write.

Jacquelyn Gardner, Ph.D, is a psychoanalyst in private practice in San Francisco, California. She has been on the faculty of the University of San Francisco and an instructor at the Institute for Psychoanalytic Psychotherapy Studies, San Francisco, California.

Beverly Greene, Ph.D, is a professor of psychology at St. John's University, New York, a certified clinical psychologist in independent practice in New York City and a fellow of the American Psychological Association, six of its divisions and the Academy of Clinical Psychology. She is a Diplomate in Clinical Psychology from the American Board of Professional Psychology and the author of over seventy-five professional publications.

Dorothy Evans Holmes, Ph.D, ABPP (Clinical Psychology), is a professor and Director of the Doctor of Psychology Program in Clinical Psychology at the George Washington University, Washington, DC. She is also a training and supervising analyst in the Baltimore-Washington Institute for Psychoanalysis.

Jerald Kay, MD, is Professor and Chair, Department of Psychiatry, Wright State University School of Medicine, Dayton, Ohio. He is the Founding Editor of the *Journal of Psychotherapy Practice and Research* and Associate Editor of the *American Journal of Psychotherapy*.

Narendra Keval, M. Clin. Psychol. and T.Q.A.P., is a consultant clinical psychologist and adult psychotherapist and he both trained and worked at the Tavistock Clinic. Currently, he is responsible for the provision of psychoanalytic psychotherapy in an outpatient clinic as part of Hertfordshire Partnership NHS Trust and also teaches psychotherapy at the University of Hertfordshire and the Tavistock Clinic. He runs a private practice and has research and publications in the field of race, culture and psychotherapy.

Deborah Y. Liggan, MD, is a freelance medical writer and journalist who analyses current multicultural interpretations of the literature. She graduated from Texas A & M University School of Medicine and received a Master's degree in management from Webster University (St Louis, MO).

Ruth M. Lijtmaer, Ph.D, is Senior Supervisor and Faculty at the Contemporary Center for Applied Psychoanalytic Studies, Fairleigh Dickinson University, New Jersey. She runs a private practice. Her latest publications are: 'Countertransference and Ethnicity', *New Jersey Psychologist*, 53, 3: 30–32 (2004); 'The Place of Erotic Transference and Countertransference in Clinical Practice', *Journal of the American Academy of Psychoanalysis and Dynamic Psychiatry*, 32, 3: 483–498 (2004).

Judith Mishne, Ph.D, is a full professor at New York University School of Social Work. Her primary foci in her many articles, books, and professional presentations are ethics and multiculturalism, and clinical work with children, adolescents and parents. She has been the honoured recipient of major awards for her contributions to the profession.

Shumona Ray, MA, is a high school teacher. She is currently pursuing her doctoral degree in education, with a particular focus on visible minority women in teaching and issues of equity and leadership in schools, at the Ontario Institute for Studies in Education at the University of Toronto. Her interests include anti-racist education, feminism/spirituality and anti-colonial pedagogy.

Adina J. Smith, Ph.D, is an assistant professor in the Department of Health and Human Development at Montana State University. She teaches in the counselling programme and is the Director of the counselling training clinic for students in that programme. Dr Smith has extensive experience conducting community outreach programmes with ethnically diverse and rural populations.

Ursula Streit, Ph.D, is Associate Professor in the Department of Psychiatry, University of Montreal. She trained in ethnology (DPhil, University of Zurich, Switzerland) and psychoanalysis (member of the Canadian and the International Psychoanalytic Society). She has carried out clinical work with migrant patients using Nathan's ethnopsychoanalytic therapy and, more recently, interpersonal psychotherapy for depression. She is involved in residents' training in transcultural psychiatry.

Richard Tan, MA, MCPP, is a psychoanalytic psychotherapist in private practice, having previously worked in the public sector. Currently, he also teaches for various psychotherapy courses in the UK, and is part-time seminar leader on the MSc in Psychodynamic Counselling programme at Birkbeck College, London University.

Nadine M. Tang is a social worker in private practice in Berkeley, California. She is an assistant clinical professor in the clinical science programme at the University of California, Berkeley, and an instructor at the Ann Martin Center in Oakland, California. She has written a number of papers on Chinese child-rearing practices, and dealing with differences in the psychotherapy setting.

Rinaldo Walcott, Ph.D, is an associate professor and Canada Research Chair of Social Justice and Cultural Studies at the Ontario Institute for Studies in Education at the University of Toronto. He is the author of *Black Like Who?: Writing Black Canada*. He is also the editor of *Rude: Contemporary Black Canadian Cultural Criticism*.

Carmen Braun Williams, Ph.D, is Assistant Vice President for Diversity at the University of Colorado. She is also an associate professor in counselling psychology, former associate dean, and a licensed clinical psychologist. Her research interest is cultural competence in psycho-therapy and in higher education. Dr Williams received her doctorate in clinical psychology in 1980 from the Pennsylvania State University.

Kris Y. Yi, Ph.D, is a practising psychologist and psychoanalyst in Los Angeles and Claremont. She is a member and co-chair of the Committee on Cultural Diversity at the Institute of Contemporary Psychoanalysis (ICP).

Foreword

Much has been written recently about problems within mainstream psychiatry arising from issues of race and culture – or to use the current jargon, ethnicity and diversity. These hover around the over-representation of black and other minority ethnic communities among people who are compulsorily detained in institutes, diagnosed as 'schizophrenic', given excessive doses of medication and so on. But in terms of numbers, people caught in the psychiatric traps are very small compared to those with mental health problems who seek help from sources other than the formally 'psychiatric' ones. And this is where psychotherapy and counseling come in.

Service users often refer to psychotherapy and counseling as 'talking therapies'. As such one may think that communication through spoken language is an essential ingredient of psychotherapy. In my experience this is not always the case. People communicate with one another in a variety of ways and, even when spoken language appears to be the main vehicle of communication, unspoken ways – so-called 'body-language' is just one of these – may be more important in the total process (of communication). Another assumption that is common is that the effectiveness of psychotherapy (or counseling) depends on the type of training or model of 'mind' that the therapist is committed to. I would contest this too. Many people who gain from seeing a psychotherapist remember the person rather than his or her model or where they trained. So psychotherapy in common sense terms is a way of helping people with (mental health) problems that is dependent on communication and relationships. The question then arises as to who could gain from psychotherapy and to what extent is it applicable in a multicultural society.

It is sometimes claimed that since psychotherapy developed in a Western cultural tradition, it is not appropriate for people from 'other' cultures. I believe that this viewpoint misses two important points. First, 'culture' is not a sort of closed system of traditional beliefs and practices that people carry around with them and pass on to their children. It is more like a dynamic and changing system of values and worldviews that people live by and create and re-create continuously – the basis on which we define our identities and negotiate our lives. So a multicultural society is one with a diversity of cultural forms derived from a variety of sources, East and West, North and South. There is no reason why a therapy derived from one source cannot be adapted or expanded to be applicable to people whose main cultural background may come from elsewhere. And suiting the therapy to the individual is a part of the expertise that a therapist should possess.

Second, human beings everywhere are creatures who cooperate to form societies and, contrary to the message of the 'selfish gene', whatever their ethnic background people have always helped others who they see as being 'like us'. Barriers to cooperation and helping each other only arise when these others are regarded as 'the other' and not 'like us' – for example because of racist misconceptions. So, in my view, it is absurd to think that just because (say) therapists in the Indian or African traditions do not adhere to a system called 'psychotherapy', interpersonal communication is not a vehicle for helping people whose ancestors came from India or Africa. In a modern Western country where psychotherapy is a service that is available for people with mental health problems, people from all cultural and ethnic backgrounds have a right to access such therapies in a form that is appropriate for them. Psychotherapy, or indeed any form of therapy that is available, should be appropriate for everyone – that is, everyone who needs it.

So when we come to consider the nature of psychotherapy and its usefulness in a multicultural society several issues come to mind. Although there have been many books and articles about these issues and the way therapists should aim to address them, some books tend to be confusing because they try to promote a particular 'brand' designated by a particular name. The editors of this book are very aware of this fact and therefore have tried to bring together information and views that could be of practical use in the field by tapping into the experience of professionals involved in delivering mental health services. The topics that are dealt with in this book cover a very wide field, including ones that are often missed out in books on psychotherapy – such as spirituality, the interpretation of subjective distress, racial conflict and religious healing – all considered in relation to psychotherapy. Further, some of the chapters address the interplay between class, gender, sexuality and race. But what is particularly important is that the views of these professionals are set in the context of a critical appraisal of the meaning of concepts like 'race' and 'culture' in the field of psychotherapy, the impact of multiculturalism on the clinical scene and the way that 'race' plays out within relationships formed during therapeutic encounters.

This is a welcome addition to the literature on psychotherapy and a book that should be of value not just to practising psychotherapists, but also to researchers in the field of mental health and indeed anyone interested in understanding better the nature of 'talking therapies' in a multicultural society.

Suman Fernando
Hon. Senior Lecturer in Mental Health
European Centre for the Study of Migration and Social Care (MASC)
University of Kent
Visiting Professor in the Department of Applied Social Sciences
London Metropolitan University

Acknowledgements

We offer our sincerest thanks and appreciation to all the contributors in this book for sharing their knowledge, expertise and clinical experiences. We would also like to thank our close friends and colleagues in Canada, the United Kingdom and the United States who in many different ways have contributed to making this work possible. In particular we wish to thank, Shukla Dhingra, Suman Fernando, Jim Fitzgerald, Beverly Greene, Bill Hall, Sharon Mier, Rinaldo Walcott, and Carmen Braun Williams.

We would like to acknowledge the help and support of, and offer our sincere thanks to, Joanne Forshaw and Claire Lipscomb of Routledge, Dawn Harris of Psychology Press, and Sue Dickinson, the copy-editor, for their tremendous help and support. The people in our lives who were patient and understanding during the editing of this book: Roisin, Maya, Tara, Zina, Daniel, Anissa Talahite and Maggie Palmer.

Introduction

Roy Moodley and Stephen Palmer

Psychotherapy and counselling have been growing at an enormous rate in the last two decades. In the 1990s, we saw a significant proliferation of counselling and psychotherapy articles, books and training courses all purporting to address the mental health concerns of culturally diverse clients and patients. Amongst these developments issues of race, culture and ethnicity are being addressed in various ways; sometimes through the popular but problematic concept of multicultural counselling and psychotherapy,[1] and at other times through the exploration of race and culture in therapy. Within this pantheon of multicultural therapies are many nomenclatures, such as: cross-cultural counselling and psychotherapy (Marsella and Pedersen, 1981); 'ethnopsychiatrie' (Devereux, 1983) and 'ethnopsychotherapie' (Nathan, 1985); existentialism in therapy (Vontress, 1985); cross-cultural counselling (Pedersen, 1985); transcultural psychiatry (Cox, 1986); transcultural counselling (d'Ardenne and Mahtani, 1989); new cross-cultural psychiatry (Littlewood, 1990); multicultural counselling (Pedersen, 1991); intercultural psychotherapy (Kareem and Littlewood, 1992); multicultural counselling (Ivey *et al.*, 1993; Pope-Davis and Coleman, 1997; Palmer and Laungani, 1999; Palmer, 2002); and multicultural psychotherapy (Rameriz, 1999).

While some practitioners focused on 'race' as a major construct, for example Afrocentric (Hall, 1995), black feminist (Pankhania, 1996), race and culture (Lago and Thompson, 1996), race and culture in person-centred counselling (Moodley *et al.*, 2004), other practitioners, such as Atkinson, Morten and Sue (1993), Carter (1995), Cross (1971, 1978), Cross, Parham and Helms (1991), Helms (1990), Ponterotto (1988) and Sabnani *et al.* (1991), have extended the discussion to include racial identity as a variable in counselling and psychotherapy.

These texts and the few journal articles which make their appearance sporadically appear to repeat some very familiar themes, viz. race and racism, culture and psychopathology, and the ethnocentric and individualistic process of contemporary psychotherapy. Furthermore, Ahmad (1993) suggests that some of the available literature in psychotherapy, psychoanalysis and psychiatry has been heavily skewed, espousing a naive empiricism and cultural reductionism that reflects the interests of the health professionals rather than the priorities of ethnic minority patients. It also seems fairly evident that most psychoanalytic literature appears to be concerned almost exclusively with white subjects, and racial difference was only an intermittent and peripheral focus of attention (Walton, 1995, p. 780). While this position reflects negatively on the profession, it may also indicate the institutional culture and tradition of the psychotherapy and psychoanalysis journals, the dearth of black editors or the general lack of papers on racial and cultural issues (Fernando, 1988).

This book, therefore, evolved out of a need to address some of these issues; to bring together some of the writers, researchers and practitioners who have published in the psychotherapy journals but particularly those who critically analyze issues of race, culture and psychotherapy. In this book, although we felt that it was not productive to reproduce 'not that again' or 'more of the same' arguments and commentaries of the critique on conventional psychotherapy, we nevertheless sought to place early in the text a few chapters which address the same issues but from a different angle. For example, we begin the book with a critique of race, culture and multiculture, followed closely by a thorough examination of contemporary multiculturalism and culturalism. But the book primarily focuses on issues such as racism in the clinical room, race and countertransference conflicts, spirituality and traditional healing issues, and issues of class, gender and sexual orientations.

HOW THE BOOK IS ORGANIZED

The book is divided into six parts.

Part A: Critical perspectives in race and culture in psychotherapy

We believed that it was critical to undertake a deconstruction of race, culture and ethnicity; critique the process of multicultural psychotherapy; and provide readers with a review of psychotherapy with black and ethnic minority patients or clients. We begin with: Chapter 1: Race, culture and other multiple constructions: an absent presence in psychotherapy, by ourselves (Roy Moodley and Stephen Palmer), in which we explore the social, cultural and political constructions of 'race', ethnicity and multiculture in the context of psychotherapy. Since these concepts have come to acquire a wide variety of meanings that allow for a flexible, fluid and multiple understanding of patients, it often creates tensions in the therapeutic encounter. Rather than explore the tensions, this chapter attempts to deconstruct in detail each of the social categories – race, ethnicity, culture and multiculture. This exploration is followed in Chapter 2: Multiculturally crazy: diagnosis in Black, in which Rinaldo Walcott critically examines the whole concept of multiculturalism and its impact in counselling and psychotherapy. Rinaldo explores the notion of interiority and exteriority of the subject through Fanon's *Black Skin White Masks* (1963) and *The Wretched of the Earth* (1967). In Chapter 3: Culturalism in multicultural psychotherapy, Farhad Dalal explores how the pursuit and obsession of 'culture' as an exclusive focus in psychotherapy becomes hegemonic. Finally, in Part A, Chapter 4: Psychotherapy across the cultural divide, Dinesh Bhugra and Kamaldeep Bhui explore the cultural divide, and suggest that the key problems in the field are to do with a lack of awareness of cultural nuances but there is a bigger problem where the therapists choose to ignore culturally sensitive and culturally developed tools of psychotherapeutic intervention and assume that their own models are readily applicable to other communities.

Part B: Governing race in the transference

In Chapter 5: Racial transference reactions in psychoanalytic treatment: an update, Dorothy Evans Holmes revisits some of the ideas and vignettes that she wrote about in a seminal paper ten years ago. Here she explores the role of race in elucidating transference manifestations as she did in her previous work. Vignettes and clinical narratives are used to illustrate the point that race can be a useful vehicle for the expression and elaboration of transference of defence, of drive derivative and of object ties. In Chapter 6: Transference and race: an intersubjective conceptualization, Kris Y. Yi argues that race-based transference in the psychoanalytic literature has been often described either as a manifestation of intrapsychic conflicts or a projection of unwanted mental content onto the racial other. These views, although helpful in some situations, exclude other possible meanings of interracial transference. Kris describes an approach based on contemporary intersubjective theories in which race-related transference is seen as one aspect of a person's ongoing construction of experience and understanding of the unique meaning of race. Kris explores the role of race and culture in the development of transference and argues that the psychotherapist needs to be aware of *culture embeddedness* in her therapeutic endeavors.

In Chapter 7: Interpretation of race in the transference: perspectives of similarity and difference in the patient/therapist dyad, Nadine M. Tang and Jacquelyn Gardner present us with their ideas about racial and cultural stereotypes in psychoanalytic psychotherapy with patients or clients from the majority culture and with those from minority backgrounds. Nadine and Jacquelyn indicate that there is some overlap in the themes of transferences to them as members of different racial minorities. They argue that for African-American therapists, projections are more often based on racial stereotypes, whereas for the Chinese-American therapist, projections are based on cultural assumptions and the principle of paying careful attention to the manifestations of racial and cultural stereotyping, by which so much can be learned about the patient's or client's inner life, to the benefit of the therapeutic work. In Chapter 8: Race in the room: issues in the dynamic psychotherapy of African-Americans by Deborah Y. Liggan and Jerald Kay, they offer in a 'narrative of race' an integrated model of psychological stress. Deborah and Jerald argue that African-American patients or clients can receive effective therapy from any culturally oriented therapist who facilitates the resolution of racial conflict. From this foundation, they propose a dynamic model in which the therapist enters the experience of the African-American patient or client and establishes fixed points of reference for the proper detection of transference/countertransference issues.

Part C: Racism, ethnicity and countertransference

In Chapter 9: Racism and similarity: paranoid-schizoid structures revisited, Richard Tan examines the importance of exploring and interpreting in the transference the unconscious dynamics of racism as present in psychothera-peutic work; in particular, the primitive defences employed against the unfolding of racist feelings when therapist and patient or client are from different racial groupings. In Chapter 10: Black, white, Hispanic and both: issues in biracial identity and its effects in the transference-countertrans-ference, Ruth M. Lijtmaer explores the idea that the more dissimilar the respective world views of the therapist–patient or client dyad, the more the work must be undertaken as a joint search for understanding and meaning. Confronted with a patient or client of different ethnic background, the therapist is compelled to look at assumptions and fantasies about the other and not rely on the analyst's own ethnicity as the primary source of identity. These ideas are examined through the exploration of a clinical case study of a Chinese patient with a Latino therapist. In Chapter 11: Black and White thinking: a psychoanalyst reconsiders race, Neil Altman begins with an analysis of race as a social construction and then follows the argument that, at a deep structural level, race and racism are organized by the same rational–irrational polarity of Enlightenment philosophy that informs psychoanalytic structural theory. In Chapter 12: Understanding unbearable anxieties: the retreat into racism, Narendra Keval explores how some patients retreat into racist thinking – as part of a pathological organization of the mind – in order to put the brakes on psychic growth and development.

Part D: Intersecting gender, race, class and sexuality

In Chapter 13: African-American lesbians and gay men in psychodynamic psychotherapies?, Beverly Greene attempts to answer the following questions: Does the social privilege or disadvantage of one identity override the other? What do individuals do psychologically to manage the demands that they declare a loyalty of sorts to one or another identity? How can we better understand the complex nature of multiple identities in this population with our current theoretical paradigms? Are psychodynamic paradigms useful in work with lesbians and gay men, people of color or both? In Chapter 14: Multiple stigmas in psychotherapy with African-American women: afrocentric, feminist, and womanist perspectives, Carmen Braun Williams describes three multicultural therapy models – Afrocentric, feminist, and womanist – and their application to psychotherapy with African-American women dealing with multiple social stigmas. In Chapter 15: Success neurosis: what race and social class have to do with it, Dorothy Evans Holmes explores success neurosis, social class and race, and the complex ways in which race and social class have real and intrapsychic impact on the establishment and cessation of success neurosis.

Part E: Spirituality, cultural healing and psychotherapy

In Chapter 16: Healing and exorcism in psychoanalytic practice by Nathan Field, Nathan explores the process of traditional healing and psychotherapy. He contends that the shaman, in reclaiming the lost soul, must at the same time do battle with the devils that hold it captive. A psychotherapist must be capable of confrontation with these devils when the occasion arises. He argues that the whole therapeutic enterprise is meaningful only to the degree that a truly human connection has been established. Judith Mishne in Chapter 17: Cultural identity and spirituality in psychotherapy discusses the critical relationship of Jewishness, spirituality and trauma. In her discussion, Judith considers the relationship between religious and personal identity, illustrating her study with a case vignette of four years of intensive psychoanalytic psychotherapy with a Holocaust survivor. In Chapter 18: Feminist spirituality, Mother Kali and cultural healing, Shumona Ray and Roy Moodley discuss the worship of the Mother Goddess and rise of feminist spirituality. Through the exploration and study of Mother Kali, the demon goddess of India, they attempt to show the potential for the feminine in the therapeutic process.

Part F: Future directions

In Chapter 19: A pluritheoretical approach: Tobie Nathan's ethnopsychoanalytic therapy, Ursula Streit discusses the work of Tobie Nathan, one of the founders of the Ethnopsychiatric approach. Tobie Nathan's recent synthesis of fifteen years of clinical work with migrant patients is presented and discussed. His clinical approach represents a unique attempt to integrate therapeutic techniques used in non-Western cultures and psychodynamic therapy by introducing three main parameters: (i) the patient's or client's mother tongue; (ii) 'traditional' etiologic theories (explanatory models) specific to the patient's culture of origin; and (iii) a group setting with a multicultural group of therapists. In Chapter 20: Cultural representations and interpretations of 'subjective distress' in ethnic minority patients or clients, Roy Moodley argues that in ascribing universal meanings of distress, a therapist may neglect the network of meanings that an illness has for a particular sufferer in a particular culture. Therapists who restrict their search to the multi(ple) cultural therapies and the variables of race and ethnicity may find themselves being limited in their repertoire of interpretations of an individual's illness. And, finally, in Chapter 21: A hermeneutic approach to culture and psychotherapy, John Chambers Christopher and Adina J. Smith explore the idea of thinking interpretively about cultural meanings and discerning their specific manifestations. John and Adina suggest that through this approach psychotherapists can be effective with clients from different cultural backgrounds and also better recognize how the dominant Western cultural outlook – individualism – influences psychotherapy theory, research, and practice.

Note

1 Multicultural therapy is problematic for a number of reasons: it excludes white people from its process (Sashidharan, 1986); it focuses exclusively on racial groups thus essentialising and reifying the category of race; it also excludes the other aspects of identity, viz. gender, sexual orientations, class, disability, and religion.

References

Ahmad, W. I. U. (1993) Making Black People Sick: 'Race', Ideology and Health Research, in W. I. U. Ahmad (ed.), *'Race' and Health in Contemporary Britain*. Buckingham: Open University Press.

Atkinson, D. R., Morten, G. and Sue, D. W. (eds) (1993) *Counseling American Minorities: A Cross-Cultural Perspective*, 4th edn., Dubuque, IA: Brown & Benchmark.

Carter, R. T. (1995) *The Influence of RACE and Racial Identity in Psychotherapy*. New York: John Wiley and Sons.

Cox, J. L. (ed.) (1986) *Transcultural Psychiatry*. London: Croom Helm.

Cross, W. E. Jr. (1971) The Negro-to-Black Conversion Experience: Towards a Psychology of Black Liberation, *Black World* 20: 13–27.

Cross, W. E. Jr. (1978) The Thomas and Cross Models of Psychological Nigrescence: A Review, *Journal of Black Psychology* 5(1): 13–31.

Cross, W. E. Jr., Parham, T. A. and Helms, J. E. (1991) The Stages of Black Identity Development: Nigrescence Models, in R. C. Jones (ed.), *Black Psychology*. Berkeley: University of California Press.

d'Ardenne, P. and Mahtani, A. (1989) *Transcultural Counselling in Action*. London: Sage.

Devereux, G. (1983) *Essais d'ethnopsychiatrie générale*. Paris: Gallimard.

Fernando, S. (1988) *Race and Culture in Psychiatry*. Kent: Croom Helm.

Hall, W. A. (1995) Counselling Black Students, in R. Moodley (ed.), *Education for Transformation*. Leeds, UK: Thomas Danby Publications.

Helms, J. E. (1990) *Black and White Racial Identity: Theory, Research and Practice*. Westport, CT: Greenwood.

Ivey, A. E., Ivey, M. B. and Simek-Morgan, L. (1993) *Counseling and Psychotherapy: A Multicultural Perspective*, 3rd edn., Boston: Allyn & Bacon.

Kareem, J. and Littlewood, R. (eds) (1992) *Intercultural Therapy*. London: Blackwell.

Lago, C. and Thompson, J. (1996) *Race, Culture and Counselling*. Buckingham: Open University Press.

Littlewood, R. (1990) From Categories to Contexts: A Decade of the 'New Cross-Cultural Psychiatry', *British Journal of Psychiatry* 156: 308–327.

Marsella, A. J. and Pedersen, P. (eds) (1981) *Cross-Cultural Counseling and Psychotherapy*. Honolulu, Hawaii: East-West Center.

Moodley, R., Lago, C. and Talahite, A. (2004) *Carl Rogers Counsels a Black Client: Race and Culture in Person-Centred Therapy*. Ross-on-Wye: PCCS Books.

Nathan, T. (1985) *Sexualité idéologique et névrose: essai clinique ethnopsychanalytique*. Paris: La Pensée Sauvage.

Palmer, S. and Laungani, P. (eds) (1999) *Counselling in a Multicultural Society*. London: Sage.

Palmer, S. (ed.) (2002) *Multicultural Counselling: A Reader*. London: Sage.

Pankhania, J. (1996) Black Feminist Counselling, in M. Jacobs (ed.), *Jitendra: Lost Connections: In Search of a Therapist*. Buckingham: Open University Press.

Pedersen, P. (1985) *Handbook of Cross-Cultural Counseling and Therapy*. New York: Praeger.

Pedersen, P. (ed.) (1991) Multiculturalism as a Fourth Force in Counseling (special issue), *Journal of Counseling and Development* 70: 4–250.

Ponterotto, J. G. (1988) Racial Consciousness Development among White Counselors' Trainees: A Stage Model, *Journal of Multicultural Counseling and Development* 16: 146–156.

Pope-Davis, D. B. and Coleman, H. L. K. (eds) (1997) *Multicultural Counseling Competencies: Assessment, Education and Training, and Supervision*. Thousand Oaks, CA: Sage.

Rameriz, M. (1999) *Multicultural Psychotherapy*. Boston: Allyn & Bacon.

Sabnani, H. B., Ponterotto, J. G. and Borodousky, L. G. (1991) White Racial Identity Development and Cross-Cultural Counselor Training: A Stage Model, *The Counseling Psychologist* 19: 76–102.

Sashidharan, S. P. (1986) Ideology and Politics in Transcultural Psychiatry, in J. L. Cox (ed.), *Transcultural Psychiatry*. London: Croom Helm, pp. 158–178.

Vontress, C. E. (1985) Existentialism as a Cross-Cultural Counseling Modality, in P. Pedersen (ed.), *Handbook of Cross-Cultural Counseling and Therapy*. New York: Praeger.

Walton, J. (1995) Re-placing in (White) Psychoanalytic Discourse: Founding Narratives of Feminism, *Critical Inquiry* 21 (Summer): 775–804.

Critical perspectives in race and culture in psychotherapy

Race, culture and other multiple constructions: an absent presence in psychotherapy

Roy Moodley and Stephen Palmer

The terms race, culture, ethnicity, multiculture, anti-racist and its related terms that act as labelling descriptors of ethnic minority clients, or as a reference to the 'Other', or as linguistic signifiers of cultural differences, and the lack of a comprehensive definition of these concepts have produced much confusion and difficulty in the practice of psychotherapy (Sue, 1997), and has resulted in the same set of multicultural competencies being used on clients regardless of their cultural or ethnic characteristics (Helms and Richardson, 1997). Carter (1995) suggests that since the influence of race and racial identity is unclear in psychotherapy, therapists experience difficulties when working with black clients. One way out of the difficulty and confusion, it seems, is to develop a more clear, meaningful and flexible understanding of race, culture, ethnicity, multiculture and the other related terms.

Developing a precise and finite definition of these terms may not be possible or desirable, given their complex history, their present reflexivity and their potential for change in the future. However, for both psycho-therapists and their clients these social constructions are essential elements within which the identity of the client is negotiated and the inter-subjective relationship is constructed. Psychotherapy with a black or ethnic minority client then becomes a site within which fixed, essential and stereotyped ideas about race, ethnicity, multiculturalism, black and multiethnicity tend to get challenged and changed. Liberal ethics of seeing all clients as equally but differentially 'ill' is interrogated by notions of social pluralism and cultural diversity.

In this chapter, we begin by considering the social construction of race, culture and ethnicity and the other multicultural terms. Throughout this discussion we attempt to intersect these terms with psychotherapy.

THE SOCIAL CONSTRUCTION OF RACE, CULTURE AND ETHNICITY

The social and cultural theories and critique on race, culture, ethnicity, racism, anti-racism and multiculturalism have been well articulated and documented (see, for example, Gates, 1992; Gilroy, 1990; Hall, 1992; Law, 1996; Mason, 1992, 1995, 1996; Solomos and Back, 1995). Although multi-culturalism and its related terms have also been discussed and critiqued by post-colonial commentators (see, for example, Bhabha, 1994; Fanon, 1952; Gilroy, 2000; Said, 1978; Spivak, 1988), there still appears to be much confusion about what is meant by these concepts (Bulmer and Solomos, 1996). The notion that race and ethnicity are not 'natural' categories (Appiah, 1989), having a biological or genetic base, is now generally accepted by most writers in this field. While in the past some researchers have favoured a (racist) genetic explanation, the overall position, however, in social and health sciences, is one of acknowledging that race, racism, ethnicity, culture and multiculturalism are socio-culturally and politically constructed and contested, allowing them to acquire a variety of meanings that allow for a flexible, fluid and multiple understanding of ethnic minority clients. From a post-structuralist and post-modernist perspective this reflexivity should allow for a creative approach to health care practice, particularly in psychotherapy and psychiatry. However, this does not appear to be the case. Ethnic minority clients are still categorized and labeled in a singular 'strait-jacket' way, often exclusively in terms of a particular continent of origin, or religious affiliation, or racial skin tone where race is seen to be equated with skin color, particularly the color black which then becomes a privileged site for the interpretations of psychopathology of African and African-Caribbean clients.

This a priori definition, reduced to a conventional Cartesian dialectic, has led to diagnostic generalizations about specific ethnic minority clients' mental health problems with the offer of non-specific treatment procedures across a wide range of culturally diverse clients. As Williams notes, 'The categories race, culture, black, have been problematised as a base on which to construct analysis' (Williams, 1999, p. 213), and she argues that such a conceptualization 'leads to a reductionist's aggregation of ethnic differences . . . [to] confuse practice through oversimplification, generating stereotypes and fostering ethnocentrism' (p. 213). In other instances, these concepts have been the signature legitimizing not only a concrete pharmacological practice with ethnic minority clients but creating an invisible screen of a liberal, post-structuralist and modernist flexibility which hides coercion and state ideological intervention of the minority client. This view is shared by Sashidharan in his critique of transcultural psychiatry. He argues:

> 'culture' or 'ethnicity' take on a special, politically loaded meaning . . . [and] invested with a new meaning these mere words or concepts suddenly become powerful tools with which the transcultural psychiatrist [psychotherapist] sets out to particularise social structures which are products of historical and political struggles. As a result, culture or aspects of people's lives and experiences are reduced to mere

manageable problems falling within the clinical or professional competence of the culturally informed practitioner.

(Sashidharan, 1986, p. 159)

Sashidharan's comments may appear to be critical of the culturally informed psychotherapist who imbues these definitions without critically examining them for their role in promoting a coercive and oppressive practice. It seems that when these terms are employed as a convenient epistemological tool for the identification of 'psychological distress' of ethnic minority clients they tend to universalize different world views thereby maintaining the status quo of Western psychotherapeutic models. Any question of difference is then presented as complex, ambiguous, contradictory and confusing, leading many professionals to avoid or dismiss cultural diversity in psychotherapy.

However, before a discussion of the relationship between these multicultural concepts and psychotherapy can be undertaken it is necessary to look at the concepts of race, culture, ethnicity and multiculturalism individually.

Race

The term race first appeared in the English language in 1508 to refer simply to a category or class of persons, without any reference to anything biological (Miles, 1982). It was only in the late eighteenth century that the word race was invested with a physical connotation, and only in the early nineteenth century that specific theories of racial types began to emerge, most notably about populations outside Europe (Alderman, 1985). Many of the ideas associated with genetics and racial differentiation during this period were founded on pseudoscientific theories that are now discredited. But at the end of the century, 'eugenicists and social Darwinists were offering "scientific" justifications for genocide as well as for imperialism . . . through which Europeans projected many of their darkest impulses onto Africans' (Brantlinger, 1985, pp. 205–217).

The person who is most noted for thinking about race has been the African-American social theorist W. E. B. Du Bois who discussed the concept of race in 'The Conversation of Races' (1897). This paper and the other writings of Du Bois have been the topic of discussion by Appiah who argues that for Du Bois, '"race" is not a scientific – that is, biological – concept. It is a socio-historical concept' (Appiah, 1986, p. 25). Appiah notes:

> Race, we all assume, is, like all other concepts, constructed by metaphor and metonymy; it stands in, metonomically, for the 'Other'; it bears the weight, metaphorically, of other kinds of difference . . . Even if the concept of race *is* a structure of oppositions – white opposed to black (but also to yellow), Jew opposed to Gentile (but also to Arab) –

it is a structure whose realisation is, at best, problematic and, worst, impossible.

(Appiah, 1985, p. 36). [italics in original quotation]

Yet it is within this impossibility that contemporary Western culture attempts to find a 'truth' about difference, meaning, genetics and culture. It is also within this problematic that psychiatry, psychotherapy and psycho-analysis are attempting to make sense of a black and ethnic minority client. Sometimes a reductionist and fixed view of race and racial difference becomes the basis for understanding the relationship with the ethnic minority client. As Henwood and Phoenix point out, 'Racial difference is neither fixed in stone nor merely illusionary, because it is the outcome of practices of (de)racialisation which position groups and subjects in more or less advantageous and discriminatory ways' (Henwood and Phoenix, 1996, p. 853).

Race, racial difference and the many forms of racism/s that are experi-enced by black and ethnic minority groups are not fixed categories, nor are they transhistorical, pointing to a time of origin or a cultural or historical specificity where the roots of discrimination and domination had begun. These ideas and ideologies are dynamic and forever changing in relation to the discursive social, economic, cultural and political practices that are operating at the time. Ferber offers a timely reminder when he argues, 'In representing race as a given foundation, we obscure the relations of power which constitute race as a foundation. Rather than taking race for granted, we need to begin to explore the social construction of race, and the centrality of racism and misogyny to this construction' (Ferber, 1998, p. 60).

For those psychotherapists who are critical or anxious about working with the ideas and ideologies of race and racial difference, Ferber, like Sashidharan (quoted earlier), emphasizes the need to see race within the context of power relations. If not, psychotherapy becomes one of 'those powerful forces that underlie the formation and perpetuation of racial and ethnic injustice in a complex and changing world' (Stone, 1998, p. 15).

Culture

The term culture covers a wide spectrum of meanings, from physical elements in a society such as buildings and architecture to abstract and metaphorical elements such as myths, values, attitudes and ideas about spirituality. According to Halton (1992), the concept of culture is so indeterminate that it can easily be filled in with whatever preconceptions a theorist brings to it. For example, Taylor's (1871[1920]) definition of culture includes knowledge, belief, art, morals, law, custom and any other capa-bilities and habits acquired by individuals as members of society. Related terms such as subculture, popular culture, counterculture, high culture, ethnic culture, organizational culture, mass culture, political culture, feminist culture, deaf culture and others, have been indicative of the complexity, dynamism and the evolving nature of the concept of culture within the disciplines of social-scientific and humanistic study. This understanding of the term culture suggests that 'culture', like race, is neither fixed nor static.

For Raymond Williams the word culture is 'a noun of process: the tendering *of* something, basically crops and animals' (Williams, 1976, p. 77). It seems that from its earliest meanings, derived from the Latin *colere* – to till, cultivate, dwell or inhabit – culture and its close ally 'colonize' became a powerful organizing influence in producing and reproducing a dominant world view amongst Europeans. As Halton says, 'Even before the nineteenth century . . . already beset by the etherealising tendencies of ethnocentric universalism . . . the Enlightenment dream of "universal reason"' was the underlying principle to the 'expression of European power' (Halton, 1992, p. 43). This ethnological origin appears clearly to describe the noun of a process, that is of expressing European power through colonization, domination, subjugation and Diaspora. This was also a time when the noun became a verb – a doing word – one in which Eurocentric ideologies were formulated to 'cultivate' not just crops and animals but other humans too. This was culture representing itself as civilization, which produced and reproduced the 'Other', as for example in *Orientalism* (Said, 1978). This kind of cultural formulation also constructed Africa as the *Heart of Darkness* (Conrad, 1902).

While there is very little agreement by the cultural commentators about the meaning of culture, there is, however, a general acceptance that culture is a process that is not static but constantly changing in time and space within a given society. An important feature of culture is that while individuals tend to express or display cultural traits, culture appears to be understood as either a coherent or incoherent society or group phenomena. The concept of culture should not be treated as a global entity but as far as possible be disaggregated into a number of discrete variables (values, ideologies, beliefs, preferences) to avoid any vagueness, multiple meanings and circular definitions. It is the global characterization of culture that offers methodological difficulties when an attempt is made to link it causally with phenomena in individual behaviour (Smelser, 1992). This latter point is particularly important in understanding psychotherapy with ethnic minority clients. A contemporary critique of psychiatry would contend that the psychiatric discourse tends to link culture with the now outdated pseudo-scientific theories on race (see Thomas and Sillen, 1972) and Western socio-biology of the culturally different client. These approaches have often resulted in particular treatments for black and ethnic minority clients, some of which would now be seen as racist (see Fernando, 1988).

In 'Trouble with Culture', Ahmad clearly defines his position on culture when he says, 'stripped of its dynamic social, economic, gender and historical context, culture becomes a rigid and constraining concept which is seen somehow to mechanistically determine peoples' behaviour and actions rather than provide a flexible resource for living, for according meaning to what one feels, experiences and acts to change' (Ahmad, 1996, p. 190). Furthermore, Ahmad argues that culture has often been used as a decoy to divert attention away from factors such as social inequalities and racism in the lives of ethnic minority communities. At the same time race, culture and ethnicity are clearly ideologically constituted and as such 'carry with them material consequences for those who are included within or excluded from, them' (Bulmer and Solomos, 1996, p. 781). So it seems that the term culture is as problematic as the term race and just as troubling as the term ethnicity.

Ethnicity

There is a tendency, in the literature, to use the terms race and ethnicity interchangeably (Mason, 1996). Furthermore, there seems to be an 'increasing use of "ethnicity" as a euphemism for "culture"' (Tilley, 1997, p. 489), in much the same way that black is used to describe African or Caribbean ethnicity.[1] In the 1990s, socio-economic and geopolitical changes in the international arena, particularly in the West, summoned ethnicity out of European 'inner-city third world hamlets' to include many European white minority groups, bringing into consciousness that the colour white, which is often forgotten in this category, is also a part of ethnicity; to the extent that in the late 1990s, according to Tilley, '"ethnicity" has become the term of the hour in political science, as we grapple with its role in domestic conflict and international security' (Tilley, 1997, p. 497). Associated terms such as ethnic cleansing, Balkans' racism, Rwandan genocide and others have come to grip our consciousness as historic events had marked the last century. Indeed, these are not new phenomena. Since the dawn of history, hegemonic masculinities have privileged particular spaces as discursive forums for patriarchy, patriarchal projections, annihilations, dissolution of the 'Other', and other similar Kleinian terms to indicate the primitive instincts. The terms have changed over a period of time but the projections have not. For example, in the first part of the twentieth century Europe experienced the Holocaust, and at the end of the century ethnic cleansing was unleashed without any recourse to human rights that have since evolved. Ethnic cleansing it seems is a metaphor for our time (Ahmed, 1995).

   The concept of ethnicity, according to Mason, found its way into political and academic discourse largely as a response to dissatisfaction with the idea of race and with the assimilationist assumptions of a focus on immigration. Since race as a conceptual and empirical idea to locate difference was proving to be problematic because of its articulation within a political discourse, the term ethnicity was more appealing and privileged because of its flexibility and inclusiveness of all those minorities that appeared to be outside the fixed meanings of race, that is South Asian, Chinese and others.

The positioning and repositioning of subjects and groups in terms of race, racism, culture and ethnicity have been seen as a cyclic process throughout the pre- and post-war periods. For example, the idea of ethnicity referred to the Irish, Italians and Jews in the early part of the twentieth century, but took on a more sinister and racialised meaning for the Jewish community. In the latter half of the century, after the migration of West Indians, East Asians, Pakistanis and Bangladeshis, the term revised itself to exclude, except for Jews, those white Europeans defined earlier, and focused negatively on Africa, Asia and the Caribbean.

It seems that individuals can go 'beyond' the realms of the boundaries and limitations set by culture, race and ethnicity, moving from fixed meanings to more imaginative ones. This question of the 'beyond' is crucial to Homi Bhabha's quest in *Location of Culture* (1994), in which he argues:

> the 'beyond' is neither a new horizon, nor a leaving behind of the past . . . What is theoretically innovative, and politically crucial, is the need to think beyond narratives of imagined origins and initial subjectivities and to focus on those moments or processes that are produced in the articulation of cultural differences. These 'in-between' spaces provide the terrain for elaborating strategies of selfhood – singular or communal – that initiate new signs of identity, and innovative sites of collaboration, and contestation, in the act of defining the idea of society itself.
>
> (Bhabha, 1994, pp. 1–2)

Bhabha's decisiveness about moving beyond the narrative of initial subjectivity may be too much of a utopian project for a number of, if not most, individuals from black and ethnic minority clients. The formulation of a new cultural space, one in which difference can mean different and equal, is a prerogative for those who are able to manage the material construction of cultural difference in the face of racism and cultural domination. The majority of ethnic minority people are caught up in a less aesthetic struggle about culture, race and ethnicity than those in the dominant (middle-class) culture. Their analysis of a culture of difference appears to be compatible with their social and economic realities of an inner-city existence. Their hope of a new sign of cultural identity is more akin to the ideas offered by Stuart Hall in his discussion of new ethnicities where he argues for,

> a positive conception of the ethnicity of the margins, of the periphery. That is to say, a recognition that we all speak from a particular space,

out of a particular history, out of a particular experience . . . we are all, in that sense, *ethnically* located and our ethnic identities are crucial to our subjective sense of who we are . . . [and] it is not an ethnicity that is doomed to survive, as Englishness was, only by marginalizing, dispossessing, displacing and forgetting other ethnicities. This precisely is the politics of ethnicity predicated on difference and diversity.

(Hall, 1992, p. 258)

Stuart Hall leaves us without any doubt that a new cultural politics of race and the experiences of racism articulate conceptions of ethnicity. This is far from the position taken by Modood *et al.* who suggest that, where 'black' and 'South Asian' have been used to describe ethnicity, 'such categories are heterogeneous, containing ethnic groups with different cultures, religions, migration histories and geographical and socio-economic locations. Combining them leads to differences between them being ignored' (Modood *et al.*, 1997, p. 227). This is precisely the kind of difference and diversity to which Hall refers. Furthermore, Modood *et al.* suggest that the way forward is to allow individuals to assign themselves into ethnic groups. Much more complex a process since, 'one of the most thorny problems in theorising about race and ethnicity is the question of how political identities are shaped and constructed through the meanings attributed to race, ethnicity and nation' (Solomos and Back, 1995, p. 16).

What seems clear as we consider the various theoretical formulations of race, culture and ethnicity is that the secondary qualifiers which come into play also need to be reconceptualized. Words like difference and diversity are themselves contested terms and need to be understood sometimes in quite specific contexts whether in health care or social policy. As Brah in her paper on 'Difference, Diversity, Differentiation: Processes of Racialisation and Gender' argues,

the usage of 'black', 'Indian', or 'Asian' is determined not so much by the nature of its semiotic function within different discourses. These various meanings signal differing political strategies and outcomes. They mobilise different sets of cultural or political identities, and set limits to where the boundaries of a 'community' are established.

(Brah, 1993, p. 200)

For psychotherapists, it seems that the key to understanding these concepts is an awareness that all these terms are constructed within changing socio-political and cultural ideologies that may have consequences for psychotherapy and clients' attitudes towards the process of change. Adhering to a rigid understanding of these terms may offer psychotherapists cognitive, emotional and professional security but may lead them to indulge in stereotyping clients negatively with dire consequences for a vulnerable client. The client, on the other hand, may from time to time alter the meaning of the concept of ethnicity during the conversations with the therapist and many times through his/her various stages of psychotherapy. As Adam says,

> Ethnic identity waxes and wanes not only in response to group members' own perceived needs, both instrumental and symbolic, but also in response to imposed identities by outsiders.
>
> (Adam, 1995, p. 463)

Individuals are often torn between the need to experience themselves existentially in the 'here and now', and the desire to be historically or psychically connected to a specific, but not too distant, past. This may be constructed in ethnic, cultural and racial terms. In essence the subjective 'self' manages both the inner psychological world and outer social, cultural and political environments. Having explored the terms race, culture and ethnicity, we now turn to the concept of multiculture.

Multiculturalism

In the 1970s and 1980s the idea of multiculturalism was the primary site within which the complex and confounding issues of race, culture and ethnicity could be theorised and practised. Much of it related to the acquisition of cross-cultural knowledge/s and competencies, and very little effort was made in the theory and the research to identify the social and political inequalities that established the relationships between the dominant culture and the ethnic minority groups. Consequently, in the 1990s, newer formulations under a new multicultural agenda began to emerge to redress the imbalances that were being seen as a result of multicultural policies in education, social care and health care. These took the form of an anti-racist project through specifically located and time-limited actions such as equal opportunities, political correctness, positive discrimination, affirmative actions and other such projects (Moodley, 1999a). Overall, however, the theory and practice of multiculturalism have always been problematic for expressing ethnic minority life experiences too simplistically or for not articulating a radical approach to cultural imperialism, racism, sexism and economic oppression (Moodley, 1999b). The problematic nature of multicultural thinking, according to Apitzsch, is that 'it seems to consist not only in its defining the main differences in society in cultural terms; but also through the fact that it is liable to underestimate those social forces that distinguish not only between cultures . . . [but create] distinctions and demarcations . . . domination, coercion and subordination, disguised behind the label of culture or "ethnicity"' (Apitzsch, 1993, p. 137). It is those social forces, underpinned by cultural imperialism, racism, sexism, hegemonic masculinities[2] and other similar projections, which individually and collectively interact to produce an environment where the ethnic minority individual is denied, 'abjected' and condemned.

So, any new formulation of multiculturalism must within its definition seek to articulate a more critical idea of difference that empowers cultural traditions, facilitates economic development, respects ethnic customs and supports non-racist values. Even with such a race, culture and ethnicity would still be ideologically constituted as they 'carry with them material consequences for those who are included within or excluded from them' (Bulmer and Solomos, 1996, p. 781). In this respect Stuart Hall (1992) attempts to construct (or deconstruct) a Derridean notion of *différance*, which in part would depend on the construction of new ethnic identities where difference is positional, conditional and conjectural. Cornel West (1990) engages this notion, in *New Cultural Politics of Difference*, in which he argues that cultural differences are neither simply oppositional in contesting the mainstream for inclusion. He maintains that cultural differences are distinct articulations produced in order to empower and enable social action for the expression of freedom, democracy and individuality (see also Grillo, 1998 for a discussion on pluralism and the politics of difference). This idea sums up the 'critical multiculturalism' of Kuper, which 'is outward looking, organised to challenge the cultural prejudices of the dominant social class, intent on uncovering the vulnerable underbelly of the hegemonic discourse' (Kuper, 1999, p. 232).

Perhaps the greatest challenge to the notion of locating a specific definition of multiculturalism comes from multiculturalism itself. The lack of a complex theorization of multiculturalism (Willett, 1998) is perhaps a testament to the fact that multiculturalism, as the term suggests, is a multiple articulation of a number of varied, contradictory and contested ideas and explanations for complex human behaviours, functions, rituals and ceremonies. Therefore any attempt to homogenize it into a singularly defined concept can only create confusion and consequently reinforce the stereotypes that multiculturalism hopes to avoid in the first place. In accepting the multiplicity of multiculturalism as an aesthetically, empirically and philosophically based phenomenon, the experiences of multiple public and private social identities; gender and racial differentials; mono-, bi-, multilinguistic articulations; polarised religious orientations and sexual pluralities of an individual (or group) can be contested, accommodated, tolerated and celebrated. Such a wide definition of multiculturalism inevitably creates a tension. The lack of permanency of identity raises fears about the fragmentation and disillusionment of the 'self' and the 'Other'. Yet, it is this fragmentation that forms the basis for psychotherapy.

THE ABSENT PRESENCE OF RACE, CULTURE AND ETHNICITY IN PSYCHOTHERAPY

The socio-cultural and political ideas of race, culture and ethnicity have been constellations around counselling and psychotherapy in the last two decades mainly through the theoretical ideas of the psycho-social constructionists and the transcultural or multicultural psychotherapists. This latter group has been very vocal in arguing that race, culture and ethnicity have been either absent or marginalized in psychotherapy (see, for example, Carter, 1995; Draguns, 1997; Helms, 1990; Jewel, 1994; Kareem and Littlewood, 1992; Sue and Sundberg, 1996; Yee *et al.*, 1993). Some of these commentators, especially the British, have followed the arguments posed in British transcultural psychiatry and cross-cultural counselling. In psychiatry, for example, Sashidharan (1990), Burke (1986), Fernando (1988), Littlewood and Lipsedge (1982[1997]) and others (see Cox, 1986) have been highly critical of the absence or marginalization of issues of race, culture and ethnicity. Where there has been an introduction of these ideas, some, particularly Sashidharan (1986), have been highly critical of the way in which they are constructed in transcultural psychiatry. Likewise, in his contention for a *New Transcultural Psychiatry*, Littlewood (1990) is also critical about the cohesive way in which race, culture and ethnicity have been used in mental (ill) health care.

In psychodynamic counselling, psychological counselling and in counselling, particularly in Britain, there appears to be an emerging visibility of the issues of race, culture and ethnicity in the theory, practice and training (see d'Ardenne and Mahtani, 1989; Lago and Thompson, 1996; Palmer and Laungani, 1999; Palmer, 2002). This includes the possibility of taking an idiographic counselling approach with ethnic minority clients, such as multimodal therapy (see Palmer, 1999). On the other hand, in psychotherapy there appears to be an obvious absence and (to put it mildly) a culture of conscious disengagement with the multicultural notions of race, culture and ethnicity. The few black and ethnic minority psychotherapists, researchers and writers are constantly calling for the inclusion of race, culture and ethnicity as variables in psychotherapy. For example, Kareem emphasizes the need for the inclusion of racial and cultural dimensions in both psychotherapy and psychotherapy training, so that 'psychotherapy does not become divisive and disintegrated' (Kareem, 1992, p. 33). Much of this discussion has focused on the absence of race as a construct in psychotherapy, particularly in the North American context. For example, Draguns (1997), Jewel (1994) and Sue and Sundberg (1996) point out that the effects of race are unknown in psychotherapy. Yee *et al.* (1993) argue that racial and ethnic influences have not been well elaborated in psychotherapy literature and practice. Carter draws attention to this fact when he says, 'Race has become less salient because mental health clinicians, scholars and researchers are more comfortable examining presumed cultural and ethnic issues than addressing racial issues' (Carter, 1995, p. 4).

While race is a critical variable, the singular attention to race alone would appear to exclude the constructions of meanings that are attributed to the other experiences of ethnic minority identities, irrespective of the limited theorization of these identities. For example, there are some South Asians who construct their identities through the concepts of culture and ethnicity rather than the conceptualizations of the notions of race and racial identity. Furthermore, Carter's singular focus on race could unwittingly reify race and give it a legitimacy and potency, thus naturalizing it as a socio-biological idea. Mason (1996) offers a caution when he suggests that in recent years race, culture and ethnicity seem to be constructed into a theoretical principle by invoking the idea of racialization, thereby naturalizing ethnic and other differences. This racialization of the dynamic experiences of ethnic and cultural differences is shaped into stable, negative constructs which are then attributed to the whole of the ethnic minority group (see also Mason, 1994, 1995).

The critical issue, however, is that although many writers argue for the inclusion of race, culture and ethnicity, very little research has been conducted to realise their potential psychologically. When multicultural practitioners argue that race, culture and ethnicity are key concepts in forming the fabric of the therapeutic discourse, within which the client is held and contained throughout therapy, social intervention strategies are considered more important than psychological ones; while conventional psychotherapists, on the other hand, effectively remove the socio-political, cultural and historical meanings of a client's life experience by relegating race, culture and ethnicity to the margins. They argue that these multicultural variables cannot explain the inner life of a client nor do they offer a modicum of psychotherapeutic explanation of a client's 'subjective distress'.

CONCLUSION

In this chapter, we attempted to examine the concepts of race, culture and ethnicity to reflect on their complexities, confusions and ambiguities in social, cultural and psychological discourses and particularly to highlight their absent presence in psychotherapy. As contested sites they constantly move their boundaries and borderlines to suit a variety of ideological positions and at the same time provide a space for a critique on their processes. The reflexivity of these concepts has further complicated an already confusing discourse on minority groups in which these constructions are often bounded together as a single, linear, Newtonian idea. The homogenizing of minority communities into a single ethnic, racial and/or cultural group, namely black and ethnic minority, has led to general developments in mental (ill) health care for these groups. These notions generate from ideological positions that evolve within narrow confines of theory and practice, thus causing commentators such as Ahmad to conclude that ethnic minority health care has always been a politicized issue in which the 'racialization of black people's health' has been 'a major industry' with 'minimal improvements or benefits to ethnic minority groups' (Ahmad, 1993, p. 18).

We also questioned the clinical usefulness of the multicultural concepts. As a result of the diversity of nomenclatures and changing vocabularies of the multicultural and multiethnic terminologies, psychotherapists are finding it difficult to adopt and implement appropriate therapeutic approaches with ethnic minority clients. The challenge for psychotherapy is to engage psychoanalytic theory in an innovative and alternative way so that the notions of multiple-identities and multiple-selves begin to evolve new epistemologies in research as well as in the actual delivery of psychotherapy. At the same time the traditional ideas that encompass race, culture, ethnicity, racism, anti-racism and multiculturalism must be 'deconstructed' and more fully theorised to provide clear psychological schemas within which new clinical paradigms and research methods can be formulated.

Notes

1 On other occasions, the word 'black' is often used interchangeably with African. For example, Graham (1999) writes in an article, 'African and black are used interchangeably in this chapter to refer to people of African and African descent through the world' (p. 251). Akande, in writing from a South African perspective, uses the term 'black' in a different way, for example 'black female students (Coloured, Indians, Africans)' (Akande, 1997, p. 391).
2 Connell defines hegemonic masculinities as, 'the configuration of gender practice which embodies the currently accepted answer to the problem of the legitimacy of patriarchy, which guarantees (or is taken to guarantee) the dominant position of men and the subordination of women' (Connell, 1995, p. 77).

References

Adam, H. (1995) The Politics of Ethnic Identity: Comparing South Africa, *Ethnic and Racial Studies* 18: 456–475.

Ahmad, W. I. U. (1993) Making Black People Sick: 'Race', Ideology and Health Research, in W. I. U. Ahmad (ed.), *'Race' and Health in Contemporary Britain*. Buckingham: Open University Press, pp. 11–33.

Ahmad, W. I. U. (1996) Trouble with Culture, in D. Kelleher and S. Hillier (eds), *Researching Cultural Differences in Health*. London: Routledge, pp. 190–219.

Ahmed, A. S. (1995) 'Ethnic Cleansing': A Metaphor for our Time?, *Ethnic and Racial Studies* 18: 1–25.

Akande, A. (1997) Influence of South African Women's Career and Traditional Goals, *International Journal for the Advancement of Counselling* 19: 389–396.

Alderman, G. (1985) Explaining Racism, *Political Studies* 33: 129–135.

Apitzsch, U. (1993) Gramsci and the Current Debate on Multicultural Education, *Studies in the Education of Adults* 25: 136–145.

Appiah, K. A. (1986) The Uncompleted Argument: Du Bois and the Illusion of Race, in Henry L. Gates Jr. (ed.), *'Race', Writing and Difference.* Chicago: University of Chicago Press, pp. 21–37.

Appiah, K. A. (1989) The Conversation of 'Race', *Black American Literature Forum* 23: 37–60.

Benedict, R. (1935) *Patterns of Culture*, 7th edn. London: Routledge & Kegan Paul, 1961.

Bhabha, H. (1994) *The Location of Culture.* London: Routledge.

Brah, A. (1993) Difference, Diversity, Differentiation: Processes of Racialisation and Gender, in J. Solomos and J. Wrench (eds), *Racism and Migration in Western Europe.* Oxford: Berg, pp. 195–214.

Brantlinger, (1985) Victorians and Africans: The Genealogy of the Myth of the Dark Continent, in Henry L. Gates Jr. (ed.), *'Race', Writing and Difference.* Chicago: University of Chicago Press, pp. 185–222.

Bulmer, M. and Solomos, J. (1996) Introduction: Race, Ethnicity and the Curriculum, *Ethnic and Racial Studies* 19: 777–788.

Burke, A. W. (1986) Racism, Prejudice and Mental Health, in J. L. Cox (ed.), *Transcultural Psychiatry.* London: Croom Helm, pp. 139–157.

Carter, R. T. (1995) *The Influence of Race and Racial Identity in Psychotherapy.* New York: Wiley.

Connell, R. W. (1995) *Masculinities.* Cambridge: Polity Press.

Conrad, J. (1902) *Heart of Darkness.* London: Penguin, 1983.

Cox, J. L. (ed.) (1986) *Transcultural Psychiatry.* London: Croom Helm.

d'Ardenne, P. and Mahtani, A. (1989) *Transcultural Counselling in Action.* London: Sage.

Draguns, J. G. (1997) Abnormal Behavior Patterns Across Cultures: Implications for Counseling and Psychotherapy, *International Journal of Intercultural Relations* 21: 212–248.

Du Bois, W. E. B. (1897) The Conversation of Races, American Negro Academy Occasional Papers, No. 2, reprinted in Philip S. Foner (ed.), *W. E. B. Du Bois Speaks: Speeches and Addresses 1890–1919.* New York: Pathfinders Press, 1970, pp. 73–85.

Fanon, F. (1952) *Black Skins White Masks*, trans. C. L. Markmann. New York: Grove Press, reprint 1967.

Ferber, A. L. (1998) Constructing Whiteness: The Intersections of Race and Gender in US White Supremacist Discourse, *Ethnic and Racial Studies* 21: 48–63.

Fernando, S. (1988) *Race and Culture in Psychiatry.* Kent: Croom Helm.

Gates, H. L. Jr. (1992) *Loose Canons: Notes on the Culture Wars.* New York, Oxford: Oxford University Press.

Gilroy, P. (1990) The End of Anti-Racism, in W. Ball and J. Solomos (eds), *Race and Local Politics.* London: Macmillan, pp. 191–209.

Gilroy, P. (2000) *Between Camps: Race, Identity and Nationalism at the End of the Colour Line.* London: Allen Lane.

Graham, M. J. (1999) The African-Centred Worldview: Developing a Paradigm for Social Work, *British Journal of Social Work* 29: 251–267.

Grillo, R. D. (1998) *Pluralism and the Politics of Difference*. Oxford: Clarendon Press.

Hall, S. (1992) New Ethnicities, in J. Donald and A. Rattansi (eds), *'Race', Culture and Difference*. Buckingham: Open University Press, pp. 252–259.

Halton, E. (1992) The Cultic Roots of Culture, in R. Munch and N. J. Smelser (eds), *Theory of Culture*. Berkeley/Los Angeles: University of California Press, pp. 29–63.

Helms, J. E. and Richardson, T. Q. (1997) How 'Multiculturalism' Obscures Race and Culture as Differential Aspects of Counseling Competency, in D. B. Pope-Davis and H. L. K. Coleman (eds), *Multicultural Counseling Competencies*. Thousand Oaks, CA: Sage, pp. 60–79.

Henwood, K. and Phoenix, A. (1996) 'Race' in Psychology: Teaching the Subject, *Ethnic and Racial Studies* 19: 841–863.

Jewel, P. (1994) Multicultural Counseling Research: An Evaluation with Proposals for Future Research, *Counseling Psychology Review* 9: 17–34.

Kareem, J. (1992) The Nafsiyat Intercultural Therapy Centre: Ideas and Experience in Intercultural Therapy, in J. Kareem and R. Littlewood (eds), *Intercultural Therapy: Themes, Interpretations and Practice*. Oxford: Blackwell, pp. 14–37.

Kareem, J. and Littlewood, R. (eds) (1992) *Intercultural Therapy: Themes, Interpretations and Practice*. Oxford: Blackwell.

Kuper, A. (1999) *Culture*. Cambridge, MA: Harvard University Press.

Lago, C. and Thompson, J. (1996) *Race, Culture and Counselling*. Buckingham: Open University Press.

Law, I. (1996) *Racism, Ethnicity and Social Policy*. London: Prentice-Hall International.

Littlewood, R. (1990) From Categories to Contexts: A Decade of the 'New Cross-Cultural Psychiatry', *British Journal of Psychiatry* 156: 308–327.

Littlewood, R. and Lipsedge, M. (1982) *Aliens and Alienists: Ethnic Minorities and Psychiatry*. London: Routledge, reprint 1997.

Mason, D. (1992) Categories, Identities and Change: Ethnic Monitoring and the Social Scientist, *European Journal of Intercultural Studies* 2: 41–52.

Mason, D. (1994) On the Dangers of Disconnecting Race and Racism, *Sociology* 28: 845–858.

Mason, D. (1995) *Race and Ethnicity in Modern Britain*. Oxford: Oxford University Press.

Mason, D. (1996) Themes and Issues in the Teaching of Race and Ethnicity in Sociology, *Ethnic and Racial Studies* 19: 789–806.

Miles, R. (1982) *Racism and Migrant Labour*. London: Routledge & Kegan Paul.

Modood, T., Berthoud, R., Lakey, J., Nazroo, J., Smith, P., Virdee, S. and Beishon, S. (1997) *Ethnic Minorities in Britain: Diversity and Disadvantage*. London: Policy Studies Institute.

Moodley, R. (1998a) Cultural Returns to the Subject: Traditional Healing in Counselling and Therapy, *Changes, International Journal of Psychology and Psychotherapy* 16: 45–56.

Moodley, R. (1998b) 'I Say What I Like': Frank Talk(ing) in Counselling and Psychotherapy, *British Journal of Guidance and Counselling* 26: 495–508.

Moodley, R. (1999a) Challenges and Transformation: Counselling in a Multi-Cultural Context, *International Journal for the Advancement of Counselling* 21: 139–152.

Moodley, R. (1999b) Psychotherapy with Ethnic Minorities: A Critical Review, *International Journal of Psychology and Psychotherapy* 17: 109–125.

Palmer, S. (1999) Developing an Individual Counselling Programme: A Multimodal Perspective, in S. Palmer and P. Laungani (eds), *Counselling in a Multicultural Society*. London: Sage.

Palmer, S. (ed.) (2002) *Multicultural Counselling: A Reader*. London: Sage.

Palmer, S. and Laungani, P. (eds) (1999) *Counselling in a Multicultural Society*. London: Sage.

Said, E. W. (1978) *Orientalism*. London: Routledge & Kegan Paul.

Sashidharan, S. P. (1986) Ideology and Politics in Transcultural Psychiatry, in J. L. Cox (ed.), *Transcultural Psychiatry*. London: Croom Helm, pp. 158–178.

Sashidharan, S. P. (1990) Race and Psychiatry, *Medical World* 3: 8–12.

Smelser, N. J. (1992) Culture: Coherent or Incoherent, in R. Munch and N. J. Smelser (eds), *Theory of Culture*. Berkeley and Los Angeles: University of California Press, pp. 3–28.

Solomos, J. and Back, L. (1995) *Race, Politics and Social Change*. London: Routledge.

Spivak, G. C. (1988) *In Other Worlds*. London: Routledge.

Stone, J. (1998) In New Paradigms for Old?: Ethnic and Racial Studies on the Eve of the Millennium, *Ethnic and Racial Studies* 21: 1–20.

Sue, D. (1997) Multicultural Training, *International Journal of Intercultural Relations* 21: 175–193.

Sue, D. and Sundberg, N. D. (1996) Research and Research Hypotheses about Effectiveness of Intercultural Counseling, in P. B. Pedersen, J. G. Draguns, W. J. Lonner and J. E. Trimble (eds), *Counseling across Cultures*, 3rd edn. Honolulu: University of Hawaii Press, pp. 335–370.

Taylor, E. B. (1871) *Primitive Culture: Research into the Development of Mythology, Philosophy, Religion, Art and Custom*. London: Murray, reprint 1920.

Thomas, A. and Sillen, S. (1972) *Racism and Psychiatry*. Secausus, New Jersey, USA: Citadel Press.

Tilley, V. (1997) The Terms of the Debate: Untangling Language about Ethnicity and Ethnic Movements, *Ethnic and Racial Studies* 20: 497–522.

West, C. (1990) New Cultural Politics of Difference, *October* 53: 93–108.

Willett, C. (1998) *Theorizing Multiculturalism*. Massachusetts: Blackwell.

Williams, C. (1999) Connecting Anti-racist and Anti-oppressive Theory and Practice: Retrenchment or Reappraisal, *British Journal of Social Work* 29: 211–230.

Williams, Raymond (1976) *Keywords*. New York: Oxford University Press.

Yee, A. H., Fairchild, H. H., Weizmann, F. and Wyatt, G. E. (1993) Addressing Psychology's Problem with Race, *American Psychologist* 48: 1132–1140.

Chapter 2

Multiculturally crazy: diagnosis in Black

Rinaldo Walcott

In this chapter I want to sketch a small intervention into the discursive and material field of multiculturalism and its practices in the West. As part of this critique I want to position two key ideas which I believe play a significant role in the psychology of the subject, i.e. the notion of interiority and exteriority of the subject. These ideas, in many ways, have been explored by Frantz Fanon in *Black Skin White Masks* (1967) and *The Wretched of the Earth* (1963). Using Fanon's ideas I will illustrate how the notions of interiority and exteriority play themselves out in the constellation of the individual subject which could easily lead to a diagnosis in Black.

INTERVENTIONS INTO MULTICULTURALISM

The discursive field of multiculturalism is characterized by both its official variant and its discursive and material effects; and simultaneously by a popular variant which is characterised by the lived everyday realities of urban multicultural spaces – that is, the intimacy of living cultural difference and its various encounters in cosmopolitan spaces. In both cases multiculturalism might be characterized as the outcome of both the post-colonial and post-civil rights moments and conditions. Thus multiculturalism has to be understood as at least one element of a response to the new crisis conditions of racial minority or subaltern self-assertiveness in metropolitan spaces (Walcott, 2003). At one level multiculturalism represents the political assertiveness of former subaltern[1] peoples for access to full citizenship in metropolitan and former colonizing countries; and simultaneously multi-culturalism also represents a new social contract on questions of race and racism in which the nation-state at the level of governmental intervention intervenes to produce various forms of equilibrium in the socio-cultural sphere of the nation and citizenship. In the latter case multiculturalism fails to achieve full citizenship for racialized others.

Nonetheless, I believe that multiculturalism, as a conceptual premise must be struggled over. As Stuart Hall (2000) puts it, 'The term multiculturalism is now universally deployed. However, this proliferation has neither stabilized nor clarified its meaning . . . multiculturalism is now so discursively entangled that it can only be used "under erasure". Nevertheless, since we have no less implicated concepts to think this problem with, we have no alternative but to go on using and interrogating it' (p. 209). In this vein then, Hall calls for a 'new multicultural political logic' (p. 209). It is this new multicultural political logic that I intend to probe. In particular, I want to suggest that a new multicultural political logic would address the psychic or interior lives of subaltern peoples. The absence of a discussion of the psychic lives of racial minorities remains one of the fundamental ways in which full citizenship and thus humanity is denied. Official forms of multiculturalism by-pass the psychic life through recourse to questions of cultural preservation and heritage. By so doing subaltern citizens are *anthropologized* as caricatures of their cultural selves and particularly disturbing social practices can often be written off or dismissed as cultural practices in an attempt to legitimize those practices as constituting a specific cultural self.

The crisis that gives rise to multiculturalism as a strategy for managing cultural and racialized difference is emblematic of a new social contract of race and racialization. The philosopher Charles Mills (1997) dubs this new social contract 'the racial contract' and he suggests that the only possible way for social justice to be achieved is if the racial contract is made visible as an organizing principle of modern life. For him the racial contract is one that is agreed to by both whites and non-whites alike. It is a process that involves both acquiescence to white forms of domination, resistance to those forms of domination, and importantly, compromises that leave in place various forms of injustice agreed to by both white elites and subaltern elites. Thus the racial contract is a complex web of interlocking and contradictory socio-cultural and psychic practices and conditions. Official forms of multiculturalism embedded in nation-state legislation are an excellent example of compromised forms of the racial contract agreed to by all parties. Such agreements do not preclude continued struggles. Thus Mills (1997) writes: 'the "Racial Contract" *recognizes the actuality of the world we live in*, relates the construction of ideals, and the *non*realization of these ideals, to the character of this world, to group interests and institutionalized structures, and points to what would be necessary for achieving them. Thus it unites description and prescription, fact and norm' (p. 130, emphasis in original). In short the racial contract is still in part a script for political struggle. When the psychic life enters the public terrain of political struggles other issues are at stake.

Because of the double-edged nature of multiculturalism for racialized others it occupies a schizophrenic place in the socio-cultural and psychic life of racialized minorities. Following Gilles Deleuze and Felix Guattari (1987) we might make a call for a schizoanalysis. By this we mean that a new multicultural political logic must make sense of subaltern desire. As presently constituted multiculturalism is a belated response to subaltern desires. Deleuze and Guattari write of schizoanalysis that it is 'the analysis of desire, [it] is immediately practical and political, whether it is a question of an individual or a group, or society' (p. 203). Placing desire within the realm of the practical and the political places new and different kinds of demands on how we might think about psychic life and how we might think about the place of psychology in cosmopolitan spaces. Thus one demand of contemporary psychology must be to recognise the relationship and contradiction between cultural heritage, cultural practices and the dictates of what makes one human. In the context of post-colonial and post-civil rights conditions I am suggesting a Fanonian 'new humanism'. Such a humanism is fully aware of the ways in which the history of racialization and domination continue to impact on contemporary conditions. But a new humanism does not give up on the possibilities of cross-human identifications and thus is fully aware of the instability of the sub-categories of the human. Thus Fanon can concede that 'The Negro is not. Any more than the White man' (1967, p. 231); or even, 'I am a man and what I have to recapture is the whole past of the world' (p. 226). Fanon is not articulating liberal humanist values; rather he is challenging the premise that blackness lives outside the category of the human. His challenge forces a rearticulation of the human and thus destabilizes it in the hope of redefining it. It is in this regard that Charles Mills (1997) writes: 'To understand the actual moral practice of past and present, one needs not merely the standard abstract discussions of say, the conflicts in people's consciences between self-interest and empathy with others but a frank appreciation of how the Racial Contract creates a *racialized* moral psychology' (p. 93). It is the logic of a racialized psychology that remains a challenge in the context of the broader issues of social justice.

Further, since the interior lives of racialized subjects are hardly ever given much credence, official forms of multiculturalism are constructed on a premise that is reserved for showcasing the very terms that make racialized groups knowable on the terrain of what can often be understood as external factors. The neglect of the interior life by official forms of multiculturalism point to the contexts for what makes us multiculturally crazy. By the latter phrase I mean that we are forced to negotiate between a number of factors, which produce a schizophrenic response to one's place within the group and the nation. Such responses complicate official forms of multiculturalism because central to the *schizo* or multiply complicated response is desire and desire always remains just beyond our reach, out of bounds. Thus the subaltern subject must negotiate between racialized conditions, personal and collective desires and various practices which position them in ambiguous relation to group(s) and nation(s) that it is assumed they naturally belong to – in short, heritage and its limits become at stake.

Thus in terms of a new political logic of multiculturalism that might account for the psychic life of racial minorities in metropolitan spaces a theory and practice that can account for both individual and collective subjectivity is necessary. As Amina Mama puts it, 'I would do this by taking subjectivities as positions in discourses that are historically generated out of collective experience' (1995, p. 82). Mama's analysis informed by Fanon's anti-colonial analysis takes as its premise a move from phylogeny and ontogeny to sociogeny, which for Fanon is a consideration of the individual in relation to a collective history. Thus as Mama states, 'Discourses are not, in other words rational. Nor are they a direct reflection of social reality. What we are seeing here is a manifestation of an identity politics of racial nationalism, in which race politics are linked to physical characteristics, an identity politics that has had a pervasive influence on black radical discourses internationally' (p. 136).

But to come to the crux of the matter here: the interior lives of subaltern subjects are given less than short shrift in current multicultural arrangements. What seems to be at stake is a theory and a practice that can provide room for individuation in the contexts of the ways in which individual subjectivities are formed in concert with collective histories. Such a conceptual premise and move would allow us to approach the issue of 'racial profiling'[2] as both a collective and individual indignity that warrants a redeployment of what is meant by the human in a new post-colonial and post-civil rights world. What is ultimately at stake is the interior life of racialized subjects who must live lives both as community members, citizens (sometimes partially), and as individuals. A multicultural psychology that might recognize the delicate balance between collective historical injustice and its individual manifestations in the present can take us quite a distance ethically.

In the remainder of this chapter I will turn to these ideas by considering culture as a whole way of life, concluding this discussion with some of the ideas offered by Fanon as ways out of the morass of modernity without recourse to a romantic notion of a before. Rather his engagement is with the urgency of the here and now. Significantly, what is crucially important (at least to me) is how Fanon comes full circle on one of the most pressing issues of how we must rethink modernity and postmodernity, that is, Africa.

CULTURE AS A WHOLE WAY OF LIFE

The grandfather of cultural studies Raymond Williams strongly suggested that culture was 'a whole way of life'. Williams made this claim on behalf of the British or English working class – a white working class, that is. Williams wrote that by culture he meant 'a whole way of life, not only as a scale of integrity, but as a mode of interpreting all our common experience, and, in this new interpretation, changing it' (p. 576, quoted in Slack and Whitt, 1992). Embedded in Williams's definition of culture is a nod or more modestly an opening to psychoanalytic possibilities, or at least the space for such possibilities to enter the conversation since working through is a kind of interpretive method. The idea of culture as a whole way of life requires taking as primary to something called culture all the different claims concerning what it means to be human, whether biological, psychic, material, economic, political and so on. So to make a leap here, for Black peoples or peoples made Black, as well as other subordinated peoples, culture is definitely imbued with a range of ingredients similar to what is suggested by Williams's definition.

Thus, in the face of making artificial separations between the life of the interior and the life of the exterior, Black peoples and other subordinated peoples have long demonstrated refusals to separate the two. Historically, scholarship on Black peoples has tended to focus on exteriority and thus the material poverty of Black life has been one of the enduring ways of assessing Black peoples' health. This focus was not unwarranted given the clear material deprivation of Black life in the Diaspora and on the continent. Black life came to be located in the lower realms of material access and privilege – this is now especially true for continental Africa.

However, the artificial separation between exteriority, read as material poverty, and interiority, which came to be read as Black cultural poverty, pointed to the necessary fallacy in making such separations. It is in fact at exactly the site of culture, in this case cultural expression, that Black and other subordinated peoples demonstrate that material poverty is not co-relative with cultural poverty. Cultural expression of Black peoples and other subordinated peoples demonstrates how such expression is indicative of a desiring subject forged in the context of multiple conflicting environmental factors. It is in fact, I would argue, at the site of culture that a theory of apprehension should make its first appearance. Culture as a whole way of life must force those of us interested in making sense of suffering, survival and healing to address the ways in which subordinated peoples continue to make pleasurable, livable lives in ongoing contexts of various forms of degradation.

Let me give an example of my claims here. In the late nineteenth century and early twentieth century only two racially identified groups have contributed any significant inventions to human civilization: Jews and Blacks. Freud (a Jew) invented the theory of psychoanalysis and Blacks in the US invented Jazz, while the only significant twentieth-century instrument, the Steel Pan, was invented in the Caribbean. These new inventions, I would argue, are symptomatic of the social, cultural and psychic position that these groups had been asked to occupy in their given geo-political environments. As inventors of jazz and psychoanalysis Blacks and Jews have proffered another story of modernity. It is a story of modernity fraught with racial conflict that references both interiority and exteriority. They have represented how culture as a whole way of life is filled with the political, the psychic, the material and the social. Before I go any further, part of the claim that I am making here is that while the science of psychoanalysis is a claim of interiority its invention can or might in fact be read as reacting to claims of exteriority. Thus Freud's contributions to understanding interiority are crucially linked to explaining the socio-cultural exteriority of being a Jew in Europe. Jazz is a music of expressive interiority. With all his flaws, the principal theorist of Black interiority is Frantz Fanon.

FANON: A DIAGNOSIS IN BLACK

Fanon concludes *Black Skin White Masks* with the statement 'O my body, make of me always a man who questions!' (p. 232). In short Fanon concludes his landmark book with an apprehension. Fanon's desire to be a questioning subject plays out itself most forcefully in what is his most influential book, *The Wretched of the Earth*. However, in *Black Skin White Masks* Fanon, who is trained as a psychiatrist, launches an attack on colonial culture and its workings. To achieve the poignancy of his attack he draws a number of archetypes which sometimes come quite close to an analysis of given types. But I think it important to state that Fanon clearly does not believe in the ontological validity of something called Black and something called white. However, Fanon is less interested in a theory of explanation for individual behavior than he is in diagnosing what ails us collectively or, put another way, what is wrong with the culture of humanity.

Thus Fanon tells readers very early in *Black Skin White Masks*:

> Reacting against the constitutionalist tendency of the late nineteenth century, Freud insisted that the individual factor be taken into account through psychoanalysis. He substituted for phylogenetic theory the ontogenetic perspective. It will be seen that the black man's alienation is not an individual question. Beside phylogeny and ontogeny stands *sociogeny*.
>
> (p. 11, emphasis added)

I want to suggest that sociogeny opens up a whole new arena of diagnosis, analysis and prognosis. If we read Fanon's sociogeny alongside Jung's collective unconscious, numerous interesting possibilities arise for thinking about the contexts of what we might call culture and thus healing within culture.

In Fanon's final prayer to make of him a man who always questions is the desire for a rethinking of the category of the Human. For me, this signal of the desire to rethink the category of the Human lies in Fanon's claim that 'The architecture of this work is rooted in the temporal' (1967, p. 12) and I believe that the claim is fully achieved in the famous chapter five 'The Fact of Blackness'. Before I turn to chapter five let me state that Fanon's language in *Black Skin White Masks* does not solidify anything related to the category of race. He is always aware of racial claims of difference as positioned within a network of power and its exercise and acquiescence to powerful authorities.

Fanon writes:

> This work represents the sum of the experiences and observations of seven years; regardless of the area I have studied, one thing has struck me: The Negro enslaved by his inferiority, the white man enslaved by his superiority alike behave in accordance with a neurotic orientation. Therefore I have been led to consider their alienation in terms of psychoanalytical classifications.
>
> (1967, p. 60)

Fanon's claim in the above statement is a refusal of calcified racial categories in favor of a language that references the ways or practices of behavior on the part of both whites and Blacks. Thus one of the central features of reading chapter five is that what is claimed on behalf of blackness and whiteness are practices that are changeable over time. We can recover from these categories if we begin the process of working through. Thus Fanon's insistence on the temporality of the work is not an invalid claim. Fanon very early in *Black Skin White Masks* articulates a common but different humanity for both whites and Blacks. For both it is a flawed humanity. And thus it is my argument that Fanon is fundamentally concerned with offering us an analysis that might produce 'new forms of human life' as Sylvia Wynter puts it in her reading of Fanon's sociogenetic intervention (Wynter, 1995).

'The Fact of Blackness' is the diagnosis of, and refusal of, a set of universals about blackness. In Fanon's refusal of the objectifying of blackness and its attendant history of internalized shame in regards to slavery and Africa he states, 'For not only must the black man be black; he must be black in relation to the white man' (p. 110). This classic analysis of how identities are constituted through each other allows Fanon to further articulate his 'new' humanist vision. Thus Fanon later tells us, 'The Negro is not. Any more than the white man' (p. 231). He is intent to unravel the facts of blackness in an effort to remake the category of the Human as something more encompassing than it currently passes for.

The Wretched of the Earth is Fanon's explication of sociogeny. If we read *Wretched* as a text meant to diagnose, analyze and offer a possible prognosis and even healing of the colonial rupture and trauma then it functions as a sociogenetic analysis. What is at stake in articulating sociogeny or the sociogenetic is an attempt to think the group and the individual at once. But the group takes primacy in this particular analysis. Additionally, sociogeny recognizes or more strongly refuses the mind/body split. And in fact *Wretched* is the text where Fanon most forcefully reconnects mind and body in their social and political contexts to offer us an analysis of the stakes of rethinking the category of the Human. He writes: 'This new humanity cannot do otherwise than define a new humanism both for itself and for others' (1968, p. 246). Embedded in the conflict that is the struggle between the colonizer and the colonized is a struggle over culture. Once both groups are liberated from a flawed way of life something else might become possible – a whole new way of life.

CONCLUSION

What we get from Fanon is a diagnosis in Black. But it is a diagnosis in Black that seeks to question the ways in which individuals and groups have been produced within the context of modernity. The impact of modernity is a struggle that Clemmont Vontress (1985) characterizes as 'culture engender[ing] frustration' (p. 25). Two of the most traumatic ruptures of cultural frustration are the attempted genocide and actual genocide of Native peoples; and the brutal violence of the Middle Passage. Those two modern ruptures – Native genocide and the Middle Passage – constitute the first instance of cross-cultural failure and thus the necessary need for cross-cultural healing and recovery. The violence at the centre of those traumas was the imposition of European conceptions of the human, a conception that rendered Natives and Blacks non-human. It has been the struggle for all those rendered non-human in a post-1492 world to regain and thus resignify what it means to be Human. Cross-cultural counselling goes a long way in producing this new humanism. At the center of reclaiming a non-oppressive concept of the Human, Africa and Native determination in its totality must be approached.

In approaching larger social dynamics of human life cross-cultural counselling must also balance the delicate relations between interiority and exteriority. Black Diaspora peoples are often addressed in terms of the exterior life (for example poverty) but often such an address comes at the expense of the interior life (psychic health). Fanon's sociogeny helps us to move towards a much-needed, but fundamentally different, response to Black psychic life. It is a response that understands the crucial role of rectifying the social as a foundational element of healing and recovery. One of the central outcomes of the post-1492 world has been that culture has become the terrain within which psychic and social life is reduced to meaninglessness or its reverse. Fanon's sociogeny moves us towards correcting this failure of human cultural practice.

Notes

1 The term subaltern has come to mean those who sit almost but not quite outside the societal systems of representation and authority. These people are subjected to unspeakable forms of oppression. Gayatri Spivak's scholarship on Indian women known as the untouchables and the Subaltern History Group made the term popular and useful in post-colonial studies.
2 Racial profiling is the practice of authorities like police officers, customs officials and immigration officers (many in security-type fields do this) deliberately targeting those who are understood as non-white as potentially engaging in illegal acts. This practice is solely based on the assumption that racial minorities are more prone to criminal behavior.

References

Deleuze, G. and Guattari, F. (1987) *A Thousand Plateaus: Capitalism and Schizophrenia*, trans. B. Massumi. Minneapolis: University of Minnesota Press.

Fanon, F. (1963) *The Wretched of the Earth*. New York: Grove Press.

Fanon, F. (1967) *Black Skin White Masks*. New York: Grove Press.

Hall, S. (2000) Conclusion: The Multi-cultural Question, in B. Hess (ed.), *Un/settled Multiculturalisms: Diaspora, Entanglements, Transruptions*. London: Zed Books.

Mama, A. (1995) *Beyond the Masks: Race, Gender and Subjectivity*. London: Routledge.

Mills, C. (1997) *The Racial Contract*. Ithaca: Cornell University Press.

Slack, J. and Whitt, L. (1992) Ethics and Cultural Studies, in L. Grossberg, C. Nelson and P. Treichler (eds), *Cultural Studies*. New York: Routledge.

Vontress, C. E. (1985) Theories of Counseling: A Comparative Analysis, in Ronald J. Samuda and Aaron Wolfgang (eds), *Intercultural Counseling and Assessment: Global Perspectives*. Toronto: C.J. Hogrefe.

Walcott, R. (2003) *Black Like Who?: Writing Black Canada*. Toronto: Insomniac Press.

Wynter, S. (1995) 1492: A New World, in V. Hyatt and R. Nettleford (eds), *Race, Discourse and the Origin of the Americas: A New World View*. Washington, DC: Smithsonian Institution Press.

Chapter 3

Culturalism in multicultural psychotherapy

Farhad Dalal

The multiculturalist agenda seeks to compensate for some of the anti-pathies and confusions arising in encounters when practitioner and patient are said to be from different cultures. It was surmised that these misunder-standings would be reduced if practitioners familiarized themselves with the patient's culture in order to relate to the material from within the patient's sense-making schemas. The reasoning behind this idea is the belief that when human beings encounter something different from themselves, something they do not understand, not only are they inclined to mis-interpret what they encounter, it also arouses in them a mixture of anxiety and hostility. In my opinion multiculturalism's focus on information and familiarization, although completely sensible in one regard, avoids con-fronting the problematic of power and renders the world more benign than it actually is.

The question I would like to enter this arena with is: when is a psycho-therapy (or psychoanalysis or counselling for that matter)[1] thought to be *not* multicultural? Consider: the very notion of multicultural suggests the possibility of its normative inverse, something which one might call mono-cultural. Similarly, the affiliated idea of 'cross-cultural therapy' implies the possibility of a therapy that remains within the tramlines of a mono-culture. On the other hand, the notion of transcultural therapy is almost the antonym of the previous two as it invokes an idea of a therapy taking place in a region beyond, outside, or prior to, culture itself in some way. I will argue that there are critical difficulties with these ideas as they are derived from the twin philosophies of individualism and internalism, which not only privilege the individual over the social group, the internal world (psychology) over the external social world (sociology), but also mistakenly take the element in each of the pairs to be the opposite of and in conflict with the other element. Also, I will argue that whatever multicultural psy-chotherapy is, it is something more problematic than the way it is usually conceived of by both its detractors and supporters.

There are two dangers we are going to be continually faced with in this discussion: the first, which I will call culturalism, is that we become fixated by culture. The other danger is that we try to do away with culture entirely to end up in a culture-free space. Both these dangers are founded on, and alternate between, two kinds of errors. The first error is one in which the division of humanity into cultures, races or ethnicities is taken to be an unproblematic given, and then the issue becomes one of 'how to negotiate these differences'. One can say that culturalism is the tendency to get mesmerized by some of the divisions between human groupings found in the *external* social world. The alternative position is one in which there is a retreat into the *internal* world of individuals in which two sorts of things are presumed. First, that one can think, work and live in some way outside social groupings as 'an individual', and second, that the internal world – although affected by the social world – is autonomous and exists in some way outside or/and prior to the social world. I will begin by probing the culture-free position.

CULTURE-FREE THERAPY

There are several rationales for this position, the first of which is the assertion that therapy takes place (or ought to take place) at a deep enough level in the psyche for there to be no need to take account of cultural configurations. Implicit in this viewpoint is a model of psyche in which culture sits 'on top' of something else in the psyche. This 'something else' is construed as an amalgam of biological inheritance mixed in with the residual effects of the individual's developmental history. This model of culture-free therapy can be called transcultural therapy. It is here that we find the universalists, who believe that there are developmental patterns (e.g. the Oedipal phase, the paranoid-schizoid position, etc.) and funda- mental psychic mechanisms (splitting, projection, part object relations, etc.) that are the same for all human beings. So, according to them, the more surface cultural differences between human groupings are of little conse- quence to deep psychotherapy. Within psychoanalytic discourse, an often- cited proponent of this viewpoint is Devereux (1953), who calls the 'deep' work psycho*analysis* and refers to the 'shallower' work as cross-cultural psycho*therapy*.

Questions of 'how' and 'why' it is that strong feelings of aggression and hostility tend to get triggered when faced with people of different cultures tend to get explained in this model by the idea of projection. What is said is that difficulties in the internal worlds of individuals get projected into something external, say those of another culture. This then is said to result in members of that cultural group being experienced as difficult in some way. This is the 'how' part of the answer. The logic of the argument then leads one to say that to understand situations in the *external* social world, one needs to attend to the processes going on in the *internal* worlds of the protagonists as it is here that the sources of discomfitures and delights in the external world will be found. For example, Melanie Klein says 'the understanding of [the individual's] personality is the foundation for the understanding of social life' (1959, p. 247). Fairbairn says 'all sociological problems are ultimately reducible to problems of individual psychology' (1935, p. 241). Winnicott says 'the basis of group psychology is the psychology of the individual' (Winnicott, 1965, p. 146).

Another of the ways that therapists manage to conceive the work of therapy taking place in a culture-free zone is through the utilization of language that has become highly abstracted. The result of speaking and thinking in abstractions is that notions become so disembodied that they appear to have no need to make any recourse to the actual lived material world. Two such abstractions that are of direct concern to our subject are those of similarity and difference. It is here that we will find the 'why' part of the answer, which begins by taking the idea that all humans have a fundamental problem dealing with difference *per se* as a truism.

Freud institutionalized this idea in his first theory of instincts. He said that the self-preservative instinct experienced the presence of anything/ anyone *different* to the self as a criticism of itself, and so felt aggressed and responded in turn with aggression to the 'difference'. Over the years there have been a number of alternative ideas proposed for the *sources* of the problem with difference. One idea is that the source of the difficulty with *difference* is to be found in the processes of primary *differentiation*: birth and separation from mother. It is suggested that because this early process of *differentiation* is a painful one, it leads one in later life to an aversion towards those who are felt to be *different*. The slide from differentiation to difference is questionable; but even if the slide has legitimacy, it does not take up the critical question: *different in what sense?* It is always the case that two people will inevitably be different by virtue of some attributes, but similar by virtue of other attributes. So an experience of being different could equally and legitimately be an experience of being similar. The question we should be attending to is how is it that we are led to have an experience of similarity in some circumstances and of difference in others – *when it is possible to have both in all circumstances?* We can see then that by speaking of similarity and difference in the abstract, it gives us the false impression that they are absolute states and opposites.

An illustration of the point is found in Tan (1993), who says that one avoids facing the fact of difference (because it is painful) by its denial. He then defines racism as the denial of difference. It seems to me that even if the first statement were an existential truth, the second is a *non sequitur*. In my opinion he mistakes the symptom for the disease because of theorizing at the level of abstractions. I would say that at its base racism is the denial of similarity – the racist's clarion call is that 'they' are *fundamentally* different from 'us' and it is because of these differences that we (naturally) cannot abide each other. However, the liberal conscience defends against conscious knowledge of having exactly these sorts of disparaging feelings by a reaction formation – by refusing to see any differences at all ('I don't see the colour – just the person'). And the reason for this is that if certain sorts of differences were allowed into consciousness this would also allow in the problematic affects that the differences are cathected with. It is for this reason that the experiences of differences are repressed.

The point is illustrated further through the idea of 'the stranger'. All infants go through a stage at around the age of six months when they experience 'stranger anxiety' during which they experience something (that looks to us) like fear, distress and hostility at the sight of strangers. It is suggested by Basch-Kahre (1984) amongst others, that the fears and hostilities one 'inevitably' experiences on meeting strangers in adult life are a reactivation of the fears and hostilities from this early developmental time. But by noticing that our reactions to strangers are not uniformly negative and fearful, we can see that the idea of 'the stranger' is also an abstraction and so obfuscates more than it explains. A young black man knocking at the door in the middle of the night is likely to elicit a very different response from that of an older white woman, although *both are strangers*. It is also the case that the response elicited will be informed by two other complexities – *who* is opening the door and *where* the door is. In other words the reactions are going to be moulded by the power-relationships between the identities of the protagonists and the meanings each is given by the context in which the meeting is taking place. So depending on who is opening the door and in what context, 'Christian' might elicit a response either of terror or of relief. Ultimately, there is no such thing as 'the stranger' *per se* as strangers are always embodied and so are inevitably invested with very particular meanings.

In sum, I have been critiquing the two axioms that the preceding models implicitly rely on: (a) that the workings of the psyche are universal and so cultural differences have little or no relevance; and (b) differences between groups of people inevitably set off antipathies between them. The culture-free position is not only untenable, it is in fact completely culture-bound. What is actually taking place is that a particular model of the psyche with its versions of health and illness, although contingent, is taken to be normative, universal and then applied to all peoples and contexts. As such, one could say that it is a form of colonialism in which one cultural view-point is used to subjugate and de-legitimate another. Thus the mere *idea* of the so-called culture-free position is in fact the expression of an ideology. As is well known, the work of ideology is to give contingent historical relations the impression of being natural relations, and so of obscuring and making invisible the workings of power.

CULTURALISM

Whilst the multiculturalist ethos quite rightly seeks to counter this kind of imperialism by endorsing pluralism, it nonetheless at times falls into the trap of reproducing problematic aspects of the belief system that it is challenging. For instance, when there are tensions between blacks and whites in some city, then it is supposed that the tensions have arisen *because* they are of different colours, and so they need to learn to *tolerate* each other. Education and familiarization are thought to promote the ability to tolerate and this leads directly to the multiculturalist rationalist decree that we are 'different but equal' and so we should respect each other's differences and, in particular, we should respect each other's *cultural* differences; there are issues with how they arise within some streams of multiculturalist discourse that ask us to 'respect cultural differences' uncritically.

A number of issues would need to be considered. First, just the use of the phrase 'British (or any other) culture' suggests a homogeneity and uniformity that simply does not exist. British culture is not a unity but a great many overlapping and contesting cultures – for example, Christian, city, county, street, garage, skate, high, and so on. True, one could say that metropolitan culture is different from that of county culture, but in doing this one is lending each of them too the illusion of homogeneity. When one looks *within* any one of these then one does not find uniformity but a muddle of contesting diversities, and when one looks within an element within the diversity, then all one finds is more diversity, *ad infinitum*. Second, it is also the case that any single individual *simultaneously* inhabits not just one but a great range and variety of contesting and overlapping cultural frames – each with their own demands and claims on the individual. Third, the fact that the boundaries of where one culture begins and another ends is very fluid: and further, as culture draws on a variety of different kinds of things to name itself, gives us another point of interrogation. Why, in a moment, is one led to make a distinction at the level of nation (say British culture) rather than a more parochial level (say Yorkshire), and, at another moment, why is it that very different kinds of distinction appear more meaningful – say psychoanalytic culture or black culture?

Given these multiple possibilities, what leads us to assert that the therapy taking place between Mr. Smith and Mr. Singh is multicultural whilst that between Mr. Smith and Mr. Jones is not? As we already noted earlier, it is possible to frame both encounters in terms of similarity as well as difference. So how and why do we come to experience one encounter as taking place across a difference and the other as within a region of similarity? Given the infinity of similarities and differences that are continually present, why is it that at one moment a particular version of something called cultural difference suddenly becomes critically significant? Further, just what is it that is being construed as a cultural difference?

The answers, I would say, are not to do with the differences themselves, but with the *functions* the processes of differentiation are being required to perform. It is not the case that one simply 'finds' cultural differences which one then finds oneself responding to. Rather, one finds oneself emphasizing certain differences in order to create a differentiation. The question one needs constantly to ask is: what and whose purpose is being served by making the differentiation here rather than there?

But what is culture? One kind of definition would be to say that cultures are established when three conditions are satisfied: first, the systematization of certain conventions, behaviours and beliefs; second, the rationale for that particular form of systematization; and third, for numbers of people to broadly adhere to these conventions and beliefs and their rationales. It follows then that those who adhere to a cultural system can be said to *belong* to that culture and so are similar to each other in that sense.

Whilst this kind of definition captures some useful things, it leaves out the issue of power. Cultures are not homogeneous unities in another sense too: they are structures consisting of systems of power relations in which the rules are such that some of the groupings within that culture fare better than other groupings. Thus in many if not most cultural systems the dice are loaded to allow men to fare better than women in almost all walks of life; it is no coincidence that in the main it is men who are allowed to become priests and thus privy to the wishes and thoughts of deities. And of course there is always a rationale as to why it *has* to be so. Hence although the 'Untouchable' and the 'Brahmin' are both part of the Hindu cultural system – they will have very different experiences of it. So a therapy taking place between an Untouchable and a Brahmin could (and perhaps should) also be called multicultural.

By bringing power into the equation one gets to see a less benign side of the schema called culture. I would say that all cultural systems are (amongst other things) the institutionalization of systems of oppression. If this is the case then one can no longer respect cultural difference in any straight-forward way, because to respect cultural difference is inevitably to endorse, and collude with, a system of oppression. The fact that the rules are insti-tutionalized means that the loaded dice are invisible and nowhere to be seen, with the result that the things that take place appear to be an outcome of 'natural' dynamics. It is no coincidence that it is usually those who are the beneficiaries of a cultural organization who tend to be its loudest defenders.

CLINICAL THEMES

The complexity of multiculturalism was brought home to me through the work with a female client 'Nargis'. She was born in the UK into a secular

Muslim family. When she came to see me she had been married for five years to someone from a very similar background. It transpired that her husband-to-be's family had thought her 'other'. They looked down on her as coming from an inferior grouping despite both families being Muslim, belonging to the same 'sect', speaking the same language, and both deriving from India. Both families would be counted as belonging to the same cultural group by most 'ethnic monitoring' instruments. Despite this the in-law family thought of her as different. The couple meanwhile thought of themselves as being part of the *same* cultural grouping. What is going on?

We could understand the in-law reaction as an example of Freud's 'Narcissism of Minor Differences' (Freud, 1921) in which he suggested that the smaller the differences between groups, the harder they had to work to sustain the differentiation. But if this is a universal mechanism, then why are the couple not caught up in it? One could of course argue that the couple's conscious experience of being similar to each other is a denial and a reaction formation against their deeper 'real' sense of being different to each other. Rather than go down this sort of internalist route, I think it more productive to think about how and why it is that the in-laws are more caught up with difference and the couple with similarity. It turned out that the boy's family were emphasizing a detail in regional differences that had meaning for them whilst growing up in India which was critical to their sense of identity in that particular socio-political context. Meanwhile for the couple, born as brown skins into the English Midlands, their sense of selves – their identities – were forged by other concerns and preoccupations. Of particular relevance to them were their experiences of growing up as Muslim (albeit secular ones) and black in a predominantly white context, and the effects of these experiences on their life trajectories; in their opinion the in-laws' perceptions were anachronistic. The modern British context tarred them all with the same brush – rudely and crudely: as 'Pakis'. One can see how the processes of marginalization and exclusion are generating a belonging category. It is the same process that has generated the hyphenated identity Black-British.

It is important to note that identity is not something fixed, but is constantly being moulded through the interactions taking place with others. When I first met Nargis she presented herself as a strict Muslim; however, it became clear very quickly that her devoutness had emerged and grown in the time of her marriage. Her shift over time from secularity to devoutness was a means of countering the denigration doled out by the in-laws by occupying the moral high ground in relation to them. She came to know the Koran and its teachings much more thoroughly than they and came to practise a daily life style that became progressively orthodox. It also became clear that she was quite unconscious of this shift as a strategy in a power struggle. Her conscious thoughts were much more about how unfair it was that they slighted her so, given how 'good' she was.

These shifts and responses are not surface phenomena but integral to the sense of self. Thus it was not the case that Nargis cynically found herself quoting the Koran at her in-laws; she genuinely came to believe (and continued to believe through the therapy) in the teachings. We can see in the whole scenario how an assortment of cultural attributes are being evoked and used variously in the power struggles between the protagonists. I would go even further to say that whenever the notion of culture becomes an issue what is taking place (somewhere) is a power struggle.

The notion of culture is continually mobilized in the service of a power struggle; the disavowal of culture also serves the same purpose. They are both means of legitimating and lending authority to particular ways of being. The following example occurred in the context of an analytic group therapy (the critique I have been developing in this chapter is based on my work in radical group analytic theory (see Dalal, 1998, 2002)).

For a variety of reasons, a black group member ('Winston') had given very little of himself in the two years since joining the group. He missed a session and on his return he told the group that he had been obliged to be with his partner the previous week, as she had just had a miscarriage. Whilst sympathetic, the other group members were also aggrieved because they had no idea that his partner had been pregnant for some months. When they challenged him as to why he had kept this significant life event to himself, he replied that it was not his intention to *hide* anything; the reason for his reticence was that in *his* culture one kept this sort of thing in the family. Following this the group fell silent.

I understand what was going on in the following way. When the group challenge Winston, the defence is to play the 'culture card' in order to close the door on any further exploration. The group fall silent because of the unspoken injunction to 'respect cultural difference', leaving them nowhere to go. We can see that in this instance the ruling to 'respect' cultural difference is being used defensively to make something sacrosanct and unquestionable. But there are also other cultures present in the room including the one we may call group analytic psychotherapy culture. The conventions of this culture, which in my role as therapist I am trying to foster, encourage participants in the direction of increasingly open communication at all sorts of levels. Hence, according to *my* group analytic culture, I read Winston's hiddenness as something needing interpreting and deconstructing; meanwhile, according to Winston culture, his hiddenness is not to be touched. Although I am challenging Winston's retreat into an idea of 'culture', it is not the case that I am occupying a culture-free position; what is taking place is nothing other than cultural conflict. What is to be done at this point?

According to the ethics generated by my professional cultural system, for me to 'respect' Winston's version of cultural difference would be to abandon him in his fortress of solitude. But neither would it be ethical to try to overpower him and break down his defences forcefully, because presumably the defences are there for reasons, even if I might think them misguided. There is also now the question: how true is Winston's claim that the conventions of his culture prohibit certain things being spoken about? It would certainly be helpful if I knew about the conventions of that culture as it would give me grounds for challenging his defensive use of a cultural convention. However, even if his claim were true, it would be the case that not everyone from that cultural background would follow the convention in that particular way and degree. It is for this reason I have been speaking of Winston culture rather than Caribbean culture. As Sudhir Kakar (1993, p. 307) says:

> what is important in the psychoanalysis, say, of an Indian patient, is not 'Indian' culture but the culture of the patient . . . [which] is not 'Indian' but is what has come down in the Punjabi culture of his social class . . . transformed by his family . . . [which] become[s] a part of his psyche. Conformity to some aspects of the broader Hindu civilization, rejection of others, and the transformation of yet others . . . [make] direct linking of the patient's 'self' with a generalized Indian culture . . . only minimally useful.

CONCLUSIONS

I have been arguing that the issue of cultural difference is always relevant as none of us has the possibility of residing in a culture-free zone. However, I have also been arguing that the relevance is not so much to do with the differences in the contents of cultural systems, but the way that the differences are used to position the protagonists in the field of power relations. In sum, I have been arguing that it is not enough to simply respect cultural differences; rather what is required is a critical engagement with the differences, and in the process risk the transformation of both other and self.

Note

1 In this chapter I use the terms 'psychotherapy' and 'therapy' to refer to notions of psychoanalysis and counselling. In doing this I am nevertheless conscious that there are a number of critical differences between and within each of these that differentiate them from each other.

References

Basch-Kahre, E. (1984) On Difficulties Arising in Transference and Countertransference when Analyst and Analysand have Different Socio-cultural Backgrounds, *International Review of Psychoanalysis* 11: 61–67.

Dalal, F. (1998) *Taking the Group Seriously: Towards a Post Foulkesian Group Analytic Theory*. London: Jessica Kingsley Publishers.

Dalal, F. (2002) *Race, Colour and the Processes of Racialization: New Perspectives from Psychoanalysis, Group Analysis and Sociology*. London: Brunner Routledge.

Devereaux, G. (1953) Cultural Factors in Psychoanalytic Therapy, *Journal of the American Psychoanalytic Association* 1: 629–655.

Fairbairn, R. (1935) The Social Significance of Communism Considered in the Light of Psychoanalysis, in R. Fairbairn (1994), *Psychoanalytic Studies of the Personality*. London: Routledge.

Freud, S. (1921) Group Psychology and the Analysis of the Ego, *Standard Edition*, 18, pp. 69–144. London: Hogarth Press.

Kakar, S. (1993) In Search of Self in India and Japan: Toward a Cross-cultural Psychology, *Psychoanalytic Quarterly* 62: 305–309.

Klein, M. (1959) Our Adult World and its Roots in Infancy, in M. Klein (1988), *Envy and Gratitude and Other Works 1946–1963*. London: Virago Press.

Tan, R. (1993) Racism and Similarity: Paranoid-Schizoid Structures, *British Journal of Psychotherapy*, 10(1): 33–43.

Winnicott, D. (1965) *The Family and Individual Development*. London: Tavistock Publications.

Chapter 4

Psychotherapy across the cultural divide[1]

Dinesh Bhugra and Kamaldeep Bhui

All brands of psychotherapy are based on their own diverse theoretical origins, yet all seek individual change through a 'human relationship'. This relationship requires some nurturing even before the assessment interview and first session; a potential patient has their potential therapist in mind before and after the first meeting; thus cultural and racial stereotypes may come into play in the mind of the therapist or the patient. Once a therapeutic relationship begins, it is reflected upon in a way which manifests itself, we hope, in change. Wolberg (1977) classified the psychotherapies into three broad categories: supportive, re-educative, and reconstructive. Supportive psychotherapy is for those who are going through a sudden transitional phase of life (a life event), and for those who have a chronic debility such that 'basic change' is unlikely to be realized but, nonetheless, their distress is disabling and painful (Block, 1986). Re-educative types of psychotherapy aim to remodel the client's thinking, behaviour and habits, and not to focus on the causation but on promotion and development of new and more adaptive forms of behaviour. Reconstructive psychotherapy aims to understand impulses and habitual styles of dealing with people which have their origins in the client's earlier environment; it increases the ability to modify repetitive failures of interpersonal relationship and to relieve distress. Ego strength improves and more appropriate defences emerge. Behaviour and cognitive therapies fall into the re-educative group. Interpretative or psychodynamic therapies will fall under the reconstructive category.

Although the psychotherapies are based on differing theoretical standpoints, the majority nonetheless relieve distress using models of treatment which arise from the developed Western world's perspective about the mind, illness, emotional distress and healing. Therefore all psychotherapies are grounded in a specific culturally determined 'model of mind' and its accompanying formulations about restitution. For example, in Freud's *The Ego and the Id*, the visual representation of the mind looks like a brain and represents a very precise, almost neurological, appraisal of the structures and functions of the mind (Freud, 1984). This brain-like representation of the mind probably has its origins in Freud's earlier profession as a neurologist and a doctor in which the precise anatomical location of dysfunction is imperative. Scientific models and symbols representing our environment and problems of living are used as the building blocks of innovative conceptual advances in understanding the world and solving our problems. These scientific models, which have their origin in human experience, are evaluated against the broader social and cultural experience of society: the collective human experience. Thus a psychotherapeutic model which develops in a particular country, a particular historical era and during a specific scientific period inevitably promotes these influences in its mental representation of the world, its notions of kinship, the self, and everyday knowledge. Distinct cultures shape the language and experience of emotions by selectively encouraging or discouraging specific sets of emotional experience which are regarded as taboo or dysfunctional within that society. A recognition that an individual, group, or family are displaying these unsanctioned behaviours or beliefs signals to other members of that society that they are ill and need help. Each society determines its own sets of sanctioned and unsanctioned beliefs and behaviours. Similarly emotional states may be invested with positive or negative value. Within each society and its broad culture, there are sub-cultures which also shape definitions of normal from abnormal, healthy from ill, in need of help or not. Hence culturally determined states of distress give rise to models of restitution which are in accord with that culture's understanding of distress (Marsella and White, 1982). For example, possession states in India can help resolve local conflicts by involving the local community in the healing process; possession becomes a means of seeking help in that specific cultural context. Knowledge that spirits of the ancestors and gods are present on earth and can possess an individual's body is a prerequisite in a society which offers the possessed person culturally compatible healing leading to relief from distress (Perera et al., 1995). In the UK we would be rather reluctant to exorcize a patient with a spider phobia or a borderline personality disorder. Even if we believed in this treatment we would have to persuade the patient of the rationale. We would have to believe that spider phobias could be cured by exorcism. Akbar (1996) writes that this form of grafting of one psychology to solve the problems in different societies with their own distinct psychologies is doomed to failure. We argue that such an adaptation of our models of understanding and relieving emotional distress is feasible; it requires courage and caution. Sue and Zane (1987) suggest that to be culturally credible we need to conceptualize problems in a manner that is consistent with the client's belief system.

CULTURAL DIVERSITY AND CONTEXT

Ethnocentrism

Any psychotherapy has to consider the individual holistically. The expectations and emerging dependency in such a relationship are important markers of transformational experience. In socially and culturally fluid situations, the therapists, when they are sensitive, can move away from a priori assumptions about the significance of ethnicity to a construction of a new set of beliefs more suited to a combination of the patient's and their own world view. One could argue that the reconstructive therapies perhaps deploy this strategy in any instance and are least likely to cause concern about the ethnocentricity of the treatment paradigm. Yet some schools of psychoanalysis have attracted considerable criticism about racist theories and practice (Dalal, 1997). Psychiatry and psychology as disciplines have also been reminded of the tendency to advance knowledge and understanding in a culturally and racially oppressive manner (Fernando, 1988; Howitt and Owusu-Bempah, 1994). These debates are increasingly heard in the public arena. Therapists need to be self-reflective and examine assumptions which might inadvertently introduce and enact an imbalance of power. An insensitive therapeutic encounter may be experienced by the client as a repetition of racial oppression and its accompanying power issues. To neglect this potential, especially early in any therapeutic encounter, would simply generate a barrier that could conclude with premature termination and treatment failure. If a patient is not able to feel believed or understood about such a sensitive issue as racist persecution then, even if the therapist believes the matter not to be significant, an insensitive disavowal of it will only lead to therapeutic barriers. The oppression of women, especially those coming from ethnic minorities in which their roles may be under immense pressures towards change, contributes to feelings of powerlessness and sometimes rootlessness; this reality also needs to be understood in the full cultural and historical context of the patient's biographical experience. Brah (1996) goes so far as to conclude that racial dialectics always include issues of gender and the two are not separate debates.

Imbalance of power

The types of communication appropriate for one culture, e.g. self-disclosure in a hierarchical doctor–patient relationship, or interaction in a group setting, may not suit another (Fernando, 1988). Bloom (1991) urges that one major problem in psychotherapy across cultures is to understand how individual fantasy is transformed into interpersonal behaviour and social patterns. Individuals internalize, evaluate and respond emotionally to social situations and relationships in accord with culturally favoured patterns. Most mainstream indigenous therapies in the West are considered to involve a systematic application of a 'scientific understanding of human nature' to the treatment of the mentally ill. In societies or groups that hold primarily religious world views, indigenous psychotherapies may well have a magico-religious basis and healing rites often merging with religious rites (Frank and Frank, 1991).

With the power that is invested generally by society in the professional, and that invested by the specific professional training, it is only too comfortable for the professional to remain in a position of supremacy and prescribe forms of understanding and treatment to the patient (Acharyya, 1992). Another complicating factor in the therapist–client dyad, where two individuals come from different ethnicities and have markedly differing cultural identities, is that of conceptualizing somatic presentations as a defence mechanism (Littlewood and Lipsedge, 1989). This may again reflect the Eurocentric bias of theory and hence of therapy provision. And yet, caution needs to be exerted in putting together a reductionist stereotype of the black patient who is being influenced by their own culture, the majority culture, personal experiences and endowments, and reactions to racial oppression (Jones, 1985). The process of identity formation includes adaptation in a real social world as well as a world of internal idealized and denigrated racial images. Maturation in a predominantly white society will, of course, have an impact on the degree to which ethnic minorities identify with and adhere to the dominant perceptions of black peoples. Thomas (1992) outlines with vivid case material how black can be seen as inferior by black children and adults because that has been their experience. Interpreting this in non-racial terms as unconscious phantasy or a ubiquitous developmental task denies the reality of formative forces in personality maturation. Kareem (1992) points out that white therapists will find it easy to dismiss racism as it has not happened to them and is beyond their internal and external experience. The patient's material can only then be accommodated and worked with if there is a preparedness to acknowledge our limitations when working with racial, ethnic and cultural minorities.

Therapeutic alliance

Therapeutic alliance is relevant across a broad range of psychotherapies. Positive identification with the therapist and components of the therapeutic interaction produce an alliance that can lead to fruitful change. Although the concept of therapeutic alliance emerges from psychoanalysis, such a working contract between the client and the therapist is essential in all therapies. The therapist contributes to the alliance in terms of both personal attitudes and professional therapeutic behaviour (see Hartley, 1985). The client brings to the alliance experiences with significant persons, degrees of self-observation and self-disclosure and cognitive processing skills. The client's capacity to form a therapeutic alliance depends upon several factors. With cognitive and behavioural therapies, for example, compliance with allocated and discussed homework will demonstrate whether meaningful collaboration is possible.

The three major problems in the formation of this alliance are to do with the therapist, the client and the disorder itself (Rush, 1985). For the client, motivation, processes of organizing information and reflective negotiation of conflict are important. Whereas initially a greater degree of directiveness is typical in all except the psychodynamic therapies, this may change as the therapeutic relationship progresses. The therapist must understand the cultural meaning of degrees of directiveness and involvement and continue to negotiate, openly and searchingly, the parameters of the therapy with the individual client. Particular techniques used in each therapy may need to be modified. For example, behaviour tasks with deadlines may be viewed as intrusive or pushy thereby leading on to feelings of confusion, frustration and lack of confidence in the therapy. At the other extreme, total flexibility and passivity in the encounter might be interpreted as incompetence by some ethnic minority groups whose model of healer is a traditional one; in this model of healing the healer asks few questions and 'knows' the problems of the patient quite quickly. A shared *world view* has been shown to be more important to client satisfaction than any other factor. Jones (1985) studied 109 black and white patients, half in racially similar therapist–client dyads and half in dissimilar ones. Therapist–client match had little influence on outcome of longer-term psychotherapy. The early phase of therapeutic alliance is perhaps the most important phase in formation of rapport and working together. It is here that the racial and cultural factors become vital. Psychotherapists working with clients of different ethnic background need to be aware of their clients' feelings about racial and cultural differences in order to facilitate effective treatment and to understand potential transference actions.

Failure in empathy may lead to an increased likelihood of negative countertransference reactions. Anti-therapeutic cultural stereotypes might emerge (Blumenthal *et al.*, 1985). Furthermore, a therapist's own knowledge and continual self-awareness are important factors in preventing personal reactions from interfering in therapy. Again the psychodynamic therapy trainings specifically attend to this, but racial and cultural attitudes may never be properly scrutinized in the therapist's personal analysis, nor in the training programmes of the training organizations. This self-understanding coupled with cultural understanding is of prime importance in a therapeutic alliance. The approach adopted by Pesechkian (1990) is to identify the rules by which a behaviour is labelled as shocking within the therapeutic encounter. Another feature of this approach is to accept that the sense of one's own body is a legitimate mode of dealing with conflicts by the way a person perceives and responds to his/her own body. Psychotherapeutic belief systems can perform a 'remoralization' function back to the dominant value system. This can therefore undermine value systems which are in the patient's culture but are identified as psychopathology within the psychotherapeutic paradigm employed.

PSYCHOTHERAPY AND CULTURE

Psychotherapy is often used to refer only to Western models of therapy. Yet various healing practices derived from prehistory have influenced psycho-therapies of the modern day. Historical and anthropological research has revealed that in 'primitive people' many concepts of modern (i.e. Western) psychotherapies exist (Ellenberger, 1970). Religious conversion, faith-healing and shamanism have features in common with psychotherapy – altered cognitive states, suggestion, cognitive reorganization and social reinforcement by the healing presence. Whatever the model of psychother-apy, there are at least some common factors in such an approach. For example:

- The client's motivation and expectations are always important to consider.
- The client's image of the therapist may deploy race as a master label through which to begin to anticipate their encounter with the therapist.
- Both client and therapist have to agree on the rationale for therapy, which then needs to be converted into a therapeutic plan.

Omission of the ethnic, racial, linguistic, cultural as well as social class dimension will only manifest in a prolonged engagement phase. One might consider that this is, in any event, a part of the work but an oversight could result in unnecessary and premature termination of treatment.

It must be emphasized that ethnicity should not be seen as a proxy marker for more important demographic, cultural, experiential and personality differences that are more closely linked to psychotherapy process and outcomes. There are no good research outcome measures and few well-validated methodologies to examine patient and setting variables, but initial work concludes that culturally sensitive therapies and trainings appear to better engage clients and increase the effectiveness of therapists (Sue *et al.*, 1994). Many patients are not offered psychotherapy because they are deemed to lack the psychological mindedness to engage in self-reflection and analysis (Coltart, 1988). There has been an extensive cross-fertilization between psychotherapy and social anthropology as disciplines, yet the most basic questions regarding the relationship between culture and psychother-apy remain unanswered (Havenaar, 1990). Thus there is no systematic formulation of the role of culture on the therapeutic process, and cultural aspects of healing have rarely dealt with psychotherapeutic practice. Frank (1961, 1974) has attempted to summarize the instrumental components common to all therapies as: (1) a special type of relationship (intense, confiding, etc.); (2) a therapeutic setting that is recognized as a place of healing and is socially sanctioned; (3) a rationale or myth that explains the patient's suffering; and (4) the procedure or ritual based on a therapeutic rationale which counteracts the causes of the suffering. Roth and Fonagy (1996) found that non-specific factors beyond the characteristics of individual therapeutic traditions account for effectiveness. These common factors are the dominant ingredient and perhaps it is in this arena of engagement of a patient, in accord with Frank's basic paradigm of healing, that Western therapies fail patients from other cultures. In particular Frank's second, third and fourth components are entirely shaped by the cultural expectations of the patient and the culture of the service. The general public's acquaintance with the set of ideas that are involved in therapy determine the readiness to use a particular form of healing. Psychotherapy-related ideas have themselves been promoted as common societal values and belief systems.

Traditional psychotherapy takes its view of humankind from descriptive psychopathology. This one-sided view is historically and culturally grounded in Western science and thought. A transcultural approach involves a more extensive alternative interpretation. According to the cultural and historical evaluation a behaviour, illness or symptom can be given a different significance (Pesechkian, 1990). It remains crucial to be aware of those cultural differences that are psychologically significant, if we wish to avoid stumbling into areas that are taken for granted in dealing with patients from Western cultures but have unanticipated consequences in patients from other cultures (Slote, 1992). For example, despite the persistent attack on the original conceptualization of the Oedipal complex (Webster, 1995) and alternative formulations of the incest taboo (Erickson, 1993), it appears that patients continue to present material which at varying levels of abstraction is consistent with an Oedipal model of conflict resolution (Britton *et al.*, 1989; Barrows, 1993; Miller, 1995). One should then consider the limitations of the cross-cultural application of this concept rather than regard the components of the Oedipal scene as incompatible with cross-cultural evaluations of distress.

Client–therapist interactions

Culture itself can influence what is perceived as mental distress and help by seeking through its definitions of normality and abnormality in a particular society, and by explaining the aetiology of certain illnesses and influencing clinical presentation (Bhugra, 1993). There is no doubt that culture can provide cathartic strategies allowing use of ecological adaptation in accord with social rules. The kind of diagnostic model required for psychotherapy across cultures involves explorations of personal and clinical phenomena within a framework that has to consider phenomenological, dynamic and existential schema within which cognitive strategies and behavioural patterns can be explained. A discrepancy in the time schedules, between what the client thinks is right and what the therapist thinks is possible, only adds to the confusion and negative experiences about the health care system.

Havenaar (1990) reports that the intense interpersonal relationship may indeed not be necessary and that the ideas around healing and the buildings or institutions can all become therapeutic transference objects; this characteristic of recovery is echoed by Frank (1974). Luborsky and Crits-Cristoph (1983) identified that those client–therapist dyads which were matched for cognitive style, religious background and age did better. Kleinman and Good (1985) report that in some cultures talking about emotions is seen as damaging and not healthy, and so a match on cultural variable enables a more rapid working therapy, thereby shortening the time required for a familiarization and 'culture-based premise-posturing'. Flaskerud and Liu (1990) report that ethnic and language matching made no difference to the therapeutic outcome other than to increase the number of sessions (language match). Their statistical model indicates that ethnic matching actually had a detrimental effect in comparison to language matching on both numbers of sessions and drop-out rates. Tesone (1996) reports that using a second language for psychoanalytic work may act as a detour with the aim of gaining distance and avoiding emotional and instinctual overload. Lloyd and Bhugra (1993) comprehensively discuss the problems as well as the advantages of ethnic matching and conclude that, as a society, we need to make a decision as to whether multicultural competencies should be part of core professional training for all, or whether 'special' services will develop and be maintained as a solution.

SERVICE ISSUES IN PSYCHOTHERAPY FOR ETHNIC MINORITIES

Due to political and social environments prevalent in the UK, ethnic minorities are less likely to receive talking therapies. There are several possible explanations. The commonest argument advanced suggests that people from ethnic minorities are not psychologically suave and sophisticated and are unable to deal with emotional issues (Carstairs and Kapur, 1976). Another argument put forward is that psychoanalytic psychotherapies are developed in the Western milieu and are therefore impossible to be used anywhere else, whereas these communities express their distress in physical, somatic and religious terms (Carothers, 1953). However, neither of these arguments is entirely correct.

It is more likely that psychotherapy services are not accessible to individuals from ethnic minorities because of physical and psychological barriers erected by the service providers. Failure to understand individual contexts and needs and trying to pigeonhole and stereotype individuals takes away the necessity to provide more culturally tailored services.

Furthermore, a lack of availability of culturally skilled psychotherapists, in general, and therapists interested and willing to work with ethnic minorities, in particular, makes the situation worse. Littlewood (1992) argues cogently that there is an underlying theme of racism which keeps therapists away from ethnic minority clients and makes them conscious of what others would think of them if they were to provide such *unfashionable* service. Jones and Jones (1970) argue that the dyad of same ethnicity therapist and client too poses insoluble problems. Schachter and Butts (1968) suggest that the biracial dyad can have a therapeutic catalytic effect and may lead to a quicker unfolding of the problem. Although the use of this style and dyad has increased in the UK, especially in the field of child adoption and fostering, this may well lead to reduced choice. Furthermore, as Littlewood and Lipsedge (1989) suggest, this method is perhaps less a solution to a complex situation than one possible option analogous to that provided by women's therapy groups. Various stages of cross-cultural psychotherapy development in the USA have been described (Comas-Diaz, 1992). In the first stage, questions were raised about the applicability and effectiveness of psychotherapy as practised by the white psychotherapists with their black clients. This then led on to a stage of empirical studies. However, these studies have many flaws including small numbers of patients and the non-random allocation of therapists, types of therapy and clients (Sue and Zane, 1988), and their outcome measures themselves did not have adequate cross-cultural validity. It must be stated that the UK psychotherapies are going through similar phases of development and assessment of their applications.

RESEARCH AND TRAINING

The data reflecting the influence of racial and cultural variables on the outcome of psychotherapy is limited and along with social class and gender needs more systematic investigation. The issue of ethnic matching between the therapist and client needs to be considered at a research and service provision level. Often therapist, patient and context variables may indeed have a greater influence than ethnicity *per se* (see Sue *et al.*, 1994 for a review of American models and research). Outcome measures along with processes of psychotherapy need to be studied. In addition, large-scale studies are essential to find the best therapy match, and to better determine an understanding of transference and countertransference experience in cross-cultural encounters. A majority of studies thus far are limited in the sample size and by their method. Training of psychotherapists, in general, in cultural, racial and ethnic norms needs to be undertaken as a matter of some urgency. Training at a general professional level should include social anthropology and understanding of sociological factors and cultural, ethnic and racial issues. The emphasis in training has to change in order to understand the role of the client's racial and ethnic background in presentation and management. Supervision of cases must include ethnic, cultural and religious factors. The training of therapists, clinicians and researchers from all ethnic backgrounds deserves to be taken seriously. The contents of training must include general principles of cross-cultural assessments and interaction, understanding of cultural norms, mores and taboos, religious and spiritual formulation, and the impact of migratory experience. On a more specific level, such training must ensure that individual therapists using their own particular brand of theoretical skills can interpret the role of culture and race in the lives of their patients. The training needs to be theoretical as well as practical. Local communities should be encouraged to become involved in putting together packages of training. These individuals can enrich training courses by bringing their experiences and their backgrounds to influence the training process and to rectify theory and service-based failure of treatment. Open discussion of racial and cultural similarities and differences in training will not only encourage awareness in trainees of their own conscious attitudes, but also enable them to understand their countertransference.

Note

1 This chapter is part of a longer version published in 1998 as 'Psychotherapy for Ethnic Minorities: Issues, Context and Practice', in the *British Journal of Psychotherapy* 14(3): 310–326.

References

Acharyya, S. (1992) The Doctor's Dilemma: The Practice of Cultural Psychiatry in Multi-cultural Britain, in J. Kareem and R. Littlewood (eds), *Intercultural Therapy: Themes, Interpretations and Practice*. London: Blackwell Scientific Publications.

Akbar, N. (1996) *Natural Psychology and Human Transformation*. Tallahassee, FL: Mind Productions and Associates.

Barrows, P. (1993) Oedipal Issues at 4 and 44, *Psychoanalytical Psychotherapy* 9: 85–96.

Bhugra, D. (1993) Influence of Culture on Presentation and Management of Patients, in D. Bhugra and J. P. Leff (eds), *Principles of Social Psychiatry*. Oxford: Blackwell, pp. 67–81.

Block, S. (1986) *An Introduction to the Psychotherapies*, 2nd edn. Oxford: Oxford Medical Publications.

Bloom, L. (1991) The Dangers of Groupism in Psychotherapy and Counselling, *Freud Museum Offprint 2*. London: Freud Museum.

Blumenthal, S. J., Jones, E. E. and Krupnick, L. L. (1985) The Influence of Gender and Race on the Therapeutic Alliance, in R. E. Hales and A. J. Francis (eds),

APA Annual Review 4: 586–606. Washington, DC: American Psychiatric Association.

Brah, A. (1996) *Cartographies of Diaspora: Contesting Identities*. London: Routledge.

Britton, R., Feldman, M. and O'Shaughnessy, E. (1989) *The Oedipus Complex Today: Clinical Implications*. London: Karnac Books.

Carothers, J. C. (1953) *The African Mind in Health and Disease: A Study in Ethnopsychiatry*. WHO Monograph Series. Geneva: WHO.

Carstairs, G. M. and Kapur, R. L. (1976) *The Great Universe of Kota*. London: Hogarth Press.

Coltart, N. (1988) Assessment of Psychological Mindedness in the Diagnostic Interview, *British Journal of Psychiatry* 153: 819–820.

Comas-Diaz, L. (1992) The Future of Psychotherapy with Ethnic Minorities, *Psychotherapy* 29: 88–94.

Dalal, F. (1997) The Racism of Jung, *Self & Society* 25(1): 4–24.

Ellenberger, H. (1970) *The Discovery of the Unconscious*. London: Allen Lane.

Erickson, M. (1993) Re-thinking Oedipus: An Evolutionary Perspective of Incest Avoidance, *American Journal of Psychiatry* 150(3): 411–416.

Fernando, S. (1988) *Race and Culture in Psychiatry*. London: Croom Helm.

Flaskerud, J. and Liu, P. Y. (1990) Influence of Therapist Ethnicity and Language in Therapy Outcomes of Southeast Asian Clients, *International Journal of Social Psychiatry* 36: 18–29.

Frank, J. D. (1961) *Persuasion and Healing: A Comparative Study of Psychotherapy*. Baltimore, MD: Johns Hopkins Press.

Frank, J. D. (1974) Psychotherapy: The Restoration of Morale, *American Journal of Psychiatry* 131: 241–275.

Frank, J. D. and Frank, J. B. (1991) *Persuasion and Healing*, 3rd edn. Baltimore, MD: Johns Hopkins Press.

Freud, S. (1984) The Ego and the Id. II, in *On Metapsychology*. Penguin Series No. 11. London: Penguin.

Hartley, D. (1985) Research on Therapeutic Alliance in Psychotherapy, in R. Hales and A. Frances (eds), *APA Annual Review* 4: 532–549. Washington, DC: American Psychiatric Association.

Havenaar, J. (1990) Psychotherapy: Healing by Culture, *Psychotherapy Psychosoma* 53: 8–13.

Howitt, D. and Owusu-Bempah (1994) *The Racism of Psychology*. Hemel Hempstead: Harvester Wheatsheaf.

Jones, A. (1985) Psychological Functioning in Black Americans: A Conceptual Guide for Use in Psychotherapy, *Psychotherapy* 22: 363–369.

Jones, M. H. and Jones, M. (1970) The Neglected Client, *Black Scholar* 5: 35–42.

Kareem, J. (1988) Outside In, Inside Out, Some Considerations in Intercultural Therapy, *Freud Museum Offprints*. London: Freud Museum.

Kareem, J. (1992) The Nafsiyat Intercultural Therapy Centre: Ideas and Experience in Intercultural Therapy, in J. Kareem and R. Littlewood (eds), *Intercultural Therapy: Themes, Interpretations and Practice*. London: Blackwell Scientific Publications.

Kleinman, A. and Good, B. (1985) *Culture and Depression: Studies in the*

Anthropology and Cross Cultural Psychiatry of Affective Disorder. London: University of California Press.

Littlewood, R. (1992) How Universal is Something We Call Psychotherapy?, chapter in J. Kareem and R. Littlewood (eds), *Intercultural Therapy: Themes, Interpretations and Practice*. London: Blackwell Scientific Publications.

Littlewood, R. and Lipsedge, M. (1989) *Aliens and Alienists*. London: Unwin Hyman.

Lloyd, K. and Bhugra, D. (1993) Cross-cultural Aspects of Psychotherapy, *International Review of Psychiatry* 5: 291–304.

Luborsky, L. and Crits-Cristoph, P. (1983) Two Helping Alliance Methods for Predicting Outcome of Psychotherapy: A Counting Sign vs a Global Rating Method, *Journal of Nervous and Mental Disease* 171: 480–491.

Marsella, A. J. and White, G. (eds) (1982) *Cultural Conceptions of Mental Health and Therapy*. Dordrecht: D. Reidel.

Miller, L. (1995) The Transition to Oedipal Adulthood: Oedipal Themes, *Psychoanalytical Psychotherapy* 9: 219–230.

Perera, S., Bhui, K. and Dein, S. (1995) Making Sense of Possession States: Psychopathology and Differential Diagnosis, *British Journal of Hospital Medicine* 53(11): 582.

Pesechkian, N. (1990) Positive Psychotherapy: A Transcultural and Interdisciplinary Approach to Psychotherapy, *Psychotherapy Psychosoma* 53: 39–45.

Roth, A. and Fonagy, P. (1996) *What Works for Whom: A Critical Review of Psychotherapy Research*. New York: Guilford Press.

Rush, L. (1985) The Therapeutic Alliance in Short Term Directive Therapies, in R. E. Hales and A. Frances (eds), *APA Annual Review* 4: 562–572. Washington, DC: American Psychiatric Association.

Schachter, J. and Butts, H. (1968) Transference and Countertransference in Interracial Analysis, *Journal of the American Psychoanalytic Association* 16: 792–808.

Slote, W. (1992) Oedipal Ties and the Issue of Separation-Individuation in Traditional Confucian Societies, *Journal of the American Academy of Psychoanalysis* 20(3): 435–453.

Sue, S. and Zane, N. (1987) The Role of Culture and Cultural Techniques in Psychotherapy, *American Psychologist* 42(1): 37–45.

Sue, S. and Zane, N. (1988) Psychotherapeutic Services for Ethnic Minorities, *American Psychologist* 43: 301–308.

Sue, S., Zane, N. and Young, K. (1994) Research on Psychotherapy with Culturally Diverse Populations, in A. Bergen and S. Garfield (eds), *Handbook of Psychotherapy and Behaviour Change*. Singapore: John Wiley & Sons.

Tesone, J. E. (1996) Multi-lingualism, Word Presentations, Thing Presentations and Psychic Reality, *International Journal of Psycho-Analysis* 77: 871–881.

Thomas, L. (1992) Racism and Psychotherapy: Working with Racism in the Consulting Room, chapter in J. Kareem and R. Littlewood (eds), *Intercultural Therapy: Themes, Interpretations and Practice*. London: Blackwell Scientific Publications.

Wolberg, L. R. (1977) *The Technique of Psychotherapy*, 3rd edn. New York: Grune and Stratton.

Governing race in the transference

Chapter 5

Racial transference reactions in psychoanalytic treatment: an update

Dorothy Evans Holmes

In 1992 I published the paper 'Race and Transference in Psychoanalysis and Psychotherapy' to address how conceptual myths and countertransference problems impose limitations on the uses patients and therapists make of race-bound transferences in psychoanalytic treatments. Since 1992, the focus on the meanings of race in treatment, real and psychodynamic, has expanded, as has the number of published works. These writings have had numerous foci. For example, there has been enlightening discussion *and* tendentious argument on what theories should guide one's interventions about race. The role of self-disclosure, the need to emphasize the external factors contributing to race in analyzing racial material, and the necessity for the psychoanalytic therapist to examine race in his or her own treatment also have been examined. Upon review of these emerging trends that are summarized below, it is clear that the body of knowledge on the workings of race in psychoanalytic treatment is richer, and that it has not as yet provided the fullness of understanding the topic requires.

The major purpose of this chapter is to extend the ongoing discussion on race in psychodynamic treatment by addressing a question raised by my work with two patients presented in the 1992 paper who returned to treatment some years after concluding their original treatment. In each case the patient returned having sustained career successes that had been highly conflictual and were significantly worked through in the original treatments. However, there was indication to return because they had not been able to achieve lasting satisfaction in intimate relationships. The question is how the patients' racial dynamics and their unfolding in the second treatments played a role in the resolution of their libidinal difficulties.

WRITINGS SINCE 1992

Theoretical debates: which approach is best?

This author's 1992 paper was written largely from an ego psychological point of view, with emphasis on Oedipal-level conflict and demonstration of defensive patterns, their underlying anxiety-laden or depressive affects and unacceptable thoughts and urges that got attached to racial content. Five cases were presented in that paper. In four of the five cases – Miss A (African-American), Ms. B (African-American) and Mr. D and Ms. E (both Euro-American) – the treatment method worked well. Common to all of the improvements was an effective engagement of the patients' racialized struggles with aggression in their careers. In the case of Mr. C (an African-American man who was characterologically more disturbed than the other patients), the treatment gained some traction around his difficulties in completing his professional degree, but the patient left prematurely. He had been severely traumatized at age six when his surrogate father (actually his uncle) was killed. He had cherished the uncle as father. He felt that his grandmother abetted this death by permitting the uncle to go to the home of his married lover, i.e. knowing that the lover's husband was home. The husband shot the patient's uncle dead. The patient lost two beloved parental figures – his uncle through death and devaluation and the grandmother through betrayal. As Mr. C expressed himself racially in very vivid terms, I will recount a vignette from his treatment and consider it from the point of view of a theoretical argument that emerged in the literature in response.

In the fifteenth month of treatment, Mr. C encountered a white woman in the waiting room for the first time. He felt that I was betraying him with her presence. This event occurred in the presence of the patient's emerging erotic transference to me which he complained was interfering with his concentration. In that context, the following exchanges took place (Holmes, 1992, p. 5):

Mr. C: What is that 'honky' doing in the waiting room?!!
Analyst: Clearly, you feel that her presence is intolerable. What's bad about her being there?
Mr. C: That you're a god damned traitor. You fraternize with the enemy!! He flailed about on the couch and cried inconsolably.
Analyst: Your great distress makes me wonder about what other betrayals have hurt and angered you so.
Mr. C: (struggling for composure): My grandmother; she let my Uncle Joe get killed!
Analyst: This painful revelation came after you experienced me as a traitor in cahoots with the white woman in the waiting room. In yesterday's session you felt your angry and sexual feelings for me were dangerous. It seems that it was easier for you at first to find me despicable and push me away rather than explore the dangers with me.
Mr. C: (chuckling, with some relief): Yeah, everybody knows all the wrong 'whitey' has done to us. I was sure you would understand that!

Analyst: Sure, racism is alive and well, *and*, at the same time, we may have an opportunity to understand how your pain goes beyond racism.

This exchange was cited by a colleague to bolster her recommendation that treatment of racial issues needs to emphasize the embeddedness of race in the culture as an intersubjective construct that influences patient and therapist and shapes the transference. Thus, according to Yi (1998), theories such as ego psychology and Kleinian psychology are misguided in that they do not emphasize the intersubjective point of view. Yi (p. 248) quotes *part of* the above exchange from Holmes' work to demonstrate that the analyst omitted the intersubjective aspect and cites the 'omission' as causal in the patient's early departure from treatment. The part of Holmes' text on the same page quoted by Yi in which the therapist did include herself in the interpretation in an intersubjectively focused way (see above, 'This painful expression came after you experienced me . . .') is strangely omitted by Yi.

Openness to the possible merits of working with race from a variety of points of view is strongly indicated in the fact that still so little is known about this topic. Of course, an appeal to such openness should not be premised on inaccurate characterizations of alternate points of view, as was the case in Yi's work, rich as it was in its own clinical examples presented from an intersubjectivist point of view. Similarly, Altman (1993) and Foster (1993) are strident and tendentious in their attack on ego psychology while they valorize a particularly narrow object-relational point of view. I review this debate in detail in Chapter 15 in this volume and to some extent in Holmes (1997). I will not repeat it here except to say that clinical material on race presented in published works since 1992 does not support the use of uni-dimensional conceptual and technical approaches. In reflection on my own work, I believe now that a pluralistic approach is indicated and I will try to demonstrate that in my discussion below of the two patients from the 1992 paper who returned to treatment (Ms. B and Mr. C).

Self-disclosure

Leary's work (1997) on the topic of self-disclosure in relation to race in psychodynamic treatment is richly evocative. She, an African-American therapist, made selective self-disclosures about race in her work with a white female patient who expressed her hostility in terms of racial slurs and racial stereotypes. She hypothesized that the self-disclosures would deepen the clinical process. Clearly, the therapist's openness to speaking about the taboo subject of race, as illustrated in the self-disclosures, did benefit the treatment in that the self-disclosures had a stabilizing effect on the working alliance. However, as I commented in Holmes (1999, p. 321): 'the case material is ambiguous on the question of the impact of self disclosure on gaining access to and resolving the patient's proneness to hostility and rage. In particular, the hostile, intrusive motivations for the patient's race-linked and non-race-linked questions . . . did not seem relieved by Leary's answers.' I think that in addition to answering her questions with self-disclosures, more in-depth work possibly could have been accomplished with a combination of a particular kind of object-relational interpretation and a drive–defense approach. Specifically, I think benefit might have accrued from first interpreting to the patient how she was experienced by the patient in racial terms (e.g. 'You experience me as a black woman who may be hypersensitive to criticisms about affirmative action programs'). Then, over time, as the patient began to find her own impulses less noxious, it could be useful to interpret to her the meanings of her questions. Specifically, it could be interpreted that she asked questions of the therapist in order to be active and thereby not to repeat the experience of having been the painfully passive recipient of her mother's hostile questions. Thus, I recommend a multi-pronged approach that adds to Leary's ego-supportive self-disclosures two kinds of interpretations – one from a modern Kleinian perspective that builds on the containing function of the therapist in an interpretive fashion and an ego psychological approach. I have come to believe that things racial in treatment are very dense and respond best to multiple approaches.

The external reality of race

Hamer (2002) has written cogently on the need to work analytically with the external reality of race in analytic treatment. As he says, because race so often is riveting and compelling it must be addressed in its reality-bound aspects. Otherwise, the therapist will be ignoring the elephant in the room. Hamer's point seems especially well-taken in cases of racial trauma, as in the case of black men being capriciously or otherwise wrongly detained or arrested, often with cruel or even physically brutal aspects. Such experiences are ego-damaging; unless the therapist fosters full exploration of the surfaces of such experiences (i.e. their external reality aspects), their deeper meanings and their relationship to and influences on internal reality may not be addressed and resolved. As Hamer says:

> the discussion of external reality within the analytic space gives us an opportunity to evaluate what is apparently outside and what apparently inside; how each influences the other; and how the space or tension between them can be made more vital for purposes of newly adaptive functioning . . . [Otherwise,] more traumatic experiences of racism obliterate the individual's ability to hold on to transitional space, where the subjective cannot be experienced as such because external reality feels so compelling.
>
> (p. 1233)

I would only add that there is always an external reality of race. The lived reality of race in Western culture is that it always asserts itself, even if in subtle ways that cumulatively may be as damaging as the more blunt and crude examples noted by Hamer. Finding that external reality to speak to can make a critical difference in the treatment situation. In the clinical material presented below, I will attempt to illustrate this point.

The therapist's own therapy as a remedy for racial 'blind spots'

In 1999 I published a paper on 'Race and Countertransference: Two "Blind Spots" in Psychoanalytic Perception'. The point of that paper was that much that can be worked with racially in treatment often is bypassed for two reasons: race often condenses scary impulses that for ordinary countertransference reasons we form counter-resistances to. Also, racial issues carry burdens beyond ordinary countertransferences. Race is embedded in our psyches *and* our culture. Its connections to the worst in us (prejudice; racism; evil) as well as to our ordinary conflicts over our impulses make us shun it. In Holmes (1999) I argue that didactic learning and supervision are necessary tools in gaining mastery as a therapist with respect to race. I further argue that they alone are not adequate, that only the therapist's own treatment attuned to racial meanings, *and for therapists of all ethnicities and races*, can help a therapist master his or her own racially related issues. Only with such mastery can therapists then fully help their patients with such issues. A way of understanding the profound and persistent resistance to race as something to be examined is made clear in Ainslie (2003). In that work, Ainslie presents a psychological portrait of one of the white men who brutally assaulted an unsuspecting black man who they then dragged to his death over three miles of dirt and asphalt roads. This case was widely reported in the popular press in 1998. Ainslie was able to identify some trauma in the background of the killer he profiled (e.g. death of his adored adoptive mother). However, he concluded: 'The frightening and disorienting fact is that such distance [between the killer and the rest of us, including therapists] is more an illusion than we care to contemplate because it subverts our need to believe in a world where logic and order prevail and where evil resides elsewhere, in some distant, confinable sphere' (p. 18).

Our own treatments are necessary lest we capitulate to conspiracies of silence with our patients around race, something we are sorely tempted to do, as Ainslie suggests. We do so because it is very difficult to own that which we, more often than not, project into blacks and others; otherwise, we would experience it as our own unworthiness and evil. We make them the containers of that evil that we cannot abide as our own. We put them in the 'distant, confinable sphere' of which Ainslie speaks. In my view, only in a competent treatment can such issues be addressed fully and resolved so that we can bear and decipher the representations of race within ourselves and in our patients – going to whatever abyssal places we must in the process.

CASE MATERIAL

Several cases will be presented briefly to illustrate both the challenges and the opportunities afforded by addressing racialized realities in therapy. Access to racially influenced constructions of inner and outer reality are not always ready-to-hand because we are strongly motivated to hide them as was just reviewed. First, I will present updates on two cases reported in 1992 – the cases of Ms. B and Mr. C, both African-American patients. I will also present material from the case of Ms. G, a Euro-American woman. Both Ms. B and Mr. C returned to treatment with me after several years away and after they had achieved some gains in, and pursuant to, the original treatment, especially in terms of achieving consolidated work identities. They returned because of continuing problems in their love lives. The third patient, Ms. G., not previously presented, came to treatment because of panic associated with aging and dread of what signs of her aging would reveal about her.

Ms. B

This patient entered treatment first with work-related and intimacy problems. The therapy dealt mostly with her career-rise as a late 20s African-American woman whose successes her family envied and which envy she responded to with masochistic approaches to her work. Race did not enter Ms. B's treatment frequently, but in the intensities of work on her siblings' envy of her meteoric career advances, there were evidences of the way her masochism was racially influenced. Her siblings lashed out at her ambition and success in racial terms whenever she frustrated them, as once when she demanded to know the purpose of the large sum of money her sister expected in the form of a loan. The sister recruited their brother to her cause and assaulted the patient with the invective, 'Super Nigger'. The patient found the high levels of professional work to which she climbed difficult to bear for other reasons. She had numerous ego weaknesses including anxiety intolerance, poor control over her anger, extreme narcissistic vulnerability, and she formed hostile–dependent attachments to men. The racial component of these problems was not prevalent or readily accessible in the first course of treatment, but came to light when she returned. She came back in the throes of a difficult marriage in which extreme verbal abuse was exchanged between the two. Within months of her return, she filed for divorce. The patient's indisputable work success at a very high level of prestige and income offered her some ego support and she began to be interested in why her relationships with men were so unsuccessful. She came to understand the desperation and contempt in the search for an upgrade of her father with whom she had been more warmly connected than with her mother. She also came to understand that she ended up fighting with most men out of fear of inevitably being let down by them. This negative anticipation was based in the fact that she could not really idealize her father given his severe alcoholism and its degraded expressions throughout her childhood (immodesty including incontinence; physical abuse of her mother). Relatedly, the patient fended off men so that they would not see the gaps in her own sense of self, the inadequate inner regulation of self and urges, and the impoverished and depriving internal objects. Much in these issues could be addressed through 'standard' ego psychological interventions. However, the repetitive failures in relationships and my sense of her desperation and waif-life quality led me eventually to include more of an object-relational approach in my thinking and listening and in my interventions. The following sequence is given to illustrate this aspect of the work:

Ms. B. was musing on the fact that she felt so hurt by the last man to rebuff her inasmuch as she had found his qualities so inviting (warmth, street smartness, kindness). She expressed regret that she had put the cart before the horse in being too demanding of him too quickly. His leaving her had put her in a tailspin in which she began again to sleep around. She was able to interrupt that slide fairly quickly in favor of examining it. I began to realize that while she had conflicted urges and guilt about her promiscuity that she could at times work with constructively in the treatment, she also suffered beyond that. Specifically, she seemed not to have an inner light to guide her; she lacked certainty or confidence about her thoughts, feelings and capacities.

Ms. B: I want to have a fabulous life with a man. I had hoped to have that with Jim (the most recent man to leave her).

Th: What would make your life fabulous?

Ms. B: We'd go places and people would notice him and then me. He's so bright. People pay attention.

Th: There's something validating about that brightness. You feel good in its midst. It's confirming.

Ms. B: (Chuckling): I'm thinking of my neighbor, Paul; he told me, 'You know, I like your quirks; they're what make you you. I liked that. That's what I wanted from Jim. That good feeling about myself

Th: At some point in life we all want that to come from particular others.

Ms. B: (Tearing up): My mom just couldn't do it and my dad wasn't there. She almost seemed ashamed of me like when my grandmother said I had bad table manners and when my aunt told her I was asking for too many things on a shopping trip.

Th: I wonder what made them so uptight about having good manners. They're important, sure, but I wonder what made them so uptight. [Here I was wondering about family background and the fact that many blacks feel they need to do things absolutely correctly lest they be harshly judged by whites. I then asked her to tell me what she knew about how her grandmother and mother grew up.]

Ms. B: My grandmother and grandfather grew up on a farm in _____ (a southern state). My grandfather kept whites away because he knew what they thought of blacks and he didn't want his family exposed to all of that.

Th: That?

Ms. B: Well, they don't think much of black folks.

Th: [In the patient's pause, I was thinking that no one really escapes the influences of harshness that often get constructed racially and then get recorded apocryphally as in the story about grandfather keeping whites away. The grandmother's and aunt's harshness and the mother's shame may have contained elements of such racially constructed harshness. I said to the patient:] As you know, up to now we have not talked much about your own personal racial experiences. Do you have anything more to share about them?

Ms. B: When I was in first grade, I had some fancy barrettes in my hair. The white girl next to me said they were hers. I told the teacher, 'no; my aunt gave them to me yesterday', but the teacher took them out of my hair and put them in the other little girl's hair.

That memory became an important pathway by which the patient reconstructed her sense of her own lack of validity. A little black girl's reality and belongings are not hers; what you are is defined by another who is more powerful; you're made into a liar and a thief when you're not. At first the transference took on these markings. Her distrust of me was intense and persistent. Interpretations that focused on her experiencing of me as like the first grade teacher who would rob her of her own sense of reality and her appeal and turn her into a bad person were helpful. Gradually, her own rage became more decipherable to her and she could own it and reshape it into constructive uses. She came to feel more real and solid. She began to associate therapy with benign personal validation that started from the outside, i.e. with what I could give her in the work but that she could then claim or not as her own. As these changes took place in the second therapy, she could let men get closer to her and she could relate to them less guardedly and more lovingly.

Mr. C

Mr. C's case is referenced earlier in this chapter in terms of his highly racially constructed world, with 'whitey' being the bearer of his own racial evils and those of the betraying grandmother. He had come to therapy originally because his integrity had been impugned, which delayed achievement of a highly coveted credential he sought. He used the first therapy well enough to re-establish his bona fides with the credentialing board that had recommended treatment and to obtain the credential he sought. His love life remained chaotic and he left treatment prematurely. The transference in that treatment was dominated by mistrust of me. Efforts to interpret the focus on 'honkies' and 'whitey' as defensive shields against his mistrust of black women were not successful. As already reviewed, Yi (1998) thought the work with Mr. C was limited by the therapist not utilizing an inter-subjectivist point of view. Indeed that point of view was not emphasized, though it was not absent. However, I think his return to treatment clarified what was missing in the first effort. He returned because of panic attacks and stalking behavior in relation to a woman he loved. In the ensuing ten years between the two treatments he had become an extremely successful lawyer. His net worth was in the millions of dollars, a feat about which he felt especially proud because his work was largely public sector work in which great wealth is not usually accumulated. He appreciated the ingenuity he showed in making his particular work pay off for the underclass and for himself. The second treatment revealed a deeper meaning, however. Since no one expected that he would have become wealthy doing the type of work that he did, he felt that he flew undetected under the radar screen, and therefore, he would not be subject to envious attack. Similarly, he had lavishly renovated his house, but its exterior was plain and the house was in an inner-city ghetto.

Mr. C returned to treatment with strong motivation to work out his problems with women. He said he was tired of his pattern of always having multiple sexual partners, but that without more than one he was subject to the panic attacks and stalking that brought him back. He exclaimed, 'I'm just a barefoot black country boy from the rural south; it's as simple as that, so why do I have so much complicated stuff going on'?! This self reference was key to the second therapy, as it enabled us to engage a core issue: he could not claim all of himself. He had to hide his economic and professional prowess and he had to deny himself the fullness of love. The diminishment of himself was motivated by a need to stay undetected for his crimes of passion that he likened to those that led to his uncle's death. This case can be conceptualized from the points of view of multiple clinical theories. However, what unlocked this case for me was recognition of this man's enforced 'littleness' that had in it inadequately developed capacity for love. We can think of this as defensive; we can think of it as being the result

of that which the culture constructs and imposes. Neither of these conceptualizations captures fully what patients such as Ms. B and Mr. C need,
which is the realization that their lived reality of race demands that they be
invalidated. The therapist must convey this because in being invalid one
cannot conceptualize oneself. Recognizing *that* race is constructed and/or
that it may be defensive in nature will not be fully mutative. Rather, the
therapist must be able to help the patient mentalize (Fonagy, 2001) *what* is
very commonly constructed, namely the painfully limited and limiting
experience of self in its nitty-gritty details. This effort involves helping the
patient mentalize the manifestations and meanings of having been stripped
of positive value and expectation (e.g. the meanings of 'I'm just a barefoot
black country boy . . .'). So, we worked on this mantra requiring of him
that he have limited success and no hope that, in his case, was represented
in not being able to have a whole relationship with one loved person. We
worked in this way for several years at the conclusion of which he had
sustained himself without panic attacks or stalking and only occasional
forays into the multiple-partnering that previously had been a driven
necessity.

Ms. G

This wealthy Euro-American patient came to me in her late 70s, referred by
her psychoanalyst who had successfully treated her nearly a quarter century
earlier for a complex character neurosis. That illness had expressed itself in
sex with her husband being conditioned on fierce verbal fighting which she
instigated. The history that shaped her psychology included severe mistrust
of men based on having been abandoned by her father after he divorced her
mother and married a close friend of the mother's. The mother despised
the patient's father; the patient took on the role of mother's companion.
At once, she felt obligated to care for her mother and stultified by mother's
control. The mother exercised control over the patient through subtle
manipulations of money and more directly through enemas that persisted
for several years into the patient's early latency. The patient tried to resist
the enemas, leading to her being held down forcefully by a troika of women
– mother, grandmother and older sister. After the 'enema period', she tried
to effect a perfectly placid demeanor in order not to show any feeling or
state that could lead her mother to try to gain control over her. She came to
me for treatment because she was panicking that her third face lift still left
wrinkles which she associated with the possibility that dangerous feelings
could be detected. Eventually, this apprehension came to be linked to race
in the following way:

Ms. G was becoming more able to express her feelings without so much
fear. She, exceptionally able to be curious and introspective, wondered why
this freedom of expression was possible after so many years. In that

context, she told me of a holiday party she was planning. She asked if I knew a particularly prominent African-American couple she was inviting. I told her that I thought I detected a disruption in the poise she had shown up to the point of wondering if I knew the couple. I wondered what occasioned her unease. With growing discomfort but straightforwardness, she commented that she had told her other guests who were white that the couple in question was black. She began to recognize that some prejudice was involved in that disclosure to the other guests and to me, since there was nothing to distinguish the couple from the other guests other than their race. She associated then to her belief that blacks are in a lower station in life 'by definition' (as socially constructed). While uncomfortable sharing these associations, Ms. G. recognized that she was very free to tell me – an African-American therapist. Why? One could assume that it was because I had, despite all, become a good 'new object' whom she trusted. The patient's further associations clarified otherwise. What she made very clear was that, consistent with her assumptions about blacks being in a lower station, I could not hurt her no matter what she said. Why? As Ms. G. said, 'As a black person you have no power.' This revelation was stunning to both of us. In processing it, we discovered a layer of contempt and racially felt domination over me beneath the surface of the patient's good working alliance with me as a trusted 'new object'. Working at the level of contempt enabled the development of a truer trust in me. It also became an important path to reworking the patient's desperate need to be 'on top' and to thereby conquer her own 'low status' feelings by whatever means available, including potential racism. Thereby, she tried to escape her mother's domination, her father's abandonment and her shame over being from a divorced family in a social echelon in which that circumstance was rare and scorned.

DISCUSSION

In the twelve years since my original paper on race and transference in psychoanalysis and psychotherapy, much has been written to clarify the various expressions and vicissitudes of race in the treatment situation. Still, race remains as embedded as ever in the human psyche and I believe it will remain so, given that our culture continues to reinforce race prejudice and racism, and thereby encourages powerful resistances to examination of these phenomena. The powerful lenses of psychoanalytic clinical theories and techniques, *all of them*, can illuminate the various roles and functions of racial constructs in the human mind, with value of doing so in its own right, that is in helping people resolve their racial issues. Furthermore, such work can provide a pathway to elucidation of the other issues in the mind that are projected onto race.

Whenever there is a possibility to work on racial constructs in the human psyche, it is imperative to do so, as the damage to perpetrator and those on the receiving end can be enormous. In the cases of Ms. B and Mr. C presented above, racist practices had robbed each of efficacy and validity. It was necessary to access and work through these racialized aspects for their treatments to be more fully mutative. In the case of Ms. G., her own potential racism was not in general leveled at African-Americans, though she could be cruel to functionaries of any racial or ethnic identity. Her race prejudice certainly did harm to herself because it had embedded in it a split-off aspect of her being, namely her own unruly need to dominate. Until it could be reclaimed – unwelcome wrinkle that it was – she could not bind her anxiety and use her aggression constructively.

The issue of race is reminiscent of the myths and realities of black holes. For years and until very recently it was wrongly assumed that whatever was taken into black holes was lost, irretrievable and indecipherable. Yes, it was said, there's energy being emitted from what has been taken into them, but that energy was considered random. It is known now that the energy from black holes can be deciphered though it is difficult to do so. For many years, we have treated race in the treatment situation similar to the antiquated view of black holes – that is, as an abyss. I hope the cases presented in this chapter and the collective work to date demonstrate otherwise.

References

Ainslie, R. (2003) A Psychoanalyst Explores the Dark Worlds of Racial Hatred, *Round Robin* 17 (Newsletter of Section I, Psychologist-Psychoanalyst Practitioners): 1; 14–18.

Altman, N. (1993) Psychoanalysis and the Urban Poor, *Psychoanalytic Dialogues* 3: 29–49.

Fonagy, P. (2001) *Attachment Theory and Psychoanalysis*. New York: The Other Press.

Foster, R. (1993) The Social Politics of Psychoanalysis: Commentary on Neil Altman's 'Psychoanalysis and the Urban Poor', *Psychoanalytic Dialogues* 3: 69–83.

Hamer, F. (2002) Guards at the Gate: Race, Resistance, and Psychic Reality, *Journal of the American Psychoanalytic Association* 50: 1219–1237.

Holmes, D. (1992) Race and Transference in Psychoanalysis and Psychotherapy, *International Journal of Psychoanalysis* 73: 1–11.

Holmes, D. (1997) A Critique of N. Altman's *The Analyst in the Inner City*. Hillsdale, NJ: The Analytic Press; 1995, *Journal of the American Psychoanalytic Association* 45: 644–648.

Holmes, D. (1999) Race and Countertransference: Two 'Blind Spots' in Psychoanalytic Perception, *Journal of Applied Psychoanalytic Studies* 1: 319–332.

Leary, K. (1997) Race, Self-disclosure and 'Forbidden Talk': Race and Ethnicity in Contemporary Clinical Practice, *Psychoanalytic Quarterly* 66: 163–189.

Yi, K. (1998) Transference and Race: An Intersubjective Conceptualization, *Psychoanalytic Psychology* 15: 245–261.

Chapter 6

Transference and race: an intersubjective conceptualization[1]

Kris Y. Yi

The psychoanalytic and psychotherapy literature on the topic of race-related transference is sparse: earlier literature dwelt on such issues as whether blacks could be analyzed (and the answer was a yes) and whether the racial difference between the analyst and the patient served as a facilitator of or a deterrence against development of true transference (Goldberg, Myers and Zeifman, 1974; Schachter and Butts, 1971). Some white analysts noted their countertransferential guilt for the social injustice suffered by their black patients and issued a caution against a tendency to explain away neurotic behaviors to the realistic effects of racism and miss intrapsychic meanings. Also reported in the literature is the presence of race-based stereotypes and prejudicial feelings in most interracial dyads: Published clinical accounts in the literature seem to lend validity to the existence of negative racial transference based on stereotypes and prejudice (Schachter and Butts, 1971; Greenson, Toney, Lim and Romero, 1982; Comas-Diaz and Jacobsen, 1991; Holmes, 1992; Tan, 1993): White therapists' fears based on stereotypes towards black patients were that their black patients were aggressive, impulsive, and lacking insights. In cases involving black and white male dyads, the black man's sexuality invariably came up as an issue: for example, Ralph Greenson, who is white, noted his countertransferential contempt towards his black male analysand's sexual activities, which he later recognized as envy (Greenson *et al.*, 1982). Similar fear and envy of sexuality were reported by Schachter and Butts (1971) in a white male analysand towards his black analyst. Other reactions of white patients to black therapists centered around feelings of superiority, hostility, paranoid fears of the black therapist's aggressive powers, and/or contempt and devaluation of the (ethnic) therapist's linguistic, intellectual competence to help the patient.

Within the psychoanalytic literature, two main types of explanations have been offered for the race-based (usually negative), transference phenomenon. These two are broadly classified as the intrapsychic drive model and the Kleinian/contemporary Kleinian model. The drive model attempts to explain the race-based transference as a manifestation of the patient's intrapsychic instinctual conflicts whereas the Kleinian and contemporary Kleinian ideas (Tan, 1993) view the patient's negative racial transference as a defensively motivated projection of the undesirable aspects of the self onto the race of the therapist. In the following I review and critique these two approaches in detail. I then propose an intersubjective view.

INTRAPSYCHIC DRIVE MODEL

In the intrapsychic drive model, black race was usually seen as a symbol of libidinal and aggressive instincts: hence black patients' race-based self-depreciation was seen as their equating their skin color with unconscious instinctual fantasies. Fischer (1971) discussed a female black patient's idealization of her white male therapist as her using the black–white racial barrier as the 'backdrop for her reawakened incestuous transference wishes and conflicts'. Fischer also discussed his own countertransferential denial of color difference as denial of aggressive and sexual impulses. A question some authors asked was whether black patients could transfer their instinctual impulses and wishes onto the white therapists or whether they would resist doing so because of the color barrier (Goldberg, Myers and Zeifman, 1974; Schachter and Butts, 1971): in the case of the three black patients with their white analysts reported in Goldberg, Myers and Zeifman (1974), the conclusion was that the racial difference was not a barrier, but a facilitator of the development of the transference. More specifically, the female patients developed eroticized, masochistic transference to their white analysts, which was understood as a defense against underlying aggressive impulses towards the analysts. The authors thought that this eroticized, masochistic transference developed rapidly due to the cultural stereotype about black aggression.

It is clear that the questions these authors focused on were consistent with their classical Freudian orientation: i.e. whether race was a conduit of libidinal and aggressive impulses and whether transference of these impulses could be established across the racial barriers. From views of object relations, self psychology, and the more recent relational theories, this classical position would be seen as too restrictive in its view of race as only carrying meaning about libidinal and aggressive instincts. The classical position leaves out the myriad of other possible meanings attached to race, for example concerning one's internal and external object relationships and selfobject needs and longings.

Furthermore, the intrapsychic drive model assumes that psychopathology involves conflicts *within* the person over unresolved childhood instinctual impulses. Here, the therapist's role is to remain a blank screen, not to interfere with the emergence of these instinctual wishes (and defenses against them). The therapist therefore believes she does not contribute to the development of the patient's attitudes and feelings. Hence, transference is considered a solipsistic event, not a relational event. This intrapsychic model of transference contrasts sharply with the more recently advanced relational view where the therapist is seen as either contributing to the development of transference, or co-constructing it together with the patient (Stolorow, Brandchaft and Atwood, 1987; Mitchell, 1988). Hence this view places emphasis on the nature and the shape of the therapist's contribution to the patient's subjectivity.

The potentially adverse therapeutic consequence of the intrapsychic drive model is that the therapist is conveniently left out from the question as to how she might contribute to the development of the race-based trans-ference. Consider the case of Mr. C, a black lawyer, reported by Holmes (1992), who, according to Holmes, leaves the analysis prematurely due to his 'severe character pathology'. In the segment she reports in detail, Mr. C. was upset at seeing a white woman in the therapist's waiting room (the therapist herself is black). Holmes reports the following exchange to have taken place:

Mr. C: What is that 'honky' doing in the waiting room?!!
Analyst: Clearly, you feel that her presence is intolerable. What's bad about her being there?
Mr. C: That you're a god damned traitor. You fraternize with the enemy!! He flailed about on the couch and cried inconsolably.
Analyst: *Your great distress makes me wonder about what other betrayals have hurt and angered you so?*
Mr. C: (struggling for composure): My grandmother, she let my Uncle Joe get killed!

(p. 5)

Holmes frames Mr. C's rageful reactions to whites as defensive in nature – more specifically, *defensive displacement* onto whites of Mr. C's experi-ences of victimization at the hands of his grandmother. This view frames the patient's experience of the analytic relationship solely in terms of the patient's past and leaves out the analyst's own contribution. Holmes does not explore the meaning Mr. C attached to seeing the white patient in the therapist's office or inquire about the significance of the perceived betrayal from a black therapist; instead, she shifts the focus away from the here and now transference to the patient's past, in essence diverting their attention from exploring in detail the apparently emotion-laden perception of his black therapist's betrayal. Furthermore, the therapist's strategy of directing him to look at other sources of his anger may have left the patient feeling scolded and judged that his rage was inappropriate to the situation. Is it possible that the therapist was feeling hurt and/or annoyed and critical of Mr. C's intense angry reactions, therefore quickly working to get him to see them as defensive and inappropriate? One wonders if this kind of interaction between the therapist and the patient, especially if they occurred routinely, is responsible for the patient's premature termination from therapy.

KLEINIAN/CONTEMPORARY KLEINIAN CONCEPTUALIZATION

Within psychoanalysis, the Kleinian school, with its dark vision of human nature, has offered perhaps the most compelling explanation for the horrors of racism, racial violence, and genocides at the societal level carried out in the various parts of the world in the twentieth century (Chasseguet-Smirgle, 1987, 1990). However, very little is written about the race-related issues in therapy utilizing Kleinian concepts. Only two writers have employed the Kleinian concepts of projection and projective identification to specifically explain race-related transference in therapy (Tan, 1993; Altman, 1995). Altman (1995) states that our culture has constructed black and white racial categories in order to create a focus for projection and introjection. The 'opposite' race creates a category of people who are 'not me' into which we can project unwanted psychic content, such as aggression, acts accordingly, which is then introjected by the other racial category of people. Altman believes that a complex moving back and forth of projective identification takes place in inter-racial therapy using race as a focus. According to Stern (1994), the term projective identification has carried both intrapsychic and interpersonal meanings. Originally conceived of by Klein as a defensive process by which the subject rids the self of unwanted mental contents, subsequent theorists such as Bion, Racker and Kernberg highlighted the communicative aspect of this concept by stressing that the subject attempts to communicate to the object via the projected material, which is felt and identified with by the object (Stern, 1994).

While the concept of defensive projection may fit some people's use of the racial categories as container for unwanted impulses, it may not explain individuals' attitudes and feelings towards race in every case. In particular, this concept, for its emphasis on defensive warding off of inherently bad innate impulses, may obscure the developmental dimensions underlying one's attitudes and feelings towards the racial other. Stolorow *et al.* (1987) point out another important potential pitfall in invoking the concept of projective identification in therapy – it may be used in a self-serving way for the therapist: by explaining away the therapist's feelings as foreign material injected by the patient's aggression and hostility, the therapist can maintain a modicum of intact self. In this scenario, there is no room for the therapist's own pre-existing vulnerabilities to cause unpleasant and painful feelings in the therapist. The adverse therapeutic consequence of 'blaming' the patient for the therapist's vulnerable feelings when race is at issue is illustrated in the following report of a clinical case by Tan (1993). Tan, a foreign-born Asian therapist, employs the concept of projection and projective identification in his work with a white male social worker patient whose work brings him into constant contact with Asian immigrant clients. Noting that his patient has a strong sense of pride in being similar to the therapist in that both are in the helping profession, Tan states that this sense of similarity 'created for him (the client) an ideal space for his projections into me of unwanted parts of himself'. Sometime into the treatment, this patient started to complain of being stuck in therapy. He also felt similarly at work, feeling useless and helpless due to his immigrant (Asian) clients' lack of understanding of the English language. Noting his own paralleling feelings of being 'extremely frustrated, and made to feel useless', the therapist set out to show that 'he (the client) was feeling hostile' towards the therapist and was attacking him to 'disarm me from doing him any good, and that, furthermore, he was only able to maintain me by feeling superior because I, like his clients, was not white'. Tan felt the client's reference to the 'lack of understanding of the English language' was a thinly disguised denigration of the non-white, foreign-born therapist. Tan goes on to say that:

> this reflects the way he dealt with his clients by seeing them with contempt and inferiority, the unbearable painful parts of himself. In particular it was very difficult for him to accept help from me (who is foreign, inferior and his client in phantasy) as this would make him feel inferior which he found intolerable. The intensity of his feeling in this regard was intensified by my saying to him that he was polite towards me in an 'obsequious' way and, as such, was in fact secreting contemptuous feelings towards me. This threw him into a state of anxiety because I had used a word which he did not understand, i.e., obsequious. He had often told me of his interest in literature and that he spent his time writing and hoped to be published one day . . . During these times, I would find myself being over-cautious with my choice of words, with an overriding feeling of inadequacy and inferiority in the use of the English language. I was surprised, therefore, when he reported to me in the next session that his being unfamiliar with the word had caused him so much shame and anger. At this point it was a touch and go as to whether he would be able to carry on with therapy as he felt extremely persecuted and pained by his intense feelings of inadequacy and inferiority.

(pp. 36–37)

From another vantage point, one can see the iatrogenic contributions to the precarious predicament this therapy ended up in: first of all, the Asian therapist assumes that the white client is looking for a ready opportunity to unload his dark, hostile impulses onto the therapist when the client feels pride in being similar to the therapist. He does not entertain the possibility of growth-oriented meaning in this patient's desire to be equal to the therapist, i.e. to be in the same league with the therapist, perceived to be competent and esteemed. In fact the therapist's assumption of the patient's destructive motivation of hostility and intent to project unwanted aspects of himself onto the therapist permeates all his perceptions of the patient. While it is certainly possible that the client was subtly feeling superior to the foreign-born, non-white therapist, the only evidence Tan uses to support this possibility is his own, apparently very strong, countertransference feelings of helplessness and insecurity. He tells the patient that the patient wants to feel superior, wants to render him impotent and useless and is being 'obsequious', to defend against this underlying hostility. This line of interpretation amounts to abusive attack on the patient. Understandably, the therapy became precarious as the patient became extremely anxious and justifiably felt persecuted in response.

INTERSUBJECTIVE CONCEPTUALIZATION

The previous sections outline the problematic aspects of the intrapsychic and Kleinian views as applied to race-related transference in therapy. The goal of this section is to provide an alternate conceptualization from the more recently advanced views, such as social constructivism (Hoffman, 1992), hermeneutics (Strenger, 1991), intersubjectivity (Stolorow, Brandchaft and Atwood, 1987), and relational theories (Mitchell, 1988), to which, for the purpose of this chapter, I will refer collectively as *intersubjectivity* theories. Although these views are certainly not synonymous, one central common assumption is rejection of the classical psychoanalytic view which equated the therapist's perception with objective knowledge concerning the client's mental state, replacing it with a view that increasingly recognizes that the therapist and the client have different sets of experienced realities, one being no more objective or valid than the other. This view holds that the therapist, far from being neutral and objective, operates out of a subjective reality that may or may not be similar to the subjective world of the client, but that nevertheless has much influence on the therapeutic process.

From these views, transference is no longer conceptualized as solely the projection of the client's feelings, drives, fantasies, and defenses onto the blank-slate therapist, but a product co-created by the subjectivities of both the therapist and the client (Hoffman, 1992). In particular Stolorow, Brandchaft, and Atwood (1987) define transference as the person's organizing activity, an expression of the rules the person uses to understand and process the information about the self, others and the world (Stolorow *et al.*, 1987). Hence, the person's attitudes and feelings regarding race are understood as one aspect of the person's ongoing construction of experience. And depending upon the patient's unique organization of experiences and psychological makeup, any number of possible meanings can be attributed to the patient's and/or the therapist's race. For some, race may not take on salience or significance while for some others it is the central pivot around which one's experiences are processed. It is my personal impression, from teaching psychology graduate students, discussions with colleagues, and work with both white and racial minority patients, that race is more important and salient to racial minority individuals than to whites. This is apparently true of therapists as well: racial minority therapists are more cognizant of race and impact of race on therapy than white therapists. And for some racial minority therapists, race may become so important that it is forced upon the clients regardless of the clients' own positions and experiences concerning race. For example, Carter (1995) reports therapy conducted by a black male therapist with a white female patient in which he insists that they look at race relationship between them over her repeated statements that race is not her main issue (pp. 205–211). The heightened salience of race for racial minority individuals may be a function of their attention to both overt and subtle racial inequalities represented pervasively at societal and cultural levels. Whites, because of the privilege that their race has accorded them in society, may not have as much reason to question the racial status quo.

Case A

A is an art historian of Jewish extraction in her 40s who sought psychoanalytic psychotherapy. She was referred to me by a colleague who let her know that I was an Asian. During our initial meetings she spoke of a deeply held sense of herself as defective at the core. She suffered at the hands of a highly volatile, emotionally and verbally abusive father and an alternatively depressed and anxious mother. Given the favored status of her two older brothers, she also thought of herself as being an outsider to her family. Her sense of being an outsider sometimes was extreme enough to make her feel like an alien, outside the human race.

As an art historian, A developed deep interest in works of those artists branded as outcasts in the society, homosexual and foreign-born artists, and her heroes tended to be foreign-born women whose art work depicted themes of alienation and oppression. A consciously acknowledged her resonance with the painful struggles of these individuals and was imbued with hope and strength by their ultimate triumph achieved in their art. And although unspoken, my status as a racial minority, a perceived outsider in the society, was a source of powerful hope that motivated her to embark on a course of therapy.

However, my racial status and foreign background were also a source of deeply held fears: she was to voice numerous concerns and fears about my being an Asian and being of a foreign background. A was afraid that since my native language was not English, I would not be able to provide precise understanding of her experience. And when my choice of words did not accurately describe her experience, she became extremely angry. A also spoke of her fear that I might be emotionally unresponsive as her impressions of her quiet Asian colleagues seemed to suggest to her. She was very vigilant and anger-prone when any signs of my emotional 'inaccessibility' were present. For example, on one occasion, she felt herself to be in a terrible internal crisis regarding performing some work tasks. In the session she was agitated and extremely angry, saying that I was like a 'wall', emotionally unmoved by her crisis and was doing nothing to help her feel calmer. A was quite prone to have one of these emotional outbursts when she perceived me to be emotionally over-controlled and emotionally blank. This line of perception was explored over and over again and was in time linked to her profoundly depressed, wooden mother, who at times appeared in A's dreams as an armless, black couch, with A being perched precariously on its edge. Repeated work in the area of repetitive transference, as described above, eventually ushered in a period of her coming forth with deeply felt longing for contact and attachment to me. She spoke of just wanting to be with me, without speaking words.[2]

Case B

B is a 40-year-old third-generation Chinese-American woman in an ongoing psychotherapy for the past year and a half. Her presenting problem was her inability to experience an intimate and committed love relationship (she had some superficial dating relationships and friendships, but was generally isolated and withdrawn from others). She was working full-time and putting herself through school, studying in an Asian discipline, with a hope of eventually having a professional career in that area. In the initial meeting, B said that she had been in psychotherapy for seven months with a white male psychologist about a year previously but had discontinued it because she often felt criticized by him. She hoped for a better experience with me, for I, as an Asian woman, might understand her better.

Over a period of time, I came to think of B as 'a woman without shadow', for her intense focus on the present with a striking indifference to her past. It seemed as if her life was contained in the present and present only with no continuity with the past. Her account of her early experiences of important others was extremely sketchy, not going beyond her one-dimensional characterization of her mother as having been critical of her school grades. I came to understand that this omission made sense as these figures provided no real acknowledgment and affirmation of B as a person. As an adult, B had been in a series of relationships, all of which were disappointments. Overall, I hypothesized that she had an enduring, extremely shameful and despairing conviction about herself as alone, unable to get close to others. This enduring sense of herself was concretized by a vivid image she had in her 20s of herself dying alone in a nursing home. In light of this, I gradually came to understand the importance our shared Asian background had for B: she sought out treatment with me imbued by a fantasied bond with me due to our common Asian background. Given her profound conviction about herself as being alone, her use of race as a basis for a possible bond with me was significant, for it carried her hope for contact and connection with another person. Given her hopelessly distant relationship with her Chinese mother and lack of other affirming relationships in her life (she once said that 'icicles' surrounded her heart), I also sensed that her hope for attachment with me was fragile and rooted in deep-seated fear that once again she will be let down.

Case C

C, a white unmarried male graduate student at a large university with 'relationship problems', sought treatment at a clinic and was assigned an Asian female therapist in her mid-20s. Even prior to their first face-to-face contact, C developed a powerful reaction to the therapist's race: he later told the therapist that when she called him to make the first appointment, he detected an accent in her English. He also said the therapist's voice was small and these were unmistakable signs of her inadequacy. In the initial face-to-face meeting, C said that he did not think the therapist could help him. He said that in his experience, Asian women were 'sexual fetish' for white men and this was evident to him from a large number of white men dating Asian women at his school. The therapist felt on one hand horrified by his blatant and unbridled racist and sexist statements, while on the other hand she struggled with feeling personally assaulted by his unwarranted attack on her. She asked him how he could have these judgments about her as passive and inadequate, since they had just met.[3] C was able to agree with the therapist that he in fact had very little knowledge of her. And, with an agonized look on his face, he began speaking about an ex-girlfriend who was an Asian, whom he perceived as passive and empty-brained. He did not respect her. However, when she suddenly left him he was devastated and fell into a profound depression. And although a number of years have passed, C had not completely recovered from this experience nor has he had any significant relationship with a woman since then. C came from an abusive family: his alcoholic father abused his mother physically and emotionally when drunk. C despised his mother who could not stand up for herself and who helplessly took the abuse. C felt tortured by his intense ambivalence toward his mother/ex-girlfriend and now his new therapist. After a couple of meetings, C decided that he felt too conflicted to continue the work and asked to be referred to a white male therapist within the clinic.

DISCUSSION OF CASES A, B, AND C

It is my experience that in cross-racial therapy dyads or in same-race dyads when both participants are of racial minority, more often than not, race becomes a salient issue. While a classically oriented analyst might be inclined to assign aggressive and libidinally related meanings to race-based transference, an intersubjective therapist entertains a much broader array of possible meanings, mindful of the person's unique history and psychological makeup of the intersubjective milieu that might have given rise to the patient's unique take on the race. Hence for C the therapist's race became linked to a helpless, dependent mother while for A, to an unresponsive, depressed, and wooden mother. For B, the therapist's Asian race was taken positively, stimulating a fragile hope for attachment.

Among the broad arrays of meanings that race may bear in therapy, it may be fruitful to give particular consideration to the larger societal and cultural milieu in which race relations are shaped. To begin with, racial stereotypes available in the general culture may enter into therapy: in the cases of A and C, negative stereotypes about Asians were quickly activated and were important organizers of their initial experiences of the therapists. For C, the young female Asian therapist evoked a 'China doll' image of Asian women, exotic sexy plaything, 'sexual fetish' of white men. For A, the stereotype of Asians as being emotionally inscrutable was eventually linked to her unresponsive, depressed, and wooden mother, which was a source of profound dread. In my experience, while it is not always pleasant to deal with stereotypes in therapy, they are invariably useful in understanding patients' relational configurations.

Furthermore, the power disparity evident in the general society between races is often reflected in the cross-racial therapy dyads as well. In A's case, aspects of this power differential relationship were organized to reflect her pre-existing internal object-relations configuration originally shaped and maintained in the power differential relationship of her relationship with her parents: the racial minority therapist was equated with A's own experience of herself in her family of origin, as an outsider, alienated and marginalized.

From the intersubjective position, if the therapist's race evokes an intense negative reaction, as was the case for both A and C, it should be understood as the therapist's race being organized in such a way as to activate fear of repetition of some aspects of the patient's painful experiences with caregivers. In the case of C, his fear of the 'China doll' therapist was that of being stuck in a relationship that could potentially repeat his extremely painful experiences with his dependent, helpless mother. For A, the therapist's race stimulated fear of an experience where her relationship with an emotionally unresponsive mother would be repeated. In sharp contrast to the Kleinian position, where patients' negative reaction is likely to be viewed as a defensive projection of inherent aggression or hostility, an intersubjective position would emphasize developmental elements underlying the negative reaction in its assumption that understanding and a gentle articulation of the patient's fears would result in the patient's feeling understood, and bring forth the patient's developmental yearnings. In A's case this was successfully accomplished, as repeated work on her fears ushered in a deepening therapeutic bond. In C's case, had he stayed in treatment, the therapist's understanding and articulation of his fears would have created an opportunity for him to experience the seemingly weak therapist–girlfriend–mother in a way facilitative to his growth.

THE THERAPIST'S RACE, HER CONTRIBUTION TO TRANSFERENCE, AND EMPATHIC-INTROSPECTIVE MODE OF INQUIRY

A relevant question to an intersubjective therapist working with race is how the therapist's race contributes to the shape and nature of transference in therapy. I believe the impact of race in this regard is profound. Perhaps not much different from the way gender influences and shapes one's identity, one's race seems to influence individuals' characteristic ways of being in the world, how they come to construe who they are in the world, and the ideals they live by. And therapists, just like anybody else, are influenced similarly by their racial background. One finds a compelling example of this when one sees that the 'truths' that psychoanalysts operate out of are not universal, but products of the world view and values of the Euro-American culture. These values include bounded, autonomous self with an affect-filled interiority, assertiveness of personal needs, personal achievement, personal identity, democracy, introspection, interpersonal equality, etc. (Cushman, 1990). How closely a patient, regardless of his racial background, personifies these values is intimately linked to the analyst's conscious and unconscious judgments about the patient's pathology or psychological health and psychotherapy goals. A number of writers have pointed out that when these values are applied to non-white patients, it may be considered ethnocentric: Frantz Fanon decried the ethnocentric nature of classical psychoanalytic theories as applied to blacks (Bulhan, 1985a). Others have pointed out the inappropriateness of applying the psychoanalytic concepts of individuation and autonomy (Yi, 1995) and of self psychology (Cushman, 1996) to Asian individuals.

Case D

D is a white woman in her 40s in a psychoanalytic psychotherapy for two years. One day she wanted to sue her boss for unpaid compensation for some extra work she did. She was in the right, for the company policy clearly called for compensation of such extra work. In outrage, D had consulted a lawyer about suing her boss. When she brought into therapy a draft of a letter to the boss threatening a lawsuit for me to read before sending it off, I had a strong feeling of aversion. She asked for my reaction to the letter, and before being able to resort to an analytically inquiring mode, I blurted out, 'Well, maybe this is our individual differences, but a lawsuit would not be something I would be thinking about.' D appeared to feel some shame initially at my less than enthusiastic support for her idea, but went on to reflect upon how she felt deeply victimized at the hands of her boss, who, like her father, was perceived to be an authoritarian, being prone to arbitrary use of power. While it seemed fruitful for D to reflect upon her intense anger at her boss and its connection to her father, I was left to wonder about my rather spontaneous, strong disapproval of, not so much her rage, but the manner in which she set about to resolve the interpersonal dispute, i.e. through a lawsuit. Upon some reflection, I came to think of this incident not as differences in our idiosyncratic personal preferences but rather a revealing example of our cultural differences: I realized that my aversion to the lawsuit was congruent with an Asian cultural preference for interpersonal harmony even at the cost of personal sacrifice and resolution of injustice through appeal to moral obligation, whereas, D's stance of lawsuit seemed to be congruent with her mainstream cultural value of asserting individual rights and resolving interpersonal problems by invoking contractual agreements. The next day, D thanked me for my 'prudent' approach to the situation and told me that she had decided not to go ahead with the lawsuit. She successfully received compensation for the extra work by speaking to the general manager of her company, who in turn brought pressure to bear on her boss. While the impact of my reaction to her idea of lawsuit was never explored in therapy thereafter, there were other opportunities to do so, as D went on to have similar experiences at work, where she felt inadequately compensated for her work, and at the mercy of her boss's arbitrary use of power. She had memories of going to her mother, when she felt abused by her father, only to be told not to cry and that her father was right after all. She felt that I too wanted her to keep quiet and not complain. By then, I was becoming *painfully* aware of my role in recreating her experience with her mother in transference.

DISCUSSION OF CASE D

D's case demonstrates the contribution the analyst's race-based culture makes to the nature and shape of the transference. From the intersubjective position, it is considered impossible for the therapist and patient not to influence each other, as attitude can be communicated, if not overtly, then subtly through gestures, postures, line of inquiries, etc. The point to be underscored here is that the analyst's racial background and associated cultural values are an important part of the analyst's subjectivity and influence her therapeutic endeavors, from her views of human nature, pathology v normalcy, to her choice of techniques and therapy goals. In D's case, it occurs to me as a strong possibility that another analyst of non-Asian background might have found D's idea of lawsuit more agreeable than I did. In fact, a Euro-Amerian therapist may be more likely to see it as an objectionable self-defeating passivity if the patient did not protest the lack of compensation for the extra work. And if the patient was an Asian who would not insist on being compensated for the extra work, what will happen to transference if the assertive Euro-American attitude were subtly (or not so subtly) communicated?

Precisely because the analyst's cultural values can not be kept out of cross-racial therapy, an analyst who is not reflective with respect to the culture-embeddedness of her therapeutic endeavors may suffer the danger of being ethnocentric. I believe what is in order is an approach that allows the analyst to gain access to the patient's subjective experiential world but also to reflect on the *culture-embeddedness* of her therapeutic maneuvers. This approach is tantamount to what some intersubjective theorists (Stolorow *et al.*, 1987) call *empathic-introspective* mode of inquiry. This term, *empathic-introspective* as opposed to empathic, places dual emphases on the therapist's attempt to *empathize*, to understand the patient's experiences from a perspective within, and on the therapist's attempt to *introspect* with respect to the role her subjective organizing principles play in understanding and shaping the therapeutic relationship with the patient.

While the empathic-introspective approach has emerged as a useful therapeutic construct, its significance in terms of working with the racially different client has not been previously recognized in the literature. Maintenance of the emphatic-introspective mode of inquiry is of paramount importance in working with the racially different client given that, when properly exercised, it requires the therapist to self-reflect on her subjective organizing principles, including her assumptions, thoughts, ideas, and feelings that are culture-bound.

CONCLUSIONS

There is no doubt that the issue of race is insufficiently explored in psycho-analytic literature. This is a problem because race is an important and salient organizer of experience for a growing number of people of different racial backgrounds who make up our patient base. Not addressing this problem would mean doing disservice to a large and growing number of individuals of different racial backgrounds who may need their therapists' assistance in understanding and exploring their feelings about their own or the therapist's race. The currently existing psychoanalysis literature on race-based transference falls broadly into the classical and Kleinian views. In this article, I hoped to have pointed out the problems with these views; the classical position, with its ideal of the blank screen therapist, may leave out the therapist's contribution to transference, and may be too restricted in its emphasis on intrapsychic meaning to the exclusion of other possible meanings. The Kleinian view is limited in its strong tendency to consider negative transference as defensive projection on the part of the patient, a defensive maneuver to dump unwanted mental contents to the racial other. The problem of blaming the patient becomes more extreme if the concept of the projective identification is invoked in which the therapist assumes that his/her negative reaction to the patient is caused by the patient's destructive impulses. In this chapter, these views are contrasted with an intersubject-ively based view, where race-related transference is seen as an instance of the person's ongoing organizing activity and where understanding of the unique meaning of race for each patient is emphasized. Treatment implications from this view were discussed with clinical examples.

Notes

1 This chapter was originally published in the *Journal of Psychoanalytic Psychology*, 15(2) (1998): 245–261. Copyright © 1998 by the Educational Publishing Foundation. Reprinted with permission.
2 And at this time, we were able to put into words for the first time her reactions to each session's ending: she spoke of feeling immobilized after each session and needing to take time to gradually get ready for her day. This immobilization was understood as her body and mind being numb, too numb from unspeakable grief, grief originally from repeated separations from her mother, who, in spite of my patient's pleadings, would leave her alone in the house to go to work each day. In the sessions, she would feel overwhelmingly sad and she would sob, sometimes with her face buried in her hands, as if feeling too ashamed of showing her feelings to me. As this is an ongoing case, the therapy goal is that a repeated working through of these affect states would lead her to be better able to recognize them and hence integrate them into her conscious mental life.
3 This response was perhaps inappropriate, for it challenged and disqualified the patient's transference perception. Upon reflection, the therapist was able to recognize that her response was based on her painful personal experiences of having been a victim of racist incidents.

References

Altman, N. (1995) *The Analyst in the Inner City*. Hillsdale, NJ: The Analytic Press.

Bulhan, H. (1985a) *Frantz Fanon and the Psychology of Oppression*. New York: Plenum Press.

Bulhan, H. (1985b) Black Americans and Psychopathology: An Overview of Research and Theory, *Psychotherapy* 22(2): 370–378.

Carter, R. (1995) *The Influence of Race and Racial Identity in Psychotherapy: Toward a Racially Inclusive Model*. New York: John Wiley & Sons.

Chasseguet-Smirgle, J. (1987) Time's White Hair We Ruffle: Reflections on the Hamburg Congress, *International Review of Psychoanalysis* 14: 433–444.

Chasseguet-Smirgle, J. (1990) Reflections of a Psychoanalyst upon the Nazi Biocracy and Genocide, *International Review of Psychoanalysis*, 17: 169–176.

Comas-Diaz, L. and Jacobsen, F. (1991) Ethnocultural Transference and Counter-transference in the Therapeutic Dyad, *American Journal of Orthopsychiatry* 61(3): 392–402.

Cushman, P. (1990) Why the Self is Empty: Toward a Historically Situated Psychology, *American Psychologist* 445(5): 599–611.

Cushman, P. (1996) More Surprises, Less Certainty: Commentary on Roland's Paper, *Psychoanalytic Dialogues* 6(4): 477–488.

Fischer, N. (1971) An Interracial Analysis: Transference and Countertransference Significance, *Journal of American Psychoanalytic Association* 19: 736–745.

Goldberg, E., Myers, W. and Zeifman, I. (1974) Some Observations on Three Interracial Analyses, *International Journal of Psycho-Analysis* 55: 495–500.

Greenson, R., Toney, E., Lim, P. and Romero, A. (1982) Transference and Coun-tertransference in Interracial Psychotherapy, in B. A. Bass, G. L. Wyatt and G. J. Powell (eds), *The Afro-American Family: Assessment, Treatment, & Research Issues*. New York: Grune & Stratton.

Hoffman, I. Z. (1992) Some Practical Implications of a Social-Constructivist View of the Psychoanalytic Situation, *Psychoanalytic Dialogue* 2: 287–304.

Holmes, D. (1992) Race and Transference in Psychoanalysis and Psychotherapy, *International Journal of Psycho-Analysis* 73: 1–11.

Mitchell, S. (1988) *Relational Concepts in Psychoanalysis*. Cambridge, MA: Harvard University Press.

Schachter, J. and Butts, H. (1971) Transference and Countertransference in Inter-racial Analyses, *Journal of the American Psychoanalytic Association* 16: 792–808.

Stern, S. (1994) Needed Relationships and Repeated Relationships: An Integrated Relational Perspective, *Psychoanalytic Dialogues* 4(3): 317–346.

Stolorow, R., Brandchaft, B. and Atwood, G. (1987) *Psychoanalytic Treatment: An Intersubjective Approach*. Hillsdale, NJ: The Analytic Press.

Strenger, C. (1991) *Between Hermeneutics and Science*. New York: International University Press.

Tan, R. (1993) Racism and Similarity: Paranoid-Schizoid Structures, *British Journal of Psychotherapy* 10(1): 33–43.

Yi, K. (1995) Psychoanalytic Psychotherapy with Asian Clients: Transference and Therapeutic Considerations, *Psychotherapy* 32: 308–316.

Chapter 7

Interpretation of race in the transference: perspectives of similarity and difference in the patient/therapist dyad

Nadine M. Tang and Jacquelyn Gardner

It is only relatively recently that issues of race and racial differences have been addressed in the psychotherapy literature. Initially, the focus was on the potential barriers to treatment that therapist and patient of different racial backgrounds might present. During the 1960s, this issue was taken up in a more exploratory way with attempts made to capitalize on the meanings that were made of race in the transference (Schachter and Butts, 1968; Goldberg, Myers and Zeifman, 1974). Only in the last twenty years has the emphasis shifted to one in which the subject of race in and of itself is recognized as being of potential value in the therapy (Holmes, 1992; Leary, 1995, 1997 and Thompson, 1995). It now provides another avenue to access unconscious ideas about the therapist if she is of a different, or even similar, racial background.

RACE IN THE THERAPY

The teaching of clinical practice has closely mirrored the changes in attitude towards race in the consulting room. Early in our training, there was no discussion of the possible implications of our being Asian-American and African-American therapists who were often assigned European-American patients. Our efforts were to remain a blank screen, and the fact of our differences was never mentioned. Adding more confusion to the issue was our experience of being assigned the Asian or African-American patients with whom it was assumed we could work better. This was rarely discussed openly, and we dutifully tried to make the best of it. As Holmes noted in her paper (1992), sometimes the patient felt that she had been assigned to someone of lower status, especially when the patient had made no such request. With the benefit of hindsight, it is hard to imagine just what we were thinking. As minority practitioners in training, we were also in the position of trying not to bring our racial differences into the consulting room. Strangely enough, the subject just never seemed to come up.

We now seem to have swung around to the view that racial differences should be raised by the therapist even if not by the patient. Numerous interns feel obligated to make mention of the fact of race, often in a way that feels artificial and forced. Once having dutifully done so, they can now proceed with the 'real' work. It is our view that race and racial differences can indeed be useful windows into the unconscious, and can provide valuable information about the transference when stereotypes are made use of. However, such work fits best in a context in which there is some evidence, often in derivative material, that this is an area of curiosity, interest or conflict for the patient, and not simply one forced upon him or her for technical reasons.

It is our belief that both these reactions towards racial differences between patient and therapist, that is not allowing it to intrude in the therapy, or always having to bring it up, are responses to the incredible anxiety that discussions of race arouse. Our experience demonstrates that the reasons for the anxiety differ for White and minority therapists. As Yi (1998) points out, for the former, the subject of race can lead to feelings of guilt for injustices suffered by their minority patients. We believe that it is also about guilt associated with White privilege. In addition, the therapist's own racial stereotypes may lead to uncomfortable feelings in the countertransference. Thus, Yi cites Greenson (Greenson, Toney, Lim and Romero, 1982) who came to realize that the contempt he felt for his Black patient's sexual exploits actually arose from feelings of envy. Another wonderful example of this is provided by Altman (2000) in his work with an African-American man who consistently bounced his checks and ultimately never paid him. With remarkable candor and thoughtfulness, Altman explored his own reactions to this treatment. 'I also got caught in a tangled web of guilt, anger, and greed. . . . I began to feel like the stereotypical greedy Jew, like the Jewish landlord feeding off the poverty-stricken residents of the ghetto' (p. 594). In an earlier paper, Goldberg et al. (1974), three European-American male analysts noticed in their work with African-American female analysands that they all charged less than they would normally have, partly in response to what was seen as their patients' early experiences of deprivation. This would imply that they too experienced some guilt, and the need to make reparations.

For the minority therapist, the anxiety may stem from a fear of racism and racist attitudes. There is tremendous anxiety associated with racial prejudice. By introducing the subject of race into the therapy, the minority therapist risks the emergence of racist attitudes. This is demonstrated when Leary (1995) comments on her patient Mr. A's feelings about Blacks and Jews. He proceeds to reveal that he saw her 'as a wild provocative woman' and was 'alternately fascinated and repelled by my hair' (p. 136). Though the freedom with which Mr. A could speak of his stereotyped and racist thoughts helped to further the therapy, we can only imagine how difficult it would be to retain one's ability to be therapeutic. As both Yi (1998) and Leary (1997) have noted, there are also the feelings of the therapist to be considered in this intersubjective arena.

The words 'nigger' or 'chink', no matter in what context they are used, make us uncomfortable. The emotional sensitivity to the word does not change whether it is used jokingly among friends, in an erudite discussion with colleagues, or overheard in a chance encounter on the street. It is the level of anxiety about such racially loaded words that in part drives the impetus to make racial differences explicit. However, it is a misguided assumption that by making these differences explicit we can neutralize the discomfort. In some clinical instances, such naming of differences can further the therapy, in others it might do the opposite. Bobrow (2002) speaks of the danger of interpretations functioning as intrusions (p. 69). It is of interest to think that interpretive comments made for the purpose of naming differences can in fact interfere with the therapeutic work.

In our observation, it is more comfortable for minority therapists to address issues of race than for their White counterparts to do so. This could be explained by the greater familiarity that minorities have had with the experience of living in both cultures (Tang and Gardner, 1999). For this reason, they are more likely to have had to deal with and talk about racial issues in the many areas of their lives In addition, Yi makes the case that 'Racial minority therapists are more cognizant of race and of the impact of race on therapy than White therapists' (1988, p. 252). Thus minority therapists are more likely to recognize the subject of race between patient and therapist, and are more likely to address it.

In an earlier paper (1999), we put forward the idea that the use of racial stereotypes by our patients was fertile ground for exploration. In many instances, the patient acted as if the stereotypes were real, and made use of these to explore aspects of themselves which they had projected on to us. In part, we provided models for identification, and in fantasy, a way out of the suffering that they experienced. The transference was very powerfully shaped by the fact of our respective races in addition to other obvious factors such as age and gender. We present here two vignettes that will serve to illustrate how the race of the therapist was creatively used by the patients to clarify their own identities. In both cases, race and its attendant meanings were an irreducible factor in the therapeutic work. The fact of racial similarity in Tang's case was only noted and explored as to its unconscious meanings six months after the start of treatment. In Gardner's case, the fact that patient and therapist were from different racial backgrounds was never really verbalized.

The fact of racial differences leads to the question as to the importance of working with someone of similar or different race, and, if different, how one deals with it in the therapy. It brings to mind a discussion with a colleague who is from Pakistan, and who wore her native dress to work.

One Caucasian patient was quite distressed about this because she felt it emphasized their differences (personal communication, Loveleen Posmentier, 2000). We believe that there are times in the therapy when highlighting differences forecloses on the potential space where the patient is able to use fantasy to feel connected or even similar to her therapist. As Jones noted, 'one's own feelings are used as an index of what another is experiencing. Since you are judged by my perception of my own feelings, if we are too different, I cannot feel what you feel' (1998, p. 475). We would argue that there are times when the illusion of similarity is vital to the work. There are many considerations that go into the decision whether to make racial differences or similarities explicit in the work. This question remains open throughout the course of the therapy, and it is up to the clinician to grapple with the issue of whether to raise the subject, and, if so, when and how. The following two case examples illustrate the different approaches and meanings of race in the therapy, and the rationale behind making race an explicit issue or choosing not to address it at all.

CASE 1: ASIAN-AMERICAN THERAPIST (TANG) AND EURASIAN PATIENT

Ms. A is a 32-year-old biracial woman who sought therapy at her fiancé's behest. She and her fiancé Mr. B were both concerned about the degree of her anger. The referral was sought after she threw a glass during an argument.

Ms. A had a one-year-older half brother. Both were born in Southeast Asia of an Asian mother, and in Ms. A's case, a European-American father. When she was approximately nine months old, her parents went to work in a different country, and they were not permitted to bring the two children to join them. An aunt and grandparents looked after them for the next three years before they could leave the country and join their parents. Of particular significance was her mother's disapproving and critical attitude to some of her behavior and preferences, saying that her choices indicated she was not smart, or that she was immoral.

In our initial meeting, Ms. A began by seeking direction, but readily spoke about her reasons for coming, and provided a great deal of her history without prompting. I had the distinct impression that she wanted to comply with what she thought I might want, and I commented to her that she seemed to work hard at being a 'good girl'. She was clearly struck by my observation, but wanted to meet with someone else whose name she had been given before committing to another meeting. It was a week before she called to schedule an appointment. She continued in once- and at times twice-weekly therapy.

Though many issues have arisen in the course of the therapy, I would like to focus on those aspects of the transference that were enhanced by the fact of my being Asian. It was not until six months into the therapy that my race was mentioned explicitly. Ms. A had noted the difference between her husband and herself in that she felt there was value in things that go unspoken. I wondered out loud if perhaps this might be culturally related to her Asian side. This led to her revealing that she never thought that she would have chosen an Asian therapist. When she sought referrals, she was given my name and that of a European-American therapist. My ethnic background was readily identifiable by my name, and she made her appointment with me out of curiosity, but assumed that she would work with the European-American therapist. She was quite surprised when she found herself wanting to work with me and cited my comment about her needing to be a 'good girl' as compelling to her.

On my inquiry about her reluctance to consider seeing an Asian therapist, she associated it with her mother's attitude of contempt for Asians. Further exploration revealed a rather complex set of feelings towards her own ethnic identity. In some ways she experienced herself as a second-class citizen because unlike her favored brother, mother and myself, she was not pure Asian. She did not trust that she had a legitimate claim to being Asian since she could not speak the language, was unfamiliar with her mother's family traditions and had never learned how to cook her native foods. In addition, her father had forbidden her mother from speaking her language once they left Asia and she was encouraged to fit in once they moved to the United States, and not to stand out by being different. She identified herself as an American, and never dated Asian men. She could not easily find a place for her own Asian side for she was either not Asian enough, or, if she was Asian, it was a denigrated part of herself.

Within a few weeks of this discussion, Ms. A confessed to having looked me up on the Internet, and in the following months she began to idealize me, saying that she wished she could be more like me, and would consider my possible opinion when she chose a scarf to wear. An encounter at an Asian takeout restaurant when I revealed that I hated cilantro (coriander) became a shared moment that she subsequently referred to as being important. She was amused by and admired the unapologetic way in which I could state a preference. Several months after this encounter, she was describing how difficult it was for her to state her desires if she didn't have a series of rational reasons for having them. Giggling, she said 'I keep thinking about your saying "I hate cilantro"'. I thought about that for a whole week, wondering, how did she say that?'

The way in which race and gender became linked was evident in her feelings about herself and men in her life. She began a session by describing her husband's renewed commitment to a dream. He had always wanted to travel around the world by bicycle, and as he described this, 'I fell in love with him again. I just thought, go for it, it was so great. That is what made me fall in love with him, it was his passion for adventure.' This had also been true of her first husband in whose adventures she had willingly participated. She associated this sense of adventure and fun to belonging to her father who had loved to travel, and gladly accepted work in remote parts of the world. Her mother was far more concerned about paying the bills, and having a stable home. The seductiveness of her father was that he was fun. In some fashion, she unconsciously identified being Asian and female as equivalent to being the responsible caretaker who couldn't have fun. It was only through a man that she could participate. This also emerged in the transference when she became intensely curious about where I would go on vacation. Subsequent discussions revealed that it was important to her that I go to more exotic or unusual destinations. It was significant that an Asian woman could decide to be adventurous, and she began to wonder why she never saw this as a possibility for herself. She questioned why she had never come up with a dream of her own.

Discussion

Though not mentioned for six months, the race of the therapist was clearly an important factor from the outset. Even when Ms. A was consciously dismissive of the idea of working with an Asian therapist, it is also clear that she had used the therapist's ethnic identity as a way to help define her own. Had the therapist not been Asian, she may readily have attributed the therapist's ability to make her own choices to being only for those of other ethnicities. The fact that the therapist and her mother were both Asian, though of different ethnic backgrounds, enabled the patient to begin to differentiate what was idiosyncratic to her mother, and what might be culturally based behavior. That the therapist was an Asian of a different culture from hers may have made it easier for Ms. A to identify with her, especially since both her mother and father transmitted a view of some Asian women as being sexualized and exploited.

It was only after the fact of our ethnic similarities and differences was made explicit in the therapy that Ms. A was able to engage in the therapy in a way that was less about pleasing the therapist, and more of an effort to establish her own sense of self. This was initially accomplished through an identification with, and idealization of, the therapist, and subsequently exploring her own ideas and opinions with greater freedom. The fact that the therapist hates cilantro became useful shorthand for the idea that one can have an opinion that needs neither justification, nor analysis, but simply is. Further, it is worth noting the possible meaning that cilantro represented. It is often associated with Asian cuisine, and something that most Asians are 'supposed' to like. The therapist's comfort with disliking something so representative of Asian food without the need to reject an

Asian identity may have modeled one possible solution to her conflicted identity as half Asian. In much the same way, she used this as a way to be more expressive of her own reactions.

The development in her ability to relate to men closely paralleled the development in the transference, from ingratiation and idealization, to identification with and finally a comfort with forging her own identity.

Throughout the course of this therapy, the clinician chose to focus on the racial similarities, even though there were also some significant differences. To the extent that we can view ourselves as more similar to each other, there is less of a threat to the fantasy of close identification. Ms. A did not present any material that the therapist was aware of that suggested that the differences were significant.

CASE 2: AFRICAN-AMERICAN THERAPIST (GARDNER) AND EUROPEAN-AMERICAN PATIENT

Ms. S is a married European-American woman in her early 30s who came to therapy because of problems in completing her graduate studies. She was moderately depressed and complained that she couldn't make use of her talents to succeed in life. She is a tall, slender woman who for the most part dressed conservatively in business attire. Ms. S complained of difficulties in turning papers in on time, along with the discomfort of frequent stomach aches and headaches, all of which she understood to be related to stress. She sought therapy after a particularly distressing meeting with her academic advisor who was questioning her about her slow progress in the graduate program. She was determined not to have these difficulties prevent her from finishing school. She chose to work with me because I had a Ph.D, making it obvious that I had been successful in graduate school. It was also implied that the therapist, as a professional woman of color, must have the capacity to overcome significant difficulties in order to become successful. Ms. S began twice-weekly psychotherapy with the objective of better utilizing her talents to achieve her ambitions. She was psychologically minded, open and free in relating her experiences.

At the time she entered treatment, Ms. S had been married for two years and had no children. She is the middle child of three girls, separated in age from her older sister by thirteen months. Although her father was a successful professional in the literary business, the family had serious financial problems due to her father's abuse of alcohol. Ms. S recalled times when money was not available to purchase school clothes for her and her sisters. Her father would spend a great deal of money entertaining clients on weekend trips which involved excessive drinking. The concerns over money, as well as the time her father spent away from home, were sources of frequent arguments between her parents. Her mother primarily devoted her energy to the home while maintaining an avid interest in the performing arts. She supported a local theater group by doing fund-raising and helped with public relations by writing articles for community newsletters.

At the outset of treatment, Ms. S vacillated between complaining on the one hand about what she had endured because of sacrificing for others, and on the other hand taking pride in her ability to be selfless. She complained bitterly that she felt invisible, unseen by the people closest to her. She felt misunderstood and that her talents and interests went unrecognized and unsupported. In particular, she felt angry with her mother for not protecting the family from the hardships imposed on them by her father's drinking. Her parents had been absorbed with the care of her older sister who suffered from acute asthma, leaving Ms. S feeling neglected. This often required emergency trips to the hospital as well as considerable home care by her parents. As a result, she received little of what she needed.

The following excerpt is illustrative of her work during the third year of treatment.

> I dreamed I was in a house I didn't recognize. I hadn't cooked and it seemed there was no food in the house to prepare. Someone came to the door offering to take care of me and it seemed he might be interested in me romantically as well. Somehow I knew he was married and unavailable. My mother has the notion that if you have a feeling you can't survive without someone, even if that person is not good for you, then you know you are really in love. I can see that I pretty much have the same idea. If I don't feel I am sacrificing for a man, then I don't feel I'm truly in love.

The dream revealed a great deal about the transference as it emerged at this stage of the therapy. Ms. S was unfed, in need and looking to me to feed her. She was asking that we create a different resolution from the one tinged with masochism apparent in the dream.

The interpretations at this point focused on bringing into her awareness this masochistic aspect of Ms. S's relationships with men. She moved away from complaining about sacrifice to presenting an unconscious resolution to her suffering in a transference fantasy thus described:

> I find myself thinking how great it would be for someone to truly know me. I can't imagine what it would be like for someone to know me well enough to know just how to cultivate my voice for singing. It makes me think how hard it is for someone to become a really great blues singer because you can't really teach someone how to sing the blues, but you can try to learn by listening to someone else's singing. If I could learn, I might be able to get free from some of the things that weigh me down and hold me back. I can imagine you as someone who would be able to sing about sad things and

turn them into something beautiful. This makes me think about my singing lessons and how hard it has been to get back to them.

I commented that 'Perhaps it was hard to get back to your lessons because you are always comparing yourself to a woman who sings better than you and you are constantly frustrated by her'. I understood the patient's inhibitions to be caused by both her idealization of the therapist and her guilt about surpassing her. This prevented Ms. S from recognizing and making use of her own abilities. The patient's rage with her mother further compounded her difficulties. The emergence of this transference fantasy constituted an unconscious communication to the therapist. The therapist's holding of this fantasy for the patient in fact soothed her while sustaining for her a vision of transcending suffering. The patient seemed to be saying, 'I know you have suffered. I am suffering. You have transcended, and knowing this enables me to transcend.'

In a later hour, she again took up the theme of frustrations in her life. 'I'm frustrated, but I'm beginning to think about these frustrations in a different way. I wouldn't be so frustrated if I didn't let myself get into these situations where I feel like I'm giving up so much and everyone is taking advantage of me. I don't have to suffer so much.' This expression of the unconscious communication in fantasy accompanied a change in the patient's internal world which she expressed in her changed view on suffering. She simply does not have to suffer as she has in the past.

Discussion

The transference fantasy of a European-American woman in therapy with an African-American therapist illustrates how the patient made use of the clinician's race in its construction. She projected onto me a life of oppression and suffering. She had entered therapy complaining of an apparent need to be in relationships in which she made important sacrifices in order to enhance her partner's life and to preserve the relationship. Through the use of interpretation, the patient became aware of her desire to identify with her mother whom she experienced as having made similar choices out of love for her daughter. She began to understand that she both wanted to give up her ambitions and pursue them at the same time. With this understanding, the transference deepened and the fantasy emerged. She felt that I was an accomplished blues singer who could teach her how to sing the blues. The idealizing fantasy imbued with the racial association to a Black, blues singer expressed the desire to transcend a position of conflict related to making sacrifices. She was convinced that as an African-American, I must have been subjected to painful experiences which I had endured and overcome. Thus if the therapist could achieve academic and professional success as an African-American woman despite all the obstacles that they face in this society, then such successes should certainly be attainable for her, a European-American woman. As the work continued, she was able to gain an understanding of her wish to turn passive into active, transforming pain into a song and no longer being a victim.

Here we see how a therapy dyad of racially different patient and therapist makes use of the therapist's race in the process of achieving some important psychological gains. Perhaps even more significantly, the patient's transference became manifest without any explicit interpretation being made about the realities of the racial differences in the consulting room. Though closely attuned to any reference to race or racial differences in the clinical material, there seemed to be a need to work 'as if' this was not an issue. Over time, as the patient talked of becoming a blues singer, I gradually became aware of two divergent pulls. One was to explore with Ms. S her unconscious motivations for becoming a blues singer. The other was to remain unintrusive, allowing her the transitional space for the creative play between patient and therapist. The decision not to make explicit the patient's use of a racial stereotype in identifying with me protected this 'space'.

CONCLUSION

Both cases described above serve to illustrate how the patients made use of the therapist's race in forging an identificatory object. In one case, the racial similarity provided a reality-based factor, while in the second case, the total racial difference made the identification one that was based on pure fantasy.

Perhaps of greater import is the question of how race was dealt with in each case. In the first, where there were clear similarities, the race of patient and therapist was quite explicit and openly discussed from fairly early on. The fact remains that there were also differences which were not dealt with. In the second case where there were clear differences, the fact of race was never mentioned. Therefore in both cases there was no discussion of the racial differences. This raises some interesting possibilities. Perhaps as noted in the introduction to this chapter, the idea of raising differences in the race of the therapeutic dyad is too anxiety-provoking, or may be seen as potentially disruptive to the process. To make it explicit may threaten to create a rift in the therapeutic alliance if the subject is not evident in the patient's material. Then, too, the heavy reliance on fantasy in the second case may argue against the therapist's introduction of the reality for fear of destroying the patient's creative use of play. As Bollas (1992) noted, 'The ego understands that unconscious work is necessary to develop a part of the personality, to elaborate a phantasy, to allow for the evolution of a nascent emotional experience, and ideas or feelings and works are sent to the system unconscious, not to be banished but to be given a mental space for development which is not possible in consciousness' (p. 74).

Perhaps what is paramount is the need for a thoughtful approach to discussions of race in the therapy. On occasion, the subject is clearly in the room, and can and should be addressed explicitly. However, there are also instances in which being explicit can interfere with a developing transference fantasy. This can change with the vicissitudes of the work and the therapeutic relationship.

References

Altman, N. (2000) Black and White Thinking: A Psychoanalyst Reconsiders Race, *Psychoanalytic Dialogue* 10: 589–605.

Bobrow, J. (2002) Psychoanalysis, Mysticism and the Incommunicado Core, *Fort Da* 8: 62–71.

Bollas, C. (1992) *Being a Character*. New York: Hill and Wang.

Goldberg, E., Myers, W. and Zeifman, I. (1974) Some Observations on Three Interracial Analyses, *International Journal of Psycho-Analysis* 55: 495–500.

Greenson, R., Toney, E., Lim, P. and Romero, A. (1982) Transference and Countertransference in Interracial Psychotherapy, in B. A. Bass, G. L. Wyatt and G. J. Powell (eds), *The Afro-American Family: Assessment, Treatment, and Research Issues*. New York: Grune & Stratton, pp. 183–201.

Holmes, D. (1992) Race and Transference in Psychoanalysis and Psychotherapy, *International Journal of Psycho-Analysis* 73: 1–12.

Jones, E. (1998) Psychoanalysis and African Americans, in R. L. Jones (ed.), *African American Mental Health*. Hampton, VA: Cobb & Henry, pp. 471–477.

Leary, K. (1995) Interpreting in the Dark: Race and Ethnicity in Psychoanalytic Psychotherapy, *Psychoanalytic Psychology* 12: 127–140.

Leary, K. (1997) Race, Self-Disclosure, and 'Forbidden Talk': Race and Ethnicity in Contemporary Clinical Practice, *Psychoanalytic Quarterly* 66: 163–189.

Schachter, J. and Butts, H. (1968) Transference and Countertransference in Interracial Analyses, *Journal of the American Psychoanalytic Association* 16: 792–808.

Tang, N. and Gardner, J. (1999) Race, Culture and Psychotherapy: Transference to Minority Therapists, *Psychoanalytic Quarterly* 1: 1–20.

Thompson, C. (1995) Self Definition by Opposition: A Consequence of Minority Status, *Psychoanalytic Psychology* 12: 533–546.

Yi, K. (1998) Transference and Race: An Intersubjective Conceptualization, *Psychoanalytic Psychology* 15: 245–261.

Chapter 8

Race in the room: issues in the dynamic psychotherapy of African-Americans

Deborah Y. Liggan and Jerald Kay

The only reality is the patient's reality, and there is a distinct reality of being Black in America. For many African-Americans, the psychodynamic formulation offering a rationale for the development and maintenance of dysfunctional life patterns includes an inflexible narrative of race. The multicultural solution does not compromise the goals established for treatment outcome or patient satisfaction. The psychological stress of being Black in America can be formulated into a narrative of race that may be used as a guide for constructing a specific biopsychosocial formulation of African-American patients in psychotherapy (Liggan and Kay, 1999). The position of cross-race therapy dyads is supported by the acknowledgement of race in the consultation room. African-American patients can receive effective therapy from any culturally oriented therapist who facilitates the resolution of racial conflict. From this foundation, we propose a dynamic model in which the therapist enters the experience of the African-American patient and establishes fixed points of reference for the proper detection of transference/countertransference issues.

HISTORY OF BLACKS IN MEDICINE

Race enters into psychotherapy in ways that parallel its operation in society. Consequently, the doctor–patient relationship is neither culturally value-free nor devoid of historical, political, and social considerations. Thus the history of Blacks in the health system has distorted medical relationships and institutions as well. The question perplexing the public is how American physicians could allow a disparate health system to evolve. Racial inferiority was taught in the nation's medical schools during the Jacksonian era (1813 to 1860). Physicians practiced according to a lexicon of 'Negro Diseases' that included conditions such as cachexia africana (dirt eating), struma africana (the 'Negro Consumption'), and drapetomania (the psychiatric disease causing slaves to run away). Professional journals were laced with articles based on unnecessary surgery, the vulgar display of

Black female nudity and genitals, slave starvation and burning experiments, and withheld treatments to observe the progression of disease. Black health reached its nadir during the reconstruction period following the civil war. The alarming death rate in this segment of the population led to the prediction that Blacks would be extinct in America by 2000AD.

Segregated medical care was reinforced with the founding in 1847 of the American Medical Association, which controlled hospitals, the medical education system, and professional societies. Although science disproved doctrines of racial inferiority by the 1920s, compulsory sterilization laws were enforced in thirty states. Hysterectomies performed on Black women for eugenic purposes came to be jokingly referred to as 'Mississippi appendectomies' in medical locker rooms. In 1964 and 1965, efforts were made to allow America's Black population access to decent, mainstream, health care. Passage of the Medicare and Medicaid legislation was intended to open the health system to Blacks, the indigent, the handicapped, and the elderly poor. At this time, the small number of Black physicians organized to start a Black hospital movement and medical society.

PSYCHOTHERAPY WITH AFRICAN-AMERICANS: DIFFERING IDEOLOGICAL PERSPECTIVES

Traditional therapists tend to view Black patients' symptoms and dissatisfactions as an expression of individual psychopathology, to be analyzed and understood in light of the patient's unique individual history. Even those therapists who are sympathetic towards Black goals may not view cultural factors as the genuine or primary determinants that interfere with a Black patient's fulfillment. While cultural limitations on Blacks may be superficially acknowledged, a patient's anger in response to these factors may be said to reflect an unhealthy sense of passive victimization that militates against constructive personal change. Thus a Black patient's sensitivity to the social and cultural roots of his/her difficulties may not be legitimized by the therapist as an important focus for treatment. Rather, racial concerns may be interpreted as the patient's defensive attempt to avoid painful inner conflict by placing the blame for personal unhappiness outside the self.

In contrast, those who identify themselves as multicultural therapists view the social and cultural context of the Black patient's problems as legitimate and an important focus of treatment. Indeed, to deny or minimize these sources of conflict is seen as inappropriate as attempts to treat Black persons while denying that racism is an ugly reality that affects us all. The Black patient's capacity to identify and respond to ways in which Blacks are depreciated, trivialized, scapegoated, or falsely defined in work and family is not viewed as peripheral to therapeutic work. Rather, the Black patient's expanded awareness of the false and constricting values, myths, and pressures that pervade the systems in which he/she operates is seen as crucial to the process of self-definition and growth. It is when a therapist fails to legitimize the patient's realistic anger and protest that the Black patient becomes further inhibited in the capacity for creative and free-ranging thought and action.

The destiny of the small class of Black physicians has been tied to the mass of Black patients throughout America's history. It was believed that they alone were endowed with the tools required to care for this segment of the population. Do people of color still believe that Black physicians are better able to relate to more diverse groups, or do they shy away from doctors who they believe have inferior training and experience? Do white patients believe that they are receiving quality medical care when their doctor is an ethnic minority? In essence, is race in the consultation room an issue in the dynamic psychotherapy of African-Americans?

Studies of treatment outcomes substantiate the assumption that therapy is often ineffective with ethnic minorities (Brantley, 1993). Blacks were cited as not appropriate for psychotherapy in that they failed to meet the criteria of verbal fluency, motivation and 'psychological mindedness'. They were deemed crisis-oriented and non-introspective, valuing environmental change rather than personal change. Blacks are further portrayed as seeking concrete outcomes rather than abstract goals with future orientation, or as preferring collective enterprise and interdependence versus independence and self-actualization (Rosen and Frank, 1962; Smith, 1989).

Regardless of one's political position, most historians agree that many dynamics occur when a physician interacts with a patient from another culture. This diversity can cause conflict and force individuals out of their comfort zone. Negative internal models of relationships include that of the Black matriarch, the emasculated Black male, the White authority figure and the Black self-rejected image. In the discussion of an African-American patient in psychotherapy, we use these negative internal models to address two controversial issues. First, to what extent are racial conflict and negative internal models of relationships incorporated into the Black patient's dysfunctional life issues? Second, can Black patients resolve issues caused by their need to function in a racially stratified society through a therapeutic alliance with therapists from other cultures (Glazer, 1998)?

Psychotherapy is modified for different age groups (adolescents – elderly); different types of mood disorders (dysthymia, bipolar disorder, antepartum and postpartum patients); and non-mood disorders (bulimia, drug abuse, borderline personality disorder, social phobia, somatization, and medically ill patients). If race enters into psychotherapy in ways that parallel its operation in society, then culture shapes individuals' experiences, perceptions, and decisions on how they relate to others. It influences the way patients respond to medical services and preventive interventions, and impacts on the way physicians deliver those services. In a society as culturally diverse as the United States, psychiatrists and others in health care delivery need to increase their awareness of, and sensitivity towards, diverse patient populations and work to understand culturally influenced behaviors. Consequently, studies examining the therapeutic dyad are not without racial bias. White reviewers predominantly state that neither race nor ethnicity impact on treatment outcome; Black investigators hold the opposite view. There have been extreme exceptions to these positions. B. Jones and colleagues (1970) and Thomas (1970) argue that the cross-race dyad poses insoluble problems and that the White therapist's efforts will be destructive to the Black patient.

The isolation of Blacks from other cultures in the therapy process is exacerbated by the politically correct concept of raceless therapy. This approach assumes that all people, regardless of race, ethnicity, or culture, develop along uniform psychological dimensions. With such purity of intention, most therapists do not view race in treatment as a serious problem. Racial concerns may be written off as naïve, outdated, or simply misguided. It is indeed difficult for therapists to examine openly and critically how their own unconscious biases and perceptions adversely affect and limit their treatment of Black patients. Yet no longer can we close our eyes to the fact that every therapist has an implicit concept of normality for Whites and Blacks that arises out of the cultural context in which he/she is embedded. As we will see in the following pages, a therapist's implicit (and often unconscious) absorption of cultural norms and values continuously affects the nature of the interventions that are made (or not made) in the course of the therapeutic process. According to this postulate, there are no cultural biases in outcome or requirement for race pairing between analyst and analysand. Social scientists describe an 'illusion of color blindness' to which a therapist may subscribe when assuming that the Black patient's culture is the same as that of other cultures. Three core problems have been identified with the color-blind therapeutic approach: (1) it disregards the central importance the patient's blackness has for him or her; (2) it ignores the impact of the therapist's whiteness on the patient; and (3) it abstracts the Black patient from the social realities of his or her experiences (Griffith, 1977).

RACE AS AN INTERPERSONAL TREATMENT ISSUE

Over the past decade, insurance companies, legislators, and funding agencies have become increasingly concerned with efficacy and accountability in regard to psychotherapy. A number of reviews of the literature on the efficacy of psychotherapy pertain to interpersonal psychotherapy (IPT). This time-limited treatment for major depression was developed, defined in a manual, and tested in randomized clinical trials by the late Gerald L. Kierman and collaborators. It has subsequently been modified for different age groups and types of mood and non-mood disorders and for use as a long-term treatment (Weissman and Markowitz, 1994). Interpersonal psychotherapy makes no assumption about the cause of depression or other disorders, but uses the connection between onset of symptoms and current interpersonal problems as a treatment focus. This raises the question: is race an interpersonal treatment issue? IPT generally deals with current rather than past interpersonal relationships, focusing on the patient's immediate interpersonal problems. It attempts to intervene in symptom formation and the social dysfunction associated with depression rather than in the patient's personality.

Interpersonal psychotherapy as an acute treatment has three phases (Weissman, 1997). The first, usually constituting the first one to three sessions, includes diagnostic evaluation and psychiatric history and sets the framework for the treatment. The therapist reviews symptoms, diagnoses depression by standard criteria, and gives the patient the sick role. The sick role may excuse the patient from overwhelming social obligations but requires the patient to work in treatment to recover full function. During the initial session, the psychiatric history includes a review of the patient's current social functioning and current close relationships, their patterns, and mutual expectations. Changes in relationships proximal to the onset of symptoms are elucidated (eg. death of a loved one, children leaving home, worsening marital strife, or isolation from a confidant). The framework for understanding the social and interpersonal context of the onset of depressive symptoms allows the therapist to link the depressive syndrome to the patient's interpersonal situation. In the middle phase, the therapist pursues strategies specific to the chosen interpersonal problem area. For example, grief is defined as complicated bereavement following the death of a loved one. The therapist facilitates mourning and gradually helps the patient to find new activities and relationships to compensate for the loss. In this way, the patient is helped to deal with the change by recognizing positive and negative aspects of the new role he or she is assuming, and assets and liabilities of the old role this replaces. The final phase of IPT, typically the last few weeks of treatment, encourages the patient to recognize and consolidate therapeutic gains and to develop ways of identifying and countering depressive symptoms should they arise in the future.

Rendon (1993) proposes that there are disorders of ethnicity just as there are disorders of identity. In an environment of extreme ethnic pathology, primitive defenses prevail. Psychological defenses may be seen as a hierarchy of mental coping processes that attempt to obtain distance from experiencing the painful event or unwelcome ruminations and feelings about past events. When an individual's ethnic identifications are conflicted, the internal response is to mobilize defense mechanisms such as denial, projection, and displacement to deal initially with the psychological dissonance and discomfort (Perry and Cooper, 1989; Smith, 1989, 1991). Maladaptive patterns in a patient's internal models of relationships influence interactions with others, expectations, and self-perception. For African-Americans, three primary internal models drive psychological defenses. These are the internal parental models, the internal model of Whites and the internal model of Blacks. One of the problems with maladaptive defenses is that they lead to limitations on information needed for adaptation. These defenses often impair the ability to resolve interracial conflict and leave the patient more vulnerable to being traumatized in future encounters with Whites. Defense mechanisms may persist even when hostility is no longer a risk. Meyers (1982) suggests that prolonged exposure to stressful conditions may lead to a chronic state of over-reactivity to events. Situations that are in fact benign for the individual may be experienced as stressful and threatening because of the perceived threat of discrimination.

INTERNAL PARENTAL MODELS

Substantial anger is frequently experienced towards the demands of intrusive mothers from matriarchal single-parent homes while the absent father role is unjudged. Attempts to dispel this model argue that the myth of the Black matriarch is based on over-interpretations of the effects of poverty on family structure and incidence of father absence. The internal model of father is a structure absent or emotionally detached from the needs of the child, leading to negative expectations of others. Black men maintain that they have been castrated by society but that Black women somehow escaped this persecution and even contributed to this emasculation. This is allegedly substantiated by the disproportionate advancement of Black women over men in the Black middle class. Both parental models influence development through difficulty maintaining a sense of self as a separate and autonomous person, and having needs from the external environment with little expectation of response. Defenses developed in relationships with the intrusive mother or the absent/passive father become rigid and obstruct adaptation to new circumstances. These defenses drive a host of behaviors: fear, anger, self-defeat, servility, and avoidance.

INTERNAL MODEL OF WHITES

The stressful effects of social oppression on members of disadvantaged groups are well documented. While multiple sources of oppression and deficiency substantially affect an individual's experience of life, it is the internal model of Whites that evokes significant anxiety within the African-American's psychological capacities. This image is distorted by the power and privilege ascribed to representations of a superior class. It is difficult to appreciate how extensively the residual bonds of slave ownership prevail in the ego structure, or how this internal model is updated with a politically correct self-image. There is a connection between primitive fantasy and racism. Doctrines of white–black and superior–inferior stratification are conceptualized as projective expressions of unconscious wishes. A similar view is held by Fischer (1971), who wrote that the black–white difference between the analysand and analyst is a significant and visible structure upon which the more basic and dynamic infantile fantasies are projected. Despite political and social reform, racial conflict is perpetuated in the unconscious motives of the opposing cultures.

The fear of inadequacy and the need to prove parity with peers may increase internal anxiety. Unconscious expectation of difficulties with whites may lead African-Americans to avoid or minimize contact to protect themselves from loss of self-esteem.

Another response to this unconscious expectation is servility. Submissive posturing and overcompliance with the wishes of perceived authority figures demonstrate concession to the traditional expectations of Whites. Many African-Americans constrain within their person a degree of anger towards the majority group. Aggressive acts clearly reflect this hostility, but often there are more subtle, self-defeating behavioral manifestations of anger. This is frequently the case with Blacks who demonstrate great potential for achievement, then sabotage their own success by creating problems to highlight imperfections and prejudice in society or their work environment.

INTERNAL MODEL OF BLACKS

African-Americans appear to have a central conflict between racial pride and an underlying image of self as inferior, primitive, and 'nonwhite'. Negative images of 'thick lips and thick minds' are portrayed in the chants of children at play and reinforced by low academic expectations. Social scientists refer to a 'pan-stupidity' syndrome, ascribed to the fear of being misunderstood, not accepted, considered ignorant or misled in relations with whites, no matter how benign they appear. The power of negative stereotypes is more pervasive than its influence on white perception of Blacks as drug dealers and welfare mothers. It extends to the core of a value system in which unacceptable behavior is 'acting Black', and beauty is 'looking White'. In its extreme, the negative image evokes a sense of shame for one's blackness. Helms (1986) defines racial identity as the portion of a person's world-view that is shaped by society's manner of attributing value to the socially ascribed group. Negative ethnic identity is characterized by using the majority group's standards as a means to judge and to accept or reject oneself. Hence the aesthetic reinforcement of 'good hair' versus 'nappy hair' and the preference of lighter skin color, mirror negative ethnic identity. In *The Rage of a Privileged Class*, Cose (1993) asks why would people who have enjoyed all the fruits of the civil rights revolution – who have Ivy League education, high-paying jobs, and comfortable homes – be quietly seething inside? To answer that question is to experience America as a land filled with attitudes, assumptions, and behaviors that make it virtually impossible for Blacks to believe that the nation is serious about its promise of equality, even for those who have been blessed with material success. The internal negative models described in the narrative of race offer an explanation of how these attitudes affect the African-American psychological being. The following case illustrates these principles.

CASE VIGNETTE

Ms. B is a 40-year-old single African-American woman in a professional school who presented with complaints of isolation in her academic program. Specifically, she felt that she had no one with whom she could talk. She complained of poor sleep with middle and terminal insomnia, tearfulness, depressed mood, decreased energy, decreased concentration and intermittent suicidal ideation over a two-month period. These symptoms started in the setting of a difficult school rotation where she felt singled out by the supervisor. The patient expressed feelings of hopelessness, stating that, despite her education and hard work, she could be reduced to 'a Negro' by any White person. She complained of being racially isolated throughout her life. She was often the only minority in her private school classes, a prestigious women's college, and graduate school. However, Ms. B denied any prior history of depressive symptoms. She described her baseline self as an energetic, perfectionistic, high-achiever who could do anything. She denied any history of an excessively irritable or euphoric mood, racing thoughts or pressured speech. Ms. B also denied any psychotic symptoms, such as auditory or visual hallucinations. There was no known family history of alcoholism, suicide or sociopathy, although her mother had several periods of symptoms consistent with depression for which she was never treated. On examination, Ms. B was reserved and guarded with pronounced sadness, decreased eye contact and little inflection in her voice.

The major stressors for Ms. B appeared to be her intense sense of loneliness and loss of self-esteem during conflicts with her supervisor. The fact that the supervisor is White represents significant distress in the way she interpreted his actions towards her, regardless of their racial intent. Ms. B's affective, cognitive, behavioral and vegetative symptoms are perhaps indicative of an endogenous type of depression. Because of her earlier experiences with Whites, she has difficulty trusting authority figures to be fair. She views herself as inadequate, defective and unlovable. Her primary defenses are regression, introjection, isolation of affect and intellectualization. Ms. B's socio-cultural background instilled in her a basic belief in the value of hard work, stoicism, and self-reliance with little dependency and autonomy, and her resistance towards a White therapist.

In early sessions, she explained that her feelings of alienation, because of her race, were a consequence of her need to protect herself due to mistrust of the intentions of others. Ms. B established the multiple meanings being Black had for her. Blackness was therefore something that made her stand out. Over the course of therapy, she came to accept her part in socially isolating herself from peers and followed a cognitive plan to connect with classmates. She came to see that her suspiciousness was healthy when it promoted caution in racially biased situations, but unhealthy when benign situations were misinterpreted. We questioned whether her need to prove parity was a defense against acceptance of herself as a Black woman. As depressive symptoms subsided, she found herself able to relate to groups of people in a new way – no longer as an outsider, but as a participant.

Discussion

A multiplicity of factors contribute to a Black patient's problems with work. The beginnings of such a summary would include intrapsychic and psychodynamic formulations; the negative impact of multicultural stereotypes; the realities of discrimination and lack of opportunity; and the impact of situational and contextual factors that affect African-Americans in White-dominated work settings. These factors all combine to make the road to professional fulfillment an especially difficult one for the Black patient.

There has been increasing recognition that ethnicity and culture play a role in the presentation, diagnosis and treatment of psychological problems (Bernal and Castro, 1994). Dysfunctional life patterns may have precipitated a number of negative schemas, which are amplifications of pre-existing learned behavior and cognitive patterns. As negative life events increase, judgments about close relationships become less favorable. The experience of racism has undoubtedly contributed to emotional distress and psychological disease for African-Americans. The biopsychosocial model of psychiatric disease postulates that psychopathology is the final common pathway of three determinants: (1) biological predisposition; (2) individual characteristics; and (3) the adaptive and adjustive reactions of a fully formed personality to stressors and deficiencies imposed from the external environment (Smith, 1989). In the case of Ms. B, there is biological predisposition, characteristics of dependency and autonomy, and social factors including stressful life events, low self-perception and less perceived support (isolation). Black patients may have defended against early negative encounters with Whites by suppression and denial. This impairs the patient's ability to resolve the experience and leaves the patient more vulnerable to be traumatized by future encounters with Whites.

RACE OF THE THERAPIST: BLACK–WHITE DYAD

While such stories and questions are interesting in themselves and may illuminate some aspects of African-American history, they may also serve to introduce the puzzling ambiguities surrounding this most basic concept of Freud's (1901) psychopathology: the unconscious determination of behavior. The unconscious determination of behavior, Freud asserted, is that conflicted and self-defeating behavior is determined by memories outside of a patient's awareness. His concept of the repressed unconscious and its power for influencing behavior became such a deeply ingrained conviction that most psychotherapists regard it as a foundation stone, and while any other part of a building may be altered or renewed, foundation stones usually are revered and left untouched. Freud acknowledged that some memories are not conscious; but we cure patients of their hysteria by transforming their unconscious memories of historical scenes into conscious ones. Freud further suggested that transference dominates the whole of each person's relations to his or her environment. Transference, by definition, cannot mean any other than persistent feelings or memories that are out of place in the here and now. They are perceptual distortions of earlier experiences most often with parents or siblings. Freud defined the central task of the psychotherapist as being similar to that of an archeologist, both of whom must dig up remnants of the past. One of Freud's most enduring contributions is that those who cannot remember early conflicts or trauma are doomed to relive and repeat behaviors throughout their lives.

The question in the case of Ms. B is common to many African-American patients in cross-race therapy: can Blacks resolve identity issues caused by their need to function in a racially stratified society through a therapeutic alliance that includes other cultures? As this vignette demonstrates, when discussing racial issues and engagement in psychotherapy, the issue of racism is an inevitable factor interwoven with multiple other concerns when the patient is Black and the therapist is White (Foulks *et al.*, 1995). Recognizing the influence of culture and ethnicity within the fabric of each individual patient's problems allows integration of the patient's experience into the process of therapy and the content of interpretations. It is important to employ strategies that minimize the perception of ethno-centricism or institutionalized attempts to devalue the Black culture. The existential approach described by Havens (1974) enables the clinician to enter the experience of people with cultures different from self. This requires exclusion of preconceptions that the patient's values and frame of reference are the same as those of the therapist.

Ms. B's references to race provided the therapist with additional points of entry to transference reactions. Comas-Diaz and Jacobsen (1991) coined the term *ethnocultural transference* to refer to the major therapeutic response that may arise for patients in intra-ethnic dyads. Although ethnocultural similarities and differences may impede rapport, they may also serve as catalysts for addressing issues such as trust, anger, acknowledgment of ambivalence, and acceptance of disparate parts of the self. Race was used by Ms. B to express transferences that represented powerful early feelings towards White people in her life. In dynamic therapy, interpretation of these projections onto the white supervisor allowed the patient and therapist to explore transference meanings of race. For example, Holmes (1992) suggested that it is possible that a Black patient would be inclined to experience the whiteness of the therapist as a prized representation of an idealized lost, never-achieved object. An outcome goal achieved by Ms. B was to reach internalization, where the racial identity becomes a flexible narrative. The case illustrates the point of many epidemiological studies, that racial issues are a major contributor to psychopathology. Outcome studies now need to demonstrate the benefits of psychotherapy in resolving racial conflict and modifying negative internal models of relationships both in cross-race and similar-race dyads.

Of particular relevance are questions about the interrelations among individual and ethnic factors as they influence people's functioning. These include ethnic group identification, reference group perspectives, degree of assimilation or acculturation, and minority or majority group status. The strength of an individual's ethnic identity either assists or impedes that patient in completing identity developmental tasks and resolution of internal racial conflict. Numerous models assess race and ethnic identity as therapy variables (Atkinson *et al.*, 1986; Cross, 1978; Pomales *et al.*, 1986; Tyler *et al.*, 1985). For example, the ethnic validity model developed by Tyler and colleagues (1985) addresses convergence, divergence and conflict between different ethnic world views. Individual attitudes about one's blackness affects perceptions and responses to self and environment. The model is noted for recognition, acceptance, and respect for the commonalities and differences in psychosocial development and experiences among people with different cultural heritages. Another concept that lends itself well to application in dynamic psychotherapy is the Cross developmental model of racial identity (1978). Cross used the concept of stages of identity to describe the different ways in which Black people may resolve the identity issues caused by their need to function in a racially stratified society. For example, the pre-encounter stage is characterized by a devaluation of Black culture. In the encounter and immersion stages there is increasing awareness and pride in Black culture. And in the internalization stage there is inner security with one's blackness and tolerance for other cultures. In a study by Pomales and associates (1986) Black patients were assessed by their level of racial identity and this level was linked to patient satisfaction and psychotherapy treatment outcome. It was noteworthy that patients in the encounter stage placed a high value on culturally sensitive counselor behavior, described as therapy which acknowledged the patient's blackness and showed openness to exploring cultural components of the problem.

Paradoxically, the potential advantages of same-race therapy are also associated with unconscious threats that may lead certain Black patients to seek out White therapists. For example, a Black patient who is involved in an intense, unresolved struggle to separate from whites may experience considerable anxiety in anticipating dependency on the Black therapist. African-Americans who lack a stable and coherent sense of identity and fear themselves to be without substance and depth usually have consolidated a repertoire of cross-race behaviors that make it easier to enter treatment with a White therapist, with whom these behaviors may help to control the anxieties inherent in beginning a therapeutic relationship. Blacks with unconscious conflicted wishes to achieve and succeed in the world may wish to avoid a relationship with a professional Black in which these conflicts will inevitably be stirred. In summary, many Blacks consider a White therapist 'safer' than a Black therapist, although this feeling may not be their conscious experience. Rather, unconscious fears of Black patients may be defensively masked by an experience of Black professionals as less capable or more authoritative than that of their White counterparts.

RACE OF THE THERAPIST: ADVANTAGES OF THE BLACK THERAPIST

A significant number of factors go into the making of a good psychotherapist that far outweigh the matter of one's race. Other things being equal (level of skill, experience, quality of training, etc.), Black patients may have much to gain in working with a Black therapist. Some of the advantages include:

1   Many Black patients find it difficult to be open with a White therapist. For example, their frankness and specificity regarding racial experiences may be limited. In general, a more honest exploration of self may be facilitated by work with a same-race therapist. With a Black therapist, the Black patient is less pulled to unconsciously fulfill stereotypical multicultural behavior that will block more creative, free-ranging work.
2   The first-hand experience of Black therapists with specifically multicultural emotional, physical, racial, and spiritual experiences may facilitate a greater depth and intensity of clinical work. African-

Americans have incorporated a great number of racially defined myths regarding the 'Black experience', which can best be explored with a Black therapist who has taken seriously the task of his/her own consciousness-raising.

3   A same-race therapist offers greater opportunities for identification. While this is an advantage for all patients, it may be especially critical for more disturbed individuals, who have not consolidated a stable and coherent sense of racial identity.

4   Affirmation by a same-race therapist has especially significant meanings for certain patients. To be accepted by another African-American in the context of a close relationship characterized by trust and mutual respect may be more 'validating' of one's worth and self-esteem than working with a cross-race therapist. This is especially the case for narcissistic Black patients with poor self-esteem who unconsciously experience White therapists (or Whites in general) as relatively more fooled by appearances than are Blacks.

Despite Black preference for racially matched therapy, there have been no studies demonstrating that African-American patients do substantially better in treatment when seen by therapists of the same racial group. Studies do show that empathy develops more naturally and there is less negative countertransference when Black therapists engage Black patients (Holmes, 1992). These sources point out that the over-identification with the patient's social situation occurring in the same-race dyads may result in reinforcement of the patient's pathology. As a minimum, there is a loss of clinical objectivity and thus inattention to the individual pathology that the patient brings to treatment. If African-Americans require racially matched therapy, major civil rights issues would be encountered in triaging and assigning minority patients to culturally specific therapies while majority patients are referred to standard treatments. Moreover, requirements to bring an equal quality of mental health care to all diverse citizens would be an organizational and quality-assurance task of daunting proportions.

CONCLUSION

Is it politically correct not to fully interpret intrapsychic conflicts in the face of racial explanations offered by therapy patients? It is more difficult for ethnic minorities to achieve good outcome from psychotherapy when their racial conflicts are not resolved. African-American patients can receive effective therapy from any culturally oriented therapist who facilitates the resolution of racial conflict. It is not the race of the therapist but the acknowledgment of race that is crucial to the therapeutic interaction.

Dynamic psychotherapy should recognize the influence of culture and ethnicity regarding the patient's emotional problems. Consequently, the integrity of the patient's diverse heritage and identity are acknowledged and respected. By integrating the contribution of ethnic circumstances on life events and psychosocial patterns, dynamic therapy neither systematically advantages nor subjugates any particular heritage.

We support cross-race therapy dyads with the acknowledgment of race in the consultation room. The pattern of exchange involved in therapy can provide a prototype of cross-ethnic exchanges (Tyler *et al.*, 1985). Many Blacks enter therapy to improve functioning within mainstream America (adaptation) without loss of ethnic identity (assimilation). In the dynamic model of psychotherapy, the therapist assumes the internal frame of reference of the patient and perceives the world as the patient sees it. The problem is articulated from the patient's perspective. This allows increased empathy and the ability to communicate empathy to the patient. The patient in cross-ethnic psychotherapy may establish early transferences based on previous formal relationships where self-disclosure was kept to the minimum required to transact an interaction. One approach used in cross-ethnic psychotherapy to overcome this resistance is having the therapist use more informal language when possible. Another method is to encourage patients to talk in therapy as they talk to their close associates. The more knowledgeable the therapist can become regarding differences in use of vocabulary, communicative gestures, expressions of distress and personal-culturally based values, the better will be the therapeutic alliance. Another tactic is to create a culture-comfortable environment. This is accomplished by the displaying of pictures, posters, artwork and other décor that reflects the cultures and ethnic backgrounds of the diverse patients served. Additionally, magazines, brochures and other printed materials in the reception area should reflect these different cultures. Printed information must also take into account the average literacy level of individuals and families receiving services. All of these efforts must enhance the primary goal of therapy, which is to provide patients with new learning experiences consistent with the multicultural mental health model.

References

Atkinson, D. R. *et al.* (1986) Afro-American Preferences for Counselor Characteristics, *Journal of Counseling Psychology* 33: 326–330.

Bernal, M. W. and Castro, F. G. (1994) Are Clinical Psychologists Prepared for Service and Research with Ethnic Minorities? Report of a Decade of Progress, *American Psychologist* 49: 797–805.

Brantley, T. (1983) Racism and its Impact in Psychotherapy, *American Journal of Psychiatry* 140: 1605–1608.

Comas-Diaz, L. and Jacobsen, F. M. (1991) Ethnocultural Transference and Countertransference in the Therapeutic Dyad, *American Journal of Orthopsychiatry* 61: 392–402.

Cose, E. (1993) *The Rage of a Privileged Class: Why Are Middle Class Blacks Angry and Why Should America Care?* New York: Harper Collins.

Cross, W. E. (1978) The Cross and Thomas Models of Psychological Nigrescence, *Journal of Black Psychology* 5: 13–19.

Fischer, N. (1971) An Interracial Analysis: Transference and Countertransference Significance, *American Psychoanalytic Association Journal* 19: 736–745.

Foulks, E. F., Bland, R. J. and Sherrington, D. (1995) Psychotherapy across Cultures, in J. M. Oldham and M. B. Riba (eds), *Review of Psychiatry*. Washington, DC: American Psychiatric Press, vol. 14, pp. 511–528.

Freud, S. (1901) Psychopathology of Everyday Life, *Standard Edition*.

Glazer, N. (1998) *We Are All Multiculturalists Now*. Cambridge, MA: Harvard University Press.

Griffith, M. S. (1977) The Influences of Race on the Psychotherapeutic Relationship, *Psychiatry* 40: 27–40.

Havens, L. L. (1974) The Existential Use of the Self, *American Journal of Psychiatry* 131(1): 1–10.

Helms, J. E. (1986) Expanding Racial Identity Theory to Cover Counseling Process, *Journal of Counseling Psychology* 33(1): 62–64.

Holmes, D. E. (1992) Race and Transference in Psychoanalysis and Psychotherapy, *International Journal of Psycho-Analysis* 73: 1–11.

Jones, B. *et al.* (1970) Problems of Black Psychiatric Residents in White Training Institutions, *American Journal of Psychiatry* 127(6): 798–803.

Liggan, D. Y. and Kay, J. (1999) Race in the Room: Issues in the Dynamic Psychotherapy of African Americans, *Transcultural Psychiatry* 36(2): 195–209.

Meyers, H. F. (1982) Stress, Ethnicity, and Social Class: A Model for Research with Black Populations, in E. E. Jones and S. J. Korchin (eds), *Minority Mental Health*. New York: Praeger, pp. 118–148.

Perry, J. and Cooper, S. (1989) An Empirical Study of Defense Mechanisms, *Archives of General Psychiatry* 46: 442–452.

Pomales, J. *et al.* (1986) Effects of Black Students' Racial Identity on Perceptions of White Counselors Varying in Cultural Sensitivity, *Journal of Counseling Psychology* 33: 57–64.

Rendon, M. (1993) The Psychoanalysis of Ethnicity and the Ethnicity of Psychoanalysis I, *The American Journal of Psychoanalysis* 53(2): 109–122.

Rosen, H. and Frank, J. D. (1962) Negroes in Psychotherapy, *American Journal of Psychiatry* 119: 456–460.

Smith, E. J. (1989) Black Racial Identity Development: Issues and Concerns, *The Counseling Psychologist* 17: 277–288.

Smith, E. J. (1991) Ethnic Identity Development: Toward the Development of a Theory within the Context of Majority/Minority Status, *Journal of Counseling & Development* 70: 181–188.

Thomas, C. (1970) Different Strokes for Different Folks, *Psychology Today* (September), 49–58.

Tyler, F. B. *et al.* (1985) Ethnic Validity in Psychotherapy, *Psychotherapy* 22: 311–320.

Weissman, M. M. (1997) Interpersonal Psychotherapy: Current Status, *Keio Journal of Medicine* 46(3): 105–110.

Weissman, M. M. and Markowitz, J. C. (1994) Interpersonal Psychotherapy, *Archives of General Psychiatry* 51: 599–606.

Racism, ethnicity and countertransference

Chapter 9

Racism and similarity: paranoid-schizoid structures revisited[1]

Richard Tan

> Identification concerns the relating to an object on the basis of perceived similarities with the ego. However, this is a complex phenomenon which has several forms. The simple recognition of a similarity with some other external object that is recognised as having its own separate existence is a sophisticated achievement. At the primitive level of phantasy, objects that are similar are regarded as the same, and the omnipotent phantasy gives rise to a confusion between self and object.
>
> (Hinshelwood, 1989, pp. 315–316)

In 'Race and Transference in Psychoanalysis and Psychotherapy', Dorothy Evans Holmes (1992), writes:

> Several issues have been suggested to account for the frequently observed tendency to not fully interpret intrapsychic conflicts in the face of racial explanations offered in therapy by patients. These issues include white therapist guilt, black therapist's over-identification with the downtrodden (a particular form of countertransference problem), and warded off aggression by patients and therapists. These limitations in therapy intervention have occurred when the patient explains a problem in its racial aspects alone, and the therapist does not seek ways to expand the patient's understanding once the racial component has been acknowledged.
>
> (p. 1)

This chapter looks at issues identified above which make it very difficult for therapists to focus on the transference relationship. In particular, it concentrates on the use of similarity as a defence against painful feelings of difference and, by extension, separation.

Racism in this context is defined as an inability to accept and acknowledge difference without attempting to control and dominate the object that is felt to be different and separate. The control and dominance aim to reenforce the phantasy that the quality of separateness does not exist. Putting it in another way, the object is perceived and experienced to be similar, leading to a distorted omnipotent feeling of sameness. The creation of similarity in this way is based on infantile phantasies of introjective controlling of the object as well as projective identification with it (Klein, 1946; Bion, 1959, 1962). Because this is such a primitive and infantile level of functioning, development is often obstructed.

If these defences are employed successfully, difference is destroyed. It is almost a form of disturbance resting on primitive defences of the paranoid-schizoid position. This is often seen in racial conflicts when rational thinking becomes impossible, and extreme hatred and violence are used in an attempt to wipe out any source of difference. Difference serves as a constant reminder of the painful infantile experience of impending loss of the 'good breast', which for some infants is unbearable. In this sense, the source of difference has to be denigrated, perhaps annihilated or made similar, in order to control the threat of painful acknowledgement of dependency needs.

In the clinical setting, the awareness of the difference between therapist and patient has then to be thought about and worked through so that progress can begin to be made. Where therapist and patient are from different racial backgrounds, the bringing about of this difference becomes crucial as cultural and racial differences are such fertile and receptive areas for projections.

Psychotherapy is about human relationships and as such both therapist and patient bring with them their own prejudices from their respective cultures and internal object relations, each unconsciously responding to the other in ways which could affect the outcome of the therapy (Heimann, 1950). As a non-white foreigner living and working in a predominantly white/English society, I found myself more often than not having to negotiate through the maze of covert and sometimes overt prejudices and discriminations of a white society. This is of course not exclusive to Black and White but present in any other cultural mix. The experience of these prejudices, which may be real or imagined via projection or projective identification, leads to an inability to access the situation realistically. An ability to contain and make sense of these feelings away from the immediacy of anxieties is essential to rational functioning. This is even more so when faced with racist feelings from patients. It is not easy, however, to get away from the immediate pressure of racist material from within and without so as to be able to think with clarity. It is often a luxury not afforded to the therapist faced with such infantile/primitive functioning when everything is felt to be immediate and concrete.

As a non-white psychotherapist, I have often then experienced this situation, whether the patient is from the indigenous population or from one of the many ethnic communities living here. Unlike the external, these prejudices have to be explored as they are the very defences which prevent the patient from benefiting from treatment. There is an added dimension in that I sometimes do not get the opportunity to work with this area of conflict with patients, as I am rejected out of hand because I am both foreign and not white, making it possible for them to cling on to these defences. The reason most often given is that due to the sensitive and intimate nature of the treatment, my being foreign meant I could not/might not be able to understand the patient's feelings. Although, we can grant a limited validity to this objection, there is also a fundamental problem which lies in the inappropriate attitude to difference. The issues arising from this single act of rejection are boundless for both the therapist-to-be and the patient. I would therefore stress the importance of understanding this from the transference relationship and that this be taken up from the outset with sensitivity from the beginning of contact.

Roland Littlewood (1988) in his paper 'Towards an Inter-cultural Psychotherapy' writes:

> As a White I am frequently approached by White patients who in the past have had a Black therapist or doctor, and who immediately told me how good it is that I am White, that I thereby had the ability and the knowledge to help them. They are puzzled by my returning to the assumption, which they see as tacit, but which I see as one aspect of their current inability to deal with their problems, whilst they see the past therapy and the Black therapist as a transient difficulty now passed.
>
> (p. 16)

I think Littlewood is referring here to the problem of identification at a primitive level which operates by creating a similarity to the object. In *A Dictionary of Kleinian Thought*, Hinshelwood writes of identification:

> Identification concerns the relating to an object on the basis of perceived similarities with the ego . . . The simple recognition of a similarity with some other external object that is recognized as having its own existence is a sophisticated achievement. At the primitive level of phantasy, objects that are similar are regarded as the same, and this omnipotent form of phantasy gives rise to a confusion between self and object . . . (The internal objects are phantasies, but at first phantasies are omnipotent, so through these phantasies involved in identification the object is the self. Actual changes in the personality come about on this basis and can be observed objectively) [t]hese primitive processes occurring very early in development when there is little distinction between activity, phantasy and reality. Phantasy 'is' reality and phantasy constructs the reality of the internal world on the basis of these primitive forms of introjective and projective identifications.
>
> (1989, pp. 315–316)

This is at the root of making racist feelings an issue in the therapeutic process where both therapist and patient are from the same racial grouping. The assumed similarity is based on perceived reality, especially so when the therapist may be having countertransference feelings in this area of the patient's psychopathology. There may well be instances when matching is necessary but it can so easily be used thoughtlessly as a projection of the therapist's own difficulties in an avoidance of thinking about someone who is different. The white patients to whom Littlewood refers may have been referred to in this thoughtless manner. Any assessment had probably ignored this possible problematic situation arising. All this emphasizes the importance of an awareness racial difference when the patient seeking help for his or her psychological problems is to be fairly and appropriately served. Disregard for the patient's needs and inappropriate referral could amount to exploitation of the patient arising from the assessor's dismissal of his own therapeutic obligations both to self and the patient.

This chapter then is about the primary problem of the disposal of differences. Whilst differences cover a host of situations, I believe racial difference is perhaps unique. Racial difference in the transference is an essential tool to be taken up and made use of in the resolution of the patient's emotional conflicts, a tool to be used *vis-à-vis* transference interpretations.

This chapter puts forward three main points:

1   Unconscious racism exists especially when therapist and patient are from different racial backgrounds.
2   Racism in the transference is a defence against growth, and it is lodged at a primitive (infantile) level of the paranoid-schizoid position.
3   It is imperative that racist feelings are interpreted in the transference.

I will now give some examples to illustrate how racist attitudes and feelings are present and brought into the therapeutic relationship and, secondly, when transference interpretations are made, how the transference is deepened in the service of a working through of the patient's problems. Because this chapter focuses on racism as a defence against growth, the clinical material presented is necessarily selective to illustrate the points raised. Other ramifications of defences present are not taken up here.

CLINICAL MATERIAL

Patient A

A is a white community worker whose work brings him in contact with members of the Asian community. He places emphasis on being a racially aware person and would readily speak up in defence of the rights of the ethnic minority population. He has a brother to whom he refers as having provincial values and whom he sees as rather ignorant in blaming immigrants for his unemployment, and the decline of English values generally. He thinks his whole family maintains this attitude, which he despises. He presented for therapy because he was having relationship difficulties with his girlfriend who was on the verge of leaving him.

He thinks that as a therapist I must be just as racially aware and open-minded as he is and that the obvious racial difference between us, and others, is not an issue. His coming to me as a foreign non-white therapist gives him a sense of validity for the job he does and reinforces his denial of any racist feelings in him. Also my being in the 'helping profession', as he calls it, allows him to feel that we are somewhat similar: doing the same job as it were. These two feelings created for him an ideal space for his projections into me of unwanted and painful parts of himself. This provides him with the opportunity to focus on the idea that we were similarly doing something positive and constructive, thereby denying the devalued and rejected parts in himself.

After one of his regular reports of his day's work with his Asian and black clients given in a rather excited way, I said to him that he felt somewhat excited as if he felt at one with me, that we were doing the same thing. He agreed with surprise and excitement as if this was a new discovery. This theme that we were 'of like minds' and therefore feeling 'good' in his therapy with me continued for some time.

Halfway through the second year of treatment, the patient started to complain of being stuck in his work and indeed his therapy, and was contemplating termination for the first time, as the therapy was not doing him any good. He felt frustrated with his work because he was made to feel helpless and useless by his clients who had quite a different approach to life, and who very often could not really understand his suggestions because of their lack of the English language. This complaint paralleled my counter-transference feelings as I was feeling extremely frustrated, and made to feel useless by his regular boasting of how aware he was of racial problems and how effective he was in this area of work (Davids, 1988). His subtly dismissive attitude towards my efforts was quite devastating. In the transference, I thought that he was complaining to me that my lack of English was a reference to my inability to understand his unconscious communication and I was therefore stuck like him with his clients. After being able to gather my analytic stance, I showed him his hostility and that his regular boasting was a way of putting me down and disarming me from being able to help him. In short, he felt that the only way to maintain the relationship with me was from a superior stance. I think this reflects the way he feels about his clients, with contempt because they are different, thereby providing a space for his projections. This made it intolerable for him to accept any help from me as this would make him feel inferior like his clients. The intensity of his feeling in this regard was amplified by my saying to him that he was polite towards me in an 'obsequious' manner and, as such, was secreting his contemptuous feelings for me. This threw him into a state of anxiety because I had used a word he was unfamiliar with. He had often mentioned his interest in literature, that he spent quite a lot of time writing and hoped perhaps to be published one day. He had a particular regard for an English writer and his clever use of words. These were times when I noticed my uncertainty and inadequacy of the English language and would become over-cautious with my choice of words as if I had something to prove to him. In the next session, I was surprised when he reported that his unfamiliarity with the word had caused him so much shame and anger that he had looked it up in the dictionary in an attempt to regain his composure. Furthermore, he had become slightly paranoid for he felt that I had used a difficult word to shame him. At this point, there was some confusion as to whether he was able to stay in therapy. He was feeling persecuted by a very harsh super-ego which did not allow him any feelings of inadequacy and of course I was to blame for this. I had caused him to feel inferior and insignificant but these painful feelings were immediately warded off by paranoid phantasies to enable him to survive.

My interpretation had made him consciously aware of the difference between us. He had, prior to this episode, been engrossed in a struggle to keep us the same. This feeling of undifferentiatedness enabled him to ward off any feelings and thoughts of envy, missing me between the sessions and holidays as if we were locked together; so that I was not a separate person with my own existence. The very obvious difference of being from different racial backgrounds and culture and their implications were dismissed, and I was felt to be in his control. The awareness of difference between us gave him the opportunity to acknowledge me as a separate person in possession of some goodness in having the capacity to contain his projections without being damaged, either by collapsing into a heap or retaliating with hostility. These were the very anxieties that he experienced within himself. The polarized feelings of omnipotence on the one hand, and the total helplessness on the other, had prevented him from being able to see that perhaps there was a middle option in his actions and responses to me. He felt incapacitated by them, impoverishing his quality of life.

Having somewhat cleared his clouded thinking, he now had to face his depressive anxieties. Had he damaged the relationship with me and had he the necessary resources to repair the damage? This became evident when he found difficulties in leaving the last session before the Christmas break. He was very concerned that something would happen during the break, that the situation between us would have changed when he resumed therapy, and that he was not certain as to whether I would be there for him. He was anxious about his ability to keep me in mind, and his hostile feelings towards me, so as not to bear the difficult feelings of separation and his need for me, in turn caused him to feel that I would retaliate. I had to remind him of the date and time of resumption of sessions.

On his return, he told me anxiously that he had sped 130 miles to keep his appointment. There are various implications about this destructive recklessness, but I will not discuss these here. Soon after this period, he revealed for the first time that his now ex-girlfriend (she had now left him), was in fact from South East Asia. When we discussed this omission on his part, he said that he did not think it was important to tell me at the time. Perhaps, I too had not considered sufficiently the importance of thinking about the obvious difference between us at the first meeting and possibly taken it up.

Patient B

B is a white European social worker who works in the UK. She often complained that she could not quite understand me because of my accent. She herself spoke with a heavy accent and was not particularly conversant with English idioms. She was surprised therefore when friends told her that they sometimes had difficulty understanding her. In her mind she spoke near-perfect English and in this respect felt that she was equal to her friends and colleagues. She had mentioned on numerous occasions that she had done very good assessments and would conclude that she had taken a lot from me in the therapy. She then acknowledged that she felt equal to the task at hand and felt somewhat similar and connected to me.

It came to light in the transference, however, that she was in phantasy, feeling superior to me, and in coming to me as her therapist, was patronisingly so. She said that she had two close black friends, a man and a woman. On an occasion when she had gone out with her black man friend for a meal, she felt that she was rather special and was proud at being seen as a liberated and intelligent white woman. She felt good at being able to portray this 'nice' part of herself. She had always prided herself on being able to treat her non-white clients with equality and thought the terms black and white were only significant in the political sense as if this had no bearing on one's personal life. In one particular session, she expressed satisfaction at having a non-white therapist and yet there was the struggle for equality as if my words and presence were persecutory in some way. On establishing that there was a difference between us as therapist and patient, and also as different people from different racial backgrounds, she was able to acknowledge that she felt ashamed to admit that I had a better command of English. This was primarily because being European she felt she had a closer affinity to the English, both being white. Although this may be true in that there was a closer link between Europeans and the English, it was nevertheless an assumption that with my being non-white I had a lesser understanding and command of the English language. Her inability to accept a relational difference between us led her to not being able to think and see me clearly. The rather painful acknowledgement of the difference between us allowed her to take back some of her projections; particularly the devalued and unwanted parts of herself as a foreigner in the UK, and more fundamentally the 'foreignness' of her feelings in her relationship with a manic depressive mother. The working through of this defence enabled her to think and see herself more clearly and she was beginning to get in touch with the pain, as opposed to complaints, of having abused herself in her relationships. This more positive approach towards her took the form of being able to assess herself and others more clearly. In the context of the work, she was more able to accept herself as foreign and yet have a place in English society instead of being some pseudo-English person whom she perceived herself to be for a long time.

The omnipotent denial of the pain and attacks on the internalised maternal object, projected into me, became less severe with the consequence that she did not have to totally hate her mother and her illness or identify with her illness to such an extent that she herself became prey to depression. She had begun to feel less responsible for her mother's fragility as well as her hostility and I was experienced as less threatening in the transference.

This unfolding process led her to express very emotionally her mother's severe illness and how it had affected her in her early life. In particular she spoke painfully of being shut out by a mother who could not bear her own depression, causing the patient to experience a deep isolation and loss. She recalled how, years before coming into therapy, she had almost got herself thrown out by a black friend of hers when, in discussing racism, she had indicated that she had struggled with racist feelings and thoughts of her own. She was very anxious that I would be just as racist as she was and, in this way, would be affected by her, just like her friend, and like her mother by her own depressive feelings.

CONCLUSION

I have been discussing the use of similarity as a particular defence against unconscious racist feelings in the therapeutic relationship, and how this is achieved through identification, idealization at the infantile level of perceiving and denigration of the good parts of the therapist via omnipotent phantasies. The deployment of projective identification is to break down the good parts of the therapist in order to achieve a similar superiority/inferiority to prevent any real emotional contact from being made, thereby avoiding the painful experience of difference and separation. Racism is here defined as the inability to accept and acknowledge difference without attempting to control and dominate the party (object) that is felt to be different and separate. In the atmosphere of racial conflicts, one then has to destroy the difference in order to preserve the survival of the self. The good bits are always under threat of being expelled due to excessive projection, and in the living situation one fears one's quality of life would be eroded due to the presence of a different person. Racism seen in this light is a defence firmly lodged in the paranoid-schizoid position.

There is an inevitable feeling of uncertainty and ambivalence about another of a different race or simply one who is different from ourselves and this is, to my mind, quite appropriate. It is, however, important to have the capacity for curiosity to learn and to find out about those who are different from us, thereby paving the way for real emotional contact. It is quite another when those who are different from us become a receptacle for internal struggles and conflicts.

In order to be efficient in our work, psychoanalytic psychotherapists are expected to have the ability to think about our countertransference feelings so as to be less influenced by our omnipotence and, in turn, by that of our patients. I think this is the first obstacle for us to be aware of before any growth can begin to take place in the therapeutic relationship.

I hope I have been able to demonstrate the importance of maintaining and working with the transference in bringing about conscious awareness of racial difference between therapist and patient, thereby enriching the therapeutic relationship. It is always more comfortable to deny that difference exists. Davids writes (1988):

> I think that we must recognise that we, like our patients, are human and are subject to the same societal pressures to turn a blind eye to uncomfortable aspects of ourselves. In the area of racial difference we are very susceptible to persuasion that 'differences don't matter,' i.e., that they do not have real psychological meaning or impact on our professional work. Of course when we are so persuaded we spare ourselves a painful struggle, something that is both understandable and human. However, in so doing we also undermine our therapeutic efficacy.

Note

1 This chapter is a shortened version due to the limitation of space. Two further clinical examples that go to clarify the issues under discussion are therefore not included in the present chapter. The original was published in *The British Journal of Psychotherapy* 10(1), Autumn 1993.

Acknowledgements

I wish to thank Dr Alberto Hahn and M. Fakhry Davids for their helpful comments and to Professor R. D. Hinshelwood for first arousing my awareness of this conflict.

References

Bion, W. (1962) Theory of Thinking, in *Second Thoughts*. London: Maresfield Reprints, pp. 110–119.

Davids, F. (1988) Two Accounts of the Management of Racial Difference in Psychotherapy, *Journal of Social Practice*, (November 1988) pp. 40–51.

Heimann, P. (1950) On Counter-Transference, *International Journal of Psycho-analysis* 31: 81–84; reprinted (1989) in Heimann, *About Children and Children No-Longer*, London: Routledge, pp. 73–79.

Hinshelwood, R. D. (1989) *A Dictionary of Kleinian Thought*. Free Association Books, pp. 315–336.

Holmes, D. E. (1992) Race and Transference in Psychoanalysis and Psychotherapy, in *International Journal of Psycho-Analysis* 73(1): 1–11.

Klein, M. (1946) Notes on Some Schizoid Mechanisms, in *Envy and Gratitude*. London: Hogarth Press, pp. 1–24.

Littlewood, R. (1988) Towards an Inter-cultural Therapy: Some Preliminary Observations, *Journal of Social Work Practice* (November): 9–19.

Further reading

Bion, W. (1967) Attacks on Linking, in *Second Thoughts*. London: Maresfield Reprints, pp. 93–109.

Caper, R. (1999) A Mind of One's Own, in *A Mind of One's Own*. London: New Library of Psychoanalysis, Routledge.

Freud, S. (1914) On Narcissism: An Introduction, *Standard Edition*, 13, London: Hogarth Press.

Freud, S. (1917) Mourning and Melancholia, *Standard Edition*, 14, London: Hogarth Press.

Freud, S. (1985) *Civilization, Society and Religion*. First published in Pelican Books 1985; reprinted 1987, London: Pelican Freud Library.

Griffiths, M. S. (1977) The Influence of Race on the Psychotherapeutic Relationship, *Psychiatry* 10: 27–40.

Klein, M. (1935) A Contribution to the Psychogenesis of Manic-Depressive States, in *Love, Guilt and Reparation*. London: Hogarth Press, pp. 262–289.

Klein, M. (1940) Mourning and its Relation to Manic-Depressive States, in *Love, Guilt and Reparation*. London: Hogarth Press, pp. 344–369.

Klein, M. (1957) Envy and Gratitude, in *Envy and Gratitude*. London: Hogarth Press, pp. 176–235.

Mattinson, J. (1975) *The Reflection Process in Casework Supervision*. London: Institute of Marital Studies.

Rosenfeld, H. (1987) Destructive Narcissism and the Death Instinct, in *Impasse and Interpretation*. London: Routledge, pp. 105–132.

Rustin, M. (1991) *The Good Society and the Inner World*. London: Verso.

Searles, H. F. (1962) Problems of Psycho-analytic Supervision, in *Collected Papers on Schizophrenia and Related Papers*. New York: International University Press, pp. 584–604.

Steiner, J. (1979) The Border between the Paranoid-Schizoid and Depressive Positions in Borderline Patients, *British Journal of Medical Psychology* 52: 385–391.

Steiner, J. (Nov. 2001) *Prejudice, Judgement and the Narcissism of Minor Differences*. London: The Melanie Klein Trust. Website: www.melanie-klein-trust.org.uk.

Chapter 10

Black, white, Hispanic and both: issues in biracial identity and its effects in the transference–countertransference[1]

Ruth M. Lijtmaer

Changes in the ethnic composition of the population and ethnic inter-marriage have resulted in a cultural and social space in which 'biracial' is increasingly viewed as a legitimate category of self-identification. 'If identity is conceptualized as an interactionally validated self-understanding, then identities can only function effectively where the response of the individual to themselves (as a social object) is consistent with the response of others' (Rockquemore, 1998, p. 199).

Appearance provides the first information about the individual to others in the context of face-to-face social interaction. It helps define the identity of the individual and to express their self-identification. It is in this process that identities are negotiated and either validated or invalidated. Therefore, it is impossible to think of identity without its ethnic nature. Strongly grounded in each individual by a growing assemblage of symbolic rituals where specific cultural values are transmitted, a culturally influenced world view is established (Javier and Rendon, 1995). These basic belief systems and culturally specific ways of relating are programmed, providing the foundation for the development of identity.

There are very few psychoanalytic articles describing the psychodynamics of a biracial treatment. In the last years the wealth of articles emphasize the white–Black dichotomy; the patient is white or Black or the therapist is Black or white. Significant works on this area are: Altman (2000); Comas-Diaz and Jacobsen (1991); Fisher (1971); Holmes (1992, 1999); Jackson and Greene (2000); Javier and Rendon (1995); Leary (1997, 2000); Perez Foster (1998, 1999) and Schachter and Butts (1968), to name a few. The common theme of these papers is the need for awareness of transference–countertransference responses when working with someone ethnically different. Most of the non-psychoanalytic papers discuss the difficulties of biracial identity develop-ment and its effects in the individual's future life.

In ethnically different or similar dyads, the therapist needs to exercise particular caution against applying his or her personal assumptions and metapsychology about minds at large. Whether the therapist's attitudes fall within the range of despondency, sadness or guilt over the patient's life circumstances, or whether the therapist's reactions run the spectrum of puzzlement, fear, ethnic prejudice or dislike, they will be detectable by our patients. 'These reactions demand scrutiny and can be a critical point of contact with the patient's transference, conflicts and resistances' (Lijtmaer, 2001, p. 73). The clinical case that follows is an example of how our identities are shaped through our social interaction with others, how biracial people whose chosen racial identity is consistently invalidated by others are at risk of psychological distress, and how our ethnic identity influences the transference–countertransference.

Being of a mixed ethnic background myself, I became more aware of my ethnic identity when I saw Joan as a patient. Therefore, before I embark on describing our mutual responses in this clinical case, there are some personal points that need to be addressed. I am from South America and was raised speaking Spanish. My ancestors came from Eastern Europe, therefore my complexion is white and I consider myself a Hispanic non-practicing Jew. This information is necessary to help readers understand the dynamics of treatment.

Definitions of terms

It will be helpful to define some terms that will be used throughout the chapter. They are: Splitting, Ego Identity, Racism, Transference–counter-transference.

Splitting of the object world occurs when there is an unsatisfactory early relationship between mother and infant because the 'good mother' is not intrapsychically available. This process 'gives rise to repeated, intense, and convincing oscillations of self-esteem that contribute to an uncertain sense of identity' (Akhtar, Kramer and Parens 1996, p. 139). Patients who have suffered traumatic experiences, including racial discrimination, use splitting as a defense to protect the self from the painful affect of being an outsider. Therefore, the self stays at the mercy of distorted or unintegrated self and other representations. The ego fragments itself into separate parts: the idealized self (and object), and the bad self (and object). Patients who use splitting, to maintain an inner sense of goodness, develop the fantasy that the badness is out there (projective identification).

Ego Identity: following Erikson (1950), ego identity refers to that aspect of the ego which, at the end of adolescence, integrates the disparate infantile ego states and neutralizes the autocracy of the infantile superego. For Erikson (1968) ego identity is an enduring psychological structure that is subjectively experienced as a psychological well-being. If identity is established through an active and reciprocal exchange between the individual and the psychological matrix in which the individual lives, identities can only function effectively when the response of the individual to themselves (as a social object) is consistent with the response to others. In contrast, individuals cannot effectively possess an identity 'where there exists a disjuncture between the identity an actor appropriates for him/herself and where others place him/her as a social object' (Rockquemore, 1998, p. 199). Biracial identity may be understood as an emergent category of identification.

Racism: prejudice and discrimination when directed at other ethnic groups are referred to as racism. Lipsky (1984; cited in Jackson and Greene, 2000, p. 110) defines racism 'as internalized oppression. It is a reenactment of a trauma that will create distress if it is not healed or discharged' (cited in Jackson and Greene, 2000, p. 110). It can be viewed as a psychological stressor that affects the daily lives of ethnic group members and subsequently interferes with psychological adaptation and functioning in the larger society, affecting the ethnic person's self-regard and interpersonal relationships. It may appear as teasing, belittling, ridiculing, stigmatizing and dehumanizing (Aponte and Wohl, 2000). Since it is frequently unconscious, the potential for racism, stereotypes and biases in the therapeutic situation is as universal as it is in the society as a whole. Following this line of thought, Moskowitz (1995) stated that 'there is no ethnicity . . . There is hatred and the need to deny our own badness, and fear of our own hatred' (p. 553).

Transference and countertransference: transference is defined as the patient's emotional reactions to the therapist based on the patient's sense of who the therapist is culturally with respect to race, ethnicity, religion, and other factors. The reader should note that this is a more broad definition. The same encompassing mode is the definition of countertransference as the therapist's emotional responses to the patient's interactions, based on the patient's race, ethnicity, religion, or the like. Perez Foster (1998) coined the term *cultural countertransference* to emphasize this point. These conceptualizations are founded in the relational perspective. From this viewpoint, the patient–therapist relationship is continually being established and re-established through ongoing mutual influences in which both patient and therapist systematically affect and are affected by each other. Therefore, the therapist's personality plays a significant role in shaping and organizing what is happening in the therapeutic situation as well as in the transference. The relational approach is particularly helpful when working with multiethnic populations because it emphasizes the cultural background of each member of the therapeutic dyad and their mutual influence.

CLINICAL VIGNETTE

Joan came to see me because of feelings of depression and self-doubt. She is a 35-year-old woman of dark complexion, born in Central America. Joan came to the United States at the age of 18 to study. She obtained an MA degree and is working in her field. Her father is French and her mother Spanish. The oldest of three, she is the only one of dark complexion in her family. She married in the USA and has a 7-year-old daughter. Her husband is from South America. Joan's native tongue is Spanish and from the beginning she addressed me in that language. She does not have much of a relationship with her siblings. Her father died a few years ago and her mother lives in Central America.

The first countertransference issue that appeared in treatment was in her initial contact on the telephone. She was looking for a Spanish-speaking therapist and when given my name she was not sure if I spoke Spanish. When I responded in Spanish she made an appointment. After I hung up I had the fantasy of Joan as being curly-haired and sensual. Her voice had a sexual texture. When we met for the first time she was well dressed, a little heavy and had curly hair. I was surprised to see her dark complexion. In hindsight, my initial fantasy of her made me think of my stereotypes of Hispanic people. I did not think of her as a Black woman speaking Spanish.

Joan comes from a well-to-do family. As a child she had nannies and domestic help. Particularly, there was a nanny whom she was very close to. She described her mother as self-absorbed, insecure and unavailable. Her father was a successful business man. He had to travel often and had to entertain frequently due to his powerful standing in the community. He had several affairs (she learned this as a young adult) and her mother was busy doing things to look more attractive and socially acceptable, to preserve her social position in the community as well as holding on to her marriage.

She remembered going to a private school and being the only dark-skinned child. She was frequently teased and made fun of because of her skin color. Before going to school she was not aware of the skin color differences, except for the times she fought with her brothers who teased her about many aspects of her, including being of dark complexion.

When she was 12 years old, two boys from the neighborhood were playing with her and they tried to rape her in an empty lot of land. She remembered trying to run away from them but she could not, and they succeeded. Full of anger and shame she ran back home and tried to tell her mother. But Joan's mother was too busy with guests and she never brought this topic to her mother's attention again. She lived in terror for many months after that. She saw those boys a few times and they screamed at her some pejoratives that contained racial implications. After the rape incident Joan became more conscious of her skin complexion. Around that time she had the fantasy that she was an adopted child, as her siblings' skin was light.

After the traumatic incident, Joan had frequently asked her mother why her skin was so dark. Joan's mother told her that they have some Black relatives and ended the conversation. It was at this juncture in her life that she started to experience herself as divided: a Black part that was bad, and a part that spoke Spanish that was good and was accepted. When relating these memories I felt sad for her. She had to experience such prejudice and discrimination so early in her life! I realized that my personal experiences of prejudice were insignificant compared to what she had gone through as a child.

Bringing up the topic of race was not difficult. Joan was making it easy for me because she was bringing all these material loaded with color. However, at first, due to my own feelings of inadequacy to talk about this topic, I was cautious to bring them up. I have to add that there was a part of her narrative that I could identify with due to some discrimination that I had suffered myself because of my ethnicity and language. Nonetheless, when Joan related those memories, they reminded me of a personal experience associated with the city I come from where there were no Blacks when I was growing up. I was surprised to see so many Black people when I migrated to the USA. How noticeable one is when the color of one's skin is different! These thoughts made me realize that Joan was touching in me areas of my experience that I had not thought of before; they shook my held beliefs about race.

After the rape incident and her mother's unavailability, Joan tried to dissociate emotionally from her family, but primarily from her mother. In retrospect, I think that her splitting was influenced by her ambivalent feelings towards her mother at an early age. Her mother was not supportive, consistent, available and reliable to help her develop a good sense of herself.

Yearning from closeness and fear of rejection came up in treatment predominantly related to her skin color, in statements like: 'When I started seeing you I was afraid that you may not want me as a patient because I am Black', or 'What made you take me as a patient?' I was surprised by her comments as I have never thought of refusing to see a patient due to their ethnicity or skin color. Those statements made me feel sad and insecure. I wondered: how can I tell her that she is a wonderful human being? Could she believe me? As a result of my internal response, I asked her how she experienced our white–Black–Hispanic relationship. She timidly responded that it was different, that I seem to care, but she still was not sure. She said that she had to be cautious trusting people, since she could not trust her mother.

In hindsight I obviously liked her and became aware of that. I think that I was fascinated by her strong observing ego, her reflective capacities and her sensitivity. I wondered if I was the mother that rejected her and dismissed her, or the nanny that abandoned her and gave her up. At the same time, was I the mother of excitement and discovery or was I the father that had an exciting secret life? I was not sure. However, this transference response of fear of rejection appeared many times at different levels. I found myself fantasizing about holding her and telling her that I was not her rejecting mother. When I became aware of my feelings towards her, I suggested looking at the positive sides of herself, her professional achievements, her being a good mother to her daughter, and her good relationship with her husband, despite the trauma she suffered. Nevertheless, initially, whenever I remarked on those issues, she stated that she knew she was different but not in a positive way, after all 'I am Black' (bad).

Around that time she learned from a family friend that she had been the product of her father's liaison with the Black nanny who had raised her. This information was devastating to her. At the same time, it explained her dark skin complexion. She was angry at her mother for having kept that as a secret. She also expressed anger towards her father for his infidelities, and his secret about her. Simultaneously and ironically, she was grateful that she was able to have a 'comfortable' home and was raised by her parents and not sent away.

A great part of the work from then on was to facilitate her connection with her mother that was loaded with anger. At times I wondered how angry she was at me. When I questioned her about that, she denied any negative feelings towards me. I saw me as her good-enough mother who accepted her white–Black–Hispanic, her biracial identity that she was struggling to integrate. After much work on these topics and the transference, she started to access more positive images of herself, and also in relation to her mother. I started to encourage her to accept herself as a total person: not Black or Hispanic Joan, but a whole Joan. It was then that she started to understand her mother's struggles to accept her father's infidelities. Joan began to recognize that racial difference had meant abandonment not only from her mother but also from the outside world. That was her past. Now, in the present, she came to comprehend her own power to make her image of herself change. Joan started to acknowledge that her biracial identity did not mean rejection in all her relationships. She could be Black, Hispanic, or both: a whole Joan.

Discussion

In this clinical case, the issue of race had significance as a result of Joan's struggles with her sense of identity. Because of Joan's negative experiences and circumstances, her self concept was split into good self and bad self. She had not experienced the cultural stability that allows identity formation to proceed (provided that the relationship with important objects is not traumatic). She had enough good in her very early experiences (with her Black-nanny-mother) to function in the world, but not enough to feel good about her biracial self. Joan's distant relationship with her mother, an almost non-existent relationship with her father, and the secrets in her family were significant ingredients in her identity confusion. There was little basis for trust in the provider (mother) making the object not trustworthy, nor was the provider an object in whom and from whom emotional investment could be expected. This is a failure in object constancy that made it difficult for her integrate her divided sense of self. The cultural upheaval that she had experienced increased her difficulties in adolescent identity formation maintaining the split of her two worlds (Akhtar and Kramer, 1998). As good and bad experiences became incorporated, she began to accept her biracial identity. Indeed, ambivalence towards the mother was profound, and rage and hateful feelings were present that initially impeded integration to occur. Another ingredient that prevented that integration was her feelings of shame and inferiority that influenced her interactions with others.

Our similarity and difference in our ethnic backgrounds were played out in the transference–countertransference. In the transference she initially idealized me because I was Spanish-speaking like her good self. Later I became the object of excitement and comfort. I guess that her negative feelings towards me, as they probably existed, were not verbalized for fear of rejection. I believe now that it might have been helpful if I had explored the negative transference more. However, I experienced resistance and concern for not repeating the rejection she had suffered. My failure to do so constitutes a countertransference resistance as a result of my anxiety about skin color differences.

My countertransference ranged from being surprised and intrigued at her skin color, sadness for her life circumstances, and warmth towards her. At times I felt cautious for fear of losing my neutrality due to my identification with her difficulties with her ethnic identity, as well as the fact that we were both immigrants. I believe now that I was more empathic because her dark skin complexion had impacted so much on her development. I still wonder what would have happened if Joan had chosen a biracial Hispanic therapist, and how the transference–countertransference matrix could have been.

Biracial individuals have multiple options (Rockquemore, 2003) that may be more difficult to recognize. Even though 'many persons make the mistake of thinking that the biracial person is fortunate to have a choice the reality is that the biracial person has to fight very hard to exercise choices that are not congruent with how they may be visually and emotionally perceived' (Root, 1998a, p. 107). Current research suggests that it is better to support biracial people in exploring both sides of their heritage in order to develop positive biracial identities and healthy psychological adjustment. In fact, taking a biracial identity is related to a more positive sense of identity, fewer psychological problems, and greater self-confidence than adopting a mono-racial label (Arnold, 1984 and Watts, 1991, cited in Gillen, Cohn and Throne, 2001). Like binocular vision, it may allow a depth perspective from two different viewpoints. Being biracial requires two processes. On the one hand, it may precipitate a conscious distancing from the stigmatized group. On the other hand, it may involve the creation of a new identity based in part upon the inability to be accepted without reservation by either composite race group. Joan's newfound biracial identity helped her find pride in her achievements and was a source of psychological resilience.

CONCLUSION

I have attempted with the clinical example to show how our identities are shaped through our social interaction with others, how being biracial and feeling comfortable with that identity is a complex task, and how our different ethnicities played a significant role in the transference–countertransference. Consequently, the intrapsychic component of ethnicity in both members of the similar/different dyad have to be explored. With this perspective in mind, I want to emphasize that racial/ethnic identity differences between therapist and patient involve issues of unconscious meaning at different levels that we have to be aware of. For that reason, 'Blackness and whiteness can be contingent and negotiable rather than static, established identities' (Leary, 2000, p. 649). Finally, 'it is crucial for the therapist to attempt to become familiar with his or her own racial attitudes and feelings, including racism, in the countertransference' (Altman, 2000, p. 601). Otherwise, these subjective states can seriously impact, derail, and even truncate the treatment process.

Note

1 Sections of this chapter were presented at the 24th Spring Meeting, Division 39, APA, April 17–21, 2004; Miami, Florida. Aspects of the clinical case appeared in 'The Psychological Effects of Treatment of Trauma on the Clinician', *New Jersey Psychologist* 54(4), 2004. Copyright © New Jersey Psychological Association.

References

Akhtar, S., Kramer, S. and Parens, H. (1996) *The Internal Mother: Conceptual and Technical Aspects of Object Constancy*. Hillsdale, NJ: Jason Aronson.

Akhtar, S. and Kramer, S. (1998) *The Colors of Childhood: Separation-Individuation across Cultural, Racial and Ethnic Difference*. Hillsdale, NJ: Jason Aronson.

Altman, N. (2000) Black and White Thinking: A Psychoanalyst Reconsiders Race, *Psychoanalytic Dialogues* 10(4): 589–605.

Aponte, J. and Wohl, J. (eds) (2000) *Psychological Intervention and Cultural Diversity*. Needham Heights, MA: Allyn & Bacon.

Comas-Diaz, L. and Jacobsen, F. (1991) Ethnocultural Transference and Countertransference in the Therapeutic Dyad. *American Journal of Orthopsychiatry* 6(13): 392–402.

Erikson, E. H. (1950) *Childhood and Society*. New York: W.W. Norton.

Erikson, E. H. (1968) *Identity, Youth and Crisis*. New York: W.W. Norton.

Fisher, N. (1971) An Interracial Analysis: Transference and Countertransference Significance, *Journal of the American Psychoanalytic Association* 19: 736–745.

Gillen, A., Cohn, L. and Throne, C. (2001) Black Identity in Biracial Black/White People: A Comparison in Jacqueline who Refuses to be Exclusively Black and Adolphus who Wishes he Were, *Cultural Diversity and Ethnic Minority Psychology* 7(2): 182–196.

Holmes, E. (1992) Race and Transference in Psychoanalysis and Psychotherapy, *International Journal of Psychoanalysis* 73: 187–219.

Holmes, E. (1999) Race and Countertransference: Two 'Blind Spots' in Psychoanalytic Perception, *Journal of Applied Psychoanalytic Studies* 1(4): 319–332.

Jackson, L. and Greene, B. (eds) (2000) *Psychotherapy with African American Women*. New York: Guilford Press.

Javier, R. and Rendon, M. (1995) The Ethnic Unconscious and its Role in Transference, Resistance and Countertransference: An Introduction, *Psychoanalytic Psychology, Special Section: Ethnicity and Psychoanalysis* 12(4): 513–520.

Leary, K. (1997) Race, Self-Disclosure, and 'Forbidden Talk': Race and Ethnicity in Contemporary Clinical Practice, *Psychoanalytic Quarterly* 66: 163–189.

Leary, K. (2000) Racial Enactments in Dynamic Treatment, *Psychoanalytic Dialogues* 10(4): 639–653.

Lijtmaer, R. (2001) Countertransference and Ethnicity: The Therapist's Psychic Change, *Journal of the American Academy of Psychoanalysis* 29(1): 73–84.

Moskowitz, M. (1995) Ethnicity and the Fantasy of Ethnicity, *Psychoanalytic Psychology, Special Section: Ethnicity and Psychoanalysis* 12(4): 547–555.

Perez Foster, R. (1998) The Clinician's Cultural Countertransference: The Psychodynamics of Culturally Competent Practice, *Clinical Social Work* 26(3): 253–270.

Perez Foster, R. (1999) An Intersubjective Approach to Cross-Cultural Clinical Work, *Smith College Studies in Social Work* 69(2): 269–291.

Rockquemore, K. (1998) Between Black and White: Exploring the 'Biracial' Experience, *Race & Society* 1(2): 197–212.

Rockquemore, K. (2003) Multiple Realities: A Relational Narrative Approach in Therapy with Black-White Mixed-Race Clients, *Family Relations: Interdisciplinary Journal of Applied Family Studies* 52: 119–128.

Root, M. (1998a) Resolving 'Other' Status: Identity Development of Biracial Individuals, in P. Oraganista, K. Chun and G. Marin (eds), *Readings in Ethnic Psychology*. New York: Routledge, pp. 100–112.

Schachter, J. and Butts, H. (1968) Transference and Countertransferenc in Interracial Analysis, *American Psychoanalytic Association Journal* 16: 782–808.

Chapter 11

Black and White thinking: a psychoanalyst reconsiders race[1]

Neil Altman

As suggested by the title of this chapter, 'Black and White Thinking', our concept of race emerges from dichotomized thinking. Race is a social construction. Race does not exist *per se* in nature, in the sense that skin color or the shape of certain facial features can be said to exist independently of our concepts. Race as a concept refers to differences in such physical characteristics, but it is at a higher level of abstraction and refers to much more than those physical characteristics. A moment's thought should make it clear that differences in skin color occur on a continuum; they are not dichotomous. Some people who are labeled black have skin that is lighter than that of some people labeled white. The same can be said about any physical characteristic used to differentiate between the 'races'. Jews were called black in nineteenth-century Vienna (Gilman, 1993) but are called white in twentieth-century United States. So, what accounts for our construction of such categories of people with an ostensibly physical basis that is demonstrably specious?

In the most general terms, people struggle with difference and similarity among themselves. On the individual level, human beings construct self–other differences, though different cultures draw the line between self and other in different places. For example, Roland (1988) pointed out that in some Asian cultures self includes the community, however defined, whereas in the United States and Europe self is individualized.

Foucault (1980) argued that every social dichotomy establishes a hierarchy. From this point of view, we establish gender and racial dichotomies so that we can put one category on top of the other for purposes of domination and control. Rationalizing racial and, arguably, gender categories in physical terms conceals the domineering intent by making the categories appear to innocently mirror nature.

I find it fascinating, by way of background, that efforts to dominate and control emerged from the European Enlightenment. The Enlightenment was a philosophical rebellion against the power of the Church. Philosophers at the time set reason as the highest value versus faith, emphasized by the Church. Eventually, European society came to rely more on a scientific than a religious world view. As part of this movement, however, rationality became nearly synonymous with the mature and the civilized. On this basis, a number of new dichotomies were set up, including the scientifically and techno-logically advanced European and North American nations versus the 'underdeveloped' 'Third World' and the rational male versus the emotional female. The splitting off of rationality from irrationality thus became the philosophical basis and justification for European colonialism and sexism. Colonialism, with its attendant racism, was justified in the name of civilizing the primitive natives, that is bringing them science, technology, and ration-ality. Kovel (1988) pointed out that structural theory in psychoanalysis also splits off the rational ego from the 'primitive', irrational id. On one hand, we can view Freud's project as subversive, critical with respect to the Enlight-enment view of humankind. That is, Freud demonstrated the tenuousness of the rational ego's control over the psychic world – the ways in which the unconscious undermines our sense of self-knowledge and self-control. On the other hand, to the extent that Freud viewed health in terms of the domination of the conscious ego over the id, he reflected and reinforced the Enlighten-ment idealization of rationality and control. Freud's scientific aspirations as a medical doctor predisposed him to privilege the ego as the site of all those functions necessary to scientific enterprise. The culmination of this trend in Freud's thought was reached with ego psychology as developed by Anna Freud and North American analysts, often under the influence of the medical model. When Freud (1933) the ego psychologist said, 'Where id was, there ego shall be', he defined the goals of psychoanalysis in terms reminiscent of the colonial mentality. In this sense, the structure of racism is built into structural psychoanalytic theory, particularly in its ego-psychological form.

Let me argue for this rather startling contention with a concrete example. Consider how ego-psychological criteria for analyzability include verbal intelligence, a variation on the theme of rationality. Other criteria of anal-yzability, frustration tolerance and impulse control, are variations on the theme of the domination of the id by the ego. When people of African, Latin American, and Asian origin are assigned the qualities of irrationality, emo-tionality, impulsivity, and so on, clearly they are devalued in psychoanalytic theory and excluded from psychoanalytic practice. It is easy enough to argue, and to demonstrate, that African-Americans, Latinos, and people from developing countries are not actually different from Caucasians in these terms. Some might argue that the problem is the biased and dis-criminatory process by which people are judged to be deficient. From that point of view, the problem is that IQ tests are biased or that inner-city people have inferior educational opportunities. I suggest that such an argu-ment does not attack the exclusionary nature of psychoanalytic theory and practice at their roots. As long as our thinking is structured by dichotomies such as rational (identified as mature) and irrational (identified as primi-tive), someone or another must be devalued and excluded.

In a sense, then, racism is built into the ways we think and speak, into the concepts and language on which we are socialized. We cannot simply dispense with our race-related concepts, however, as racial categories have become social realities. Whether or not they have any basis in physical reality, the concepts have taken on a life of their own as people have identified with labels such as black, white, African-American, and so on, and developed very real senses of group identity based on these categories. As we begin to talk about race in clinical practice, the problem that lurks in the background is how to recognize the social reality of race without losing sight of the way in which our conceptions of racial differences are based in and perpetuate oppressive and discriminatory social arrangements.

Before turning to more clinical considerations, I note that my discussion so far has to do with how our thinking and thus our experience are structured by networks of concepts that existed long before we were born and into which we were socialized early in life. Insofar as these conceptual networks, like those having to do with race, perpetuate oppressive social arrangements, one might say that we are all inadvertently socialized to be racist, to take for granted the discriminatory practices of our society.

The individual, however, is not destined to be a prisoner of the language and concepts within which he or she is trained to think and to experience. There are subversive currents and concepts within our culture and our language; the individual, as well, has the capacity to reflect on preconceptions, even those ingrained during early socialization. The most important clinical implications of what I am saying are that we should expect to find racism in our countertransference and in our thoughts and feelings generally and that reflection on our countertransference is an essential element if we wish to deal with race in our therapeutic work. I now illustrate these points with two clinical examples, one from my own practice and one from Leary (1997).

CASE STUDY: MR. A

A colleague referred Mr. A,[2] an African-American man, to me, a Jewish, white man, for help with panic attacks and marital difficulties.

In our first few sessions, Mr. A told me about having grown up in the South Bronx as a tough, out-of-control street fighter. His parents had given up on him, as he saw it, and sent him into foster care when he was 10 years old, where he was physically and sexually abused by members of the extended foster family. At age 12, he returned to his parents and vowed to turn over a new leaf. There, despite continuing to hang out with a group of tough kids who got into nearly daily fights, he began to achieve in school. He graduated from the local high school with high honors and then went to an Ivy League college on an academic scholarship. After completing an Ivy

League law school degree, he opened a general practice taking on cases that he felt furthered progressive social causes. As it happened, I knew the neighborhood in which Mr. A grew up; I had worked there for many years. I never mentioned to Mr. A that I was familiar with the South Bronx, but I felt a bond with him based on my experience with people there, and I tremendously admired him for what he had accomplished in his life given the way the deck had been stacked against him in many ways at the outset.

One of the problems that preoccupied Mr. A when I first began seeing him was that his father was asking him to return some money, tens of thousands of dollars, that the father had given him. Mr. A's father was recently remarried. In Mr. A's view, his father's new wife was trying to exploit her husband by getting him to reclaim the money so she could have it. Mr. A was tremendously angry at this woman. As he talked about the situation, what also came into focus was his anger at his father for allowing the wife to damage Mr. A's financial situation in this way. Mr. A believed that his father had similarly stood by and allowed his first wife, Mr. A's mother, to send Mr. A into foster care as a child. As angry as Mr. A was, he refused to express his anger to his father and did not resist giving the money back. He anticipated that his father would listen to him sympathetically but would ultimately defer to his wife.

Meanwhile, Mr. A was missing our appointments and bouncing checks he wrote to me. For business reasons, he regularly canceled with me at the last minute. After the first time his secretary called to cancel an appointment, I began to explain that I charge for such missed appointments. Mr. A stopped me by saying that he expected to pay for them; after all, he said, I had been there waiting for him. I went on to ask him to call me in person when he canceled, rather than have his secretary call me; I said I wanted to talk personally with him when he canceled. He agreed to this and said that he knew he was trying to avoid a confrontation with me by having his secretary call. The referring colleague had mentioned a fee that Mr. A had told her he could pay weekly. I regarded this fee as moderate – not close to my full fee but not close to the lowest fee I was accepting either. Mr. A and I had agreed on this fee in our first meeting. Then, his first check bounced. He claimed to be mystified and said he would look into the matter at the bank and would bring me cash the following week. The next week, he duly brought me cash, and said something vague about the bank's being a tool of the capitalist system. This comment struck a chord of guilt in me: I felt like a tool of the capitalist system in my pursuit of his money. This guilt distracted me from inquiring into just what he meant or how it happened that the check had bounced. I let the comment pass. Over a period of months, this sequence of events became a pattern. Early on in the treatment, he called to warn me that something may have gone wrong at his bank, and to ask that I call him immediately if his check bounced. The check bounced. I called, and he brought cash the next time. During the third month, a check bounced, but Mr. A didn't call to warn me. I asked him to pay me in cash, and I summoned up the courage to say that we had to look at the situation – every check he wrote me over three months had bounced. In retrospect, I wonder why it took me so long to confront Mr. A.

Even before the first check had bounced, I had the marginal thought that Mr. A would not pay me. I cannot be sure of all the sources of this thought, but I believe my thinking went something like this: I can't believe that this man, who has fought his way up from poverty and who still struggles to make ends meet, is going to give substantial sums of money to a privileged person like me. At a somewhat deeper level was a racially prejudiced thought: I thought of him as more likely not to pay me because he was black. Feeding this thought were, I think, classism and stereotypes involving black people, irresponsibility, and criminality. I also got caught in a tangled web of guilt, anger, and greed. A complementary anti-Jewish stereotype was activated as well. I began to feel like the stereotypical greedy Jew, like the Jewish landlord feeding off the poverty-stricken residents of the ghetto.

In the face of my sense of shame about all these feelings, it was difficult for me to confront Mr. A about the bounced checks. I was afraid that doing so would expose all these prejudices, would reveal both my own greed and my sense of him as out to not pay me. My professional self was still in control, however, and I confronted him: 'Every check you have written to me has bounced.' Mr. A said that he would bring cash from now on, he would not let this happen again. I said that the most important thing is that we understand what is happening between us. He said no, the most important thing is that my needs be taken care of. I was shocked – he thought that taking care of my needs is the most important thing? Why were we there? With the benefit of hindsight, I can see that he may have been indicating that he thought I was putting my needs ahead of his – and that he was accepting this situation consciously, but protesting unconsciously via the bounced checks. At the time, though, I guiltily felt that there was some truth to his statement about the priority of my needs. Distracted and confused by this sense of guilt, I said, 'What about your needs?' He said that he felt his needs were being met, that he was quite satisfied with my availability and understanding as a therapist. I pressed on. I said I wondered if he resented paying for the numerous sessions he had not attended – in this way, his needs were not being met at all. He returned to his idea of the justice involved in paying me for the missed sessions (i.e. I had set aside the time and waited for him).

At this point, feeling somewhat frustrated, I decided to take a leap far beyond where Mr. A was consciously at the moment. I said, 'You know, the situation that develops when you bounce a check is like that between you and your father. I know that, unlike your father, you eventually pay me. But when you bounce the check, it puts me in your position in relation to your father, having been promised some money, feeling that I got it, and then having it withdrawn. I think you may, without intending it, be letting me know something about how it feels to be you in relation to your father.'

I might have emphasized his identification with his father more, but I was trying to attenuate – by emphasizing his role as victim rather than as perpetrator of a wrong – what I was afraid would be experienced by him as an attack. Mr. A looked stunned. He stared at me for a moment, then acknowledged that that was an interesting slant on what was happening. Then he said that what he was most concerned about was his pattern of letting relationships die. He said that, throughout his life, after a certain point, he would stop calling people. It was only those who didn't give up, who kept calling and calling him, who became lasting friends. He provided an example and said that he did not want the same thing to happen to us, and that that was why he was concerned about staying on top of paying me. As the session ended, I was encouraged that he had both described the threat to our relationship and expressed a determination to make the relationship work. I was also daunted by the complexity and possible insolubility of the situation: pursuing him for money would be the way I would 'keep calling him' but would also be the way I would be letting him down by putting my needs ahead of his. I finish this vignette by describing how our regular meetings ended after eight months of treatment. After missing two sessions in a row, which he had never done before, Mr. A arrived for the first session of a new month; I expected, or hoped, that he would pay me then for the previous month (actually, for the previous two months). Arriving late, he said that an important meeting had run long and that he hadn't had enough time to go to a cash machine. Would I take a check for both months – a check that he guaranteed would not bounce – or would I rather wait until next week for cash? I felt caught between a rock and a hard place. If I took the check, I would be giving him enough rope to hang himself; if I said I would wait for cash, there was every likelihood that he would not show up the next week or two, and I would have to wait longer than I was comfortable with for the money. I took the check. As I reached out and took it, I had a strong sense that our relationship was doomed. In retrospect, I wonder why I did not 'freeze' the situation in place and reflect on what had developed between us. The bottom line is that I had reached my limit with Mr. A. I needed the money, and I was angry.

The next week, after I received a notice from my bank that Mr. A's check had bounced, his secretary called at session time to say he could not attend and to schedule a new appointment. I said that I wanted to speak with Mr. A directly. He did not call me back. Over a period of weeks, he failed to respond to my calls, then letters. I began sending bills, more bills, and, after eight months, a statement of my intention to sue him in small claims court if he did not respond. I eventually did sue him, and obtained a judgment against him (he did not show up in court). He did not pay even after being served with the judgment.

Discussion

I am aware that this case can be discussed in terms of an enactment of internalized relationships with Mr. A's father and mother, without reference to a racial element. One might say, as I did at one point to Mr. A, that he was promising me money and then reneging as his father had done to him. I then came to feel cheated and abandoned, as he had felt with regard to his father. I believe that he may also have felt that I took advantage of him, as he paid for missed sessions (certainly my countertransference was such that I was ready to believe that he felt that way). We had discussed these dynamics, so that the ideas were available to conscious reflection. The real action, however, was on the unconscious level, as the dynamic organized our interaction in the 'trenches' of the emotionally supercharged events that transpired between us. In the end, we both felt abandoned by the other, which in various ways probably replicated facets of his having been sent away to foster care.

So why add a racial element to our understanding of this case? One answer to this question is, for me, that it was just there. Beyond this basic fact, adding the racial element, in my view, deepens and expands this sort of dynamic understanding and roots it more firmly in the here-and-now flow of unconscious communication. I think about the racial factor first of all in terms of projective and introjective processes. My prejudicial image of Mr. A served a defensive, projective function for me by protecting my preferred self-image as a responsible, solid citizen. Meanwhile, Mr. A, I speculate, had internalized such denigrated images of himself as a black man. Within our interaction, this process was reinforced as Mr. A presumably identified with my covertly racist image of him. He might have inferred that I held such an image of him from, for example, my delay in confronting his bounced checks, as if I were bending over backward to deny that I found his behavior to be irresponsible. On his side, Mr. A may also have had a defensive interest in attributing to me a derogated image of himself that he may have unconsciously held. Perhaps Mr. A had a racist (though plausible) preconception of me – that I would exploit and demean him while pretending to be helping him. All these preconceptions that we presumably had about each other got actualized between us, so that preconception and reality came to coincide too much for us to reflect on the internalized scenarios that we each held, in a way that would allow for a significant degree of perspective.

One reason I feel justified in assuming race-linked preconceptions of me and of himself on Mr. A's part is that we are both shaped by the same society, with its racial and racist stereotypes. I (Altman, 1995) and others such as Cushman (1995) and Greenberg (1991) have referred to society in this way as a sort of third person in the room. Both Mr. A and I knew that racism is in us, at some level, simply because we are members of North American society. If we said that racism is 'out there', in racist society, and not 'in here', in our very psyches, we would be splitting off and denying an important 'bad object' experience between us. This is not to deny that we don't also hate this racism, strive to transcend it, and have loving, admiring, and identificatory feelings across racial lines. It is precisely because we do have such a multiplicity of feelings that societal racism does not shape us in any sort of monolithic way. Society is itself not monolithic in its racial attitudes, or in any other respect. So we are all under social influence, and yet we each consciously and unconsciously pick and choose which aspects of that influence to be shaped by, as well as bring to bear our own powers of resistance, creativity, and agency. Going further with the idea of a third person in the room, I think of Ogden's (1994) concept of the analytic third, by which he means an intersubjectively created space in which patient and analyst are both created anew within their interaction. Ogden looks to his own reverie processes for clues as to the unconscious transformation processes that have taken place in him within any particular analytic third. One can regard my racist and anti-Semitic 'reveries' as my entrée into the intersubjectively created analytic third in this case, in which Mr. A had become the deprived, oppressed black man seeking recompense through anti-social activity (in the manner described by Winnicott, 1956, when he discussed stealing as a sign of hope) and I had become the greedy Jew chasing after money, taking what was rightfully his. Mr. A presented himself as looking after my needs, but, finally, the joke was on me.

On another level, my resistance and anxiety about becoming the greedy Jew, as well as my fear of becoming the oppressive white man, led me to delay confronting Mr. A about his bounced checks or taking up the issue of racism with him. My level of anger may also have made the specter of racist violence too powerful a fantasy. Within our intersubjectively created third space, one of us was to be victimized, and the other was to be the victimizer. It is fascinating how intersubjectively generated third and societal third coincide in this case and how the dyadic interaction is subsumed within the analytic third.

I believe that it might have been helpful if I had used my awareness of racism in myself to explore more explicitly race-linked feelings between us. My failure to do so may well constitute another modality in which my racism, along with my anxiety about my racism, was transmitted. Nonetheless, I have argued that my attempt to be aware of my own racism was an indispensable first step toward engaging the unconscious communication between us and toward becoming aware of the dynamics within the third space between us, the intersubjective societal third. I am not necessarily advocating explicit disclosure of such feelings and images to patients.

Rather, I am advocating the use of the analyst's hostility and contempt to tune in to extremely problematic aspects of the unconscious interaction, which by virtue of their very unacceptability become of the highest importance analytically. If we do not confront such feelings in ourselves, we do not stand a chance of being able to process such interactions therapeutically in words and in action.

In the case illustration, I demonstrate, I hope, that my own racism worked in tandem with the patient's negative self-image – based on an identification with his father and perhaps his own racism – to create a powerful dynamic in our relationship. My racism was a piece of the unconscious interaction, perhaps most evident to the patient in the form of the defense against it (i.e. my delay in confronting him about his bounced checks).

I am not advocating explicit disclosure of the analyst's feelings. It should be clear that I believe that such feelings make a strong impact on the patient without their being talked about explicitly. I also believe that any necessary working through on the analyst's part can be done as part of his or her self-reflection and through the ways in which he or she repositions himself or herself in the interaction.

Although I wish an end to racism were possible, I believe that, given the present state of society and the human psyche, it should be taken for granted that none of us will be able to overcome our personal racist attitudes altogether. Thus, I am advocating that clinicians become familiar with their racism, not that they overcome their racist feelings and attitudes. The danger in implying that clinicians can and should overcome their racist feelings is that they will mistake their conscious goodwill and good intentions for a thoroughgoing nonracist attitude. As with countertransference in general, no sooner do we deal with one of its manifestations than another appears from the unlikeliest quarter. If it were not so, the analyst's unconscious would have disappeared. Psychoanalysis, in the version that most appeals to me, teaches that no one's unconscious, including the best analyzed analyst's, will ever disappear. Racism, then, will not be dealt with by any finite list of its manifestations against which we can attempt to immunize or guard ourselves. It is better that we take the attitude that racism is always there and that vigilance is always required. For most of us, liberal veterans of the Civil Rights Movement and other causes, the danger of an insidious unconscious racism is far greater than consciously held racist attitudes.

CONCLUSION

As psychoanalysts we are in a unique position to study this pervasive phenomenon in ourselves and others, and can help round out the picture with our sensitivity to unconscious factors. In his paper, 'Hate in the

Countertransference', Winnicott (1947) advocated that analysts take for granted that they are going to hate their patients, just as parents should take for granted that they are going to hate their children. In his inimitably and deceptively simple fashion, Winnicott listed eighteen good reasons parents hate their children; Winnicott believed that if analysts or parents deny that they hate their charges, they will deal with them in a 'sentimental' manner (i.e. in a syrupy sweet, patronizing manner that smacks of reaction formation). By contrast, sublimation as a defense takes aggression and destructiveness for granted and transforms it, turns it toward constructive ends. The Kleinian idea of reparation is similar. The Kleinian depressive position occurs when people take responsibility for their destructiveness and recognize that they can have destructive feelings, impulses, fantasies, and actions toward people whom they also love. Thus arises guilt, which in its constructive form can give rise to reparative actions. A relationship that accommodates hatred and provides for reparative action is stronger than one that denies hatred and thus becomes brittle. Denial of hatred very often implies denial of love. We can acknowledge our hatred when we recognize our love as a counterforce, when the motivation for repair is also strong. Even a racial difference built on projective mechanisms implies that the other race has been invested with aspects of our own psyches. We both love and hate the group that contains us. The violence and destruction visited upon black people by white people historically in the United States impose a burden of guilt on white people that may promote efforts to disown individual responsibility for further hatred on the part of white individuals. These efforts are understandable but, I believe, counterproductive. My effort in this chapter has been to advocate that we, as clinicians and otherwise, make room for racism, as well as love between the races, in the interest of promoting constructive, reparative action that will have a firm foundation.

Notes

1 A longer version of this paper was published in *Psychoanalytic Dialogues* 10(4): 589–605, 2000. Copyright © The Analytic Press. Reprinted with permission.
2 The identifying information about this man is very heavily disguised. In my view, the dynamics of the case are accurately preserved, but I recognize that disguising identifying information always runs the risk of distorting aspects of the patient, and of my interaction with the patient, that are clinically significant. In my view, this risk is inevitable, given the need to preserve confidentiality.

References

Altman, N. (1995) *The Analyst in the Inner City: Race, Class, and Culture through a Psychoanalytic Lens*. Hillsdale, NJ: The Analytic Press.

Cushman, P. (1995) *Constructing the Self, Constructing America*. New York: Addison Wesley.

Foucault, M. (1980) *The History of Sexuality*. New York: Vintage.

Freud, S. (1933) Dissection of the Psychical Personality. *Standard Edition*, 22: 57–80. London: Hogarth Press.

Gilman, S. (1993) *Freud, Race, and Gender*. Princeton, NJ: Princeton University Press.

Greenberg, J. R. (1991) *Oedipus and Beyond*. Cambridge, MA: Harvard University Press.

Kovel, J. (1988) *The Radical Spirit*. London: Free Association Press.

Leary, K. (1997) Race, Self-Disclosure, and 'Forbidden Talk': Race and Ethnicity in Contemporary Clinical Practice, *Psychoanalytic Quarterly* 66: 163–189.

Ogden, T. (1994) The Analytic Third: Working with Intersubjective Clinical Facts, *International Journal of Psycho-Analysis* 75: 3–19.

Roland, A. (1988) *In Search of Self in India and Japan: Toward A Cross Cultural Psychology*. Princeton, NJ: Princeton University Press.

Winnicott, D. W. (1947) Hate in the Countertransference, in *Collected Papers: Through Paediatrics to Psycho-Analysis*. New York: Basic Books, 1958, pp. 194–203.

Winnicott, D. W. (1956) The Antisocial Tendency, in *Collected Papers: Through Paediatrics to Psycho-Analysis*. New York: Basic Books, 1958, pp. 306–315.

Chapter 12

Understanding unbearable anxieties: the retreat into racism

Narendra Keval

This chapter attempts to explore how some patients retreat into racist thinking as part of a pathological organization of the mind whose aim is to put the brakes on psychic growth and development (e.g. O'Shaughnessy, 1981; Steiner, 1993). The patient can sometimes experience the therapist's presence, his or her interpretations or changes in the boundaries of the treatment as unwanted intrusions because it threatens an inner equilibrium which is designed to keep the psyche undisturbed.

Frantic attempts are often made to barricade themselves by projecting their infantile anxieties into perceived salient differences of the therapist that are viciously attacked. This type of defensive organization can provide a temporary retreat from unbearable anxieties but the patient is ultimately stuck from moving forward in their mental and emotional development.

Minor differences such as the colour of one's skin are sometimes chosen as an immediate target of a racist attack possibly because developmentally the skin offers the most basic type of 'holding' or containment (Anzieu, 1989), one that serves to potentially bind the most primitive parts of the personality in the earliest stages of life to give the feeling of being contained in one's skin (Bick, 1968).

A racist attack targeted at the skin colour of the therapist may tell us that the 'psychic skin' of the patient may have been breached in treatment, giving rise to early infantile anxieties that are often defended against by a retaliation that aims to give the therapist the sense of what it feels like to be intruded and narcissistically wounded. Elsewhere I have suggested that a minor difference such as skin colour as a visible sign of difference can upset an inner equilibrium by triggering unconscious anxieties to do with the recognition of dependency and separation from the maternal object in the first instance and subsequently to the recognition of the triangular relations between the parents.

Such a recognition can result in a narcissistic rage that emanates from what is perceived to be an injury or insult to the self (Keval, 2001).

PSYCHIC AND GEOGRAPHICAL RETREATS

Pathological organizations of the mind offer a space which acts like a shelter from both persecutory and depressive anxieties that the experience of separateness can bring to the fore (Steiner, 1993).

They are brought into play when the individual is unable to cope with anxieties of a paranoid-schizoid (p-s) nature such as fragmentation and chaos or the pain of mourning that the depressive position (d) gives rise to (Klein, 1946). All manner of differences and potential conflicts in the self are hated because movements in either direction represent potential changes in the self. One way in which this is dealt with is to obliterate the object representing these differences and potential threats to the self by a retreat into racist thinking.

Whilst there is much suffering in the choice to remain inside the retreat, the relative comfort offered by the illusion of permanence seems to override the anxiety of coming out of the retreat and continuing the developmental journey as represented by making emotional contact with the therapist.

Freud (1937) was preoccupied with this problem in 'Analysis Terminable and Interminable' when he attempted to understand the reasons behind his patient's preference to cling to their own versions of reality in the face of understanding even when this was at the expense of an impoverished and crippled life.

Our experiences in the consulting room would confirm this picture when we witness our patients' struggle to keep things the same often at any cost. These highly organized defences where destructiveness plays a key role have come to be known as narcissistic object relations in which recognition of dependency and separateness is viciously attacked (Rosenfeld, 1971), racist thinking and feeling being one of many modes of functioning to keep the psychic retreat intact.

We can often sense a menacing atmosphere in the way some patients describe the way they are gripped and seduced by parts of themselves which can only be described as a 'corrupt gang', offering easy painless solutions to their life difficulties that aim to keep everything same and familiar versus the inevitable pain of mourning that conflict, change and growth involve. It is often voiced in terms of a predicament between risking the feelings of shame, embarrassment and humiliation of being exposed versus the relief offered by remaining in the retreat at the cost of much frustration and despair. In the course of an analysis or therapy we often listen to all manner of differences such as geography, social class, sexual and generational that enter the preoccupations of our patients to convey important aspects of their inner functioning and can point to the type of anxieties which dominate their thinking at any given moment. The case I present here illustrates this point well. For example, geographical spaces and boundaries are often imbued with such rich meanings that it is difficult not to conclude that the passions aroused in defending these spaces and territories must also echo an area of the mind that is being defended. A vicious hatred often follows in the wake of the racialization of these internal and external spaces (Cohen, 1993). Whilst Freud thought the narcissism of minor differences between people was relatively harmless, he seemed to underestimate the power of the destructive forces that could be unleashed when unconscious phantasies behind internal and external spaces are punctured.

A phantasy that underpins racist thinking is related to attacking any awareness to do with difference or separateness. The object of racial hatred represents a threat to this phantasy and therefore has to be eliminated. To be at the receiving end of this type of assault is to experience an attack on your sense of self, everything that makes you a person with a distinctive identity. In a nutshell you are not allowed to be your self (Fanon, 1967; Davids, 1992; Tan, 1993). Increasingly, psychoanalysis has been interested in what kind of impact these defences against anxiety can have on the growth and development of the mind itself, the subject of the next section.

RACISM AND MENTAL SPACE

If we examine racist thinking closely, most notably in the form of racial stereotypes, you cannot help but be struck by its simplicity. It rests on the principle of splitting a world into neat categories such as black and white thinking with no room for ambiguity or complexity. You are either with us (the 'goodies') or against us (the 'baddies'), a familiar rhetoric amongst our politicians in the current so-called 'war on terrorism'. There is no room here for a third position, a middle ground which suggests that this type of thinking only accommodates dyadic relationships. Triangular relations are felt to be too threatening because it introduces a further position or mental space to think from, introducing more complexity and reality into the matter. It is this reality that pathological organizations resist and there are developmental reasons for this state of affairs that contemporary analysts have been exploring.

In order to keep the integrity of a pathological organization intact certain types of knowledge or 'facts of life' (Money-Kyrle, 1968) have to be kept out of awareness. Minor differences which are attacked in racism are part of a defence against the recognition of major differences such as the sexual differences and the differences of generations. Developmentally, this means that the discovery and recognition of mother as a separate person on whom one is dependent is one step away from a further recognition that she has an independent mind and life of her own, particularly a relationship with her partner, introducing parental sexuality and the Oedipus Complex. In this way a link has been made between the 'epistomophilic drive' (Klein, 1946), the inbuilt curiosity to explore the mother's body and the discovery of the parental intercourse (Britton, 1989).

Working through of the depressive position which recognizes the separateness of mother also parallels the working through of the Oedipus Complex with all the anxieties of exclusion, envy and jealousy that this situation can bring to the fore. It is thought that this discovery or its obstruction has profound consequences for the way mental space is structured affecting the capacity to comprehend and relate to reality. The triangular situation introduces new challenges that provoke anxiety in the child's mind. If the anxieties of feeling excluded from the parental relations are manageable it introduces different possibilities, that of being an observer of the parents' relationship and allowing oneself to be observed in relation to another.

This is dependent on the individual's capacity to play with different configuration of links between objects in the mind, i.e. become curious about these links and what they give rise to, which in turn is thought to determine whether mental space expands with curiosity or contracts if the anxiety that links give rise to is too intolerable. In this way the quality of an individual's thinking is thought to be determined by the degree of separateness achieved (Segal, 1957). This means that changes from two-dimensional to three-dimensional thinking will depend on the type of anxieties dominating the individual at any given moment.

Depth to thinking refers to the capacity to think symbolically, particularly in relation to dimensionality that enables the differentiation of inside and outside spaces, subject from object, mindlessness to mindfulness, and the integration of past and present experiences including the comprehension of time, space and ultimately our mortality.

In a similar way I am suggesting that the racist imagination or state of mind captures the struggle to avoid making this two-pronged discovery which involves an attack on the recognition of the links in object relationships. Just as objects are not allowed to come together in the mind so do thoughts representing these objects, affecting the way mental space is structured and ultimately limiting the possibilities for growth and development of the personality.

The following case study tries to illustrate some of these ideas, in particular how the patient oscillates in her mind between the paranoid-schizoid and depressive positions as evident in her thinking in the course of a session and how racist thinking is brought into play as part of a retreat into a pathological organization of the mind when both claustrophobic and agoraphobic anxieties become too intolerable for her. I have mentioned only those aspects of the patient's material that are relevant to the main themes of this chapter.

CASE MATERIAL

Ms. B was a woman in her late twenties who wanted help for her panic attacks, which started when she and her Spanish boyfriend accepted her mother's offer to let them stay with her whilst they saved money to buy their own home. Ms. B spoke of how she felt a little superior to her boyfriend because he needed her help to settle into this country. I learnt that Ms. B's father died from an illness whilst he was in hospital during her teens and, although she described her relationship to him as frosty, it was clear to me that there was much regret on her part for not visiting him before he passed away. Right from the start of our meeting Ms. B felt intimidated by the prospect of coming to see me in an outpatient clinic in an area which she imagined was typically middle-class in contrast with the area in which she lived, an impoverished council estate where she spent most of her life growing up. When she came to her session she looked as if she had made a special effort with her appearance and was eager to please.

In this particular session she was preoccupied with this contrast by describing the area in which she lived as 'scum', compared with an adjacent area in which she spent long periods playing as a child. She referred to this as 'posh dicky'. She began to tell me how this area was associated with people who were clearly better off in all sorts of ways, namely wealth, access to books and knowledge about the world and having the luxury to travel and discover foreign places. In short, this was everything she wanted for herself but she saw her mother as the main obstacle to the possibility of a different and more rewarding life. She said she left school early because she got pregnant at 16 years, which took her life in a different direction as she became a young mother working in a local grocery store to earn a living. It was revealing that she became pregnant not long after her father's death and saw these early years as having to cope with a baby and trying in her omnipotent way to fill the gap that her father's death had left in the family.

Ms. B described the 'scum' area in which she lived as racist and associated this with her mother and sister who could not stand the sight of blacks or Asians. Her mother told her that if she brought a black man home she would be kicked out. Ms. B did not think of herself as a racist because she said she had Asian and black friends but her white friends disagreed and reminded her that calling them 'pakis' behind their back could hardly let her off the hook.

She was however adamant that it was her mother and sister who denigrated Asians and black people but admitted that she joined in the racist conversations that frequently took place in their home so that she did not feel too left out. As she was telling me this she said she was 'two-faced' when it came to her loyalty to her black friends. She thought quite insightfully that much of her mother and sister's hostility was not just to do with racism but about anything different, such as ideas, people or places. She said they preferred the same old ways of doing things whereas she wanted to try and experiment with doing things differently. She brought an example of this when she described how excited she was about doing a

Reiki course and learning from her teacher who was very knowledgeable but, if she was to be seen talking to her in the street by her white friends, how she would die of shame and embarrassment. She said this teacher came from 'those groups of people who were dirty tramps and social security scroungers on child benefits'. She recognized how terribly two-faced she could be and sometimes wished if life could be simply black and white like the way her mother and sister thought. She was aware that things were more complicated in life but often lacked the courage to speak her mind.

She brought a further example of her predicament. Her attraction to her Spanish boyfriend was evidence to her of her willingness to be different. What I later came to learn was that this boyfriend regularly taunted her in a rather sadistic way for her physical appearance. She reacted to this abuse by becoming 'superior', teaching him how to speak 'proper English' and thus putting him in his place.

She gave a further example of this difficulty when this boyfriend boasted that he came from a race that was pure and uncontaminated by foreigners, unlike the British. This conversation became all the more difficult for her when her mother responded to her boyfriend's comments by saying that these foreigners were not British at all. Ms. B tried to argue with her mother that some of her black friends were indeed British because they were born in this country. However she began to feel that she was being singled out and started to feel terribly alone in her thinking. Her next association was how dangerous it was to speak out and be different as she witnessed the consequences of doing this when her boyfriend was beaten up by her own relatives living in the area.

Discussion

Ms. B's preoccupation with the conflicting feelings about the two geographical spaces are connected with what these spaces represent in her internal world, particularly the nature of the objects that reside in them and the enactment of this internal situation with me in the transference. This is evident in the conflict she experiences of feeling superior to me, her brown therapist in a middle-class area, whom she both needs and despises. These were the two faces of herself that she found difficult to reconcile. My presence as an Indian man breached her defences and put her in touch with what petrified her most, her vulnerablity and need for my help in tandem with her curiosity. Potentially, I represented to her something she needed and wanted for herself, an independence of mind that she could use to grow as a separate person in her own right but it involves much painstaking emotional work that she would rather not undertake, namely acknowledging me as a separate person on whom she was dependent for help. Whilst she conveyed a sense of helplessness and grievance against her 'racist mother' for obstructing her life, it becomes clear that she is partly identified with her mother's racist thinking and in that sense allied to this part of herself that obstructs any developmental work by hiding in the retreat of her pathological organization.

This defensive organization has a huge bearing on the question of her identity as a woman separate and different from her mother which is expressed in the notion of same and old familiar ways of doing things versus the prospect of becoming more separate and curious with her mind.

We learn that her panic attacks started with the thought of living with her mother under the same roof, most probably a re-experience of an earlier panic as a child to do with the feeling of being trapped inside a mental and physical space shared with her mother that she called 'scum' and racist, an internal space where she felt her own sense of self was suffocated. The prospect of leaving this space and becoming more of a separate person with her own mind filled her with dread, illustrating the 'claustro-agaraphobic' dilemma in this patient (Rey, 1979). The absence of her father who could have been a potential ally in her wish to become more separate at a crucial stage of her adolescent development seems to have sealed her fate.

In her black and white thinking she contrasts this with the area which she referred to as 'posh dicky', a space in her mind which is resided in by her father and in transference with me and the analytic process ('the unknown/ unconscious or foreign'), a source of curiosity, excitement and much envy riddled with anxiety and contempt. This conflict between being the same as her mother or different, which would also involve acknowledging and identifying with aspects of her father (the 'posh dicky') in a triangular relationship, is at the heart of her crisis in identity, a crisis that manifests in the panic at the point of moving into her mother's house. It is possible to see here how this conflict between the two spaces (posh and scum) are also aspects of herself which do not sit comfortably with each other. The anxiety she experiences when she oscillates from one to the other either contracts her thinking or expands with curiosity at any given moment.

This is also a crisis that becomes 'racialized' in the transference with me but is not readily available for personal scrutiny because of the extent of splitting, denial and projection into her mother. In short she believes that it is her racist mother who has thwarted her life and prevented her from moving forward but it is in fact her own internal racism that aims to avoid the knowledge of particular facts of life, such as her dependency on others and the necessity of working through her Oedipal conflict to arrive at her own identity.

She finds it difficult to acknowledge *her* hatred of separating from her mother, preferring instead a paranoid solution in which she was on the run from the 'racist scum mother' into whom she projected her hatred of difference and curiosity. In this way she tried to carve out a sense of being separate by saying to herself it is her mother and not her who is racist by using an alibi such as her foreign boyfriend to side-step her own racist thinking.

However, this relationship with her boyfriend, which could be seen as having the potential for a healthy development, seems also to be a retreat into a pathological organization where she could 'fend off' her mother (and p-s anxieties) by using the boyfriend as a wedge but it is aimed to cover up the truth of her racist attitude, which is designed to keep the brakes on her development but create an illusion of maturity. The attempt at the cover-up of her racist thinking comes to haunt her in the way her separation difficulties become re-enacted with her boyfriend who too displays hostility towards other people that are different, this time directed at her physical appearance and weight. It tells us that hiding in the shadows of the racist attitude is a whole multitude of differences that are hated and despised. The space with her boyfriend offers her a temporary refuge but of course she has ensured that he is dependent on her help to speak English. In this way she becomes the 'mother of her mother tongue', residing inside the retreat in a superior way but cut off from meaningful contact with reality.

To face the prospect of true separation is filled with dread as she conveys in her comments that she lacked courage to speak her mind in the face of much danger. She would have to make the developmental step of making a two-pronged discovery, first acknowledging her feelings of dependency on both her mother and father/therapist and secondly the recognition that both had a life of their own in the past when father was alive, a relationship that she was not privy to.

I would argue that Ms. B defended herself from this internal reality by a split she formed and could reside over in a superior way between an internal parental couple called 'posh dicky' and 'scum' that she kept in war with each other by her own racism to avoid painful and unbearable feelings of being excluded and helpless like a child. The needy and dependent aspects of her own personality are precisely what she could not bear to acknowledge and defended herself against by viciously attacking her much-admired Reiki teacher/therapist whom she called a 'dirty scrounger on child benefits'. I expect it was precisely her emotional child benefits that were abruptly cut off from her when her father died quite suddenly in hospital. Instead of mourning his loss she replaced this process by getting herself pregnant and in her omnipotent phantasy replaced her father by becoming a parent to her baby.

This crumbled and revealed her fragile and immature personality when she could not hold her ground and panicked at the prospect of being in close physical proximity to her mother. She said she still felt like a little girl when in the company of her mother. In other words she did not feel she had enough of a backbone to stand up to her mother (and boyfriend), a backbone she would have developed further if she had allowed herself to think about the significance of the loss of her father in her life.

Ms. B's internal predicament is all the more painful because, as she sees it, to come clean with her feelings about black or Asian friends would be tantamount to betraying the integrity on which her psychic retreat was built. Being two-faced meant she could declare her loyalty to her allies in the form of her racism but only secretly declare her more humane or tender feelings for me and others on whom she was dependent for help, such as her teacher and more fundamentally her mother and father. Being two-faced also meant she could escape punishment by her racist allies, the 'thugs' in her mind, who could not tolerate any acknowledgement of difference or separateness and therefore any possibility of growth and development. For instance, it ensured that she remained sealed off from the 'posh dicky' world of her father, a world of curiosity, discovery and learning that she was so keen to embrace but not before she allowed herself to recognize the significance of her father which would have completed the Oedipal triangle.

However, by keeping the internal couple warring in her mind, thoughts representing these objects could not come together either, therefore links in her thinking could not be formed, sustained or enjoyed, affecting her curiosity and capacity to think. The movements she made in her thinking which showed some recognition of the error of her ways suggested a small but growing capacity to tolerate the anxieties of the depressive position before it got hijacked.

The other consequence of keeping the Oedipal triangle incomplete was to fall prey to the racist thinking without an internal ally, such as an identification with a strong father who could have helped her to have the courage to speak her mind instead of giving in to an attitude of cruelty and hatred towards herself and others who were different.

CONCLUSION

When anxieties to do with separation become too overwhelming for the self, racist states of mind are often brought into play as part of a 'military arsenal' of a pathological organization whose aim is to attack any awareness that leads to psychic growth. This type of offensive defence can provide a mental retreat or sanctuary that is often expressed in the type of splitting that results in the idealization and denigration of external geographical spaces. A patient is presented who illustrates this splitting and racism in her preoccupation of geographical areas which unconsciously linked up to her perception of the parental couple from whom she was struggling to become separate. This got played out in the transference with me in the way that I was perceived as a source of curiosity representing her wish to move forward in her development versus an object that was despised because it upset her inner equilibrium. At a deeper level she was attacking what I have referred to as a two-pronged discovery, that would have led to an awareness and experience of herself and others as separate human beings.

References

Anzieu, D. (1989) *The Skin Ego*. London: Yale University Press.

Bick, E. (1968) The Experience of the Skin in Early Object-Relations, *International Journal of Psycho-Analysis* 49: 484–486.

Britton, R. S. (1989) The Missing Link: Parental Sexuality in the Oedipus Complex, in R. S. Britton, M. Feldman and E. O'Shaughnessy (eds), *The Oedipus Complex Today*. London: Karnac Books.

Cohen, P. (1993) *Home Rules: Some Reflections on Race and Nationalism in Everyday Life*. The New Ethnicities Unit, University of East London.

Davids, M. F. (1992) The Cutting Edge of Racism: An Object Relations View, *Bulletin of the British Psychoanalytic Society* 28(11).

Fanon, F. (1967) *The Wretched of the Earth*. London: Penguin Books.

Freud, S. (1937) Analysis Terminable and Interminable, *Standard Edition* 23, pp. 209–253.

Keval, N. (2001) Understanding the Trauma of Racial Violence in a Black Patient, *British Journal of Psychotherapy* 18(1).

Klein, M. (1946) Notes on some Schizoid Mechanisms, *International Journal of Psycho-Analysis* 27: 99–110.

Money-Kyrle, R. (1968) Cognitive Development, *International Journal of Psychoanalysis* 49: 691–698; reprinted in *The Collected Chapters of Roger Money-Kyrle*, Perthshire: Clunie Press, 1978, pp. 416–433.

O'Shaughnessy, E. (1981) A Clinical Study of a Defensive Organisation, *International Journal of Psycho-Analysis* 62: 359–369.

Rey, J. H. (1979) Schizoid Phenomena in the Borderline, in J. Leboit and A. Capponi (eds), *Advances in the Psychotherapy of the Borderline*. New York: Jason Aronson, pp. 449–484.

Rosenfeld, H. (1971) A Clinical Approach to the Psychoanalytic Theory of the Life and Death Instincts: An Investigation into the Aggressive Aspects of Narcissism, *International Journal of Psycho-Analysis* 52: 169–178.

Segal, H. (1957) Notes on Symbol Formation, *International Journal of Psycho-Analysis* 38: 391–397; reprinted in *The Work of Hanna Segal*. New York: Jason Aronson, 1981, pp. 49–65.

Steiner, J. (1993) *Psychic Retreats: Pathological Organisations in Psychotic, Neurotic and Borderline Patients*. London, Routledge.

Tan, R. (1993) Racism and Similarity: Paranoid-Schizoid Structures, *British Journal of Psychotherapy* 10(1).

Intersecting gender, race, class and sexuality

Chapter 13

African-American lesbians and gay men in psychodynamic psychotherapies?[1]

Beverly Greene

In this chapter I will examine the notion that psychodynamic theoretical approaches are mutually exclusive to successful psychotherapy with members of culturally diverse populations that can be exemplified by African-American lesbians and gay men. I also examine the discrepancies between theory and practice that can be a function of the dominant cultural identities of most mental health professionals, a failure to acknowledge the influence of social privilege, therapist shame and guilt. I analyze this issue in the context of a persistent assertion of a meritocracy in the United States that is mythical. Included in this analysis is also a consideration of some of the dynamics that are intrinsic to a legacy of social injustice for racial and sexual minorities. Mental health institutions exist as a part of a culture that verbally espouses pride in its 'melting pot' of different cultural groups; however, for most of our history it has practiced cultural insensitivity (Strickland, 2000). Comprising primarily dominant cultural beings, institutional mental health in the United States has historically conceptualized differences from dominant cultural groups as deviant and pathological. Only recently have psychological paradigms come to view human development and behavior as something that can have many different outcomes that are not viewed as inherently pathological simply because they are different from those of dominant cultural groups. These ideas formed the core of the development of multicultural and diversity initiatives in contemporary psychology and psychotherapy.

Cultural diversity and multiculturalism are the concepts that are used to describe the study of ethnoracial, gender, sexual orientation, age, disability and other cultural differences between groups. These human differences or distinctions have little intrinsic meaning. It is a social context that gives them meaning (Greene, 2003). In Western culture race, sexual orientation and these other aspects of human diversity are deemed of great importance by social scientists and they are often viewed as both explaining and justifying the positions people hold in the social hierarchy. In the context of psychotherapy, their salience must be determined by how much of a difference these differences actually make in people's lives, at a given time, how they are understood and what they come to mean to the client. For African-American lesbians and gay men this leads to questions about how race and sexual orientation contribute to their position in the social hierarchy and what they must do to negotiate the social barriers associated with social marginalization. Given the relational nature of social status it also raises questions about the effects of the theoretician or clinician's position in that hierarchy. How does the theoretician's subjective social positioning, their awareness of it or lack thereof affect their development of theoretical paradigms. Furthermore, how does it effect their view or awareness of the social hierarchy, and their understanding of their place in it? What is reenacted in the therapy process when the clinician is a member of, or strongly identifies with, a privileged and dominant group and the client is/does not? I contend that there is the potential for the normative social power relationship to be reenacted.

Practitioners and theoreticians get their information about others from the same places that clients get that information. Deeply held beliefs about ourselves and others are shaped by many complex sociopolitical and economic variables and realities that may have little to do with accurately reflecting the true nature of identity. Our descriptions may be designed and used to serve other than noble purposes in a larger system of dominant/privileged and subordinate/marginalized relationships. Both therapist and client alike are all affected by a cultural mythology that has been developed to explain differences in our relative positions in the social hierarchy, as well as to justify social injustice by creating and maintaining discrepancies in social power. In the myth of meritocracy, achievements by members of privileged groups are usually attributed to individual efforts, and rewards for those efforts are seen as having been earned and deserved. Jordan (1997) observes that a myth of earned power and meritocracy was developed by the members of the dominant culture to justify their right to discriminate against and limit social opportunities for people who were different. When these myths are accepted, all people are viewed as getting whatever they deserve. People who are in positions of power are seen as deserving of the privileges associated with their position. People who are powerless, disadvantaged, vulnerable and who are exploited are presumed to be getting what they deserve as well. This includes blame, punishment and contempt for their circumstances. Both client and therapist have their own personal stake and role in these beliefs. The reality of life against a backdrop of dominant and subordinate relationships extends to the practice of psychotherapy, institutional mental health and the development of psychological theories. This naturally included psychodynamic paradigms.

CRITIQUES OF PSYCHODYNAMIC APPROACHES WITH CULTURALLY DIVERSE POPULATIONS

Because of their blatantly ethnocentric, sexist and heterosexist assumptions about development and behavior, psychodynamic paradigms have been assailed as mutually exclusive to the treatment of diverse ethnoracial group members, women, and sexual minorities (Abramowitz, 1997; Mattei, 1996). African-American lesbians and gay men are individuals who represent the convergence of three major identities (two for gay men) that have been pathologized by institutional mental health. Abramowitz (1997), Adams (2000), Altman (1996), Jackson (2000), Moncayo (1998), and Leary (2000) offer critiques of psychodynamic theories for limiting definitions of a normal family or marriage to the Western nuclear model, and for defining normal psychosexual development as having only heterosexual outcomes; for their exclusive focus on the individual and on individuation, minimizing the importance of relationships and connections; for failing to analyze the real and not just symbolic sociopolitical context of the patient's life as if it either has no effect on their intrapsychic development or as if the effects must inevitably render the patient a psychological cripple. Leary (1997, 2000), Mattei (1996), and Thompson (1996) argue that these ideas are attributable to early classical formulations that viewed people as if their culture was not a core piece of their psyche and only in terms of culture's symbolic and not realistic aspects. This failure to name and critique social pathology and the interactive relationship between the individual and a hostile social milieu was correctly assailed as a glaring omission. It was, however, glaringly omitted from most mainstream psychological analyses of behavior.

When any psychotherapy paradigms simply legitimize the social status quo rather than examine it critically, they become instruments of social oppression and control. In this context, people who step outside of the roles that are socially proscribed for them and often limit them they are pathologized and may even be deemed dangerous to dominant group members. In this context, men and women whose primary erotic attractions are to members of their own sex are deemed 'ill' because normal gender is defined in part by erotic attraction to the other gender (Glassgold, 1992). In addition to lesbians and gay men other socially oppressed people also received diagnoses that blamed them for their misery. A more detailed analysis of the ways that this applies to African-American lesbians and gay men may be found in Greene (2000). When used in traditional ways this paradigm also failed to identify real social barriers associated with race, gender and sexual orientation that African-American lesbians and gay men are confronted with. When members of socially disadvantaged groups are labeled defective, if they internalize those labels they become less likely to look outside of themselves for causes of their misery. They become less likely to seek social change by challenging the status quo. When they do reject their discriminatory treatment, that appropriate rejection is cited as more evidence of their defect. This process also rationalizes the need to continue maintaining barriers to social opportunities for them. This process, which is a kind of psychological colonization, is facilitated by organizing behavioral and cultural norms around the dominant cultural group. Doing so serves to obscure social as opposed to individual pathology as well as one's socially constructed and not natural placement on the lower end of the social hierarchy.

While critiques of psychodynamic models are warranted those models have been expanded, transformed and modified in ways that address some of their intrinsic biases and make them of greater use in therapies with clients like African-American lesbians and gay men, as well as other clients who are members of socially marginalized groups. A detailed analysis of works that document revisions and expansions of traditional models is beyond the scope of this discussion; however, the reader is referred to Abramowitz (1997), Altman (1996), Chodorow (1989), Greene and Boyd-Franklin (1996), Greene (1997, 2000), Hall (2002), Jackson and Greene (2000), Jordan (1997), Leary (1997, 2000), Moncayo (1998), Ratigan, 1995), Thompson (1989, 1996), and Yi (1998) for examples of innovations.

Despite these innovations, psychodynamic therapies are still assailed as being intrinsically unsuitable for psychotherapy with clients of color as well as lesbian, gay and bisexual clients and women. When we examine the aforementioned works, as well as many others, and when we consider what takes place among many of our colleagues in practice, we see there is great diversity in the way that psychodynamic models are taught and are practiced. I will briefly explore what I consider more salient factors that contribute to this perception of them, why some practitioners continue to practice as if those paradigms remain unchanged over the last thirty years and challenge what I find are often misconceptions about psychodynamic theory and practice.

MISCONCEPTIONS ABOUT PSYCHODYNAMIC THEORIES

One misconception about psychodynamic theories is the assumption that there is one unified theory upon which everyone agrees. Psychodynamic theories are really a constellation of different theoretical perspectives that have common origins in Freud's psychoanalytic theory of neurosis. Leary (2000) describes psychoanalysis as a method of inquiry that raises questions and seeks by listening to the client's narrative to determine the unconscious meanings of developmental and social experiences. Mental operations are presumed to operate in such a way that feelings and impulses that would be anxiety-provoking or unacceptable to the ego if consciously experienced will be kept out of awareness or disguised by psychological defense mechanisms that operate unconsciously. As a part of this framework, affective processes are presumed to be endowed with an autonomy that permits them to be detached or displaced from or onto objects of greater or lesser significance (Campbell, 1989, Greene, 1997). Psychodynamic methods of inquiry rest on interpretive theories of mental processes that are unified primarily around the notion that unconscious processes exist and can be important determinants of behavior and affect (Greene, 1997).

Psychodynamic formulations commonly assume that clients can change their behavior if they understand their unconscious contributions to that behavior. Despite many common elements however, the practical application of the diverse theoretical approaches that can be appropriately labeled psychodynamic range from the most orthodox to those heavily influenced by feminist theory. Furthermore, the salience of intrapsychic dynamics does not mitigate the importance of understanding the way that gender, sexual orientation and ethnocultural identities are directly relevant to the shaping of the patient's intrapsychic elements and their social world, particularly but not exclusively when they are tied to social disadvantage. Specifically, we need to know how the patient interacts with and understands their social world, what it elicits in the client, what the patient's identities elicit in others in their world and how they all reciprocally influence and shape the intrapsychic world. Clients who are different in ways that are disparaged by society face a range of additional psychological tasks and challenges that must be understood by the therapist regardless of their theoretical orientation. This understanding cannot be accomplished if the therapist focuses exclusively on intrapsychic mechanisms at the exclusion of the social contexts and realities. Furthermore, the exclusive focus on the intrapsychic is not a requirement of psychodynamic therapy. This raises an important question as to why many practitioners and theoreticians continue to practice as if this were so.

Critiques of early work such as classical theory ignore numerous new formulations such as intersubjective (Yi, 1998), contemporary object relations (Adams, 2000), relational and feminist (Jordan, 1997; Leary, 1997, 2000) analyses of theory. Many of these innovations in theory seek to apply a broader range of possible meanings to any patient's behavior, as well as different potential outcomes from the same developmental circumstances. They do not limit themselves to analyses of behavior as a function of the patient's personal psychology alone. They include an analysis and consideration of the integral effects of the larger societal and cultural milieu in which identity and relationships around race, sex, sexual orientation, class, etc. are shaped. Perhaps what is most important is that new approaches presume that the subjective positioning of the therapist is not objective or neutral, but rather that therapist and client each view the world via their own cultural lens. Their analyses are also situated in the explicit consideration of the effects of sociocultural variables on the shaping of theoretical paradigms of pathology and health, as well as diagnostic nosologies. Hence, anything that influences a person's characteristic ways of being in the world, how they come to see who they and others are or can be is 'grist' for the mill. In contemporary paradigms the therapist seeks to understand the client's experience with the view that differences are seen as different perspectives rather than 'right' or 'wrong'.

THE THERAPIST'S SUBJECTIVE CULTURAL POSITIONING AND SHAME

The culture of psychodynamic psychotherapists

Psychodynamic psychotherapists are influenced by their own personal cultural identities as well as the culture of psychodynamic theory. Like any other culture, psychodynamic theory and theorists are embedded in a cultural matrix that is not objective, but rather is embedded in a larger Western, masculine, bourgeois, intellectual culture with its own language, rules of belonging and standards of normalcy (Abramowitz, 1997; Fancher, 1993; Moncayo, 1998; Strickland, 2000). It is by definition subjective. Psychodynamic thinking emerged out of a modernist and positivist scientific tradition that has tended to ignore its own cultural relativism and bias (Abramowitz, 1997; Leary, 2000). Abramowitz (1997) has argued that early, classical psychoanalytic theory grossly neglected the exploration of the psychodynamics of subjective cultural positioning without which you cannot understand the patient's reality. In the case of African-American lesbians and gay men, the patient's identities represent a convergence of sexuality, gender and ethnic role identification and enculturation that can only be truly understood in the context of the sociopolitical reality that constructs the meaning of those identities. For example, if the erotic attraction to the other sex were not a part of our culture's definition of gender normalcy, we would not likely have the same concept of or interest in what we consider sexual orientation. This is not unique to psychodynamic theory. This is true of any other theory of institutional mental health (Strickland, 2000). None of our theories of human behavior are free of cultural bias. Theoretical paradigms are products of the culture they emerge from, hence they cannot be unbiased, objective or neutral. In their practical application we must ask where the limitations and biases are and how we use new knowledge to improve on those limitations. This is true of therapies and paradigms on the other end of the conceptual continuum as well. Kwate (2002) observes that Cognitive Behavioral and Rational Emotive therapies have been viewed as if they are based on objective assessments of behavior and rational, linear thinking. It is as if the therapist's subjective sociocultural positioning is separate from rather than a part of the equation. The assumption is that they are less vulnerable to cultural bias, indeed culture does not seem to matter at all. When rational thought as opposed to emotion is viewed as the catalyst for scientific progress and healing with the attendant value of mastery over nature, human interests over the interests of nature or the interest of living in harmony with the natural world, cultural bias is flagrant. Cartesian thinking is not culture-free or unbiased. It represents a particular way of viewing the world that is embedded in a specific philosophy or ideas about how the world works. Consider an African world view, 'I am, because we are' in contrast to the Cartesian notion, 'I think, therefore I am'. In the former, relationship and connection is a fundamental ingredient in existence in contrast to the latter. Cartesian philosophies exemplify the mind–body, mind–spirit dualism that is not a given for many cultures throughout the world. The assumption that they represent a form of cultural neutrality is a continued failure to examine the subjective cultural positioning of psychological theorists, their theories and their assumptions about human behavior.

American psychotherapies have been for the most part, ethnocentric, androcentric and heterocentric. Psychodynamic modalities are no exception. Every theory of psychotherapy has evolved out of theories of human behavior, in a specific cultural context, where women, people of color, members of sexual minorities, people with disabilities and other socially disadvantaged groups have not been among the teachers, theoreticians, practitioners or architects of that discourse. When members of these groups were present they represented such small numbers that their voices were often silenced in many ways. Strickland (2000) observes that the contributions of people who are not male, white and European have not been appreciated. Their contributions are excluded from theory, ignored by method and punished by conclusions drawn from reductionistic experimental paradigms that are not proficient at explaining complex patterns of development or behavior. Many of those who are were among a stark marginalized minority created innovations in this work, however they often practice in a kind of psychodynamic closet. Jordan (1997) observes that breaking from traditional paradigms can leave us feeling doubtful about our expertise, vulnerable to criticism and threatened with disconnection and isolation from professional peers if we are cut off from our community of professional colleagues. This can be particularly difficult for practitioners and theoreticians who are members of marginalized groups as they may already feel their intellect rendered suspect and their acceptance contingent on their going along with the status quo.

While the ethnocentric, classist, sexist and heterosexist practices of traditional psychotherapies have changed over time, it is fair to say that psychodynamic theories and practice have been the slowest to change their espoused views, particularly with regard to sexual minorities. Strickland (2000) observes that theories and methods were designed to be replaced. Theory must always be a work in evolution that while conceptually stable also possesses the capacity to allow the same information to be viewed or understood from multiple perspectives. Psychodynamic thinking emphasizes the importance of being able to view the same data or behavior as something that can have many different origins and therefore many different meanings, determinants or explanations. The process of therapy itself involves asking what the issue or symbol means to the individual client with the assumption that the same narrative or story can have multiple meanings and origins depending on the client's history or perspective. While many clients may share similar determinants of behavior, the outcomes are not deterministic.

The task in therapy is to elicit that client's unique narrative or story. The client's history and perspective is by definition going to be 'colored' by race and ethnicity and the history of racism, sexism, heterosexism in the United States as well as its manifestations in the life of the client and significant figures in the client's life. Hence, the exploration of this material has never been antithetical to psychodynamic thinking, it is quite consistent. Why then has exploring this material been so controversial?

Social privilege and the therapist's countertransference

Thompson (1989) writes that the failure to explore sociopolitical realities has been more a function of the therapist's countertransference resistance, and is not an inherent limitation of the theory itself. Competent clinicians do not practice in theoretical or cookbook fashion. While they use their theoretical understandings to guide their work they also allow their experiences with clients to inform what they have learned theoretically and make modifications accordingly. Those who suggest they must be true to the theory in its most fundamentalist interpretation, with indifference to, or at the expense of, the patient, should be viewed with suspicion. Theory represents a guide to practice decisions, it is not an absolute determinant. An additional problem is that changes in theory and pedagogy do not automatically result in changes in practice, for many of the reasons discussed here that are connected to having or identifying with a privileged identity. It is the failure of the therapist, often a dominant cultural being by virtue of sex, sexual orientation and race, to allow for sufficient self-examination around their own privileged identities, or wish for them, and the ways it affects their subjectivity that is problematic, not simply the theory *per se*. How the therapist is raced, gendered, sexually oriented, etc. affects what they choose to see and what they choose to avoid just as it does in the client. Similarly, theoreticians' understanding of the order of the world, via their subjective cultural lens, informs the theoretical explanations they put forth about human behavior and its meaning. It is important to understand the nature of constituents of social power and privileged identities to understand why this is so.

Social privilege, disadvantage and the therapist's shame and guilt

Discrepancies in social power may be understood as representations of social privilege and social disadvantage. I contend that the need to deny the existence and meaning of those power differentials is often a key ingredient in the need to maintain silence around the institutional oppression associated with ethnic differences, gender and sexual orientation. When required to analyze societies' realistic power differentials and injustices and their meaning in patient's lives, but moreover, in their own lives, we observe that many clinicians and theoreticians experience discomfort with the process and avoid it. For many people, acknowledging a locus of privilege or social advantage is associated with shame.

In this discussion I connect the subjective cultural positioning of psychodynamic theoreticians, as members of institutional mental health, to their identities as primarily dominant/privileged cultural beings (i.e. white, middle- to upper-class, heterosexual and male). These observations may also apply to some members of marginalized groups who identify with and wish for privileged identities. They may also apply to those who may need to avoid confronting the lack of power and control that can be implied in acknowledging one's victimization. I also connect their subjective cultural positioning to their inability or reluctance to acknowledge either their cultural positioning or its influence on their views of what is pathological and what is healthy. I contend that this positioning contributes to the reluctance to explore these issues in the lives of culturally diverse clients.

African-American lesbians and gay men are positioned at the juncture of ethnicity, gender roles and sexual orientation in a society that has been invested in maintaining the dominant cultural status quo around these identities. Who they are challenges many cherished beliefs about who people should be, how men and women should behave and what it means if they do not. Those dominant cultural values have historically been reflected in mental health institutions and paradigms. Those paradigms invoked and expressed by dominant cultural beings refused to acknowledge their own subjective cultural positioning and invoked the position of objective scientist instead. In this context, the systemic determinants of social privilege and disadvantage are usually invisible and if materialized are denied by those who are in power and who benefit from them. The therapist who needs to deny their own locus of social privilege may need to avoid recognizing a patient's locus of social disadvantage as a significant contributor to their problems, rather than their personal deficiency.

Johnson (2001) argues that privilege is not just a problem for those who do not have it but is also for those who have it because of its relational nature. When someone is unfairly privileged by social systems and gets something they do not deserve, someone else is unfairly disadvantaged and does not gain something they do deserve. Each member of this dyad will have feelings about the inequity. This is implicated in our understanding of the ego ideal of the therapist/theoretician.

Moncayo (1998) suggests that it is important to acknowledge that just as there are dominant/majority and non-dominant/minority groups in society, those same hierarchical divisions may be found within what can be seen as a psychoanalytic culture as well. It is usually the majority voices that are most privileged and often deemed to speak for the entire culture. It is also those most privileged who have access to the venues that define the salient aspects of the work itself. I will return to this point later. This phenomenon has been observed even in psychotherapies that emerged out of a need to reject dominant cultural analyses. For example, Feminist theory emerged out of a need to address the realities and consequences of patriarchy and sexism in institutional mental health for women therapists and clients. It also attempted to challenge traditional therapies with the view that women's subordinate social status was a factor in the mental health problems of women. Despite these worthy beginnings, early formulations of Feminist theory were developed and articulated by those women who were most privileged (middle- and upper-middle-class, well-educated, white and hetero-sexual). Hence, they were assailed for their failure to represent the full spectrum of diversity among women.

Similarly, Afrocentric models of therapy emerged out of an attempt to address the failure of traditional therapies to include a consideration of the role of African cultural derivatives, race and the management of racism in any attempt to comprehend the psychologies of African-Americans. None-theless, they too were assailed for failing to represent the full spectrum of diversity among its members. The reality of sexism is largely ignored. Hence the complex gender-coded nature of racism for African-American men and women has been inadequately addressed. Heterosexism and its effects on the mental health of African-American lesbians and gay men was and continues to be virtually ignored (Greene, 2000; McNair, 1992; Williams, 1999). In both models, theory was articulated from the lens of the group's most privileged members, to the exclusion of many group members whose other identities were not only socially marginalized outside of the group but within it as well. In Greene (1997, 2000) I discuss the clinical presentation of these issues as well as the ways that different aspects of these approaches and psychodynamic theory may be successfully integrated into the treatment of diverse clients like African-American lesbians and gay men.

It is fair to say that although they have changed over time, the dominant and most privileged voices within any community may be slowest to change. Perhaps this happens because change can mean a loss of privilege. There are many disagreements within psychodynamic psychology that take place in the pages of academic journals and gatherings that are rarely heard outside of that 'culture'. Often dominant views and perspectives are presented as if everyone is of like mind about them and as if they are naturally correct. Like any culture or group, every member of the group is not of like mind and every member does not subscribe unswervingly to all of the traditional beliefs espoused by the group's dominant and most powerful members. It may be more difficult, however, for dissenting voices to find their way into professional forums that are often controlled by gatekeepers who hold more traditional views.

SUMMARY AND CONCLUSION

In summary, psychodynamic paradigms have much to offer the treatment of African-American lesbians and gay men as well as other members of marginalized groups. Understanding the unconscious has the power to free people to be more authentic, to integrate disparate parts of themselves in whole, to be more present, productive, creative and free to make conscious, informed choices about what they do, how they go about life and who they choose to have in their lives. Psychodynamic paradigms can also be useful in understanding the dynamics of power between privileged and disadvantaged groups. Jackson (2000) observes that its focus on how people cope and defend in response to pain and trauma in early life is useful in helping patients who belong to socially disadvantaged groups cope with the trauma of social oppression. Root (1992) discusses social oppression as a form of insidious trauma. These dilemmas can characterize the lives of African-American lesbians and gay men as members of a multiply marginalized and socially traumatized group. Psychodynamic therapy can be a powerful tool when it validates a client's accurate perception of social as well as personal injustice and exploitation in addition to the feelings elicited by such treatment. Its can be useful in assisting patients at developing conscious adaptive strategies for addressing ongoing forms of social as well as personal trauma. Ultimately psychodynamic therapies can be useful in helping clients to make distinctions between what they have been told about themselves and what is true.

Note

1 This chapter was previously published in the *Journal of Lesbian Studies* 8(1/2), (2004): 57–77, as 'African American Lesbians and other Culturally Diverse People in Psychodynamic Psychotherapies: Useful Paradigms or Oxymoron?' Copyright © Haworth Press, New York. Reprinted with permission.

References

Abramovitz, S. (1997) A Discussion of Lesbians and Psychoanalytic Culture and a Response to Kassof's Treatment of a Homosexual Woman, in A. Goldberg (ed.), *Conversations in Self Psychology*. Hillsdale, NJ: The Analytic Press, pp. 231–243.

Adams, J. M. (2000) Individual and Group Psychotherapy with African American Women: Understanding the Identity and Context of the Therapist and Patient, in L. C. Jackson and B. Greene (eds), *Psychotherapy with African American Women: Innovations in Psychodynamic Perspectives and Practice*. New York: Guilford Press, pp. 33–61.

Altman, N. (1996) The Accommodation of Diversity in Psychoanalysis, in R. Perez Foster, M. Moskowitz and R. A. Javier (eds), *Reaching Across Boundaries of Culture and Class: Widening the Scope of Psychotherapy*. Northvale, NJ: Jason Aronson, pp. 195–209.

Campbell, R. (1989) *Psychiatric Dictionary*, 2nd edn. New York: Oxford University Press.

Chodorow, N. (1989) *Feminism and Psychoanalytic Theory*. New Haven, CT: Yale University Press.

Fancher, R. T. (1993) Psychoanalysis as Culture, *Issues in Psychoanalytic Psychology* 15(2): 81–94.

Glassgold, J. (1992) New Directions in Dynamic Theories of Lesbianism: From Psychoanalysis to Social Constructionism, in J. Chrisler and D. Howard (eds), *New Directions in Feminist Psychology: Practice, Theory and Research*. New York: Springer, pp. 154–163.

Greene, B. (1995) Addressing Racism, Sexism and Heterosexism in Psychodynamic Psychotherapy, in J. Glassgold and S. Iasenza (eds), *Lesbians and Psychoanalysis: Revolutions in Theory and Practice*. New York: Free Press, pp. 145–159.

Greene, B. (1997) Psychotherapy with African American Women: Integrating Feminist and Psychodynamic Models, *Smith College Studies in Social Work* 67(3), (June): 299–322.

Greene, B. (2000) African American Lesbian and Bisexual Women in Feminist-Psychodynamic Psychotherapies: Surviving and Thriving between a Rock and a Hard Place, in L. C. Jackson and B. Greene (eds), *Psychotherapy with African American Women: Innovations in Psychodynamic Perspectives and Practice*. New York: Guilford Press, pp. 82–125.

Greene, B. (2003) What Difference does a Difference Make? Societal Privilege, Disadvantage, and Discord in Human Relationships, in J. Robinson and L. James (eds), *Diversity in Human Interaction: A Tapestry of America*. New York: Oxford University Press.

Greene, B. and Boyd-Franklin, N. (1996) African American Lesbians: Issues in Couples Therapy, in J. Laird and R. J. Green (eds), *Lesbians and Gay Men in Couples & Families: A Handbook for Practitioners*. San Francisco, CA: Jossey-Bass, pp. 251–271.

Hall, M. F. (2002) Race, Gender and Transference in Psychotherapy, in F. Kaslow (ed. in chief), J. J. Magnavita (vol. ed.), *Comprehensive Handbook of Psychotherapy Volume 1: Psychodynamic/Object Relations*. New York: John Wiley & Sons, pp. 565–584.

Jackson, L. (2000) The New Multiculturalism and Psychodynamic Theory, in L. C.

Jackson and B. Greene (eds), *Psychotherapy with African American Women: Innovations in Psychodynamic Perspectives and Practice*. New York: Guilford Press, pp. 1–14.

Jackson, L. C. and Greene, B. (eds) (2000) *Psychotherapy with African American Women: Innovations in Psychodynamic Perspectives and Practice*. New York: Guilford Press.

Johnson, A. G. (2001) *Privilege, Power and Difference*. Mountain View, CA: Mayfield Press.

Jordan, J. (1997) Relational Therapy in a Nonrelational World, *Work in Progress, No. 79*. Wellesley, MA: Stone Center Working Paper Series.

Kwate, N. O. (2002) Assessing African Centered Mental Disorder: Validation of the Cultural Misorientation Scale, *Dissertation-Abstracts-International:-Section-B:-The-Sciences-and-Engineering*.

Leary, K. (1997) Race, Self-Disclosure and 'Forbidden Talk': Race and Ethnicity in Contemporary Clinical Practice, *Psychoanalytic Quarterly* 66: 163–189.

Leary, K. (2000) Racial Enactments in Dynamic Treatment, *Psychoanalytic Dialogues: A Journal of Relational Perspectives* 10(4): 639–653.

McNair, L. D. (1992) African American Women in Therapy: An Afrocentric and Feminist Synthesis, *Women & Therapy* 12(1/2): 5–19.

Mattei, L. (1996) Coloring Development: Race and Culture in Psychodynamic Theories, in J. Berzoff, L. M. Flanagan and P. Hertz, *Inside Out and Outside In: Psychodynamic Clinical Theory and Practice in Contemporary Multicultural Contexts*. Northvale, NJ: Jason Aronson, pp. 221–245.

Moncayo, R. (1998) Cultural Diversity and the Cultural Epistemological Structure of Psychoanalysis: Implications for Psychotherapy with Latinos and other Minorities, *Psychoanalytic Psychology* 15(2): 262–286.

Ratigan, B. (1995) Inner World, Outer World: Exploring the Tension of Race, Sexual Orientation and Class and the Internal World, *Psychodynamic Counselling* 1(2), (February): 173–186.

Root, M. P. P. (1992) The Impact of Trauma on Personality: The Second Reconstruction, in L. S. Brown and M. Ballou (eds), *Personality and Psychopathology: Feminist Reappraisals*. New York: Guilford, pp. 229–265.

Schachter, J. S. and Butts, H. F. (1968) Transference and Countertransference in Interracial Analysis, *Journal of the American Psychoanalytic Association* 16: 792–808.

Strickland, B. R. (2000) Misassumptions, Misadventures and the Misuse of Psychology, *American Psychologist* 55(3), (March): 331–338.

Thompson, C. (1989) Psychoanalytic Psychotherapy with Inner City Patients, *Journal of Contemporary Psychotherapy* 19(2): 137–148.

Thompson, C. (1996) The African American Patient in Psychodynamic Treatment, in R. Perez Foster, M. Moskowitz and R. A. Javier (eds), *Reaching across Boundaries of Culture and Class: Widening the Scope of Psychotherapy*. Northvale, NJ: Jason Aronson, pp. 115–142.

Williams, C. B. (1999) African American Women, Afrocentrism and Feminism: Implications for Psychotherapy, *Women & Therapy* 22(4): 1–16.

Yi, K. Y. (1998) Transference and Race: An Intersubjective Conceptualization, *Psychoanalytic Psychology* 15(2): 245–261.

Further reading

Franklin, A. J. (1993) The Invisibility Syndrome, *Family Therapy Networker* 17(4) (July/August): 33–39.

Chapter 14

Multiple stigmas in psychotherapy with African-American women: afrocentric, feminist, and womanist perspectives

Carmen Braun Williams

Multicultural counseling theories have elucidated the experiences of marginalized populations – e.g. women, people of color, gays and lesbians, working-class people, people with disabilities, and other stigmatized groups – and deepened our understanding of the psychological impact of oppression. These theories have contributed significantly to our knowledge of the effects of social, political, gender, racial, economic, and historical factors on personal and cultural identity (Arredondo, Toporek, Brown, Jones, Locke, Sanchez, and Stadler, 1996). The ongoing quest for personal identity – the need to 'claim the *I*' (Cliff, cited in hooks, 1992, p. 46) in a climate replete with pejorative images – is a process with distinctive challenges for members of stigmatized groups.

Multicultural theories emerged as alternatives to eurocentric analyses of the experience of marginalized people. Eurocentric theories privilege certain race, class, and gender variables over others (e.g. white, middle-class, heterosexual, and masculine) and proffer designated socialized traits – individualism, independence, and autonomy – as hallmarks of mental health. Multicultural theories, on the other hand, find strength and value in a broad cultural range of psychological and behavioral characteristics.

Nevertheless, despite their valuable contributions, multicultural approaches tend to address cultural variables in isolation of one another. Namely, they examine gender, race, sexual orientation, and class separately, rather than the interplay among them. Thus, the lives of people with multiple stigmatized identities are compartmentalized into fragmented cultural categories that do not mirror real life (Constantine, 2002; Croteau, Talbot, Lance, and Evans, 2002; Harley, Jolivette, McCormick, and Tice, 2002; Moradi and Subich, 2003). Consequently, eurocentric and multicultural perspectives share a limitation in that the complex manner in which multiple stigmas operate in the lives of individuals is largely unexamined.

As Constantine (2002) cogently stated, 'Current models of mental health care often do not allow for the processes by which individuals with multiple oppressed identities arrive at a positive overall sense of cultural identity' (p. 211). Recent counseling literature has begun to address the problem of unidimensional, non-integrated perspectives on cultural identity (Constantine, 2002; Croteau *et al.*, 2002; Harley *et al.*, 2002). Yet, further attention to therapeutic limitations of compartmentalization of cultural variables clearly is needed. Also needed are therapeutic strategies that support clients who wish to embrace multiple stigmatized cultural identities.

In this chapter, the author (1) examines the strengths and limitations of two prominent culturally based counseling theories – afrocentrism and feminism – for therapy with African-American women, (2) discusses the usefulness of 'womanist' (i.e. African-American feminist) models for counseling African-American women balancing the competing demands of different cultural communities, and (3) proposes clinical strategies that seek to bridge the multiple stigmatized identities of African-American women.

STRENGTHS AND LIMITATIONS OF AFROCENTRISM AND FEMINISM

Afrocentric and feminist counseling theories emphasize the strength and value of characteristics purportedly embedded in African-Americans and women, traits devalued in the broader social context. Afrocentric theory, based on traditional African cultural patterns of spirituality, communalism, fluid time-orientation, emotional expressiveness, harmony with nature, and interdependence (Mbiti, 1990; White, 1984), advances the belief that adherence by African-Americans to traditional African cultural patterns mediates against the negative psychological effects of racism. Similarly, 'cultural feminism', the 'ideology of a female nature or female essence' (Alcoff, 1988, p. 408) asserts that qualities such as emotional relatedness, empathy, and nurturance characterize women's ways of being, knowing, care-giving, and moral decision-making, and are sources of emotional strength (Belenky, Clinchy, Goldberger, and Tarule, 1986; Chodorow, 1978; Gilligan, 1982; Jordan, Kaplan, Miller, Stiver, and Surrey, 1991; Miller, 1986).

These multicultural models offer important psychological antidotes to racism and sexism. Specifically, they enable people of color and women to begin to undo the psychological damage wrought by the internalization of racist and sexist social images (Williams, 1999). Given that both afrocentrism and feminism developed out of the impulse to offer alternatives to eurocentric, masculinist counseling ideology, it is ironic that these theories are themselves guilty of failing to integrate diversity. That is, cultural feminist descriptions of women reflect socialized characteristics associated with educated White women (Bohan, 1993; Comas-Diaz and Greene; 1994; Landrine, 1995; Reid, 1993) rather than *all* women. Similarly, afrocentric theory centers on the experience of African-American men with little attention to gender differences (e.g. Asante, 1992; Nobles, 1991; White, 1984).

These paradoxes are relevant for psychotherapy with African-American women in a number of ways. The African-American woman seeking a whole sense of self amidst a myriad of social stigmas is hampered by multicultural theories that replicate some of the same limitations of eurocentric models. These limitations, elucidated below, include the tendency to (a) 'essentialize', or claim as inherent, certain socialized cultural variables, and (b) 'privilege' certain social traits over others by presenting them in dualistic, oppositional terms. To the extent that these biases are played out in social discourse, African-American women may feel pressure to choose only *one* aspect of their identity (e.g. race *or* gender) as core to their being and to minimize other key aspects of self. They may also feel as if they must declare allegiance to only *one* community or risk being viewed as a cultural traitor.

'ESSENTIALIZING' CULTURAL VARIABLES

Both afrocentrism and feminism make assumptions about 'fundamental attributes that are conceived as internal' – i.e. 'essential' (Bohan, 1993, p. 7). For example, behaving in conformity with socialized gender patterns, or 'doing gender' (Bohan, 1993), has created the illusion of differences between women and men that are not inevitable, but nevertheless are experienced as 'natural' and become self-reinforcing (Bohan, 1993; West and Zimmerman, 1991). Pollitt (1992) argued that not all women are nurturing, caring, and relational, yet feminist discourse encourages such a view. Conversely, non-conformity with prescriptive gender roles, or gender-bending, renders individuals suspect if not outright deviant in the eyes of those who advocate adherence to expected roles. As a result, women may feel pressure to be nurturing and relational, and men independent and emotionally detached, and discouraged from exploring the full range of emotional possibilities.

These so-called feminine and masculine traits, in addition to creating false distinctions between men and women, have been applied across racial lines. Consequently, feminist theory's focus on experiences of white, middle-class women (Comas-Diaz and Greene, 1994; Landrine, 1995), when applied out of context to African-American women, has resulted in African-American women being viewed as inadequate if not abnormal (Comas-Diaz and Greene, 1994). Similarly, because afrocentric theory generalizes to all African-Americans traits assumed to be inherently and essentially African (Asante, 1987, 1992; White, 1984), those who do not conform are considered deviant (Asante, 1987).

A fundamental problem with such essentialist constructions is their failure to account for social context (Gergen, 1985, 1991; Nicholson, 1990), or, for that matter, contradictory evidence. Indeed, contradictory evidence often is attributed to flawed individuals rather than flawed theories. As such, afrocentric and feminist perspectives lay claim to a collective experience that tends to silence difference and create new, within-group categories of 'other'. Labeling so-called afrocentric traits as authentic or natural serves to marginalize African-American women whose feminist values may be inconsistent with an afrocentric focus. Similarly, feminism's focus on gender marginalizes women who seek to extend feminist discourse to address issues of race and racism.

'PRIVILEGING' CULTURAL VARIABLES

When afrocentric and feminist standards are invoked, implicit hierarchies deem those who conform to be more authentically African-American or feminist than those who do not. As suggested above, a tacit hierarchy in feminist psychology privileges the experiences of White middle-class women (Landrine, 1995) and marginalizes women of color. As Laura Brown (1994) stated, feminist therapists 'have tended to develop theories by and about women of European heritage and then simply comment in passing that what they have said probably applies to people from other oppressed groups as well' (p. 69). These incomplete conceptualizations perpetuate an implicitly hierarchical feminist paradigm that privileges examination of gender and relegates race as secondary (Williams, 1999). Women of color, critical of this pattern of racism embedded in feminist theory, have spurred efforts to make feminist psychology more inclusive (Brown, 1994; Brown and Root, 1990; Comas-Diaz and Greene, 1994; J. V. Jordan, 1997; Landrine, 1995; Landrine, Klonoff, and Brown-Collins, 1992; Reid, 1993; Reid and Comas-Diaz, 1990; Turner, 1997).

A similar hierarchical process is reflected in afrocentric discourse. Afrocentric behavior is privileged while non-afrocentric behavior is deemed to be deviant (Asante, 1992, p. 45), thus encouraging conformity, ostracizing individuality, and creating categories of 'rightness'. These hierarchies of racial privilege and correctness, which rarely address gender, create tensions among African-Americans who gauge one another's appearance, interests, and affiliations according to adherence to rigidly prescribed behavioral modes. Afrocentric discourse on homosexuality, illustrative of such tenets of correctness, reflects homosexuality as deviant, derived from 'European decadence', and most appropriately responded to with antagonism (Asante, 1992, p. 57). African-American women who happen to be lesbian will find little if any affirmation in afrocentric approaches to psychotherapy.

Clearly, the privileging of a single cultural variable as central to self-definition is a limitation of both afrocentric and feminist theories, at least as it applies to individuals with multiple stigmas. Neither afrocentric nor feminist frameworks present complex analyses of the interaction of race, gender, or other stigmatized variables on identity. Criticizing feminist therapy for this lack of integration, Brown (1994) stated, 'Feminist therapy cannot arise from a theory that would require someone to choose which aspect of her identity is the one to be liberated while others lie silenced, unattended to, or rendered marginal' (p. 69). Similarly, the lack of an integrated, multi-variable analysis in afrocentric theory is remarkable when one considers that afrocentric theory examines African-American family systems in the absence of a specific analysis of women (Williams, 1999). Indeed, there is virtually no mention of women or analysis of gender role socialization and its impact on relationships and family dynamics (see Nobles, 1991; White, 1984).

African-American women are thus caught between competing constructs: to ally with either afrocentrism or feminism may necessitate silencing a central component of their identity. False separations are constructed in which traits are presented as opposites and overlap between groups is ignored. White (1990) noted that afrocentric frameworks create 'an untenable binary opposition. Europeans are materialistic while Africans are spiritual; Europeans abort life while Africans affirm it' (p. 84). This construction relies on images of African-Americans as having no interaction with White culture, a proposition that has no basis in reality (hooks, 1992; White, 1990).

CASE SCENARIO

Tianna is a 19-year-old biracial woman with light skin tone, grey eyes, and light brown, wavy hair. Upon entering therapy, she was in her second year of college at a large university in the West. She lived in a campus dormitory in her first year and formed a number of close, racially diverse friendships. Nevertheless, Tianna reported feeling alienated from many of her African-American peers: specifically, that her physical appearance and feminist leanings were not 'black enough' for some, and that her middle-class background marked her as classist and elitist by others. Similarly, Tianna also frequently felt guarded with white peers, often bracing for the possibility that racist assumptions or statements against African-Americans would be made in her presence before they realized that she was African-American.

Tianna's father was a United Nations ambassador and her mother an international journalist. Tianna's background included extensive travel to many parts of the world and immersion in many different communities and cultures. In fact, by 19, Tianna had lived in the United States only three years, including her first year in college. In the countries her family lived in, Tianna was less aware of stigma associated with her racial background than her gender, but nevertheless felt fairly comfortable in a variety of cultural contexts. During summers as a teenager, her volunteer relief work in impoverished communities fueled her political activism against economic inequities, class disparities, and patriarchy.

In terms of racial identity, Tianna's African-American father and European-American mother chose not to overtly influence Tianna's decision about how to identify racially. They did, however, encourage her to view herself as they viewed themselves, as 'citizens of the world', attuned to global social, economic, and political issues. Tianna's choice to identify as African-American occurred in college and was, for Tianna, a decisive political statement. She felt it was important to disclaim her ostensible white skin privilege by being explicit about her identity as a woman of color.

Still, Tianna felt embattled by having constantly to defend herself against others' assumptions about her based on her appearance. She also found herself often feeling apologetic and defensive among African-American peers about her class background and feminism, and trying to win their approval by suppressing these aspects of herself. With whites, their subtle and sometimes overt racist statements, uttered without any apparent misgivings, began to make Tianna feel cautious and untrusting. Tianna longed to find a way to handle these interactions more comfortably and competently – a way that did not deplete her emotionally.

STRATEGIES FOR ADDRESSING MULTIPLE CULTURAL STIGMAS

Several psychological themes have been identified in the clinical literature on African-American women. These themes include emotional isolation (Boyd-Franklin, 1989; Greene, 1994; Turner, 1997); stress (Greene, 1994; Mays, 1985); internalized oppression (Gainor, 1992; Greene, 1994; J. M. Jordan, 1997), resisting racism (Comas-Diaz and Greene, 1994; Fischer and Shaw, 1999; Landrine, 1995; Tinsley-Jones, 2003), and, more recently, integrating multiple identities (Constantine, 2002; Croteau, Talbot, Lance, and Evans, 2002; Harley, Jolivette, McCormick, and Tice, 2002; Moradi and Subich, 2003).

Womanist traditions offer useful tools for working with African-American women therapeutically (Williams, 1999). Womanism, first coined by Alice Walker (1983), is an alternative to afrocentric and feminist approaches. Derived from African-American female culture with its commitment to survival and emotional strength, womanism offers a model that addresses the simultaneity of racism, sexism, and classism as experienced by African-American women. It is a model in which race, class, gender, and sexual orientation are understood as interactive, not isolated, in women's lives.

Womanist models of resistance and strategies for survival offer useful antidotes to the multiple stigmas confronting African-American women (Williams, 1999). Significantly, since womanist models reflect integrated analyses of race, gender, class, and sexual orientation (Brown-Douglas, 1993), they address African-American women's lives more holistically than do afrocentric and feminist models. Furthermore, to the extent that womanist models avoid conceptualizing patterns of resistance as *inherent* to African-American women, they transcend essentialist constructions and circumvent the problems associated with afrocentric and feminist approaches discussed above (Williams, 1999).

Although womanist theoretical conceptualizations have yet to be applied systematically to psychotherapy, examples have appeared in the literature (see Carter and Banks, 1996). Womanist strategies of community building, self-determination, compassion, and empowerment through interpersonal connection as key modes of resistance to oppression (Cannon, 1988; D. S. Williams, 1993) offer rich possibilities for therapeutic interventions with African-American women clients. An important task for counselors is '[r]etrieving this often hidden or diminished female tradition of catalytic action' (D. S. Williams, 1993, p. 26) and applying it in their work with African-American women clients, particularly clients like Tianna struggling to maintain an integrated sense of self.

In the following section, the author's application of three key womanist themes in psychotherapy is described: (a) the significance of social and historical context; (b) social justice activism; and (c) networks of support and connection. These themes, used as strategies for therapy with Tianna, were particularly useful in addressing her concern about maintaining self in a climate of fragmentation.

SOCIAL AND HISTORICAL CONTEXT

When working therapeutically with African-American women, it is essential for therapists to assist their clients in recognizing the sociocultural origins and impact of racism, sexism, classism, and other forms of oppression (Semmler and Williams, 2000). Drawing connections between current struggles and the historical experience of African-American women is a particularly powerful womanist intervention (Williams, Frame, and Greene, 1999). Womanist activism occurred historically in a climate of overt stigma and oppression. Womanist accounts reflect a process of maintaining self in the face of overwhelming hostility and discrimination.

Tianna was struggling to maintain her sense of self and emotional strength among peers who projected racist and classist assumptions onto her and saw only pieces of her rather than her complexity. A focus of Tianna's therapy was helping her to 'disown' the projections of others, understand them contextually, and draw strength from the accounts of other African-American women. In this phase of Tianna's therapy, her therapist introduced her to African-American women writers such as Audre Lorde and bell hooks who describe their challenges and successes with integrating multiple social stigmas. These and other African-American activist women's writings were sources of comfort and strength for Tianna.

SOCIAL JUSTICE ACTIVISM

An essential feature of psychotherapy with African-American women struggling to maintain a sense of wholeness in an oppressive cultural environment is helping them to separate what is personal from what is contextual (or political). Tianna's activism was grounded in her choice of identity as an African-American woman committed to fighting racism, sexism, and classism. Although she was initially hesitant to confront peers' assumptions about her, she learned to do so in ways that reflected her willingness to stand up for herself. For example, after several weeks of therapy, Tianna described an incident in which a black friend implied that Tianna's light skin protected her from and rendered her unable to understand the kind of racism that most blacks experience. Tianna, after several role-plays in therapy, was able to respond to statements such as these with more tolerance and acceptance – and more compassion.

Compassion, a theme that is at the center of African-American social activism, was instrumental in helping Tianna maintain a healthier perspective on these sorts of interactions. According to Tinsley-Jones (2003), 'when processing racism, it is helpful to think of ourselves as compassionate witnesses to each other and to our clients' (p. 185). It was helpful for Tianna to be reminded that everyone is at a different place in their journey toward understanding and enlightenment. Reminding herself of the historical quest for humanity by African-Americans helped to strengthen her compassion for others and commitment to confronting racism.

CREATING NETWORKS OF SUPPORT AND CONNECTION

The emphasis on emotional wholeness, psychological strength, and resilience – and their centrality to African-American women's historical struggles – is at the core of womanist theory. Another central feature is interconnection, particularly among women. Modes of psychological resistance to oppression identified in womanist discourse include reliance on women-centered networks of emotional support and care-giving, spiritual faith, and a healthy construction of self (Boyd-Franklin, 1989; Collins, 1990; D. S. Williams, 1993). Tinsley-Jones (2003) stated, 'Racism is slippery; it seeks to stay underground, to perpetuate itself, and often to make us feel defeated. To do this work, we need to be in the company of our allies, and in this, color does not matter' (p. 185).

Tianna's therapy included ongoing exploration of possibilities for new connections with others who might offer support and understanding. It was clear that Tianna had forged strong friendships. However, her friends, through no fault of their own, were not always able to help her to process her experiences with multiple social stigmas. Upon her therapist's recommendation, Tianna looked into a new multicultural student organization at the college, a mixed race and gender group committed to social justice. As Tianna's therapy came to a close, she had been to several meetings and had begun to find new avenues of emotional support and connection.

In contrast to womanist perspectives, neither feminist nor afrocentric theories consider the full social context for African-American women. Because feminism and afrocentrism focus almost exclusively on *either* gender *or* race, therapists practicing from these perspectives might have failed to address the interaction between racism, sexism, and classism that defined Tianna's struggles. Feminist therapists might have focused on Tianna's feminist ideals without adequately examining her racial identity development, or helped Tianna explore her experiences with sexism without adequately addressing her experiences with racism. Afrocentric therapists might have challenged Tianna's claim to an authentic African-American identity, given her mixed-race heritage, and encouraged her to adopt African-centered values in order to become more authentically black.

CONCLUSION

Successful psychotherapy with African-American women clients demands an understanding of and attention to cultural context. Afrocentric and feminist theories have made major contributions to understanding how social constructions of race and gender impact mental health. Nonetheless, because race and gender are compartmentalized in afrocentric and feminist discourse, yet coexist in real life, these theories are limited in their analyses of the relationship among multiple cultural variables. The case example of Tianna demonstrates the therapeutic potential of womanist approaches for addressing multiple stigmatized identities.

In Tianna's case, her psychotherapist was also a mixed-race woman who identifies as African-American. Certainly, their shared racial and gender background contributed to the success of the therapy. However, it is the author's belief that any therapist who takes seriously the task of learning and examining the personal, institutional, and cultural impact of multiple stigmas will be prepared to work effectively with clients struggling with these difficult, multidimensional issues.

References

Alcoff, L. (1988) Cultural Feminism versus Post-Structuralism: The Identity Crisis in Feminist Theory, *Signs: Journal of Women in Culture and Society* 13: 405–436.

Arredondo, P., Toporek, R., Brown, S. P., Jones, J., Locke, D. C., Sanchez, J. and Stadler, H. (1996) Operationalization of the Multicultural Counseling Competencies, *Journal of Multicultural Counseling & Development* 24: 42–78.

Asante, M. K. (1987) *The Afrocentric Idea*. Philadelphia, PA: Temple University Press.

Asante, M. K. (1992). *Afrocentricity*. Trenton, NJ: Africa World Press.

Belenky, M. F., Clinchy, B. M., Goldberger, N. R. and Tarule, J. M. (1986) *Women's Ways of Knowing*. New York: Basic Books.

Bohan, J. S. (1993) Regarding Gender: Essentialism, Constructionism, and Feminist Psychology, *Psychology of Women Quarterly* 17: 5–21.

Boyd-Franklin, N. (1989) *Black Families in Therapy: A Multisystems Approach*. New York: Guilford.

Brown, L. S. (1994) *Subversive Dialogues: Theory in Feminist Therapy*. New York: Basic Books.

Brown, L. S. and Root, M. P. P. (1990) *Diversity and Complexity in Feminist Therapy*. New York: Harrington Park Press.

Brown-Douglas, K. D. (1993) Womanist Theology: What is its Relationship to Black Theology?, in J. H. Cone and G. S. Wilmore (eds), *Black Theology: A Documentary History, Volume Two: 1980–1992*. Maryknoll, NY: Orbis Books, pp. 290–299.

Cannon, K. G. (1988) *Black Womanist Ethics*. Atlanta, GA: Scholars Press.

Carter, R. T. and Banks, E. E. (1996) Womanist Identity and Mental Health, *Journal of Counseling and Development* 74: 484–489.

Chodorow, N. (1978) *The Reproduction of Mothering*. Berkeley, CA: University of California Press.

Collins, P. H. (1990) *Black Feminist Thought*. New York: Routledge, Chapman & Hall.

Comas-Diaz, L. and Greene, B. (eds) (1994) *Women of Color: Integrating Ethnic and Gender Identities in Psychotherapy*. New York: Guilford.

Constantine, M. G. (2002) The Intersection of Race, Ethnicity, Gender, and Social Class in Counseling: Examining Selves in Cultural Contexts, *Journal of Multicultural Counseling and Development* 30: 210–215.

Croteau, J. M., Talbot, D. M., Lance, T. S. and Evans, N. J. (2002) A Qualitative Study of the Interplay between Privilege and Oppression, *Journal of Multicultural Counseling and Development* 30: 239–258.

Fischer, A. R. and Shaw, C. M. (1999) African Americans' Mental Health and Perceptions of Racist Discrimination: The Moderating Effects of Racial Socialization Experiences and Self-Esteem, *Journal of Counseling Psychology* 46: 395–407.

Gainor, K. A. (1992) Internalized Oppression as a Barrier to Effective Group Work with Black Women, *Journal for Specialists in Group Work* 17: 235–242.

Gergen, K. J. (1985) The Social Constructionist Movement in Modern Psychology, *American Psychologist* 40: 266–275.

Gergen, K. J. (1991) *The Saturated Self: Dilemmas of Identity in Contemporary Life.* New York: Harper Collins.

Gilligan, C. (1982) *In a Different Voice: Psychological Theory and Women's Development.* Cambridge, MA: Harvard University Press.

Greene, B. (1994) African American Women, in L. Comas-Diaz and B. Greene (eds) (1994), *Women of Color: Integrating Ethnic and Gender Identities in Psychotherapy.* New York: Guilford, pp. 10–29.

Harley, D. A., Jolivette, K., McCormack, K. and Tice, K. (2002) Race, Class, and Gender: A Constellation of *Positionalities* with Implications for Counseling, *Journal of Multicultural Counseling and Development* 30: 216–238.

hooks, b. (1992) *Black Looks: Race and Representation.* Boston, MA: South End Press.

Jordan, J. M. (1997) Counseling African American Women from a Cultural Sensitivity Perspective, in C. C. Lee and B. L. Richardson (eds), *Multicultural Issues in Counseling: New Approaches to Diversity.* Alexandria, VA: American Counseling Association, pp. 51–63.

Jordan, J. V., Kaplan, A., Miller, J. B., Stiver, I. P. and Surrey, J. L. (1991) *Women's Growth in Connection: Writings from the Stone Center.* New York: Guilford.

Landrine, H. (ed.) (1995) *Bringing Cultural Diversity to Feminist Psychology: Theory, Research, and Practice.* Washington, DC: American Psychological Association.

Landrine, H., Klonoff, E. A. and Brown-Collins, A. (1992) Cultural Diversity and Methodology in Feminist Psychology, *Psychology of Women Quarterly* 16: 145–163.

Mbiti, J. S. (1990) *African Religions and Philosophy*, 2nd edn. Portsmouth, NH: Heinemann.

Miller, J. B. (1986) *Toward a New Psychology of Women.* Boston, MA: Beacon Press.

Moradi, B. and Subich, L. M. (2003) A Concomitant Examination of the Relations of Perceived Racist and Sexist Events to Psychological Distress for African American Women, *The Counseling Psychologist* 31: 451–469.

Nicholson, L. J. (ed.) (1990) *Feminism/Postmodernism.* New York: Routledge.

Nobles, W. W. (1991) African Philosophy: Foundations for Black Psychology, in R. L. Jones (ed.), *Black Psychology.* Berkeley, CA: Cobb & Henry, pp. 47–63.

Pollitt, K. (1992) Are Women Morally Superior to Men? *The Nation* 28: 799–807.

Reid, P. T. (1993) Poor Women in Psychological Research: Shut Up and Shut Out, *Psychology of Women Quarterly* 17: 133–150.

Reid, P. T. and Comas-Diaz, L. (1990) Gender and Ethnicity: Perspectives on Dual Status, *Sex Roles* 22: 397–408.

Semmler, P. L. and Williams, C. B. (2000) Narrative Therapy: A Storied Context for Multicultural Counseling, *Journal of Multicultural Counseling and Development* 28: 51–62.

Tinsley-Jones, H. (2003) Racism: Calling a Spade a Spade, *Psychotherapy: Theory, Research, Practice, Training* 40: 179–186.

Turner, C. W. (1997) Clinical Applications of the Stone Center Theoretical Approach to Minority Women, in J. V. Jordan (ed.), *Women's Growth in Diversity: More Writings from the Stone Center*. New York: Guilford, pp. 74–90.

Walker, A. (1983) *In Search of our Mothers' Gardens*. New York: Harcourt, Brace, Jovanovich.

West, C. and Zimmerman, D. H. (1991) Doing Gender, in J. Lorber and S. A. Farrell (eds), *The Social Construction of Gender*. Newbury Park, CA: Sage, pp. 13–37.

White, E. F. (1990) Africa on my Mind: Gender, Counter Discourse and African American Nationalism, *Journal of Women's History* 2: 73–97.

White, J. L. (1984) *The Psychology of Blacks*. Englewood Cliffs, NJ: Prentice-Hall.

Williams, C. B. (1999) African American Women, Afrocentrism, and Feminism: Implications for Therapy, *Women & Therapy* 22: 1–19.

Williams, C. B., Frame, M. W. and Greene, E. (1999) Counseling Groups for African American Women: A Focus on Spirituality, *Journal for Specialists in Group Work* 24: 260–273.

Williams, D. S. (1993) *Sisters in the Wilderness: The Challenge of Womanist God-Talk*. Maryknoll, NY: Orbis Books.

Chapter 15

Success neurosis: what race and social class have to do with it

Dorothy Evans Holmes

Success neurosis is a complex concept. Freud first elucidated ideas on the subject in 1916 in his discourse on character types. He offered that success wrecks those individuals for whom it triggers residues of their childhood 'criminal' intent. In 1919, Freud further clarified the concept by suggesting that it is a punishment by which unconscious Oedipal guilt is expiated. Other early writers such as Fenichel (1945) followed Freud's lead in implicating Oedipal guilt as the principal etiologic factor in success neurosis. In 1936, Freud suggested that his disavowal of the existence of the Acropolis upon mounting it was a manifestation of success neurosis. It is of particular interest for this chapter that Freud linked his disavowal of the Acropolis with the economic circumstances of his youth thus, 'It seemed to me beyond the realms of possibility that I should travel so far – that I should "go such a long way". *This was linked up with the limitations and poverty of our conditions of life in my youth*' [italics added] (Freud, 1936, p. 247).

Freud's acknowledgment of the intrapsychic ramifications of 'real' factors such as poverty is a fitting introduction to the core of this chapter, that is to the exploration of how race and social class standing come to affect the building blocks of personality and conflict. It is my experience that for many patients their class and their minority status play primary roles in determining the intrapsychic meanings of success and failure. It is also my view that these meanings and the real-life experiences with race and/or social class that shape them become internalized as components of success neurosis and become part of the resistance to its resolution.

RACE, SOCIO-ECONOMIC STATUS AND SUCCESS NEUROSIS

To understand the role race and class can play in the formation of success neurosis, it is important to recognize the material reality of racist domination and oppression in the Western world. Galatzer-Levy and Cohler (2002) have written convincingly about the disturbances to the core identity of gays and lesbians owing to the social pressures of growing up in a heteronormative world. Similarly, I suggest that racial minorities and those from humbler socio-economic beginnings suffer intrapsychic difficulties, including success neurosis, as a function of growing up in a Euro-American-normative and affluence-normative world. As Frosh (1989, p. 247) pointed out, a racist society has a major stake in keeping racial minorities unsuccessful and in devaluing lower-class status because racists find it convenient to make 'blackness, femininity and the unconscious [stand for] the subversion of mastery'. Here, it is important to note that racism is not about race alone. It encompasses any and all aspects of humanity which one group uses opportunistically to dominate and diminish another group, including gender (Dias and Chebabi, 1987; Holmes, 2002). Seeking to succeed by breaking away from such domination and diminishment is to expose oneself to dangers. Failing to succeed or wrecking one's success may be adopted as a way of binding the aggression that would be necessary for escape but for which retaliative aggression would be severe. For example, actual attacks (as in police brutality or various forms of institutionalized racism such as housing discrimination and glass ceiling effects) often are riveting and compelling realities. As Szekely noted (1960, p. 49): 'Success and danger are very closely connected.'

Ordinary (neurotic) intrapsychic dangers related to the vicissitudes and calamities of growing up (e.g. Oedipal dangers) may draw the 'real' dangers into the intrapsychic realm. As Frosh noted (1989, p. 225), all of us are subject to internalizing 'the power relationships that are structured into the social world'.

THE THEORY OF SUCCESS NEUROSIS UPDATED

Beyond Freud's contribution in his paper about his disavowal of the Acropolis, Horney's (1936) work bears notice. She viewed success neurosis as a form of negative therapeutic reaction that derived from conflicted aggression and superego pressures. More recent literature is focused on a discussion of a broader range of developmental and conflictual problems thought to be implicated in success neurosis. Examples include Frank's (1977) work on the role of pre-Oedipal factors in success neurosis (Frank, 1977) and Szekely's efforts (1960) to show the effects of trauma on success neurosis (e.g. failure to neutralize aggression and libido).

Levy *et al.* (1995) built on Szekely's work to elaborate the symptom picture for patients with success neurosis whose capacities for neutralization have been thwarted. Levy *et al.* studied patients who had experienced traumas during the separation–individuation phase and who as adults suffered from success neurosis. They determined that such patients wrecked their successes in states of inflated narcissistic self-sufficiency in which promotions and other successes were subject to disruption by grandiose excitement and manic exhibitionism. Schafer (1984) found similarly that those wrecked by success experienced masochistically entrenched suffering that was organized by 'an extravagant ego ideal with respect to which the self must always fall short; a severe superego with respect to which every pleasure must be paid for with painful guilt and self-destructiveness, and the sexualization of suffering itself' (p. 399).

How, then, do we relate the developments of theory of success neurosis, including the findings about underlying severe ego damage, with the race and class factors at the center of this writing? It is important to keep in mind that for patients in downtrodden groups, the ego is subject to the domination of the superego structured by ordinary neurotic influences *and* those of dominant, dominating and diminishing social groups as well.

PSYCHOANALYTIC TREATMENT, SUCCESS NEUROSIS, RACE AND SOCIAL CLASS

The prevailing literature puts great emphasis on modification of the dire effects of racism through exposure to good new objects. This approach is best exemplified in the work of Foster (1993) and Altman (1993). For the various ways in which urban poor patients may wreck their treatment (e.g. failures to show for appointments), Altman recommended that the analyst's role is to determine 'what sort of object the analyst is . . . [for the patient] and how to strike the proper balance between new and old objects to facilitate analytic work' (p. 40). Both eschew absolutely the value of working from an ego-psychological point of view, while Bergman (1993) cautioned that Altman's dismissal of ego-psychological points of view is facile. Her point was that it is necessary to build a bridge between object-relations approaches and ego-psychological ones when addressing the entrenched suffering of the urban poor.

In my review of Altman (Holmes, 1997), I argue that patients need the benefits of all existing clinical theories. Writers such as Altman, Foster and, to some extent, Bergman emphasize a narrow range of object-relational theory having to do with the containing function of the therapist as good new object, to relieve pressure on the patient from his or her enormous rage. Indeed, the analytic therapist must be able to function as a container, *but more is required and some patients are capable of more.* First though, I need to point out the difficulties in a therapist becoming a new object in the eyes of the patient cohorts in focus in this chapter. The therapist to such patients, of whatever race, ethnicity or class origin, has by dint of having become a therapist, embodied significant identifications with the dominant culture, including attitudes about race and class. The patient intuits this fact and will, on the basis of it, as well as on the basis of projection, view the 'new object' *not as good*, but as filled with venomous rage and its corollaries of prejudice and racism. An interpretive approach that is informed by these facts and understands the narcissistic vulnerabilities in such patients is one that sees containing as a necessary early step aimed at stabilization of the patient. Gradually, in an established environment of safety the patient may be able to begin to recognize these noxious forces as existing not only in the therapist and the outer world but in him- or herself as well. So, an object-relational approach that contains and then facilitates ego expansion is necessary, as in the therapist-focused interpretive approach of Steiner (1993).

What is the more that is necessary beyond becoming a good new object to persons wrecked by success in whom race and class pressures play primary roles? Recognition of wounded narcissism is paramount. Levy *et al.*, Frank and Szekely (reviewed above) point to the need for techniques that address self-psychological instability in patients for whom class and race are important factors in their treatment. Such factors add to the narcissistic vulnerability of patients. This fact is noted well in the work of Thompson (1995). She focused on an African-American professional male patient who suffered great narcissistic injury resulting from early aban-donment by his mother and from feelings that as a black man it was unbehooving for him to be successful. Thompson saw his difficulties as stemming from a coalescence of conflicted intrapsychic issues, self-regulatory issues, and societal oppression. Moskowitz (1995) also notes the need to be cognizant of 'the terrible costs in narcissistic injury paid by those who are traumatized by oppression' (p. 551). Similarly, regarding crises of narcissism, Schafer wrote, 'self psychological considerations may help gain access to fear of a latent grandiose self and of latent exhibitionism . . . [One must show] a keen attentiveness to the mix of oedipal and preoedipal factors in these narcissistic crises' (pp. 401–2).

Thus far, we have brought our treatment approaches current to include the role of multi-faceted object-relational approaches and self-psychological points of view. It is also important to point out why a focus on ego psychology is of particular importance for the subjects of this chapter. The work of Gray (1994) is particularly germane, for his work is focused on the ways in which the ego's freest uses are limited by the patient's defensive reliance on condemning and affection-seeking elements in the superego. He pointed out that patients are prone to re-externalizing threatening superego activity onto the person of the therapist. For the subjects of this chapter, such defensive use of the therapist is especially likely because the potential for aggression to be defensively turned on the self comes from two sources: the ordinary neurotic conflicts found in all patients plus internalizations of the condemning and dominating other inherent in racism. On this point,

Gray's technical approach is especially sage: 'I take the position that optimal analysis of the superego . . . is best achieved by perceiving and interpreting superego manifestations mobilized during the analytic situation, primarily as part of the ego's defensive activities' (1994, p. 120). Gray further pointed out that without such an approach patients remain crippled in the self-observing and conscious executive capacities of their egos, and thus in their potential for mastery of their urges and motivations, especially aggression.

Gray's contributions help us further to see that the popular object relations-derived recommendations for treatment of racially or economically downtrodden patients are too restrictive, as has already been reviewed. What Gray adds is that the limited use of object-relational approaches as advised by Altman *et al.* does not address the ego-restricting multiple, complex frustrations imposed on patients living in a racist society. Experientially, for these patients, success is inextricably entwined with domination. Thus, to become free to succeed requires disentangling oneself from the feeling that one is 'fraternizing (that is, identifying) with the enemy' by being aggressive since all aggression is likely to be viewed as essentially bad, if not evil.

Succeeding requires mastery of the material reality of racism and of the internalizations of its condemning aggression and the aspersions it casts on one's sexuality. Since all of these factors limit effective use of one's capacities, they are likely to be enlisted by the ordinary causal factors in neurosis to increase inhibition. For example, guilt over one's erotic feelings for a parent or over one's wishes to triumph over a sibling is likely to be magnified by the guilt and self-doubt which racism sets up in the mind of the downtrodden patient. Thus, racism can play a major role in the onset of success neurosis and in resistance to its cure. That is, since racism is so 'real', it may be more ready-to-hand to think of one's downtrodden status as caused and perpetuated by the material reality of racism alone. Such is safer than to think of the real fact of racism as having been drawn into the intrapsychic world. To accept the latter is to accept the presence of a dreadfully burdensome form of internalized racism (e.g. frightening aggression expressed as self-hate or as a horribly disturbing unruly rage) working in cahoots with intrapsychic elements common to all neurotic illness.

Therapeutic work which is focused on all of the interacting factors and their uses to fend off dangerous urges is essentially a task aimed at ego expansion such that patients can learn to manage and use their motivations and urges successfully, without the taint of racism spoiling success. Gray's work makes clear that the limited object-relational approach already critiqued (with singular emphasis on therapist as good new object) used alone would run the risk of iatrogenically increasing the patient's reliance on a superego-dominated defense. This is so because patients are prone to defensively exporting their aggression to their therapists and to look for the therapist to be the good new object (i.e. superego-dominated search for the beneficent other) or the bad new object (i.e. superego-dominated search for the punishing other). Psychic equilibrium may be accomplished in this manner. However, if the treatment was limited to this approach for patients in the more normal-neurotic to moderately characterologically disturbed range, the gains they could make in treatment in conflict resolution, acquisition of richer object-relational capacity and robustness of self might be stymied.

What is gained by working in the prescribed ways to include expanded object-relational work, Gray's ego-psychological work and self-psychological perspectives? I believe that by so doing, the patient achieves freedom for self-observation and conscious control of capacities and urges which had been encumbered by neurosis. The attainment of freedom in one's mind, that is the freedom to use all of one's resources and powers, is a powerful antidote to the denial of such freedoms imposed by prejudice and racism. In the search for such higher-level functioning, we need to rely on the benefits afforded by multiple clinical theories and techniques that are used alternately as the clinical situation demands. Here, I am recommending a pluralistic approach as discussed cogently by Pray (2002).

CLINICAL ILLUSTRATION

A case report follows to illustrate a way of understanding and working with patients whose downtrodden identity and conflicts related to race and/or class kept them from knowing and realizing the horizons to which their minds could take them.

This is the case of Ms. Smith, who as a single African-American woman began analysis at age 30 with complaints of multiple failures in intimate relationships with men who humiliated and left her. She also expressed that she was feeling stressed by her work as an associate in a very high-profile, super-competitive advertising firm. Ms. Smith minimized her ambition, and just as analysis began, changed jobs to take a position as a public relations specialist in a corporation in which she thought she would not have to compete. She suffered from an anxiety disorder with narcissistic features.

Ms. Smith was the oldest of five children including one brother who was the second youngest. Ms. Smith's mother gave birth to the next youngest sister when Ms. Smith was 18 months old, at which time her mother suffered the first of several depressions that recurred over the course of the patient's childhood and adolescence. My patient felt that her mother loved and indulged her less than she did her three sisters and brother. She defended against envious aggression towards her mother and siblings with altruistic surrender, especially to the sister closest to her in age. For example, she declined lessons in horseback riding in favor of her sister, and could defeat her sister in competitive swimming practice, but not in actual competition. At the beginning of fifth grade, my patient was made to transfer to a mostly black public neighborhood school. The patient understood this move as face-saving for her father who was a member of the local school board. In the new school the patient felt like an outsider when her classmates rejected her on the basis that she had lighter skin color than the majority of them. She continued to excel academically, but failed socially by hiding her quite good looks with calculated inattention to her grooming and dress. With this self-effacement and abnegation she tried to arrest the guilt she felt for the perceived and real advantages she had over her schoolmates – both in terms of higher social class and over-valued light skin color; she began to cultivate a downtrodden self. She expressed the latter by capitulating to her next youngest sister, especially in sports.

At times, Ms. Smith's transference reactions included the expectation that I would treat her badly by depriving her of the maternal nurturing she had always sought. The dread was racialized in that she thought that my deprivation of her would be based on the fact that I am a medium-brown-skinned African-American woman and that I would envy her light skin color as her schoolmates had. The work on this transference manifestation included unpacking her racialized reactions in several ways:

1   I acknowledged its 'realness' among African-Americans as a source of envy and divisiveness. In so doing, I contained her feelings as a good new object does.
2   In addition, as her suspicion of me decreased, she began to idealize me. Within the safety of that idealization, she could begin to examine her sense of herself as devalued and denigrated. She traced these states to how she felt in the inferior school of her middle-school years. She came to understand that the emphasis in her thinking (that the darker-skinned and poor kids hated her) was in part a projection of her anger towards her parents for having placed her in an inferior school. Deeper still, she came to realize that she had felt placed into an inferior (impoverished) position in the family (e.g. too brief a period as the only child and too long a period of her mother's repeated withdrawals into clinical depression). The interpretive approach taken came as much from an informed object-relational framework as it did from an ego-psychological one. For example, I made use of Steiner's (1993) object-relational approach in which painful states are not just contained by the therapist, but also are interpreted, but first in their projected form in what he calls 'therapist-focused' interpretations. So, I would say to the patient, 'You experience me as being hateful towards you as your downtrodden, lower-class schoolmates were.' As the patient stabilized

in the treatment, she was able to move more to a consideration of such feelings as being in herself.

3   I interpreted the complex defensive meanings of race and class for the patient, including their uses as a displacement away from the ways she felt set apart from her family, that is by what she experienced to be their indifference to her needs and their impoverishment of her. Eventually, she was able to make use of an interpretation that she riveted herself to the limitations and hatred imposed by racist society as a displacement and projection away from the envy she felt towards family members. She came to see that this was especially so concerning the loving bond that she felt existed between her mother and next youngest sister.

As Ms. Smith worked through the complex ways in which she relied on race and racism (including internalizing the stigma of lower-class status to reinforce her feelings of being oppressed), her motivation to succeed became more freed up, albeit with periodic regressions and symptoms. For example, she became able to run for and won the presidency of the local chapter of a black women's civic organization. To effectively challenge the incumbent on her mismanagement of a major issue, the patient needed to secure a copy of the organization's by-laws. Hurriedly, en route to a meeting, she arranged to have a colleague pass her the by-laws through a window of the colleague's townhouse. As Ms. Smith reached up for the document, she fell down and shattered her knee. She came to understand that in hurting herself she was turning on herself the underlying unacceptable aggression in her ambition, including her wish to get rid of her troubling rival who symbolically represented her sister, behind whom she had often 'fallen' in their youth.

Introjected racism – that is, light skin color as a criterion for success and a source of envy – was often the surface of the work for this patient, and working in the various ways just illustrated provided a pathway to the understanding of the patient's neurotic illness. For example, after many such efforts in the middle of her nearly seven years of analysis, the patient recalled a fact of her early life that had been told to her by an uncle many years before, but had been repressed until midway through her analysis. The fact was that when the patient was three years old, her uncle observed her run up to her then 18-month-old sister and knock her off the patient's play horse, causing her younger sister to cut her lip and bleed profusely which horrified the patient. The patient then worked through the aspect of her altruism that was a reaction formation against her hostile aggression towards the sister. This insight contributed to her being able to acknowledge her aggression consciously and to use it judiciously, as in extricating herself from an exploitative financial arrangement with the same sister, an arrangement she had made early in the analysis to reinforce forfeiture of her freedom.

Discussion

I have attempted to show that race and low expectations associated with lower social class status enter the intrapsychic realm. They are used to bind unpleasure coming from three sources: actual experiences with racism in relation to race and social class, the internal self and object representations of those realities; and ordinary neurotic conflicts. I have tried to illustrate two propositions about the material reality of living in a culture of perpetual racism: that it becomes a causal link in the onset of success neurosis for those on the receiving end of racist practices and that it adds to the resistance to cure. Given the palpable, unrelieved and insistent presence of racism, it becomes a powerful source of resistance since its reality and its wretchedly damaging effects are so obvious and are ever present as a personal frame of reference. It is relieving for the neurotic or otherwise compromised ego, especially in the management of aggression, to fix on the irrationalities, specifically the brutalities of others. As Sandler noted (1990, p. 874):

> Even if the presences in fantasy are persecuting, guilt-making ones, they nevertheless have the function of *carrying the individual's own projected aggression* [italics added] while at the same time providing a background feeling of safety.

In the main current writers recommend the use of an object-relational point of view that emphasizes providing the patient with a good new object to quell unrest inasmuch as the good new object promotes 'reciprocal interactions' (Foster, 1993). To the extent that such an approach can have binding mutative effects, it must be viewed as a first step for patients who can do more insightful work. The other steps include interpretations of internal objects v. the therapist as good new object just containing the patient's projected object representations, and the use of self-psychological and ego-psychological methods for patients who can do more insightful work.

With the use of a clinical case, I have tried to demonstrate the efficacy of a pluralistic theoretical approach. This approach includes a multi-pronged focus on internal objects, the self and the ego. Apropos 'ego', the focus is not on adaptation *per se* but on encumbered functions and capacities that can be freed by the recommended methods despite the patient's stubbornly adherent success neurosis.

I will conclude by quoting an African-American woman who came to recognize that the powers of her mind were greater than those of the obstacles related to race and class that others sought to place in her path. I refer to Dr. Ruth Simmons who became President of Brown University in 2000. She is the first African-American to lead an Ivy League University. Upon being named to her post (President of Smith College, 1994), she commented, 'It was clear in the Jim Crow South that I (daughter of sharecroppers) was not to expect opportunities, *but I knew that my mind could take me anywhere* [italics added]' (Simmons, 1994). For our patients who have been similarly circumstanced, we need to engage as much of their total psyches in treatment as possible. We need to include the self, a multi-faceted approach to their internal objects and their egos in order to aid them to find and to claim the fullest possible freedom in their minds. This work needs to emphasize all encumbering influences, including the manifest and dynamic meanings of race and social class.

References

Altman, N. (1993) Psychoanalysis and the Urban Poor, *Psychoanalytic Dialogues* 3: 29–49.

Bergman, A. (1993) Ego Psychological and Object Relational Approaches – Is it Either/Or? Commentary on Neil Altman's 'Psychoanalysis and the Urban Poor', *Psychoanalytic Dialogues* 3: 51–67.

Dias, C. and Chebabi, W. (1987) Psychoanalysis and the Role of Black Life and Culture in Brazil, *International Review of Psychoanalysis* 14: 185–202.

Fenichel, O. (1945) *The Psychoanalytic Theory of Neurosis*. New York: Norton.

Foster, R. (1993) The Social Politics of Psychoanalysis: Commentary on Neil Altman's 'Psychoanalysis and the Urban Poor', *Psychoanalytic Dialogues* 3: 69–83.

Frank, H. (1977) Dynamic Patterns for Failure in College Students, *Canadian Psychiatric Association Journal* 22: 295–299.

Freud, S. (1916) Those Wrecked by Success, *Standard Edition*, 14: 316–331.

Freud, S. (1919) A Child is Being Beaten, *Standard Edition*, 17: 175–204.

Freud, S. (1936) A Disturbance of Memory on the Acropolis, *Standard Edition*, 22: 239–248.

Frosh, S. (1989) The Racist Subject, in S. Frosh (ed.), *Psychoanalysis and Psychology*, pp. 207–256.

Galatzer-Levy, R. and Cohler, B. (2002) Making a Gay Identity: Coming Out, Social Context and Psychodynamics, *The Annual of Psychoanalysis* 30: 255–286.

Gray, P. (1994) *The Ego and Analysis of Defense*. New York: Jason Aronson.

Holmes, D. (1997) A critique of N. Altman's *The Analyst in the Inner City*. Hillsdale, NJ: The Analytic Press; 1995, *Journal of the American Psychoanalytic Association* 45: 644–648.

Holmes, D. (2002) 'Glass Ceilings': Their Origins, Psychodynamic Manifestations and Consequences in Women, in B. Seelig, R. Paul and C. Levy (eds), *Constructing and Deconstructing Women's Power*. London: Karnac Books.

Horney, K. (1936) The Problem of the Negative Therapeutic Reaction, *Psychoanalytic Quarterly* 5: 29–44.

Levy, S., Seelig, B. and Inderbitzin, L. (1995) On Those Wrecked by Success: A Clinical Inquiry, *Psychoanalytic Quarterly* 64: 639–657.

Moskowitz, M. (1995) Ethnicity and Fantasy of Ethnicity, *Psychoanalytic Psychology* 12: 547–556.

Pray, M. (2002) The Classical/Relational Schism and Psychic Conflict, *Journal of the American Psychoanalytic Association* 50: 249–280.

Sandler, J. (1990) On Internal Object Relations, *Journal of the American Psycho-analytic Association* 38: 859–880.

Schafer, R. (1984) The Pursuit of Failure and the Idealization of Unhappiness, *American Psychologist* 39: 398–405.

Simmons, R. (1994) First Black President Chosen for a 'Seven Sisters' School, *Washington Post*, December 16.

Steiner, J. (1993) *Psychic Retreats*. London and New York: Routledge, Ch. 11.

Szekely, L. (1960) Success, Success Neurosis and the Self, *British Journal of Medical Psychology* 33: 45–51.

Thompson, C. (1995) Self-Definition by Opposition: A Consequence of Minority Status, *Psychoanalytic Psychology* 12: 533–546.

Spirituality, cultural healing and psychotherapy

Chapter 16

Healing and exorcism in psychoanalytic practice

Nathan Field

> The psychotherapist is the true successor to the exorcist . . . he is concerned not only with the 'forgiveness of sins' but also with the 'casting out of devils'.
>
> (W. R. D. Fairbairn)

The incentive to write this chapter was prompted by an uncomfortable piece of self-observation. The proper attitude for the practice of psychotherapy is, as Freud termed it, one of 'benevolent neutrality'. But when I reflected how I actually functioned from patient to patient and session to session it was evident that I deviated from this ideal on many occasions. My attitude varied from one patient to the next, and even within the same session could shift from the empathic to the confrontational and back again. Most disturbing was the recognition that with some patients I was often inclined to be challenging while with others it was difficult not to be empathic.

In the empathic mode I listened very closely but said little; it was as if I were engaged in holding the patient within my understanding, as a mother might hold her baby. Some interpretations felt like a kind of feeding, as if I wished to infuse the patient with calm and well-being. There were often long, comfortable silences which could deepen into an intimate dreaminess; virtually nothing happened, yet patients would remember these episodes as 'nourishing', even 'blissful'. I certainly enjoyed these intimate silences and, to allay my guilt at what felt like self-indulgence, I privately hoped my patient might derive some healing from the experience.

Whereas in the confrontational mode the climate was decidedly cooler, even bracing; the patient was not held close but was 'over there', sharply etched, separate; my voice had acquired a keener edge, my eyes and ears alert for unconscious evasions, denials, confusions and manipulations. Especially memorable were those sessions where the patient manifestly sabotaged the therapeutic process. At such times I felt the presence of something stubborn, destructive, perverse; a malign force that I was determined to expose and defeat. More than once I had the bizarre fantasy that I was engaged in a kind of exorcism.

Both states seemed a long way from the dispassionate objectivity required of the analyst, yet both the 'benign healer' and the 'forceful exorcist' proved, on occasion, to be therapeutically effective. Empathic listening seemed to relieve very agitated patients of their panic, while those I challenged might later express their gratitude that I was prepared to do battle with something they had always hated in themselves. I began to reconsider whether what I had often feared was a serious lapse from good practice might actually be an appropriate therapeutic response to that patient at that moment? The healer and the exorcist of earlier ages had been ready to engage deeply with their patients and even to risk their own souls on their behalf. A closer look at the current analytic literature might reveal that these archaic, non-analytic, modes of treatment persisted to this day amongst analytic practitioners of our own generation.

A BRIEF LOOK AT TRADITIONAL HEALING

Psychoanalysis, which began with Freud, is little more than a century old and therefore still in its infancy when compared to traditional healing which can be traced back to the beginnings of human society. Traditional healing is still actively practised at the present time in pre-technological communities all over the world. In Western societies there also exists a multiplicity of 'alternative' medical and spiritual healing methods, usually associated with holistic health philosophies, neo-religious cults and charismatic religious movements. While the range of traditional healing techniques is enormously diverse, they all subscribe to a central presupposition about human nature. The scientific model, on which modern medicine is based, treats the body as a physical object that works in the manner of a machine. Thus there exists a wide range of medical specialists for every bodily organ: heart, lungs, liver, eyes, brain, bones, etc., supported by state funding and medical insurance. Traditional healing makes the radically different assumption that within (or beside or around or beyond) the physical body there exists another 'body' that can be neither seen nor touched but which profoundly affects both our mental and physical health. This other body has been called by many names: the subtle body, the etheric body, the psyche, mind, soul, spirit, self, the will to live, etc. It is doubtful if there exists a language that does not make reference to this mysterious entity or power. In modern times it has been called *élan vital* (Bergson), the *It* (Groddeck), the *Id* (Freud), *libido* (Jung), *orgone energy* (Wilhelm Reich), or simply the *Unconscious*. Each of these terms carries a somewhat different connotation yet they all point to an indefinable core concept; while none of them adequately captures the underlying reality, each could be regarded as reflecting the differing modes in which this reality has been experienced and conceptualized. For the purposes of this chapter I shall call it by the ancient name widely used in India: *prana*.

Pranic energy is sensed among the population at large in the form of 'vibes'. More specific responses may be experienced by those who are especially open to its presence; many describe it as akin to heat; others as an internal vibratory flow. This flow can vary in intensity from the mildly pleasant to the ecstatic, hence those who have experienced it never quite forget it and some are inclined to seek it again and again. The writer D. H. Lawrence, for example, was one of many creative artists who was singularly responsive to its presence which he sensed in nature, in people, and even inanimate objects. Along with Wilhelm Reich and practitioners of Tantric yoga, Lawrence found access to his most sublime pranic experiences in sex. The close association between prana and sexual energy has long been noted and has constituted a serious deterrent to research into its healing potential (Chertok, 1988). When Mesmer's activities were investigated in 1784 it was noted that many of his female patients rapidly went into a state akin to sexual arousal, culminating in convulsions reminiscent of orgasm. This connection with sexuality was a major factor that led orthodox medicine to repudiate Mesmer's healing methods. In our own day, psychoanalysis has emphasized the sexualized quality of transference and is equally alert to its dangers. There appears to be an undeniable area of overlap between pranic and sexual energy: while they are confusingly interwoven, closer investigation reveals that they are not in fact identical.

Another type of psychic sensitivity claims to 'see' prana with paranormal vision, and describes it as a kind of radiation emanating from the body. The bulk of the aura is said to extend about six feet around each individual. This is well within the physical distance between patient and therapist in the consulting room, and may have bearing on their unconscious interaction. The colours of this complex flow of energy around the body or particular organs are said to reflect states of health as well as states of mind. Pranic radiation seems connected with actual electrical charges in the body, especially those emitted by the brain. Research with bio-feedback apparatus suggests a close connection between prana, electricity and brain waves, although prana cannot be measured directly on any known apparatus. Again, while prana manifests in ways analogous to electricity, the two forces are not the same.

Pranic energy is paradoxical in yet another respect: it feels connected with the innermost area of our personal life yet at the same time it seems immeasurably beyond the personal. Experience of it frequently evokes feelings akin to religious awe. Jung dealt with this paradox by distinguishing between the personal unconscious (which he identified with the Freudian 'id') and the collective unconscious which has affinities with notions of a 'world soul'; he likewise differentiated between 'self' and Self;

or normal dreams and archetypal dreams. They are undoubtedly different yet bafflingly interconnected.

Is pranic energy a reality or an age-old delusion? Certainly it seems difficult to make sense of a 'subtle' body that exists prior to our physical body; of a form of energy that certain people feel within themselves and others claim to see with paranormal vision; that functions like electricity but cannot be measured; that feels both personal yet supra-personal; that heals but can, if uncontrolled, damage and destroy; that evokes associations of intense sexual arousal but equally of the Holy Spirit; that can be reached through dreams, personal rapport, meditation, prayer, drugs, hypnosis, and a variety of other ways known from time immemorial. In whatever mode pranic energy is envisaged all healing practitioners accept that our mental and physical well-being is fundamentally dependent on it and therefore seek ways to understand, generate and control it. One basic finding seems to be that excessive activity of the thinking processes inhibits its flow both in the healer and the recipient. Hence traditional healing invariably took place in states of relaxation or in various altered states of consciousness.

In the Asclepian healing rites of ancient Greece the sufferer, after suitable psychological preparation, would enter the temple of healing, lie down on a pallet, and fall into a healing sleep. The god Asclepius would come to him, advise on the treatment to be followed or himself heal the illness. Alternatively the afflicted part might be touched, kissed or licked in the dream by a dog or snake, and the patient would later awake, cured.

Anton Mesmer, a celebrated healer who discovered hypnotism, likewise effected his cures outside of consciousness. He became known through his cure of a severely afflicted young woman who, in the course of her first treatment, went into a hypnotic trance and felt streams of energy flowing down through her body. Mesmer was convinced that this energy emanated from his own person since he directly felt its presence within him. He called it 'animal magnetism'. Mesmer's method aimed to provoke a series of crises in the patient, each of which would prove to be less severe than its predecessor until they eventually disappeared and the patient was considered cured. In Mesmer's view, disease originated in the unequal distribution of the 'magnetic fluid' in the body and his technique aimed to restore its correct equilibrium.

Mesmer's 'animal magnetism', which came out of his personal experience, is very similar to the ancient Chinese concept of *chi*. 'Chi is the primordial life force itself . . . also known as prana, sperm, ovarian or kundalini power' (Chia, 1983). The Taoist or yogic techniques envisage generating this vital energy by means of mental exercises and directing it upward from the sexual centre at the base of the spine through successively higher power centres known as chakras. The benefits are claimed to be improved physical and mental health, rejuvenation, longevity, and ultimately spiritual liberation. Those with an abundant store of this precious fluid can heal others by the 'jump lead' effect; by passing repeated charges of 'chi' through the body of the healee they stimulate their life force. This time-honoured method sounds like a benign version of the use of ECT in mental hospitals. It may also have been the source of Mesmer's healing effect. The most ancient of the traditional healing techniques, shamanism, is perhaps also the most extraordinary. The shaman's principal function is the retrieval of lost souls. According to ancient belief, the soul may be stolen by an evil spirit, especially during sleep; it is the shaman's job to track it down, bargain with its captors, and return it safely to its owner. There is abundant documentation of shamanic healing from every part of the globe. The procedures vary from tribe to tribe and country to country, but in all of them the shaman is required to enter into a state of trance. This is the reverse of the Asclepian or Mesmeric method where it is the patient, not the healer, who goes into trance. Eliade (1964) describes characteristic practices among the tribes of Siberia:

> the Tremyugan shaman begins beating his drum and playing the guitar until he falls into an ecstasy. Abandoning his body, his soul enters the underworld and goes in search of the patient's soul. He persuades the dead to let him bring it back to earth by promising them the gift of a shirt or other things: sometimes he is obliged to use more forcible means. When he wakes from his ecstasy the shaman has the patient's soul in his closed right hand and replaces it in the body through the right ear.

Shamanic healing certainly seems a far cry from anything a psychotherapist might recognize. Could we possibly find any points of contact between the above example and contemporary psychotherapy?

HEALING IN ANALYTICAL PSYCHOTHERAPY

I suggest we must first ask if there exists any modern equivalent to the condition known as 'loss of soul'? In his description of the schizoid personality Fairbairn, one of the founders of object relations theory, offers the following profile: 'the individual begins to tell us that he feels as if there were nothing of him, or as if he had lost his identity, or as if he were dead, or as if he had ceased to exist' (Fairbairn, 1952). Schizoid pathology manifests in varying degrees: it ranges from transient episodes of 'looking on at oneself' in an embarrassing situation, through a distressingly persistent 'plate glass feeling', leading to an overwhelming sense of futility and meaninglessness. Finally, there are the frankly schizophrenic conditions of depersonalization and derealization which Fairbairn describes as the 'ultimate psychological disaster', namely 'loss of ego'.

If there is one undisputed finding to emerge from the mass of studies on infant development, it is the disastrous consequences of parental failure in early life. The clinical implications were clearly spelled out in Fairbairn's 1941 paper, 'A revised psychopathology of the psychoses and the psycho-neuroses'. In it he proposes that all major psychological disorders can be best understood as defences against 'loss of ego'. Winnicott made a similar statement when he asserted that schizophrenia was an 'environmental deficiency disease'. Guntrip elaborated how the failure to develop a primary bond between the infant and its mother resulted in a profound, though often disguised, absence of the will to live. Bowlby's extensive studies reinforce the same message. Although Jungian terminology differentiates between 'ego' and 'self', in Fairbairn 'loss of ego' refers precisely to the same condition as the age-old notion of the 'loss of soul'. This would bring object relations theory, which is an integral part of psychoanalysis, very close to the presuppositions of traditional healing. It means that psycho-logical treatment has essentially to do with a primary connection that speaks to the soul, that renders life meaningful, and in the absence of which, especially in childhood, we fall ill.

Nevertheless current psychoanalytic research still concentrates on the facilitation of insight. It may be argued that understanding is the highest form of love; but we must remember that while insight may be an instru-ment of love, without the pre-existing primary connection it remains much less meaningful. For Freud love, in the form of positive transference, had its value in holding the patient in the treatment while the painful process of unmasking the id went on. He never saw it as a therapeutic agent in its own right. Indeed love could become a serious obstacle if the patient attempted to re-enact with the analyst the infantile attachments of the past instead of simply remembering them.

The vast literature on transference and countertransference, while never denying the importance of the analyst–patient relationship, in fact rarely describes it in a straightforward manner. With few exceptions, the phobic anxieties around countertransference result in the jargon-ridden, neo-scientific language of mental mechanisms. Even in the papers of Fairbairn and Guntrip the analyst's care and love are never openly acknowledged, they are only implied. Balint, who emphasized the necessity of primary love, rarely gives us a glimpse of how things really felt inside his consulting room, beyond admitting that 'when the patient is nearing the area of basic fault' the atmosphere can become 'highly charged'.

Yet even from the earliest years of the psychoanalytic movement, and in spite of Freud's admonitions, the therapeutic value of the mutual involve-ment of analyst and patient held an important place. Ferenczi's descriptions of the effect of his 'relaxation technique' show patients falling into trance-like states (1930). Ferenczi also attempted heroic treatments which included a close professional intimacy with selected patients. Freud viewed these experiments with profound disquiet and their subsequent failure confirmed his scepticism.

Jung explicitly incorporated the 'personal factor' into his therapeutic procedure, but it was this approach that, in the case of Sabina Speilrein, brought him into considerable professional discredit. Yet Jung's intense personal involvement with this severely disturbed young woman, his readiness to meet her at deep levels of his inner life, may well have been the crucial factor that healed her. If she suffered damage at his hand, in her view it was not through their intimate connection so much as Jung's panicky withdrawal from it. Given Jung's attitude that the analyst heals through his personality, analytical psychologists have generally found it less difficult to admit their involvement in the analytic relationship and can use such words as 'healing' or 'soul' without too much embarrassment.

Amongst the psychoanalysts perhaps none is so self-disclosing as Harold Searles. The crucial phase of interaction with his schizophrenic patients, which he describes as 'pre-ambivalent symbiosis' (1965), is simply a technical name for the primary healing relationship. In like manner Margaret Little advocates a total commitment of the analyst's self in the therapeutic relationship. The quality that characterizes the work of these analysts (and others whom space precludes me from quoting) is their trust in some pre-existing healing power in themselves and in their patients, and their readiness to become deeply involved in the therapeutic process in order to mobilize it.

In my own clinical experience schizoid personalities are not always manifestly withdrawn: they may be openly talkative or convey the impression of earnest self-examination. But within very few sessions I find it increasingly difficult to sustain any real interest in what they talk about. Sooner or later a cold, almost nightmarish, deadness takes over, in which the absence of an inner connection between myself and patient is almost palpable. Any interpretation that comes to mind feels either self-evident, unutterably banal, or just meaningless. It is as if the absence of a communicational matrix denudes even the most insightful interpretations of any relevance. With most patients this happens intermittently; with others it pervades session after session.

Direct efforts to engage with the patient frequently prove counter-productive. But if neither questioning nor interpreting have any effect, how are we to deal with the situation? Bion advocates the cultivation of a state of reverie. Jung talks of a 'lowering of consciousness' in order to reach a 'participation mystique'. Searles disclosed that he gradually learned to allow himself to sit in silence for whole sessions with patients and not even think about them. Balint spoke of a 'harmonious and interpenetrating mix-up'. I find this can sometimes be reached by letting the mind slip into neutral, even to wander, and let the silence unfold without anxiety. In this state of free-floating inattention my unconscious seems to steal up on the patient's unconscious, rather like the entranced shaman of old.

Very often states of unrelatedness affect me like a powerful anaesthetic, and I find myself overcome by acute drowsiness. When this occurs with markedly schizoid patients it is a singularly unpleasant experience: I feel cold, almost bloodless, as if near to dying. I long to sleep but something in the patient absolutely forbids me to do so. The same phenomenon has been described by Dennis Brown (1977) and others. It is worth commenting that whereas pranic or 'life' energy can be felt as warmth, or seen as light, or waves of psychedelic colour when your eyes are closed, negative 'anti-life' states induce an uncanny coldness and greyness. Exorcists frequently refer to the sudden drop in temperature felt in the presence of diabolical influences. Mystical literature often refers to fragrances of unearthly beauty, including the 'odour of sanctity', while the records of diabolical possession remark on the presence of singularly foul smells. Among therapists, more than one colleague has assured me he can 'smell' a schizophrenic. It may be that any of the sensory modalities could be involved. All these non-ordinary sensory responses might be thought to relate essentially to the 'subtle body' but are translated into sensory experience via the physical body.

My own reaction to a schizoid-type patient is to be flooded by a sense of utter pointlessness, as if the spirits of death and negativity have become active forces in the room. I have little doubt that in these phases I am experiencing, either paranormally or through projective identification, my patient's own 'soulless' state, and the accompanying inner torment. One response is to acknowledge to the patient the state I have fallen into, and explore its intersubjective nature together, as if we have joined forces to defeat a common enemy. With other patients I may just drift off into my private thoughts and trust that we can both fall into the same dreaminess, let it deepen and even doze off. Marked shifts in the affective state may then occur: cold unrelatedness changes mysteriously to positive rapport. On one memorable occasion, in the company of a habitually silent, very schizoid woman, I felt myself actually slipping into a trance. I let it deepen, even though the room had become little more than a blur. At this moment the patient remarked: 'I keep thinking I want to eat your foot. It's funny . . .' and gave a little laugh. My trance cleared instantly, and for the first time, albeit briefly, she looked and sounded normal.

Similar states of drowsiness and disconnection may impose themselves in supervision sessions. It almost always emerges that this had happened between the supervisee and his or her patient, but had not been acknowledged or explored at the time. The phenomenon has been called 'parallel process' and is not uncommon. But the fact that it manifests in this way gives the impression of an unattached complex or spirit that passes from one individual to the next until it can be made conscious or otherwise absorbed.

Broadly speaking, primitive man suffered from two sorts of mental illness: possession and loss of soul. In cases of possession the victim is thought to have been invaded by a spirit, often several, usually the spirit of a dead relative. In some cases the possessed individual remains aware of his original self but 'feels a spirit within his own spirit'; in other cases there is total loss of identity. His features change and take on a striking resemblance to his possessor; voice and speech likewise correspond with uncanny similitude. It should be remembered that not all possession is unwelcome: in cases of mediumship trance states can be induced in order to allow a benign spirit to bring messages of comfort or counsel. But in many cases the spirit is manifestly malignant and cannot voluntarily be expelled. The ancient method of countering possession is exorcism; it has been practised for several thousand years, in particular by peoples of the Mediterranean basin: Jews, Muslims and Christians.

The exorcist's first task is to compel the spirit to say his name. Once this is known the exorcist will forcibly command the spirit to depart. A vivid description may be found in Aldous Huxley's (1952) account of an exorcism by Fr. Barre in 1632 of Sister Jeanne, prioress of the convent at Loudun:

> Speaking through the lips of the demoniac, Asmodeus revealed he was entrenched in the lower belly. For more than two hours Barre wrestled with him: 'exorcise thee, most unclean spirited every onslaught of the Adversary, every spectre, every legion, in the name of our Lord, Jesus Christ, be thou uprooted and put to flight from this creature of God'. And then there would be a sprinkling of holy water, a laying on of hands, a laying on of the stole, of the breviary, of relics. 'I adjure thee, ancient serpent, by the Judge of the living and the dead, by thy maker, by the maker of the world, by him who has the power to cast thee into Gehenna, that from this servant of God, who hastens back to the bosom of the Church, thou with the fears and afflictions of thy fury, speedily depart.'

It will be seen that the exorcist does not speak in his own name but on behalf of the Higher Power that he represents. While encouraging the unfortunate victim he bullies and cajoles the demon who may, as in this case, show great cunning and tenacity. In fact Sister Jeanne was possessed by several demons for many years and was treated by a succession of exorcists, the last of whom, Fr. Surin, himself became infected by the demons he had driven out.

The exorcism of Christoff Haitzmann, which also dates back to the seventeenth century, is especially interesting because the documents describing his condition were analysed by Freud (1925). One day, while in church, Haitzmann was seized by frightful convulsions. On interrogation he revealed that nine years before he had entered into a Pact, 'written in blood', with the Devil. It was a strange agreement. Unlike Faust, who was promised earthly power, knowledge, and the love of beautiful women, Haitzmann confessed to bartering his eternal soul for the curious privilege of becoming the Devil's son – 'the sonne of his bodie' – for nine years. The term of his Pact had now become imminent. Haitzmann pleaded that only the Grace of Mary, Mother of God, could save him from the Devil's clutches. Accordingly he was sent to the monastery of Mariazell where he underwent a prolonged period of prayer and expiation. On 8 September, the birthday of the Virgin, the Devil appeared before him in the form of a winged dragon and handed him back his Pact.

However Haitzmann's troubles did not end there. Leaving Mariazell, he took lodgings with his sister. Within months he was tormented by tempting visions of rich banquets and fair courtesans. These alternated with terrifying threats from Christ himself that he renounce the world and all its temptations. Haitzmann returned in despair to Mariazell, claiming he had yet to redeem an even earlier pact with the Devil, this one written in 'black ink'. After yet more prayer he received this document back too, torn in four pieces, from the hands of the Holy Mother herself. Thereafter he remained at Mariazell as a lay brother, safe with the reverend fathers from the temptations of the world.

Freud comments that: 'cases of demoniacal possession correspond to the neuroses of the present day. What in those days were thought to be evil spirits to us are base and evil wishes, the derivatives of impulses which have been rejected and repressed.' This would certainly apply to Haitzmann's Pact in black ink where he was tempted by oral and sexual impulses, but it sheds no light on his extraordinary Pact 'written in blood' whereby he could be the Devil's own son. Freud observes that Haitzmann had become depressed on the death of his father and comments: 'the man who has fallen into melancholia on account of his father's death must have loved that father deeply. The more curious then that he should have come by the idea of taking the Devil as substitute for a loved parent.' Freud makes sense of this by referring to the ambivalence inherent in all human relationships: dependency, love and gratitude on the one hand; fear, disappointment and hostility on the other. If the latter was predominant in Haitzmann's case, he still preferred a diabolical father to no father at all ('better the devil you know . . .').

Fairbairn comments that Freud's emphasis on Haitzmann's pleasure-seeking libido obscures the underlying significance that Haitzmann's pact with the Devil was that he sought a father. The case, he suggests, supports the object relations point of view in that: 'it admirably illustrates the difficulty encountered by the psycho-neurotic or psychotic in parting from his bad objects.' Given the unresolved debate between proponents of drive theory and object relations theory, Haitzmann's two pacts – the first in black ink, the second in blood – lends credence to the idea that we may become possessed by two kinds of devil: a 'drive-theory' devil deriving from repressed libidinal impulses and an 'object-relations' devil in which the bad object has been defensively introjected. Alternatively Haitzmann's eventual salvation could be described in object relation terms by saying that he was only freed from his sick attachment to a bad object represented by his hated father by finding a good object in the shape of the Holy Mother. In a later comment on this case, Ron Britton (2005) observes that Freud noted that in Haitzmann's paintings of these hallucinatory meetings the devil was depicted as having breasts, and in one, 'a large penis ending in a snake'. Britton concludes that Haitzmann's attachment to his father included a deep longing for a mother, and that Haitzmann's devil represented what Melanie Klein called a 'combined object'.

Fairbairn wrote very persuasively of the addictive attachment to bad objects, and the practice of psychotherapy bears this out. It is a constant source of amazement how many patients repeatedly seek out painful situations, cling to them or to their memory, and somehow contrive to subvert satisfactory relationships into unhappy ones. How can we account for this strange but universal compulsion which flies in the face of the pleasure principle? Fairbairn suggests that our attachment to bad objects is our defence against the dread of an even worse possibility: the loss of ego, inner emptiness, a state we somehow know about but cannot think about or begin to describe. This defensive addiction appears most clearly in the 'negative therapeutic reaction' when the patient would seem to sabotage the therapist's best endeavours. It is as if a spirit of negativity pits itself against the life force that the therapy tries to mobilize. I can recall one instance in which my patient, with what felt uncannily like diabolical obstinacy, retorted: 'Say what you like – I will not yield to you!'

In the face of such perverse resistance a benign 'healing' attitude is quite ineffectual and frequently abused. The therapist who tolerates such abuse merely discredits himself in the eyes of the patient, who is driven to denigrate him still further. It is due to this unrecognized attachment to bad objects that healing alone frequently fails to be effective. In these situations the confrontational style of psychoanalysis, with its readiness to unmask and challenge, is of the greatest value. Searles (1965) observes:

> the relationship between patient and therapist must gradually grow . . . strong enough for the therapist to be able to endure the fullest intensity of the patient's hostility . . . and, complimentarily, I have found it an equally essential part of this phase that the therapist finds himself gradually coming, step by step, to express openly – even though not as often as he feels it – the very fullest intensity of his own hatred, condemnation, and contempt towards the patient.

Winnicott (1949) took the same position when he stated that objective hatred, free of personal bias, may be a necessary response to the patient's destructiveness, and goes even further when he adds:

in certain stages of certain analyses the analyst's hate is actually sought by the patient, and what is then needed is hate that is objective. If the patient seeks objective hate he must be able to reach it, else he cannot feel he can reach objective love.

In practice it is far from easy for those in the helping professions to express hatred towards a patient, however objectively. In each of the following examples the 'neutrally benevolent' analyst was plainly driven to the limit:

> In his third year, he (the patient) suddenly ground to a halt, and fell violently silent, exuding ever stronger black waves of hatred and despair. . . . His gaze, when he glanced at me, was shifty, evil, and terrified. He was as if possessed. . . . I carried dark and heavy projective identifications, to put it one way, which I tried in vain to decode to him, until I was almost as saturated in despair as he was. One day, without thinking it out clearly . . . I simply and suddenly became furious and bawled him out for his prolonged lethal attack on me and on the analysis. I wasn't going to stand for it a second longer, I shouted, without the remotest idea at that moment of what alternative I was proposing. This outburst of mine changed the course of the analysis.
>
> (Coltart, 1986)

Dr Coltart remarks that her patient 'was as if possessed'; it is my contention that the patient really was possessed by a malevolent internal object which the therapist spontaneously exorcized. Here is a similar example:

> She sat stony-faced, never making eye contact with me. As the session wore on I felt her growing disdain, and the tension between us increased . . . I felt totally impotent. . . . I would remind myself she was a woefully unhappy person, arrested in her emotional and psychosexual development, damaged and deprived by the early loss of her mother and by having been left with a cruel and insensitive father.
>
> (Epstein, 1979)

Many therapists will recognize a familiar situation up to this point. After suffering this treatment for some considerable time the analyst consulted one of his supervisors, who responded with a single sentence:

> 'Why don't you use the voice of her father, but not his intention?' This statement was sufficient to dissipate the image I had created of my patient as a vulnerable, love-starved child. I now saw her as a nasty, withholding, contemptuous, uncooperative bitch, and I reacted to her

accordingly. . . . I challenged her stony silences, asking her how in hell she expected me to make any progress in therapy if she refused to talk. . . .? When she exuded contempt I identified it and testily asked her what it was all about. . . . I informed her, with annoyance, that I would be making no further effort to engage her, but that I would respond when she would resume talking. With this change in my behaviour, Marcia's progress was rapid.

(ibid)

A thoroughgoing use of confrontation was developed by Davanloo who specialized in short-term psychotherapy. From the very first encounter onwards he advocates challenging every resistance, evasion, confusion or denial as it arises. If this provokes the patient to anger, so much the better. The open expression of anger appears to rapidly purge the patient of his self-destructive negativity and surprisingly opens the way for the expression of warmth and the strengthening of the therapeutic alliance. Davanloo explicitly warns the therapist against slipping into that type of 'symbiotic transference' which Searles, Balint and others regard as valuable when dealing with schizophrenic or narcissistic disorders. Davanloo's short-term technique (which he recommends for only carefully selected patients) was hailed by Malan as the greatest innovation in psychoanalysis since the discovery of the unconscious, although few analysts have ventured to practise it. From the perspective adopted in this chapter it might be regarded as the contemporary application in psychotherapy of the age-old technique of exorcism.

CONCLUSION

From the earliest years of the psychoanalytic movement analysts have, broadly speaking, inclined to be either healers or exorcists. Jung, Ferenczi, Rank and Reich seem to speak with the characteristic voice of the healer. In their approach there is an implicit trust in the healing power of relationship, an emphasis on the patient's own creative potential, a readiness to engage. Whereas those analysts, like Karl Abraham, who strictly followed Freud's advocacy of analytic detachment, maintain a greater distance between themselves and their patients, while often focusing on the negative aspects of the infantile psyche. This latter tradition set the tone of the classical analytic approach which is rigorously maintained by Melanie Klein and her followers. The Kleinian school actively challenges resistance to insight, the resort to manipulation, seduction and all the carefully hidden expressions of negative transference. In their determination to 'name the devils' and their readiness to confront them, they take the characteristic stance of the exorcist.

While healing and exorcism are very different modes of functioning, it would be a misleading simplification to see them as mutually exclusive. The healer, in striving to retrieve the patient's lost soul, must at the same time do battle with the devils that hold it captive. The exorcist, even as he drives out the demons, prays earnestly for the soul of the sinner. The overly empathic psychotherapist will fail where no attempt is made to purge the patient of his bad inner objects. The robustly confronting psychoanalyst, even though he or she maintains safe analytic boundaries, will also fail without sensitive understanding based on a truly human connection. The difficulty is to move freely between these two modes and to see them as complementary aspects of a single process.

References

Britton, R. (2005) The Use of Theological Concepts in Psychoanalytic Understanding, in N. Field (ed.), *Ten Lectures on Psychotherapy and Spirituality.* London: Karnac Books.

Brown, D. (1977) Drowsiness in the Counter-transference, *International Review of Psycho-Analysis* 37: 344–346.

Chertok, L. (1988) Psychotherapy, Suggestion and Sexuality, *British Journal of Psychotherapy* 5(1): 94–104.

Chia, M. (1983) *Awaken Healing Energy Through the Tao.* New York: Aurora Press.

Coltart, N. (1986) Slouching towards Bethlehem, in Gregorio Kohon (ed.), *The British School of Psychoanalysis.* London: Free Association Books.

Eliade, M. (1964) *Shamanism.* Princeton University Press

Epstein, L. (1979) The Therapeutic Function of Hate in the Countertransference, in L. Epstein and A. H. Finer (eds), *Countertransference.* London: Aronson.

Fairbairn, W. R. D. (1952) *Psychoanalytic Studies of the Personality.* London: Routledge and Kegan Paul.

Ferenczi, S. (1955) *Final Contributions.* London: Hogarth Press.

Freud, S. (1923) A Seventeenth Century Demonological Neurosis, in *Standard Edition,* 19. London: Hogarth Press.

Freud, S. (1925) A Neurosis of Demoniacal Possession in the 17th Century, in *Collected Papers,* 4. London: Hogarth Press.

Huxley, A. (1952) *The Devils of Loudun.* London: Chatto & Windus.

Searles, H. (1965) Phases of Patient-Therapist Interaction, in *Collected Papers on Schizophrenia.* New York: International Universities Press.

Winnicott, D. W. (1949) Hate in the Counter-transference, *International Journal of Psychoanalysis* 30: 60–75.

Further reading

Ellenberger, H. (1970) *Discovery of the Unconscious.* New York: Basic Books.

Chapter 17

Cultural identity and spirituality in psychotherapy[1]

Judith Mishne

Books, journals, classes, conferences, and psychotherapy training programs devoted to multiculturalism make little, or no mention of Jews, Jewish issues, or anti-Semitism. Langman (1999) notes the incongruity of this omission, especially because there are so many Jews in the field of counseling and psychology (see also, Dominguez, 1994; Klein, 1976; Siegel, 1991; Weinrach and Thomas, 1996). Jewish clinicians appear to be over-represented as providers of social and therapeutic services, and Jewish populations are seen to be over-represented clients. This perception has been erroneously assumed, making it appear that there is no need for any focus on the Jewish minority population during one's clinical training. The oft-cited rationale for this situation is that because Jews are not 'people of color' and can 'pass' in the white world they are part of the dominant culture and are not so oppressed and thereby not included in discussions of discrimination and diversity. This suggestion of the invisibility of Jews and their unique differences and/or that they can 'pass' could be seen as one of many forms of anti-Semitism. Seemingly, Jewish oppression does not fit the current established categories of racism and economic oppression. Beck (1991) notes the need to rethink our categories and suggests the politics behind categories, i.e. stereotypes which deny the reality of poor Jews, Jews of color, and Jews who are visibly recognized by their yarmulkes and clothing.

Another form of anti-Semitism is the trivialization of Jewish suffering. Herz and Rosen (1982) note an interesting difference between the experiences of suffering of Irish and Jewish families: 'In Irish families . . . the assumption is that one suffers because one deserves punishment for one's sins. For the Jewish family, the predominant view is that one suffers because of what the world does to you. Suffering is even a form of sharing with one's fellow Jews. It binds Jews with their heritage, with the suffering of Jews throughout history' (p. 367). These authors reflect on the centrality of suffering for the Jewish families who survived the Holocaust, and how there is an inter-generational transmission of pain and sorrow, passed onto their children, now designated as 'second generation Holocaust survivors'.

Defining and/or categorizing Jews has included considering them to be a religious group, an ethnicity, or national group. 'Perhaps the closest any identification can come is to view the Jews holistically as a culture' (Lemish, 1981, p. 28).

CLINICAL IMPLICATIONS

As with any racial, ethnic, religious or cultural group, clinicians must be aware of their attitudes and feelings about the minority group the client represents, as well as their own conflicted or negative feelings about their own personal identity. A matched therapeutic dyad is no guarantee for successful ongoing work. 'Assigning a Jewish client to a Jewish therapist can never assume to be a good match' (Langman, 1999, p. 300). There are too many varieties of Jews to expect that this characteristic alone suffices. Langman (1999) observes that some Jews fear being judged by another Jew for being 'too Jewish' or 'not Jewish enough'. Langman quotes Bindler (1996), an Orthodox Jewish therapist, who noted that his own Orthodoxy produced mixed results, even with Orthodox clients, who feared differences in their levels of Orthodoxy. In order to work with Orthodox Jews, a clinician needs an understanding of the spectrum and specifics of Jewish Orthodox identity, as well as awareness and sensitivity to the history of anti-Semitism, the client's Jewish experience, and world view.

The place of religion and/or cultural identification is a critical question in working with Jewish clients. Spero (1996b) cautions about some patients who might present symptoms of excessive shame, self-hatred, the need to be vilified, and excessive obsessing about sin and guilt. Such behaviors commonly reflect unhealthy religiosity. Optimally, this issue of a patient's religious practices and beliefs are examined non-judgmentally as part of the ongoing diagnostic assessment which is integral to all therapy efforts.

Additional to the above-noted possible symptoms are common problems connected to life experiences, with resultant poor self-esteem, sense of marginality and insecurity, as the aftermath of stigma, stereotype, and persecution. When treating Jewish patients, clinicians commonly encounter Holocaust survivors and their children. This population has received more attention in the clinical and research literature than any other Jewish population. Working with this population presents clinicians with unique and difficult challenges. Early research suggests that many mental health professionals avoided this topic and engaged in a conspiracy of silence with their clients (Danieli, 1980; 1984, p. 24). Avoidance is only one response; other countertransference responses include rage, dread, horror, recurrent nightmares, defensive numbness, and idealizing survivors as heroes or denigrating them as passive victims. In my own work with Holocaust survivors, and with Hidden Children of the Holocaust, I can attest to all of the above-noted overpowering emotions and responses (Mishne, 1995, 1996, 1997).

CASE PRESENTATION

(To preserve confidentiality this case has disguised all identifying data)

Presenting problems, family background and significant environmental events

Mr. A, in his mid-50s, sought therapy as he had, intermittently throughout his life, after his adolescent flight from Berlin, one year after 'Kristallnacht'. His parents were modern Orthodox German Jews, educated, cosmopolitan and very successful in business and commerce. Earlier, when the persecution and discrimination towards Jews in Germany began, they, like so many, experienced denial, then shock, as discriminatory laws, restrictions and confiscation of property began. The Nuremberg Laws were enacted, legalizing anti-Semitic measures. Mr. A painfully described his memories of his adolescent terror and shock, when witnessing the rampage, destruction, and burning down of his synagogue. Mr. A vividly recounted living through the terror of this period. He also described terrifying recurrent memories of beatings and stonings from endless gangs of Hitler youth. He and his sister were ousted from their school, and moved to an ultra-Orthodox, unfamiliar Jewish school. His family's financial circumstances plummeted severely as Jewish stores were boycotted, causing his once wealthy parents to have to borrow to scrape by. Despite this financial plight, they did provide him a Bar Mitzvah in 1937. In adolescence, Mr. A was deeply committed to being a Jew and he very much idealized being Bar Mitzvahed. He could recount missing soccer games and skating to endure Cheder and Hebrew classes and private instruction in moral Judaic teaching and musical reciting technique. At age 14 he left Berlin by train. His last sight of his mother was her tearful face at the train station as she ran along with the departing train for her final sight of her son. The children made it over the border where trains were routinely met by representatives of Dutch Jewish refugee committees. Several months later, Mr. A's sister joined him in a holding camp in Rotterdam which was run by the Dutch Catholic Church to help Jewish refugee children. From there they were sent to England and foster care, under the auspices of the Jewish Agency. Despite extensive correspondence and endless efforts to procure help for his parents for years, Mr. A never saw his parents again; both perished in separate concentration camps.

At the time that Mr. A began treatment with me, he was very successful monetarily, but generally dissatisfied with his life. His artistic frustration and lonely personal life felt overwhelming and he had great guilt about not being able to rescue his parents. Mr. A complained about his life-long identity problems, and his disconnecting himself from any and all Jewish institutions and affiliations. He preferred to consider himself a Humanist, especially in the newer chapters of his life when he moved to the United States to make a fresh start. Mr. A never 'passed' or kept his Jewish background 'in the closet'. Rather, I believe he exemplified what Diller (1980) called 'Jewish identity rejection', defined as 'a state of psychic imbalance in which an aspect of identity, namely the fact of one's Jewish background, is not fully integrated or accepted by the self' (p. 41). The phenomenon is said not to typically involve internalized anti-Semitism or total negativity towards Jewishness, but rather conflict and ambivalence. 'If the satisfaction derived from being a Jew does not compensate for what is lost (by being Jewish) one may ultimately begin to resent that part of one's identity' (ibid.).

Because Mr. A had experienced prior bouts of psychotherapy, and was a sophisticated and self-aware person, he attributed this dissociation to the Holocaust and loss of nearly every relative. He spoke of losing all faith in God and dropping Judaism from his life. My own recent speculations, years after my work with Mr. A, coincide with these views of his and some reflections by Hammer: 'To be conscious of an identification that is associated with such terror . . . carries with it the threat of annihilation which may be too painful for many people to endure' (1995, p. 207).

Assessment

I refer to the diagnostic guidelines of religious patients, set forth by Spero (1985). Mr. A presented with key problem areas typical of this group of disaffected Jews. Although Mr. A had originally been a modern Orthodox Jewish child and adolescent, the trauma of the Holocaust occurred in his adolescence before he had established 'identity consolidation' (Erikson, 1950) and his resolution was 'a new religion', which he scrupulously adhered to, namely his brand of 'Humanism', which contained 'behaviors and beliefs that were somehow related to overall lifestyle' (Spero, 1985, p. 20). Spero (1985, 1996b) says that while this characteristic is in itself not necessarily pathological, it is necessary as a basic criterion. Mr. A's new 'religion' was of rapid onset and involved Mr. A's 'severing family ties' (1985, p. 20). Mr. A ultimately gave up trying to rescue his parents and ceased denying the evidence that they had perished in concentration camps. When that occurred, he states he 'threw in the towel' and abruptly cut any and all connections with God and/or anything Jewish, and 'vehemently' became a 'universalist' or 'Humanist'.

Mr. A reflected an inappropriate balance between religiosity and psycho-social development. He reflected a mix of oral-narcissistic religiosity, anal religiosity and phallic and Oedipal religiosity (Spero, 1985, 1996b). In his search for narcissistic satisfaction, he maintained a disavowal of God, a hyper-cathexis of the self, and 'concomitant withdrawal of interest in healthy interpersonal relations' (ibid., p. 21). He could be hypomanic, grandiose, entitled, and subject to narcissistic rageful explosions. Anal religiosity was reflected by his 'obsessive preoccupation with right and wrong, sin, guilt, scrupulosity, etc.' (ibid.). Phallic and Oedipal religiosity appeared manifest in conflicts related to sexual relations and sexual experimentation. Mr. A had a range of homosexual fantasies and dreams, as well as numerous actual brief homosexual experimentations over several decades, none of which were in the context of a meaningful ongoing relationship or sustained connection. He pondered whether he had any actual attraction to males, or rather in fact, was simply defying Orthodox Jewish condemnation of homosexuality. He had numerous and lengthy monogamous relationships with a number of women.

Overall, Mr. A reflected uneven self-esteem, i.e. a disorder of the self, and in accord with Kohut's (1971) conception, did not withdraw from the external world, and direct libido inward, onto the self via self-preoccupations, hypochondrias, and the like. Instead, he repeatedly formed attachments of a most desperate intensity due to his need for objects to serve the function of stabilizing a threatened sense of self. Kohut's view was that the patient's central pathology concerned the self and its archaic narcissistic objects. Significant objects are not experienced as separate and independent from the self, yet unlike borderline patients, those Kohut considered narcissistically disordered have attained a cohesive self and have constructed cohesive-idealized archaic objects. These patients, unlike borderlines, are not subject to profound or irreversible disintegration. They possess narcissistic vulnerability and resultant depletion, depression and disintegration anxiety (Kohut, 1977; Tolpin, 1978). Because of their vulnerability, such patients cannot consistently regulate their self-esteem, or sustain normal levels of anxiety, excitement, and grandiosity. They are subject to embarrassment, self-consciousness or severe shame (Kohut, 1971). Ideals and values are frequently faltering and ambition and exhibitionism generally drive such patients. Failures large and small can cause mortification, rage, envy, and self-destructive interpersonal relationships.

Mr. A was aware that he had never enjoyed a passionate Oedipal attachment to his mother, or genuine identification with his father. He often said his emotional problems began before the traumata of the Holocaust and that his initial primary attachment was to the domestic employed by his parents, i.e. his caretaker, given his mother's unavailability due to her extensive involvement and employment in the family-owned business. Mr. A also suffered life-long rage at his father for not having been one of the many Berlin Jews with the foresight to flee Europe before the advent of horror and inhumanity. This rage caused him great shame and guilt, particularly because he, at age 14, had been so resourceful and self-directed in arranging his and his cousin's successful flight to safety. He hated having 'surpassed' his father, and hated himself for having contempt for this 'gentle, caring man'.

The treatment process and treatment relationship

Mr. A seemed to quickly form a therapeutic alliance, given his acceptance of the need to deal with internal problems. It appeared based upon a new and correct relationship, 'a fund of trust' (Basch, 1980, p. 133), whereby the patient views the therapist as a significant person they are willing to work with. At times the alliance felt like one made by an adolescent where I was viewed and used as a trusted adult friend or educator (Meeks, 1971), or ego ideal, role model or transitional parent (Ekstein, 1983). In the instance when there has been early parent loss, the parental role is less transitional and more lasting, and manifest in the transference. Because of the devastating losses of family in adolescence, in many ways Mr. A appeared arrested at this point, developmentally.

Mr. A was a willing and eager patient but often was most demanding, entitled, aggressive, and denigrating. Much focus was on the traumata and unbearable losses during and after the Holocaust and the stressors of alienation and aloneness during the years in England, and since the move to the United States. Transference and countertransference phenomena reflected the vicissitudes of clinical work with a vulnerable patient suffering from profound narcissistic pathology. Because of the overwhelming trauma during adolescence and the resultant lack of identity consolidation, he often went up and down manifesting the most primitive or more mature types of transferences. The merger transference, reflective of the most primitive narcissistic pathology, was evident in Mr. A's experiencing me as part of his grandiose self, a mere extension of him, whereby he needed total control of the treatment and felt entitled to rageful outbursts if he felt thwarted. Countertransference reactions were feelings of being totally taxed and drained by the necessity of boundless patience, restraint and demonstrations of empathy. At times I felt very guilty, to feel angry at a patient who has suffered so profoundly. As the treatment progressed, Mr. A demonstrated capacity for an alter-ego twinship transference, which is reflective of greater maturity. There is less archaic emergence of the grandiose self, a greater degree of separateness between patient and clinician and a better ability to demonstrate partnering and working together. Over time, eventually the treatment gradually reflects the impossibility of the perfect twin, i.e. finding another with identical views and feelings. The mirror transference is the most mature form of narcissistic transference with the therapist recognized as separate. In this form of transference, admiration and praise is sought for the patient's narcissistic gratification. This more mature transference was evident in the final fourth year of treatment.

The use of and examination of the transference and countertransference phenomena during the treatment was particularly significant in regard to the major focus on Mr. A's identity crisis and religious disorder. The extent of Mr. A's psychological and religious disorder was manifest by his attempts, early in the therapy, to foist on me and force-feed me his Humanist religion, which, as expected, was coupled with his denigration of my apparent attachment to my Jewish identity and cultural and religious observances, discernible to him by my changing appointments as needed for Jewish High Holiday Observances, and seemingly, on occasion, reacting with poorly concealed facial expressions to his tirades about all things Jewish, including the State of Israel, which he likened to a Fascist regime. His rage and contempt for my academic vacation spent visiting and teaching in Israel was boundless. For a very lengthy period he was literally in a narcissistic volcanic rage, and it called for my endless self-restraint to monitor my responses and to keep in mind this man's object losses and terrors about abandonment when he faced my five-week visit to Israel at the end of his first year in treatment. He radiated rage and scorn when it became apparent that I had close, familial, professional and friendship ties in Israel, and had traveled there many times. It should be noted that while he raged about my Jewish origins and affiliations, he manifested a split, i.e. a double standard, because indeed he had sought, as usual, a clinician he trusted to be familiar with the Holocaust, and experienced in clinical work with Holocaust survivors, and 'only a Jewish therapist would do'. Seemingly, during the first year in treatment he wanted me to be merged with him, to be a Jew like him, discarding any and all ties with Judaism and a Jewish identity.

Spero (1985, 1996b) recommends an ego assessment in regard to examination of conflict and autonomous pathologic behaviors expressed through religious beliefs and practices. The actual religious beliefs, ideals and practices must also be evaluated via non-judgmental analysis, and the transference and countertransference reactions must be recognized and monitored. Mr. A's ego functioning in regard to psychological and religious issues initially reflected inadequate defenses that could not bind in anger and depression. He could not consistently self-observe and sort out cause and event, and be aware of splits and incongruities, e.g. having a reasonable, respectful demeanor about all religions, save the Jewish religion. Jewish religious holidays and rituals commonly generated shame and guilt in Mr. A, until his final year in therapy, when he chose to actually return to an identification as a Jew, and to engage in Reformed Jewish practice and observances.

A great deal of therapeutic work and focus was on the transference and countertransference responses, examining and analyzing and learning about Mr. A's self-state and my own reactions to this patient's behaviors and transference manifestations. Previously I had considerable experience in working with Holocaust survivors and had developed a genuine capacity to avoid the conspiracy of silence and to contain countertransference responses upon hearing about unspeakable horrors patients had witnessed or experienced (Danieli, 1980; 1984). I have worked with many patients who vented rage and grandiosity, but Mr. A was and remained one of the most taxing patients I have ever encountered. Ultimately he also proved to be a very gratifying patient to work with.

In keeping with a self-psychology perspective, my goal was to rehabilitate the self-structure, and not engage in the suppression of symptoms by persuasion or education (Kohut and Wolf, 1978). No attempts were made to censor Mr. A or exhort him to make behavioral changes. In regard to his religious and identity disorder, I did 'not randomly select isolated religious practices or ideas as targets for criticism or for the imposition of (my) values and practices. Rather, I encouraged this patient to express himself freely and completely and to integrate the analytic, self-reflective process' (Spero, 1985, p. 38). The therapeutic goal was not the alteration, modification or removal of the patient's religious practice but to aid him 'to achieve a less conflicted state of belief' (ibid., p. 41).

By the end phase of treatment, Mr. A demonstrated a more cohesive self through a process Kohut (1977) called transmuting internalizations. With increased tolerance of feelings that previously caused shame and anxiety, Mr. A felt less helpless, hopeless and overwhelmed. During the often arduous course of treatment, Stolorow's (1975) injunction proved invaluable. It is helpful 'to recognize that (patient's) narcissism is literally in the service of the psychic survival of the self, enabling the therapist to endure his humble and at times thankless role in the narcissistic transference of being nothing more than the embodiment of a function which the patient's mental apparatus cannot yet perform itself' (p. 184). It also seemed that because I could accept the inevitable occasion of being perceived as being mistaken and failing him, Mr. A would not continuously need to fight and argue. The therapeutic task attempted throughout was not to avoid any and all experiences of selfobject failure, but to attempt to understand them 'within the unique perspective of the patient's subjective world' (Stolorow, Brandchaft and Atwood, p. 187 and p. 131).

Mr. A's life changes and accomplishments were numerous and I believe most impressive and gratifying to him. He made a rapprochment to extended family members, and assumed the responsibility of providing funds for college for the son and daughter of two of his cousins. He undertook a major artistic creative venture. This creative endeavor appeared to be his route back to his Jewish roots and resumption of his Jewish identity. His more positive and stable self-esteem and improved object relations enabled him to make a second marriage, something he had longed to be able to do.

Mr. A's development of empathy for himself and others indicates an internalization of a 'new edition of what one takes as possible between self and other' (Saari, 1986, p. 171). He seems to have benefited from the curative effect of the 'correctional emotional experience' (Kohut, 1984, p. 78) provided in his treatment. Returning to his familial roots and personal Jewish identity was very moving to hear him describe, especially his tentative, more confident membership and participation in services and activities in a Reformed temple when he made an affiliation.

CONCLUSIONS

In this chapter, I have presented the treatment of a Jewish older male patient, a Holocaust survivor, who for decades following the trauma of the War had renounced his Jewish identity and discarded all connection with his Jewish cultural roots and religious beliefs and practices. At the conclusion of a four-year course of treatment he reconnected with his Jewish identity and religious and cultural practices. I have reported on the diagnosis and treatment of a patient whose religious beliefs and shifts were deeply enmeshed in his 'core psychological and interpersonal conflicts' (Spero, 1985, p. 5). I have used the case study material because this sort of clinical presentation provides a particularly 'solid basis for understanding the place of religion in the dynamics of human life' (Casey, 1938, p. 452).

Many clinicians avoid religious clients, or dismiss issues of religion as irrelevant, and/or as evidence of immaturity, or as pathological, due to lack of familiarity with various religious belief systems, or due to negative countertransference responses or conscious biases based on prior held ideological pre-commitments. Appropriate clinical interventions with religious patients must be based on a recognition of or consultation about normal and pathological religious beliefs and an ability to evaluate inter- and intrapersonal imbalance from the perspective of the patient's cultural and ethical background. Management of transference and countertransference in regard to religious or anti-religious behaviors and beliefs calls for maximum self-awareness and appropriate non-directive empathic listening and therapeutic restraint.

In this period of increased immigration and corresponding ethnic, cultural, racial and religious diversity and multi-culturalism, consideration of religious matters must be included in our efforts to provide culturally competent, sensitive empathic clinical interventions, which avoid the errors of generalizations and stereotypes.

Note

1 A version of this chapter was previously published in *The Journal of Lesbian Studies* 8(1 and 2): 57–77.

References

Basch, M. (1980) *Doing Psychotherapy*. New York: Basic Books.

Beck, E. B. (1991) The Politics of Jewish Invisibility in Women's Studies, in J. Butter and J. Walter (eds), *Transforming the Curriculum: Ethnic Studies and Women's Studies*. Albany, NY: State University of New York, pp. 187–197.

Bindler, P. (1996) Clinical Manifestation of Religious Conflict in Psychotherapy, in M. H. Spero (ed.), *Psychotherapy of the Religious Patient*. Northvale, NJ: Jason Aronson, pp. 121–139.

Casey, R. P. (1938) The Psychoanalytic Study of Religion, *Journal of Abnormal and Social Psychology* (33): 437–452.

Danieli, Y. (1980) Countertransference in the Treatment and Study of Nazi Holocaust Survivors and their Children, *Victimology: An International Journal* 5: 355–367.

Danieli, Y. (1984) Psychotherapists' Participation in the Conspiracy of Silence about the Holocaust, *Psychoanalytic Psychology* 1: 23–43.

Diller, J. (1980) Identity Rejection and Reawakening in the Jewish Context, *Journal of Psychology and Judaism* 5: 35–47.

Dominguez, V. (1994) A Taste for the Other: Intellectualizing Complicity in Racializing Practices, *Current Anthropology* 35: 333–338.

Ekstein, R. (1983) The Adolescent Self during the Process of Termination of Treatment: Termination, Interruption or Intermission, in M. Sugar, S. Feinstein, J. Looney, A. Schwartz and A. Sarosky (eds), *Adolescent Psychiatry Vol. II: Developmental and Clinical Studies*. Chicago: University of Chicago Publishers, pp. 125–146.

Erikson, E. (1950) *Childhood and Society*. New York: W.W. Norton & Co.

Hammer, B. (1995) Anti-Semitism as Trauma: A Theory of Jewish Communal Trauma Response, in K. Weiner and A. Moon (eds), *Jewish Women Speak Out: Exploring the Boundaries of Psychology*. Seattle: Canapy Press, pp. 199–219.

Herz, F. M. and Rosen, E. J. (1982) Jewish Families, in M. McGoldrick, J. Pearse and J. Giordano (eds), *Ethnicity and Family Therapy*. NY: Guilford Press, pp. 361–392.

Klein, J. W. (1976) Ethnotherapy with Jews, *International Journal of Mental Health* 5: 26–28.

Kohut, H. (1971) *The Analysis of the Self*. New York: International Universities Press.

Kohut, H. (1977) *The Restoration of the Self*. New York: International Universities Press.

Kohut, H. (1984) *How Does Analysis Cure?*, in A. Goldberg and P. Stepansky (eds). Chicago: University of Chicago Press.

Kohut, H. and Wolf, S. E. (1978) The Disorders of the Self and their Treatment: An Outline, *International Journal of Psychoanalysis* 59: 413–425.

Langman, P. F. (1999) *Jewish Issues in Multiculturalism: A Handbook for Educators and Clinicians*. Northvale, NJ: Jason Aronson.

Lemish, P. (1981) Hanukah Bush: The Jewish Experience in America, *Theory into Practice* 20: 26–34.

Meeks, J. (1971) *The Fragile Alliance: An Introduction to the Outpatient Psychotherapy of the Adolescent*. Baltimore, MD: Williams and Wilkins.

Mishne, J. (1995) Hidden Children and their Families: Memoirs of a Unique Group of Holocaust Survivors. Keynote presentation at *The 5th Clinical Conference of the Committee on Psychoanalysis in Clinical Social Work: Mind Memories and Metaphor: Psychoanalytic Explorations* 10/29/95.

Mishne, J. (1996) Cherished Children: Analysis of the Resilience and Vulnerability of Hidden Children of the Holocaust. Keynote presentation at *Self Help Annual Meeting: Working With Holocaust Survivors*.

Mishne, J. (1997) Memories of Hidden Children: Analysis of Two Case Studies of Resilience, *Journal of Social Work Policy in Israel* 9–10: 101–128.

Saari, C. (1986) *Clinical social work treatment: How does it work?* New York: Gardner Press.

Siegel, R. J. (1991) Introduction: Jewish Women in Therapy: Seen but Not Heard, in R. J. Siegel and E. Cole (eds), *Jewish Women in Therapy*. Binghampton, NY: Hayworth, pp. 1–4.

Spero, M. H. (1985) *Psychotherapy of the Religious Patient*. Springfield, IL: Charles C. Thomas.

Spero, M. H. (ed.) (1996a) *Psychotherapy of the Religious Patient*. Northvale, NJ: Jason Aronson.

Spero, M. H. (1996b) Diagnostic Guidelines for Psychotherapy of the Religious Patient, in M. H. Spero (ed.), *Psychotherapy of the Religious Patient*. Northvale, NJ: Jason Aronson, pp. 19–60.

Stolorow, R. D. (1975) Towards a Definition of Narcissism, *International Journal of Psychoanalysis* 56: 179–185.

Stolorow, R. D., Brandchaft, B. and Atwood, G. E. (1987) *Psychoanalytic Treatment: An Intersubjective Approach*. Hillsdale, NJ: Analytic Press.

Tolpin, M. (1978) Self Objects & Oedipal Objects: A Crucial Developmental Distinction, in *Psychoanalytic Study of the Child* 33: 167–84. New Haven: Yale University Press.

Weinrach, S. and Thomas, K. (1996) The Counseling Profession's Commitment to Diversity-Sensitive Counseling: A Critical Reassessment, *Journal of Counseling and Development* 74: 472–477.

Chapter 18

Feminist spirituality, Mother Kali and cultural healing

Shumona Ray and Roy Moodley

The critique on race, culture and psychotherapy has been well documented (see, for example, Moodley, 1999; Bhugra and Bhui, 1998). A radical critique of traditional psychoanalysis has been conducted by feminists, especially on questions of rationality, objectivity and scientific accountability. Through a radical interrogation of patriarchy, masculinities and 'men' these scholars accuse psychotherapy of being androcentric and gender-insensitive and creating sexual dichotomies (see, for example, Braidotti, 1994; Irigaray, 1985; Mitchell, 1974). While the critique of masculinities is not universal across all forms of psychoanalysis and psychotherapy work cultures, they have nevertheless been part of the theoretical discourse of these disciplines (see Frosh, 1994) leading many clients to consider more feminine forms of healing in the masculine process of psychotherapy.

This move away from the 'talking cure' which is governed by the 'law of the Father' is supporting what Whitmont (1983) calls the 'return of the Goddess'. In the turn towards the feminine, seen metaphorically as the 'return to the body', the worship of the mother Goddess is a movement in the liberation of the repression of the feminine. Through this process the idea of the divine in women and the power of healing of the feminine is acknowledged and celebrated. This process is now referred to as 'feminist spiritualities'.

Goddesses from all periods of history now appear to be part of the Pantheon of Goddesses creating a more evolved, holistic and sophisticated view of feminine spirituality, divinity and healing.[1] Amongst these numerous Goddesses is the Hindu Goddess Kali, the Goddess of destruction and creation. She is represented as the mother who offers both the 'good' and the 'bad' breast, providing a site within which the binary divisions of psychotherapy, i.e. masculinities/femininities, male/female, heterosexual/gay, mentally ill/normal, etc., can be interrogated and displaced. In her role as the container of female masculinity she lays bare the underbelly of hegemonic masculinity and its discontents in conventional psychotherapy.

In this chapter we will explore the movement (cult) of the mother Kali, since there appears to be a recent upsurge in the popularity of this Goddess in the West, and the potential the Goddess Kali has as a symbol of healing and empowerment for women (and men). First, we look at feminist spiritualities that have become critical sites for the evolution of a new consciousness that privileges the feminine. Second, we discuss the historical representation and interpretation of spirituality and healing as the masculine form of God, the Father, Son and Holy Spirit, and the failure of this masculine approach. And finally we explore the various attempts to address the feminine aspect of the divine, particularly through the notion of the Goddess as the Divine Mother and Sacred Feminine. We develop this idea through the narrative of the Goddess Kali.

FEMINIST SPIRITUALITIES

Feminist spiritualities seem to include a wide spectrum of ideas, attitudes and objectives; at one end are the reformers, men and women from established religions, viz. Christianity and Judaism, who seek to reform their cultural traditions of practice by eliminating gender bias and by acknowledging the oppression, exclusion and contributions of women throughout history (Nelson, 2002). Such reforms include: ordination of women priests; apology and restitution to Aboriginal communities; lesbian marriages; and others. At the other end of the spectrum are the radicals or the 'Goddess Feminists'. These radicals seek to refashion/reshape existing beliefs, practices and myths or create new ones to fit their own cultural, political and social agendas (Groothuis, 2004). Indeed, these 'Goddess Feminists' are part of the bigger feminist movement and its evolution in its various phases. Groothius argues that the sacred texts and scriptures from the Western tradition do not teach a universal principle of female subordination. This has been the case throughout history.

However, even long before the Industrial Revolution gender roles had been constructed and reconstructed through the dominant structures of hegemonic masculinities. In more recent times too, the Goddess feminism appears to be unfashionable given the consumerist and materialist nature of society, and its non-religious culture (Rowland, 2002).

Feminist spiritualities, then, arise from the research and practices of radical feminists to extend the boundaries and borderlines of consciousness, desire, affectivity and the imagination. As Whitmont says,

> they are to contribute a new step in the evolution of consciousness . . . establish the value of inwardness, and of affirmation . . . and able to integrate – woundedness, pain . . . joy and beauty . . . clarifying feelings, fantasies, and desires regardless of their moral or aesthetic implications.
>
> (Whitmont, 1983, p. 197)

We do not suggest in any way that any one particular archetype from the Pantheon of Goddesses is more therapeutic than another in approaching psychological, physical, or mental health issues, but we do emphasize that alternative ways of viewing spirituality and healing which speaks to the lived experience of women and men from different cultures is imperative in contemporary health care.

GOD: THE FATHER, SON AND HOLY SPIRIT

The Judaic-Christian tradition has for centuries served to legitimate a sexually imbalanced patriarchal society that has portrayed God as male, i.e. 'God the Father'. This image has 'in turn rendered service to this type of society [patriarchal] by making its mechanisms for the oppression of women appear right and fitting' (Daly, 1971, p. 1). Since God (together with his son and holy ghost) is in charge of the nature of things, their divine plan and order of the universe is constructed as masculine and patriarchal, leading to a male-dominated religion, culture and society.

According to feminist spirituality, this process has occurred over a length of time and in several stages prior to the Christian era. In the beginning, matriarchy was the basis of humankind's natural state and the original religion was a form of nature-based polytheism that related everything to a Great Mother (a Great Goddess) (Nelson, 2004). This Goddess had three aspects: Maiden, Mother and Crone (based on the three faces of the moon), and women were considered to be an earthly incarnation of this Great Goddess. This period (over 25,000 years) saw the invention of the first tools, domesticated fire and animals, and use of plants for healing (all performed by women since women gave birth to and provided for children) (Gimbutas, 1999).

The next period was characterized by women who were Shamanic Priestesses and whose vital role included mediating between the community and its deity (Gimbutas, 1996). Women engaged in this role were responsible for channeling the creative energy of the Goddess into the material world through sacred rituals and trance dances. In their trance-state, these shamans and seers were required to use their enhanced awareness for keeping the channels open between the individual, the group and the cosmos.

At the end of the Paleolithic Age, a paradigm shift occurred as Goddess worshippers in Egypt and Crete were invaded by tribes of war-like, male-dominated nomads, who subdued their culture and subjected them to worshipping a new male god (Nelson, 2004). This shift from worshipping an Earth-based mother Goddess to a male god in the sky led to a shift in power from women to men, as men became the rulers and priests, and began to introduce new laws (for example, forms of marriage that were designed to control women and establish patriarchy). During this era of patriarchy, land ownership which previously was the basis of women's power now landed in the hands of male (father-to-son inheritance). Male gods were introduced by male priests who strictly forbade any return to the old ways of worship. From this time forward, all women were publicly considered to be the private property of men, and women were forced to subjugate themselves to male narcissism, greed and abuse of power (Woodman and Dickson, 1996, pp. 204–205).

Christianity, for example, with its inherent belief in the divine as masculine, 'sought to separate the unwanted qualities of irrationality from reason, by interpreting the reason/irrationality binary as a gendered structure (where reason is masculine and the irrational is feminine)' (Rowland, 2002, p. 60). This practice, which continued with the Enlightenment, had without a doubt a very negative effect on women and the way in which they were perceived and represented throughout the centuries. It also led to a culture in which 'we are starved for images that recognize the sacredness of the feminine and the complexity, richness and nurturing power of female energy' (Rowland, 2002, p. 63).

In addition to this, women for centuries have been barred from participating in ritual leadership and from having religious authority in many of the world's major religions. This of course has had the obvious effect of undermining female power in many societies, through the institution of legal codes that justified subordinating women. Most of the world's 'major' religions, for example, explicitly say that the image of God in the human imagination is uniquely male, and then draw arguments for sustaining women's oppression from this (Daly, 1971, p. 1). Such beliefs tend to reinforce the notion that men should dominate religion and spirituality, and that women should adopt more passive virtues (for example charity, meekness, obedience and humility). Mary Daly in 'After the Death of God the Father' (1971) suggests that the major task of the women's liberation movement has been the exposition and criticism of this male-centred heritage. This analysis, then, sets the stage for the evolution of the feminine as the centre point from which newer forms of spirituality would emerge, healing the collective wounds of women, and reclaiming the lost sense of sacredness and the divine. As Barbara Biziou in 'A Path to the Goddess through Ritual' says, 'in accepting, honoring and meeting our own physical and emotional needs, we honor the Goddess, we learn to communicate our feelings openly . . . and we then move into the trusting, rather than the controlling possessive heart' (Biziou, 2004, p. 1).

Goddess feminists today consider the present age to be a time of Renewal or Rebirth, a time to integrate and embrace matriarchy and patriarchy, and to achieve a balance between the two. As Whitmont (1983) says, 'the patriarchal achievements of the past must not be overthrown, but integrated into this new outlook' (p. 197).

GODDESS: THE DIVINE MOTHER AND SACRED FEMININE

Goddess feminists believe that Goddess energy is now struggling to be recognized, affirmed and utilized in different parts of the world. This energy is an important source of Inner Peace for the entire earth and its beings, as Marija Gimbutas says:

> The Goddess gradually retreated into the depths of forests or onto mountain tops, where she remains to this day in beliefs and fairy stories. However alienation from the vital roots of earthly life ensued, the results of which are clear in our contemporary society. But the cycles never stop turning and now we find the Goddess reemerging from the forests and mountains, bringing us hope for the future, returning us to our most ancient human roots.
>
> (Gimbutas, 2001, p. 321)

This shift in consciousness which is happening in all cultures is being played out in different ways in the specific social, cultural and political contexts of these cultures. Even in cultures which are perceived in the West to be contrary to 'feminist spiritualities' the notion of the mother and its 'reemerging from the forests and mountains' to bring 'hope for the future' is returning individuals to their 'most ancient human roots'. For example, in the Islamic tradition, Allah has two principal names – Rahman and Rahim which mean Compassionate and Merciful. Indeed, both of these names are derived from the root Arabic word that denotes womb (Burkhardt, 1995). Tobie Nathan (2005) also refers to the Djinn (invisible being capable of occupying the body and controlling the psychological functioning of a person) as a womb. The Djinn he suggests both comes from the earth and arises from women.

In Mahayana Buddhism (like other iconic forms of the Buddha as a masculine sitting deity) there is a recognition that the Mother as Prajnaparamita, the boundless and unfathomable Mother of all Buddhas, is present (Hixon, 1993). The early Gnostic Christians, for example, put much emphasis on the Virgin Sophia who is the feminine embodiment of Wisdom (Matthews, 1992), and the Chinese have Kwan Yin (the Goddess of Mercy) (Boucher, 1999). By pursuing love and devotion to the Mother in any of Her forms, the individual will eventually arrive at a state of peace and contentment (Cook, 1997). In these earlier mythologies, the Mother was seen as that which gives birth to all creatures and that which gives life to all of the earth (Gimbutas, 2001). Although worship of the Goddess has virtually disappeared, the worship of Kali still goes on, and not just in India. We discuss this phenomenon next.

MOTHER KALI: GODDESS OF DESTRUCTION

The worship of Shakti as the Divine Mother is one of the four principal sects of Hinduism. The Hindu concept of the Goddess is similar to the Tantric belief that the creative force behind all existence is female in the form of the Goddess *Shakti*. The philosophy of elevating the female principle above the male, at all levels from the cosmic to the terrestrial, is termed shakta or tantrika (tantric) which considers the many female Goddesses as coming from the one single female principle, The Goddess. She is the energizing force that stimulates the masculine potential which is seen to be dormant or even dead without her. It is said that the God Shiva without his Shakti is a corpse (Shava).

Shakti, the pure cosmic energy that generates and activates the universe, takes on the form of *devis* (or various female Goddesses) who each represent the different qualities of her primal energy. Whether she is represented in her benign form (as *Durga* – the ultimate and independent Goddess) or in her ferocious state (as *Kali*, the Goddess of destruction), she is the force behind life itself, and is sometimes shown as the divine consort of a male deity (Jacobson, 2002). In her creative aspect she is *Saraswati*, the patron of sixty-four arts one should cultivate in life; as *Gauri,* she is the deity representing purity and austerity; and as the temptress *Mohini*, she is the divine seductress who initiated the act of love responsible for creation.

However, as the awe-inspiring and fearless *Kali* she represents the destructive phase of the eternal cycles of birth, death and rebirth and the transcendental nature of womanhood (Kelly, 1998). In this context, all women are believed to be embodiments of the divine and as such are to be honored and recognized as the womb of life and creation, the keepers and transmitters of knowledge. It is for this reason that worship of the Goddess (in all her manifestations) is so popular in different parts of India and so dynamic and adaptable.

Her name is Chamunda, popularly known as Kali,[2] the terrifying Goddess and the destroyer of evil. Kali is often portrayed as the beautiful Amazonian figure standing on a buffalo, clearly symbolic of her aggressive preeminence. The 50 letters of Sanskrit (which Kali wears as a garland of human heads) appears on the petals of each lotus. Sometimes, 'in her archetypical form, Mother Kali often has no iconographic image but is represented by a stone block or even mound' (Mookerjee, 1988, p. 71). At other times Kali could be seen as a dark blue stone, or the color blue-black like other fierce deities of Asia, for example the Goddess Palden Lhamo in Tibet, a wrathful form of Tara. But elsewhere too the Goddess takes on these colors; in Mexico, for example, the Goddess Coatlique is represented as a great stone with a head of twin serpents, a necklace of human hands, hearts, and feet, and a skirt of writhing snakes (Robinson, 1997).

In India, worship of the Goddess varies in different regions and among different castes, depending on the form of the Goddess. Mother Kali, for instance, has been traditionally worshipped in some parts of India with animal sacrifice, as well as spirit possession and fire-walking in the South (McNeal, 2003, p. 241). Such acts of devotion are often associated with specific aspects of each particular Goddess, which (in the case of Mother Kali) reminds her devotees of some aspect of human life (e.g. frailty and imperfection). Other deities that are worshipped differently include *Sasthi* (the protectress of children), *Sitala* (the Goddess of smallpox and other epidemics), and *Manasa* (the snake Goddess) who are all taken as different aspects of the supreme Goddess (Cook, 1997). One aspect shared by all of these forms is the paradoxical nature of the Goddess. Each one is considered to be a source of both worldly illusion and its bondage (or *Maya*), and of the knowledge that sets one free. As McNeal says in *Encountering Kali*, 'she is the *Shakti* of bondage and the *Shakti* of liberation' (McNeal, 2003, p. 243). As such, her energy continually plays out between life and death, happiness and sorrow, health and disease, love and hate.

Shakti's embodiment of these polarities seems to offer answers to these paradoxes. As a 'good enough' mother she sometimes punishes her children, but she also gives something back. As McNeal says, 'Her left hand continually takes away what her right hands puts in place and her right hand continually replaces what her left hand removes' (McNeal, 2003, p. 243). Thus, in times of suffering or distress, the worship of the divine mother allows for an integration of the shadow and a clearer understanding of the varied and complex meanings of illness and cure seeking (see Good and Good, 1982; Moodley, 2000).

MOTHER KALI: A SYMBOL OF HEALING

In Hindu mythology, Kali is represented as the mysterious source of life and death and is also seen as an important source of healing (Jacobson, 2002).

In the West, Kali is gaining immense popularity as feminists and New Age practitioners look to Kali as a symbol of what patriarchy has tried to repress in women (qualities such as anger, uninhibited sexuality and empowerment) (Nelson, 2004). Many women today, not necessarily from the Hindu tradition, look to Kali for strength, inspiration and healing. Kali (who is said to embody both good and evil, love and hate, creation and destruction) is now 'used by many women as a way of helping them heal emotional divisions in their lives' (Kripal and McDermott, 2003, p. 276). As the Goddess of ferocity, passion and danger, Kali is also taken to be a symbol of the darkness and anger within people. Thus some patients who are suffering from the after-effects of sexual abuse or from diseases, such as

HIV-AIDS, for example, are acknowledging her as a route to mental and emotional healing. In light of this, the past few decades have seen the proliferation of many resource materials on Kali, especially for those who are seeking healing through alternative means.

Terri Kelly in 'Kali as a Symbol of Transformation in Conflict Resolution' (1998), also discusses how the transformative facets and activities of Kali can be a useful role model for contemporary progressive models of conflict resolution, e.g. 'transformative approach' and narrative therapy (Kelly, 1998). In the transformative approach to interpersonal conflict resolution, an immediate resolution to the problem is not sought after but rather the empowerment and mutual recognition of both parties involved. This means considering the views, perspectives and experiences of each party and understanding how the other sees the problem at hand. Kelly sees the Kali story as useful here, because it uses the analogy of ashes (from the cremation ground) to illustrate that we are all the same – 'a pile of ashes', and that in order to make room for fresh perspectives there must also be some destruction (Kelly, 1998). Also, the imagery of Kali moving around all sides of the cremation ground to get a full view of her enemies is useful for facilitating the bringing to consciousness of all aspects (facets) of the conflict (Kelly, 1998, p. 3). Finally, Kelly finds the symbol of Kali useful in cutting across issues of sexism, as Kali is a role model of strength and resolve for both Hindu men and women of India.

Another area where the story of Kali is useful is in resolving conflict in an interpersonal or family setting. According to Kelly, the narrative therapy here is powerful in that stories have the power to release and change (Kelly, 1998). Once again, Kali would be a complement to this model as she represents the processes of change and transformation using various 'magical powers'. Kali also destroys blocks placed by the ego, represented by Kali's six enemies: lust, anger, greed, delusion, envy and pride (Kelly, 1998). In this way Kali, as a symbol of transformation and healing, can be a useful model for healing in contemporary progressive therapy. In *Aphrodite's Daughters* (1997), Bonheim explores the concept of woman, the Goddess, body and sexuality which she summarizes as follows:

> Our Soul (by which I mean the portion of our Self that is engaged in the process of blossoming through Space and time) does not simply sit in a body like water in a jar. Rather it merges with the body, so that each permeates the other, as the golden color of a sunflower permeates its petals . . . In the same way, our soul acquires a particular coloring and fragrance by virtue of inhabiting a female or male body. The soul of a woman vibrates with a different frequency than that of a man . . . Men and women may be headed for the same ultimate destination but we travel different paths.
>
> (Bonheim, 1997, p. 1)

Clearly the whole notion of feminist spirituality and the Goddess feminist movement has provided us with the opportunity to rethink critically the binary theories of gender and culture outside the tradition of a post-Christian monotheistic experience. The great Goddess herself is not a feminine version of monotheism, which creates a binary by casting out so much that is 'other' (Rowland, 2002).

CONCLUSION

In this chapter we will have attempted to explore the movement (cult) of Kali and healing. Kali, as a mother Goddess, while appearing in various (dis)guises of gender – androgynous, masculine, feminine, bisexual and transgendered – is constructed to disrupt and interrupt the binary construction that so often constricts gender and culture. The Goddess (in any form) reminds us of the potential we all have for change. Even transformed therapists themselves can experience change in the 'indulgence' of Goddess feminism. For example, Sara Spaulding-Phillips, a psychotherapist, talks of her personal journey, healing and transformation in 'Firework: A Hawaiian Guidebook to the Goddess' (1997). She shares her story about a ho'oponopono, a 'setting-things-right' healing ritual, in one of the sacred caves of the Big Island of Hawaii. During this ceremony she enters the cave, 'the womb of the Goddess Pele', the Fire Goddess. She has this to say of the experience:

> The time was a powerful transition for me . . . I was still clinging to the last remnants of patriarchal orientation and to an identification with masculine values such as heroic pursuits, domination, and linear and hierarchical thinking . . . I burned with a need to reclaim my own connection with my female authority . . . (on leaving the cave) . . . A great feeling of peacefulness floods over me, washing me new. *With or without my broom, I will fly*.
>
> (Spaulding-Phillips, 1997, pp. 239–254, italics in original)

Perhaps feminist spirituality is getting us to come full circle (with or without the broom) to celebrate and remember all the Fire Goddesses who were burnt at the stake during the reign of the dark god in human history, and now women (and men) are free to fly into the metaphysical realm and be transformed and reborn through the healing power of the Mother Goddess.

Notes

1 The archaic Goddesses of both love and war are also part of this movement, such

as Innanna of Sumer, Anath in Canaan, Ishtar of Mesopotamia, Sekhmet in Egypt, Morrigan in Eire, Pallas in Greece, Bellona in Rome and Shakti and Kali in India. As archetypes from the depths of the unconscious psyche these god-desses are surfacing to reassert their roles as the compassionate guides of transformation of consciousness; or the Goddess may appear in 'play and dance as Artemis, allure as Aphrodite, domesticate as Vesta, or be maternal as Demeter. She may function as Athena by furthering civilization and skills, or be concerned with comfort and the relief of misery as Mary' (Whitmont, 1983, p. 197).

2 Kali was created by the Goddess Durga, the slayer of the buffalo demon. Seemingly Kali comes from the forehead of Durga. And where did Durga come from? The Gods are said to have been troubled by a powerful demon which took the form of a black water buffalo. As gods, they were impotent to quell the demon. With their combined wrath condensed and became female, the Goddess Durga. Each God then gave to her his most powerful weapon. She then killed the black water buffalo and the devil that lived with it. Then she called forth all the consort of the Gods from their masters and incorporated them into herself, thus establishing her supremacy over Gods and demons. This multiple, dominant and supreme female is always depicted as an aggressive but beautiful woman, shown plunging a spear or trident into the buffalo-demon.

References

Bhugra, D. and Bhui, K. (1998) Psychotherapy for Ethnic Minorities: Issues, Contexts and Practice, *British Journal of Psychotherapy*14(3): 310–326.

Biziou, B. (2004) A Path to the Goddess through Ritual. http://www.soulfuliving. com/path_to_the_goddess.htm. Accessed June 26, 2004.

Bonheim, J. (1997) *Aphrodite's Daughters: Women's Sexual Stories and the Journey of the Soul*. New York: Fireside/Simon Schuster.

Boucher, S. (1999) *Discovering Kwan Yin, Buddhist Goddess of Compassion*. Boston: Beacon Press.

Braidotti, R. (1994) Of Bugs and Women: Irigaray and Deleuze on the Becoming-Woman, in C. Burke, N. Schor and M. Whitford (eds), *Engaging with Irigaray: Feminist Philosophy and Modern European Thought*. New York: Columbia University Press.

Burkhardt, T. (1995) *Introduction to Sufism*. London: Thorsons.

Cook, P. M. (1997) *Shaman, Jhankri and Nele*. New York: Ellipsis Arts.

Daly, Mary (1971) After the Death of God the Father, in *Commonweal*. Pittsburgh: Know.

Frosh, S. (1994) *Sexual Difference: Masculinity and Psychoanalysis*. London: Routledge.

Gimbutas, M. (1996) *Gods and Goddesses of Old Europe, 6500–3500 BC*. Los Angeles: University of California Press.

Gimbutas, M. (1999) *The Living Goddess*. Los Angeles: University of California Press.

Gimbutas, M. (2001) *Language of the Goddess*. New York: Thames & Hudson.

Good, B.-J. and Good, M.-J. D. (1982) Towards a Meaning-Centred Analysis of Popular Illness Categories: 'Fright-Illness' and 'Heat Distress' in Iran, in A. J. Marsella and G. M. White (eds), *Cultural Conceptions of Mental Health and Therapy*. Dordrecht: Reidel.

Groothuis, R. M. (2004) Sexuality, Spirituality, and Feminist Religion. http://www.gospelcom.net/ivpress/groothuis/sfem.htm. Accessed June 26, 2004.

Hixon, L. (1993) *Mother of the Buddhas: Meditation on the Prajnaparamita Sutra.* Illinois: Quest Books.

Irigaray, L. (1985) *Speculum of the Other Woman,* trans. G. G. Gill. Ithaca, NY: Cornell University Press.

Jacobson, S. B. (2002) Kali: Goddess of the East Meets Western Feminism and Why She is Not Evil. http://www.geocities.com/Wellesley/Garden/1073/WOK/editorial1.html. Accessed June 26, 2004.

Kelly, T. L. (1998) Kali as a Symbol of Transformation in Conflict Resolution. (Unpublished paper, Portland State University, July, 1998) Portland.

Kripal, J. J. and McDermott, R. F. (eds) (2003) *Encountering Kali: In the Margins, at the Centre and in the West.* Berkeley: University of California Press.

McNeal, K. (2003) Doing the Mother's Caribbean Work: On Shakti and Society in Contemporary Trinidad, in J. J. Kripal and R. F. McDermott (eds), *Encountering Kali: In the Margins, at the Centre and in the West.* Berkeley: University of California Press.

Matthews, C. (1992) *Sophia: Goddess of Wisdom.* London: Thorsons.

Mitchell, J. (1974) *Psychoanalysis and Feminism.* Harmondsworth: Penguin.

Moodley, R. (1999) Psychotherapy with Ethnic Minorities: A Critical Review, *Changes: International Journal of Psychology and Psychotherapy* 17(2): 109–125.

Moodley, R. (2000) Representation of Subjective Distress in Black and Ethnic Minority Patients: Constructing a Research Agenda, *Counselling Psychology Quarterly* 13(2): 159–174.

Mookerjee, A. (1988) *Kali: The Feminine Force.* New York: Destiny.

Nathan, T. (2005) The Djinn: A Sophisticated Conceptualization of Both Pathologies and Therapies, in R. Moodley and W. West (eds), *Integration of Traditional Healing Practices in Counseling and Psychotherapy.* Thousand Oaks, CA: Sage.

Nelson, D. (2002) The Many Faces of Kali. http://www.iloveulove.com/spirituality/hindu. Downloaded June 26, 2004.

Robinson, J. S. (1997) The Dark Feminine: Death in Childbirth and Entry into the Shamanic Realm, in D. F. Sandner and S. H. Wong (eds), *The Sacred Heritage: The Influence of Shamanism on Analytical Psychology.* New York: Routledge.

Rowland, S. (2002) *Jung: A Feminist Revision.* Cambridge: Polity Press.

Spaulding-Phillips, S. (1997) Firework: A Hawaiian Guidebook to the Goddess, in D. F. Sandner and S. H. Wong (eds), *The Sacred Heritage: The Influence of Shamanism on Analytical Psychology.* New York: Routledge.

Whitmont, E. C. (1983) *Return of the Goddess: Femininity, Aggression and the Modern Grail Quest.* London: Routledge and Kegan Paul.

Woodman, M. and Dickson, E. (1996) *Dancing in the Flames: The Dark Goddess in The Transformation of Consciousness.* Boston: Shambala.

Part F

Future directions

Chapter 19

A pluritheoretic approach: Tobie Nathan's ethnopsychoanalytic therapy

Ursula Streit

Studies trying to determine universal characteristics of healing revealed the close relationship between basic cultural concepts and specific forms of treatment and underline the importance of shared or complementary models of illness and therapy held by patient and healer (Frank and Frank, 1991; Littlewood, 1992; Prince, 1976; Torrey, 1986; White and Marsella, 1982). However, clinics specialized in intercultural therapy still mainly use Western forms of therapy, i.e. psychodynamic therapy and/or family therapy (Gailly, 1991; Karem, 1992) or, as in work with refugees, 'traditional' and Western forms of therapy are used simultaneously or successively but they are performed by different therapists (Hiegel, 1991; Moore and Boehnlein, 1991); this suggests that an integration of Western and non-Western forms of therapy is still difficult.

What are the conditions allowing integration of cultural differences in clinical work and what are the consequences of such an undertaking? The work of Tobie Nathan[1] seems particularly interesting: more than twenty years ago he started this kind of adventure by developing a clinical setting including theories and techniques of non-Western cultures, mainly from Africa, and psychodynamic therapy (Nathan, 1986, 1988a, 1993, 1994). This approach had a profound impact on Nathan's view of mechanisms involved in psychotherapy which, in turn, influenced his work with migrant patients (Nathan, 1994, 1998, 2001). The aim of the present chapter is to describe and discuss this exemplary 'parcours'.

PARAMETERS OF PSYCHOANALYTIC THERAPY FOR WORK WITH MIGRANTS FROM NON-WESTERN CULTURES: STRUCTURE AND FUNCTION OF ETHNOPSYCHOANALYTIC THERAPY

Nathan's initial goal was to use psychoanalytic therapy with migrant patients from non-Western cultures. However, he was well aware of the cultural specificity of psychoanalysis: 'psychoanalysis' etiologic theory focuses on a psychic interiority (analytic material only consisting of psychic reality – dreams, images, emotions, fantasies – situated inside the individual), the individual being seen as fractured (composed of identificatory cores and antagonistic instincts), whereas in non-Western etiologies, for instance in sorcery, the individual is seen as whole, an entity, but its boundary (envelope) is fragile and can be penetrated'[2] (1986, pp. 171–172). Nathan tried to adapt psychoanalytic therapy to work with immigrant patients by introducing three main parameters: (i) the patients' mother tongue; (ii) the use of a group setting; (iii) the use of 'traditional' etiologic theories.

The first parameter, the use of patients' mother tongue, seems obvious: 'spontaneously the patient's thoughts are produced in that language' (1993, p. 50). Nathan also points out that a language only learned as an adult tends to be operational (opératoire) and hence is less linked to emotions. The presence of a translator being compulsory, a dyadic therapeutic relationship was no longer possible. Furthermore, as mentioned by Nathan, the second parameter, the use of a group setting, is coherent with a sociocentric conception of the person and explanatory models, or, as called by Nathan, 'traditional' etiologic theories, in which the conception of pathology involves the family and the group (1993, p. 20). As 'these etiologies and associated therapeutic interventions govern mediations between different universes (for example the ordinary world and the "extraordinary" world of supernatural beings) and are incompatible with a dyadic therapeutic setting' (1993, p. 51), the patient needs to be surrounded by a group.

The third parameter, i.e. the use, in the clinical context, of etiologic theories and references to social institutions specific to the patient's culture (system of kinship, sayings, etc.) alternatively with the psychoanalytic discourse seemed not only possible but necessary in light of Devereux's theory of complementarism (Devereux, 1972). According to this theory a double but non-simultaneous discourse is required to describe certain facts with a maximum of precision. This idea is translated by the following therapeutic procedure: for each patient the group of therapists tries to answer two questions, i.e. (a) what is the patient's problem according to psychodynamic theory? and (b) how would his problem be explained and treated in his culture of origin? In the beginning Nathan stressed the necessity for therapeutic interventions and interpretations to be ambiguous (1988a, p. 97) to allow their content to correspond to psychoanalytic theory and also to make sense according to explanatory models specific to the patient's culture; later on Nathan puts more emphasis on the importance of a dialogue between representatives of the theoretical frameworks used (1998a).

The procedure of ethnopsychoanalytic therapy is the following: the members of the group, co-therapists of various cultural background, fully trained professionals (psychologists, physicians, psychiatrists, educators, ethnologists, etc.) are already seated in a circle when the patient and the therapist in charge of the former enter the room and join this circle; often, members of the patient's family are also present. The co-therapists are cultural mediators or culture brokers: they speak various languages, are able to handle etiologic theories specific to their culture of origin and they understand the logic of 'traditional' therapeutic interventions (1994, p. 129). At the beginning of the session the leader of the group invites the professional in charge of the patient (or the patient's representative) and the members of the patient's family to present their vision of the patient's problem. The patient's help-seeking behavior is also explored: for instance did he ask members of the family living in the host country and those remaining in the home country what they think about his problem? It is also important to know if traditional healers have been consulted. Often co-therapists mention how the patient's difficulties would be explained in their own group or what a healer might have said. Also, very often, sayings or proverbs are used that express in an indirect way, possible contributing factors to the patient's problems. Even though all co-therapists participate, the co-therapist from the same cultural context as, or similar to, the patient plays a particularly important role and references to the patient's cultural background predominate. Questions as well as interventions are translated into his mother tongue (if he is very fluent in the host country's language, only particularly significant parts of the session are translated). At the end of the session the leader of the group proposes a new explanation or a new etiologic theory presented as a 'story'. At times instead of presenting a 'story' explaining the problem, the use of an object or of a ritual is prescribed (1993, p. 61); this enhances contact with the patient's cultural frame of reference or group of origin.

The use of the patient's mother tongue and of representations specific to his culture helps to reconstitute the patient's cultural universe and contributes to the cultural 'holding', the fundamental dynamic function of the group, i.e. psychological and cultural holding. The circulation of interpretations implicitly demonstrates that meaning varies according to cultural contexts (1993, p. 53). The therapeutic setting also comprises an implicit paradoxical statement: the only common characteristic of all therapists is for all of them to belong to another circle – a metaphoric one – i.e. to their cultural group (1994, p. 131). According to Nathan, these two propositions (implicit to the setting and the procedure) 'help the patient to understand or to "experience" that he does not talk like a universal human being but like a Soninké of Mali, from the village of Kharta, in the region of Khayes' (1994, p. 131).

The emphasis on mediation between different cultural universes is coherent with Nathan's view of migrant patients' basic problem described as follows:

migrants are forced to the splitting of two cultural referential systems. At first this splitting is necessary and useful; however, for the parents this process of splitting becomes more rigid and leads to a true splitting of the ego as defined by Freud, when their children adopt the cultural referential of the host culture. On the cognitive level, this kind of splitting means not to be able to establish mediation between two referential universes. When a migrant is faced with psychopathological suffering he then no longer can use the old code to express his problem; therefore he tries to explain his problem on his own and is unable to express his losses and inner conflicts

(1994, pp. 131–132)

As stressed by Nathan, 'a therapeutic setting that focuses on the identification of circles of "membership" (appartenance) and on the mediation between them, should be appropriate for the dilemmas migrants face' (1994, p. 132).

In the early years Nathan worked with adults who often were diagnosed as alexithymic, hysteric, or seen as using somatization for so-called 'secondary' gains and who often were referred to his group as a last resort. Clinical work helped to show that their symptoms are part of complex theoretical systems (1993, p. 32). Further experiences showed that this clinical approach was also helpful in the treatment of post-partum depression and post-partum psychoses as well as of problems related to the mother–child relationship and problems presented by migrants' children (Nathan, 1986, 1988a, 1988b, 1993).

In one of his most recent syntheses of his work entitled 'We are not the only ones in the world' ('Nous ne sommes pas seuls au monde', 2001) Nathan points out that this approach, now called 'ethnopsychiatry' has always been 'an experimental field of mediation between treatments immigrants bring and Western therapies' and he describes ethnopsychiatry's theoretical bases as follows: (1) not to allow oneself to disqualify "local psychopathologies"; (2) to try to highlight the value of the implicit theories of these treatments; and (3) to commit oneself to demonstrate that these treatments also offer solutions to technical problems of therapists everywhere' (2001, p. 76).

CONSEQUENCES OF A PLURITHEORETIC CLINICAL SETTING

To respect 'local psychopathologies' means that it is imperative to better understand these theories' contents, structure and function. As illustrated by Nathan's work, this effort may also lead to a better understanding of one's own theories and to interesting hypotheses on fundamental aspects of 'traditional' and Western psychotherapies.

Several 'traditional' theories are described in Nathan's book entitled *Le sperme du diable* ('The sperm of the devil', 1988), for instance 'possession by a genie, a demon, an ancestor', 'sorcery', 'fright and loss of one's soul', 'transgression of a taboo'. Even though, according to Nathan, 'primarily they seem to be forms of "know how" and not elaborated theoretic systems' (1988a, p. 101), for example sorcery is 'a metapsychology whose main function is to serve as a therapeutic framework offering a certain type of psychotherapy' (1988a, p. 113). This theory 'represents a coherent and homogenous therapeutic framework and uses the logic of primary processes while integrating them in ordinary life, using material proofs and objects' (1988a, p. 124). Nathan suggests that an etiologic theory 'represents a sort of story that suggests a solution: it is used to describe a pathologic incident. However, the chronology of this story is not linear, it is paradoxical and introduces the function of 'après-coup'. He also stresses that the function of 'traditional' etiologies is very different from medical etiologies' function: the latter wrap up diagnostic investigations while the former represent a 'stimulation to talk' (faire parler); they stimulate questions and do not put an end to the search of meaning (1988a, p. 146); furthermore, a given problem can be interpreted according to various etiologic theories.

Nathan's concept of 'traditional' (non-Western) etiologic theories and Kleinman's concept of explanatory model seem quite similar, but Kleinman focuses on the content of explanatory models considering them mainly as 'representations of the cultural flow of life experiences' (Kleinman, 1988, p. 122) while Nathan insists on 'traditional' etiologic theories' function as a container or as a form of diagnostic system in the sense of Kleinman's definition of diagnosis as an interpretation of the patient's illness according to a theoretical system. Characteristics and functions of 'traditional' etiologic theories seem to be similar to those of retrospective narrative truth in analytic-hermeneutic psychotherapy (Kirmayer, 1994). According to Kirmayer narrative truth 'refers to the construction of a coherent story out of current experience and the events of a life. . . . The efficacy of narrative truth lies in its ability . . . to situate illness in an ongoing story that affirms core personal and societal values' (Kirmayer, 1994, pp. 198–199). It seems that a key aspect of a psychic problem stems from a lack of meaning that can be shared with others or, as put by Nathan: 'suffering is solitude in meaning' (1994, p. 112).

To introduce 'traditional' therapies in the clinical setting made it possible to highlight their value; their similarities with forms of Western therapies became more evident. An analysis of therapeutic mechanisms in non-Western therapies and psychoanalysis represents a first step in Nathan's exploration of possible contributions of 'traditional' treatments to a better understanding of fundamental structures and mechanisms of therapy. Nathan's analysis of the formal structure of symptoms and of therapeutic procedures suggests that the mechanism of reversal is present in 'traditional' therapies and in psychoanalysis (1994). Mediation seems to represent another important therapeutic mechanism. In non-Western therapies a supernatural world usually described in basic myths is used to give meaning to the patient's symptoms; therefore, a form of mediation between the ordinary and the extraordinary world is needed (1994, p. 148). The third major therapeutic mechanism identified consists in a way of thinking, i.e. analogical reasoning. Nathan states that analogical thinking is induced by the therapeutic setting (analogical thinking in act) and is used in the therapist's propositions (interpretations, prescriptions, constructions) (1994, p. 120). The main conclusions of Nathan's analysis focusing on the pragmatics of therapies are summarized in the following hypotheses:

1   The etiologic theory, the material therapeutic setting and/or an active object, i.e. a formal container, induce logical processes such as analogical thinking, mediation and reversal (1994, p. 132/133) which always are set to work in a universe that can be technically manipulated (1994, p. 149).

2   'In order for a therapeutic process to take place, i.e. the patient's expulsion from the ordinary universe, inductions in other sectors need to duplicate the basic therapeutic idea illustrated by the therapeutic setting; therefore the manipulation of objects, of the therapist's or the patient's body, repeat the logic inscribed in the material setting' (1994, p. 145).

The use of a pluritheoretic clinical setting helped Nathan to discover the purely instrumental function of all forms of theory: a clinical approach in which a given fact is interpreted differently according to various cultural (theoretical) contexts illustrates that theories or 'theoretical statements we believe to be descriptions of the observed object's nature only represent part of the instrument necessary for the observation to take place' (1994, p. 72). As mentioned by Nathan, this clinical setting illustrates well Devereux's suggestion (1980) according to which 'it is never possible to observe the object itself, only the interaction of three factors: a given observer, the instrument of observation – the psychotherapeutic relationship and its theoretical and technical a priori – and the object itself' (1994, p. 72). Ethnopsychoanalytic therapy highlighted that in psychopathology no neutral observation is possible because the fact is created by the theory used. ('Anna O. + Freud = typical case of hysteria; Anna O. + Jewish Ashkenazi tradition = typical case of a possession by a dibouk', 1994, p. 303). Nathan concludes that the way to think of a patient represents a deliberate influence on the patient since the theory does not describe the fact but creates it and he suggests that all forms of therapy represent an influence of the patient (1994, p. 27).

In one of his recent writings, the chapter entitled 'Elements of psychotherapy' ('éléments de psychothérapie', 1998), Nathan tried to define common elements of all forms of therapies and he presents the following definition of psychotherapy: 'a procedure destined to influence and modify in a radical, profound and permanent way a person, a family, or simply, a situation by using a "therapeutic intention"' (1998, p. 12). This definition applies to 'scientific' psychotherapies as well as 'traditional' therapies, the latter often previously seen as based on 'beliefs' or 'suggestion'. According to Nathan, a psychotherapy 'is not a discussion between persons . . . initiating emotional discharge or cathartic reorganizations . . . psychotherapy is a conceptual war: a conflict whose outcome is to adhere to a theory' (1998a, p. 17). 'The therapist's ideas shared with his colleagues . . . "are the major motor of influence"' (2001, p. 14). The procedures used – manifest actions, questions asked, etc. – have to be seen as means to incarnate the theory. Nathan suggests that: 'whether the therapist tries to convince his patient or whether he just lets the patient reveal himself, the procedure is always a demonstration of the theory used' (2001, p. 15).

This view of psychotherapy led Nathan to the following definition of an interpretation: 'part of the meaning emanating from the therapist that respects two basic obligations: (1) to impose the idea that the therapist knows the origin of the problem, its ecology, and that he is in control of this theory; (2) to convince the patient that he, the patient, can give up the knowledge of the problem' (1998, p. 17). He suggests that an interpretation is defined by its function and can be based on words but that an interpretation can also consist in gestures, actions or mimics (1998, p. 20). 'The active ingredient of an interpretation is not its content but the process put in motion by it and that forces the patient to adhere to the therapist's theory' (1998, p. 22).

Nathan also points out that all therapists master abstract and complex theories with the following characteristics: expertise, causality, and the capacity to use events to create a story (1998, p. 33). According to Nathan 'the therapist is always the carrier ("porteur") of a myth of the creation of mankind and of the world – of a cosmogony – told and demonstrated incessantly in his way of being, in his actions and his therapeutic words' (1998, p. 50). In these myths the way to create and the difficulties in doing so are described. According to Nathan, scientific therapists could not heal if they did not have a myth of creation; he points out that Freud described in 'Totem and taboo' what happened at the beginning of the world, Freud's hypothesis being based on Darwin's theory of evolution (1998, p. 55). However, as stressed by Nathan, this myth does not describe the beginning of one specific world but of the entire world, the ancestor being the Darwinian ape, an ancestor of all human kind (1998, p. 56); Nathan concludes that it seems difficult for therapists adopting this myth to acknowledge the difference or 'otherness' ('l'altérité') and, therefore, everybody is seen as identical (1998, p. 58).

In regard to therapeutic techniques, according to Nathan the following basic differences between Western and non-Western theories are crucial: in

Western cultures, characterized by the existence of a single universe, disorder is seen as a sort of illness located inside the individual, whereas in non-Western cultures, comprising multiple universes, the disorder is dissociated from the individual, it is attributed to the intention of the invisible (1995, p. 56).

CONCLUSION

The present example of a specific clinical approach for psychotherapeutic work with migrant patients developed by Nathan illustrates an attempt to take into account the well-known fact that in all cultures we find coherence between culture, specific ways to express distress, to explain the latter and to treat it. The main characteristics of Nathan's psychotherapeutic setting are the use of patients' mother tongue and its pluritheoretic nature, i.e. the use of psychoanalytic theory and 'traditional' etiologic (non-Western) theories. This clinical setting made it possible to give meaning to idiosyncratic experiences by using culturally authorized interpretations, as is usually done in symbolic healing (Dow, 1986; Kleinman, 1988). As suggested by Nathan's analysis of therapeutic mechanisms, it seems that in ethnopsychoanalytic therapy, like in other forms of therapy, the principal theoretical idea is illustrated by the material setting and is duplicated with the help of inductions in the therapeutic procedure. The material setting, i.e. the use of a multicultural group of therapists which, if possible, includes at least one co-therapist whose culture of origin is similar to the patient's cultural background comprises the induction that it is necessary to use one's own cultural referential systems in order to give meaning to one's suffering; this setting also suggests that mediation between different cultural referential systems is possible since therapists of various cultural origin are united in the same therapeutic space. These main theoretical ideas are also illustrated in the therapeutic procedure used: the patient's problems are interpreted according to theories specific to his culture of origin and also according to other cultural referential systems represented in the group. The latter illustrates that interpretation of a problem varies according to different cultural groups. In other words, the therapeutic procedure is coherent with the logic of migrant patients' main difficulties, particularly those depriving them of the access to explanations coherent with the cultural structure of their symptoms and their difficulty of mediation between cultural universes. More recently, Nathan emphasized that ethnopsychiatry aims not only to understand the subjective suffering of the patient, but also to define the theories that contain the patient's suffering and that structure him (2001, p. 98). Despite the lack of research data, clinical experience suggests that this clinical approach brings good results with patients who could not be helped using 'scientific' Western therapies; Nathan's approach is also employed outside the center directed until recently by himself (in other parts of France, other European countries and also in Quebec).

As emphasized by Nathan, despite the use of 'traditional' etiologic theories, ethnopsychiatry does not promote 'traditional' techniques with migrant patients: 'ethnopsychiatry means to practice diplomacy in the universe of psychiatry' (2001, p. 89), in the sense that 'the therapist needs to become a diplomat who is aware of the conflict between his own theories and techniques and those used in the group the patient belongs to' (1998, p. 93). Nathan stresses that 'to see the patient as a member of a group does not mean that he is no longer seen as a unique individual, or to reduce the individual to his culture and to make him prisoner of it' (2001, p. 107). 'The universality of all human beings is an evidence' (2001, p. 108), 'the important differences to study are in the objects, i.e. objects created by the group, such as languages, therapeutic systems, therapeutic techniques, etc.' (2001, p. 109).

Nathan's approach does not focus on issues of discrimination and racism; nevertheless, these aspects seem to be dealt with indirectly: to unite professionals from several minority groups might help the patient feel less marginal in regard to the dominant culture. Furthermore, as mentioned by Nathan (1988a), the use of 'traditional' etiologic theories in the context of an official institution of the host country means that the dominant group recognizes their value. Furthermore, as put by Nathan, 'in our time of globalization the problem of psychotherapy is the following: how to proceed, in a way that my techniques and concepts do not insult those who have different roots, different referential systems, different "objects", without losing my own tradition of rationality?' (2001, p. 89).

Although, as pointed out by Nathan, it is possible for a patient to consult any kind of therapist (2001, p. 276), it seems plausible that it is important to take into account the therapeutic systems that have structured the internal world of the patient (2001, p. 86). Nathan suggests that 'a therapeutic proposition aiming at a reconstruction of the identity: (a) needs to accompany closely the patient's actual experiences; (b) has to take into account the pressure of his circle ("entourage") and (c) has to inscribe the patient as a member of his social group' (2001, p. 281).

Notes

1 Nathan, who is a professor of clinical psychology at the University 'Paris VIII', first trained in sociology and anthropology, then in psychology and psychoanalysis (Ph.D in psychology, thesis directed by Georges Devereux; 'Doctorat d'état ès Lettres et Sciences Humaines', thesis directed by Didier Anzieu; Société psychanalytique de Paris); in 1979 he began the development of a clinical approach specific to migrant patients (mainly from North Africa, West Africa and the Caribbean Islands) called 'consultation of ethnopsychoanalysis' (psychopathology department at Avicenne Hospital, Bobigny). In 1988 he established a

similar clinic in the mother and child welfare area (Département de l'Enfance et de la famille du Conseil Général de la Seine Saint-Denis). Since January 1993 he has been director of the Centre Georges Devereux (a centre of care, teaching and research in ethnopsychiatry at the University 'Paris VIII'). This institution provides psychological assistance to immigrant families mainly from Africa and the French-speaking Caribbean islands, but also from francophone islands of the Indian Ocean, from Turkey and South-east Asia. The majority of the families are referred by social and medical services (Protection Maternelle et Infantile, L'Aide Sociale à l'Enfance, La Sauvegarde de l'Enfance et de l'Adolescence) but also by the judicial system (Tribunaux pour Enfants et Protection Judiciaire de la Jeunesse). The clinical work focuses on three main aspects: the explanation of the family's problems (if necessary, individual therapeutic work with certain family members is added); the re-establishment of links with the milieu of origin; and assistance in the relationship with the various governmental services in charge of the family.

2 All quotations from Nathan's work are my own free translation.

References

Devereux, G. (1972) *Ethnopsychanalyse complémentarise*. Paris: Flammarion.

Devereux, G. (1980) *De l'angoisse à la méthode dans les sciences du comportement*. Paris: Flammarion.

Dow, J. (1986) Universal Aspects of Symbolic Healing: A Theoretical Synthesis, *American Anthropologist* 88: 56–69.

Frank, J. D. and Frank, J. B. (1991) *Persuasion and Healing: A Comparative Study of Psychotherapy*, 3rd edn. Baltimore, MD: Johns Hopkins University Press.

Gailly, A. (1991) Problèmes liés au contexte multiculturel de la relation soignant-soigné, in J. Leman and A. Gailly (eds), *Thérapies interculturelles: L'interaction soignant-soigné dans un contexte multiculturel et interdisciplinaire*. Brussels: De Boeck-Wesmael, pp. 95–115.

Hiegel J. P. (1991) Coopérer avec des médecins traditionnels asiatiques. Un métissage de savoir, *Nouvelle Revue d'Ethnopsychiatrie* 17: 23–52.

Kareem, J. (1992) The Nafsiyat Intercultural Therapy Centre: Ideas and Experiences in Intercultural Therapy, in J. Kareem and R. Littlewood (eds), *Intercultural Therapy: Themes, Interpretations and Practice*. Oxford: Blackwell Scientific Publications, pp. 14–37.

Kirmayer, L. J. (1994) Improvisation and Authority in Illness Meaning, *Culture, Medicine and Psychiatry* 18: 183–214.

Kleinman, A. (1988) *Rethinking Psychiatry: From Cultural Category to Personal Experience*. New York: The Free Press.

Littlewood, R. (1992) How Universal is Something we can Call 'Therapy'?, in J. Kareem and R. Littlewood (eds), *Intercultural Therapy: Themes, Interpretations and Practice*. Oxford: Blackwell Scientific Publications, pp. 38–56.

Moore, L. J. and Boehnlein, J. K. (1991) Treating Psychiatric Disorders among Mien Refugees from Highland Laos, *Social Sciences and Medicine* 32(9): 1027–1036.

Nathan, T. (1986) *La folie des autres: Traité d'ethnopsychiatrie clinique*. Paris: Dunod.

Nathan, T. (1988a) *Le sperme du diable, éléments d'ethnopsychothérapie*. Paris: Presses Universitaires de France.

Nathan, T. (1988b) La migration des âmes. *Nouvelle revue d'ethnopsychiatrie* no. 11, 25–42.

Nathan, T. (1993) *Fier de n'avoir ni pays ni amis, quelle sottise c'était: Principes d'ethnopsychanalyse*. Grenoble: La Pensée Sauvage.

Nathan, T. (1994) *L'influence qui guérit*. Paris: Editions Odile Jacob.

Nathan, T. (1995) Manifeste pour une psychopathologie scientifique, in T. Nathan and I. Stengers (eds), *Médecins et sorciers*. Paris: Les empêcheurs de penser en rond, pp. 9–113.

Nathan, T. (1998) Eléments de psychothérapie, in T. Nathan, Alain Blanchet, Serban Ionescu and N. Zajde, *Psychothérapies*. Paris: Editions Odile Jacob, pp. 11–96.

Nathan, T. (2001) *Nous ne sommes pas seuls au monde*. Paris: Les empêcheurs de penser en rond/Le Seuil.

Torrey, E. F. (1986) *Witchdoctors and Psychiatrists: The Common Roots of Psychotherapy and Its Future*. New York: Harper & Row.

White, G. M. and Marsella, A. J. (1982) Introduction: Cultural Conceptions in Mental Health Research and Practice, in A. J. Marsella and G. M. White (eds), *Cultural Conceptions of Mental Health and Therapy*. Dordrecht, Reidel, pp. 3–38.

Chapter 20

Cultural representations and interpretations of 'subjective distress' in ethnic minority patients[1]

Roy Moodley

The question of representing and interpreting 'psychological distress' or 'subjective distress' is one of the most difficult to measure and least understood variables in psychotherapy (Barkham *et al.*, 1996). As a result it continues to generate much of the research in this area (see, for example, Aveline and Shapiro, 1995; Dryden, 1996; Roth and Fonagy, 1996; Toukmanian and Rennie, 1992), but the focus seems to be confined to mainstream patients' groups; with ethnic minority patients appearing to be under-researched, and some of the major 'issues' concerning this patient group tend to be untheorized (Moodley, 2000).

If 'psychological distress' is difficult to measure generally in psychotherapy, investigating it in ethnic minority patients would present numerous challenges and limitations to researchers and practitioners alike. The challenges of course are always present, whether one is researching or practising psychotherapy with ethnic minority patients, but the limitations only begin to surface when psychotherapeutic ideas are applied to this patient group without any reference to 'the network of meanings that an illness has in a particular culture' (Good and Good, 1982, p. 148) or how 'distinct cultures shape the language and experience of emotions' (Bhugra and Bhui, 1998). Although the relationship between 'psychological distress' and culture is primary in shaping the illness representation of the patient, it is the psychotherapist's understanding of the patient's cultural influences in illness representations that is called into question. A view in which culture is construed to be reductive, absolute and anthropologically fixed can problematize the therapeutic process by limiting the world view of the psychotherapist or engage a therapist to interpret culturally sensitive material in a stereotypical way.

'Race', culture and ethnicity are discursive and contested sites within which the patient can be made ill as well as engage in meaningful psychological transformation. When ethnic minority patients' cultures are seen as 'living and lived-in cultures with all their vitality, complexity, complementaries and contradictions, cultures that are empowering, changing, challenging, and flexible . . . rather than lifeless, limp, cellophane-wrapped and neatly tagged cultures' (Ahmad, 1996, p. 199), then psychotherapists will be challenged to construct new meanings (of plurality and multiplicity) within contemporary psychotherapy. It may be that a patient's understanding of these issues is much more sophisticated than some of the research methods being employed; which leads Leventhal *et al.* (1980) to suggest that a patient's behaviour, in dealing with illness, can be studied in the context of the patient's own illness representation, coping and adaptation.

In this chapter, I will discuss the illness representation perceptions of Leventhal *et al.* (1980), Leventhal and Diefenbach (1991), Leventhal, Nerenz and Steele (1984), Scharloo *et al.* (1998), and Alladin (1999). This will be followed by looking at culture and illness representations, and the interpretations of subjective distress in ethnic minority clients.

ILLNESS REPRESENTATION MODELS

Research concerning how individuals think about health and illness has been steadily growing with many different terms being used for the same concept, namely patient's schema, illness representation, illness concept and illness perceptions (for example Leventhal *et al.*, 1980; Scharloo *et al.*, 1998). There seems to be a correlation between the ideas individuals have about health and illness, the ways in which they manifest their distress and the clinical, medical and social processes that are available to deal with these concerns. The research that has been conducted in the health sciences area has attempted to map out an individual's representation of illness and situate it in context. For example, in medical sociology where research has concentrated on 'lay accounts', the emphasis has been on social factors (see, for example, Blaxter, 1983; Calnan, 1987), and in health psychology where research has concentrated on 'illness representations', the focus has been on cognitive models (see, for example, Lau and Hartman, 1983; Leventhal *et al.*, 1980; Leventhal *et al.*, 1997; Scharloo *et al.*, 1998; Levine, 1999). In general, illness models can be conceptualized as 'generic and organised cognitive representations or schemata that derive from prior experiences in the medical domain and guide the processing of information in a fashion that is consistent with the prior knowledge' (Schober and Lacroix, 1991, p. 12; cited by Scharloo *et al.*, 1998, pp. 573–574).

According to Scharloo *et al.* (1998), the theory and research concerning how individuals think about health and illness can be traced back to Leventhal *et al.*'s (1980) ground-breaking article, 'The Commonsense Representation of Illness Danger'. In this article, Leventhal *et al.* argue that a patient's behaviour, in dealing with illness, can be studied in the context of the patient's own illness representation that is largely based on concrete symptom experience. They suggest that 'the patient's symptoms, his beliefs and their determinants, and his beliefs about treatment form an organised and more or less coherent theory of illness. The degree of organization will vary from person to person as will the ability to verbalize the organization. The patient's statements may not be identical with his underlying beliefs' (pp. 16–17). According to Kemp *et al.* (1999), within this model 'patients actively construct a cognitive representation of illness and regulate coping in ways consistent with this representation . . . the model views illness-related coping and adjustment as the result of an ongoing process in which patients integrate illness-related information with existing cognitive structures to form an illness representation' (p. 45). It seems, then, that patients create cognitive models or schemas of their illness which in turn become the basis for the way they cope and adapt in their day-to-day lives. This is a process of self-regulation according to Leventhal and his colleagues (1980).

Research on the structure of illness perceptions by Lau and Hartman (1983), Leventhal *et al.* (1980), Leventhal and Diefenbach (1991), Leventhal, Nerenz and Steele (1984) and Scharloo *et al.* (1998) consistently suggest the five following dimensions:

- *identity*, the label placed on the illness and its symptoms, and the knowledge/s of the symptoms associated with the illness;
- *causes*, ideas about how one gets the illness;
- *consequences*, the expected outcome in terms of physical, psycho-social and economic implications;
- *timeline*, ideas about the duration of the illness;
- *controllability/cure*, belief about the extent to which the illness can be cured or controlled.

These dimensions can be formulated into an illness representational scale to measure cognitive representations of illness perceptions. Nerenz and Leventhal (1983) suggest that the central issue in understanding illness is to examine how people integrate their experience of illness with their general self concept. Elsewhere, Leventhal *et al.* (1997) examine the notion of illness representation and its relationship to representations of the self.

Another illness representation model that is similar to the one suggested by Leventhal *et al.* (1980) and Scharloo *et al.* (1998) is the nine-point Ethnomedical Model proposed by Alladin (1993, 1999). Alladin advocates its use in transcultural psychotherapy and counselling, arguing that it 'can be more universally applied without doing violence to other cultures . . . is a personally orientated paradigm that could facilitate therapeutic dialogue and increase transcultural sensitivity' (Alladin, 1999, p. 99). The Ethnomedical Model is tabulated below:

- sickness conception
- body function beliefs

- well-being criteria
- causal/healing beliefs
- medical practice/efficacy beliefs
- recognition of health needs
- reliance on self-treatment and diagnosis
- cooperation with health advice
- acceptance of suggestions for health care

According to Alladin, this model places culture at the core, permeating every aspect of an individual's illness representation as well as healing system.

All the models discussed above raise important questions in relation to notions of 'race', culture and ethnicity and issues of self identity, especially the black identity theories of psychotherapists, such as Cross (1971, 1991) and Helms (1990). This investigation may yield interesting results, particularly in relation to Levine's (1999) experiments on identity and illness, that confirm (the earlier findings) that changes in the frame of reference of social identity can lead to shifts in the way people evaluate illness.

Other studies have shown that patients manifest a socially constructed view of their ill-health which emphasizes social relations in terms of dominance and subordination (see, for example, Stainton-Rogers, 1991), while others point to culture and its relationship to mental (ill) health (see, for example, Rack, 1982). While illness representations have a social component (culturally available information about illness), explaining long-term changes in the way people sense symptoms is problematic. Levine argues that it is difficult to explain 'changes that appear to be a function of shifts in immediate social context' (Levine, 1999, p. 64). Clearly, considerable care needs to be taken when interpreting clinical and research material regarding the social and cultural dimensions, and their impact or influence on mental (ill) health, especially in relation to 'race' where the groups concerned, namely minority groups, do not themselves participate in the construction of these discourses.

CULTURE AND ILLNESS REPRESENTATIONS

Although the association between culture and mental illness had been made by the early Greek and Arab physicians, it was not until a three-volume treatise by the Arab historian and philosopher Ibn Khaldun (1332–1406 [1967–68])[2] in the fourteenth century, that a serious reference was made linking culture and mental illness (Murphy, 1986). For example, social, economic and political variables are not seen to be important in psychotherapy, or at least not sufficiently theorised to explain some of the 'psychological distresses' experienced by patients, as Ibn Khaldun had observed. Understanding these distresses cannot be done in isolation from the patient's socio-cultural environment and the associated network of meanings that Good and Good (1982) talk about. They maintain that, 'the meaning of illness for an individual is grounded in . . . the network of meanings an illness has in a particular culture' (p. 148). This idea appears to be similar to the five stages of illness representation that Lau and Hartman (1983), Leventhal *et al.* (1980), Leventhal and Diefenbach (1991), Leventhal, Nerenz and Steele (1984), Scharloo *et al.* (1998) and Alladin (1999) discuss. Applying the basic ideas of these models in cross-cultural studies would reveal that ideas, beliefs and cultural practices of (being) existence contribute to the way in which an individual thinks about illness. As Bhugra and Bhui note,

> Distinct cultures shape the language and experience of emotions by selectively encouraging or discouraging specific sets of emotional experience that are regarded as taboo or dysfunctional within that society. A recognition that an individual, group, or family are displaying these unsanctioned behaviours or beliefs signals to other members of society that they are ill and need help.
>
> (Bhugra and Bhui, 1998, p. 311)

It seems that a collective socio-culturally based identification and naming of an illness is inextricably linked to the perceptions of other members of the patient's family, cultural and ethnic group and the wider society. A public display or expression of a particular 'psychological distress' will determine or validate the condition whilst at the same time providing the necessary resources for a cure. This kind of scenario, in which the psychological expression is constituted as part of the social and political experiences, may direct an individual patient's therapy into deeper layers of his or her cultural resources. A patient's representations may also reveal that a cure is not possible for the individual self, until the causes are controlled/cured at the social, cultural and political levels. Vaughan puts it this way, 'The individual's body may act as a conduit through which social tensions and raptures are expressed . . . [and] must be ultimately solved at the level of the social group if the illness is to be cured' (Vaughan, 1994, p. 292).

The interplay between the individual and society is, no doubt, a complex one and one that has been unacknowledged by psychiatry and, to a lesser extent by psychotherapy. In fact, this position has been constrained by some of the theories of psychoanalysis. For example, Littlewood argues that psychiatric approaches 'lack any rigorous theory for dealing with the dialectical interplay of biology and human society, or for examining the relationship between psychopathologies and its own procedure of research and practice' (Littlewood, 1990, p. 309). Furthermore, he asserts that, whilst psychoanalysis acknowledges the relationship between biology and society, it is nevertheless constrained by the theory itself disregarding ethnographic data and universalizing particular theories, namely the Oedipus complex in matrilineal societies.[3]

CULTURAL BELIEFS AND CURE SEEKING

According to Schober and Lacroix (1991), a close correlation exists between a patient's cultural beliefs about his or her illness and between his or her understanding of the treatment of such distress. They suggest that generic and organized cognitive representations or schemata are derived from prior experiences in the medical domain that guide the processing of information in a fashion that is consistent with the prior knowledge. In other words, knowledge/s about psychotherapy and its effectiveness will contribute to ethnic minority patients help-seeking strategies. A patient's representation of 'psychological distress' is not only schematically constituted through the experiencing of symptoms, naming it, and understanding the causes but also constituted through the range of treatment/s available for the cure. While the patient's socio-cultural and ethnic belief system informs her or his ideas about health and illness and the levels of sophistication of this understanding, it is also dependent on the method of cure that is available to the patient, such as traditional healing methods, complementary medicine, Western conventional medicine, psychiatry and psychotherapy.

The availability of one or many of these cures will contribute to the conceptualization of illness by the patient and the particular way in which this is expressed to the therapist. It also seems possible for patients to conceptualize and present their 'psychological distress' in cure-related ways. In other words, a patient is able to construct and present depression, for instance, in a different way to a Western therapist than to a traditional healer. Of course depression is experienced and labelled differently in different cultures, a fact that is often forgotten when ethnic minority patients enter Western psychotherapy. This point is made by Pilgrim, who is critical of the universal assumptions of notions of distress that are found within Western psychiatry and psychotherapy. He suggests, 'Deviation expressed from the Western norm is then described as a distortion of reality. Consequently, because Asian people talk in terms, say, of "a falling heart" this is construed by Western psychiatric commentators as a disguised or distorted ("somatised") version of another "true" condition (i.e. depression)' (Pilgrim, 1997, p. 74). In South Asian culture where the heart is central to the culture, there is a separation between the notion of 'the sinking heart' (*dil ghirda hai*) and sadness (see Fenton and Sadiq, 1993; Krause, 1989). The idiom of the 'sinking heart' may be regarded by contemporary observers as a metaphor for depression, but for Asian patients it

may be a dialectal interplay between the body as a social site and the ideas/
philosophy of cultural morals and values. Kleinman's (1997) 'Somatomoral
Framework' appears to offer an explanation. The 'sinking heart' experience
may be seen as an inextricable link between the psychological, physiological
and the moral-religious aspects of a patient's life.

Many ethnic minority patients are able to make a choice between the two
different modes of therapy – the traditional cultural healing and conventional Western psychotherapy. They are able to experience traditional
healing as well as Western counselling and psychotherapy, presenting 'psychological distress' to each therapist appropriately. This suggests that
competing and contradictory cures can be held alongside one another or in
tandem with each other without necessarily creating conflict in the patient.
It seems that patients are comfortable with Pierre Bourdieu's (1990) notion
of the 'polythetic' (many positions).

INTERPRETATIONS OF SUBJECTIVE DISTRESS

Communicating, conceptualizing and (in)validating experiences of 'psychological distress' of the patient has been the historical function of
psychotherapists irrespective of his/her orientation viz. psychoanalytic,
psychodynamic, cognitive behavioural, humanistic, feminist, etc. It involves
both technical skill as well as a deepened knowledge of the theoretical
awareness of a particular orientation. In turn, each particular orientation is
governed by its own set of empirically or theoretically validated criteria for
successful outcomes – seeking in the patients a more 'integrated and
together' personality. For example, psychoanalytic psychotherapy following
Klein, Winnicott, and others developed 'object relations theory' to
emphasize the 'vertical split' between the good and bad parts of the self
which in turn get projected into the world. This was seen as a development
from Freud's preoccupation with the 'horizontal split' between the conscious
and unconscious mind. For a psychoanalytic psychotherapist constructing
meaning through the idea of the 'vertical split', it is not an issue about
remembering what has been forgotten, but one of recognizing and accepting
those parts of the self that have been disowned (Holmes, 1998). These
theoretical ideas offer each therapeutic orientation a conceptually unique,
historically specific and culturally focused identity and one in which the
therapist can (in)validate the patient's utterances and his/her own
communications.

But for the ethnic minority patients who do not conceptualize a vertical
or horizontal split of the self, can psychotherapy interpretations make any
sense? Some studies (Asuni, 1986; Buhrmann, 1986; Fernando, 1988;
Littlewood and Lipsedge, 1982 [1997]) report that ethnic minority groups
use a different conceptual model to represent their illnesses. For example,

Asuni in comparing African traditional healing methods with the European model suggests that the 'why' questioning and interpreting of conflict and illness is given more emphasis than the 'how' model used by Western therapists (Asuni, 1986, p. 314). Buhrmann, with reference to the Nguni people of South Africa, observed the difference between Western methods that divide illness into different categories of somatic, psychological and psychosomatic, and those of black people that do not. They do not split themselves into good and bad parts but express their distress as, 'when part of me is ill, the whole of me is ill' (Buhrmann, 1986, p. 26), irrespective of what the illness is. Conceptualizing and presenting 'psychological distress' in this way may also be indicative of the social nature of illness presentation.

For the psychotherapist to communicate, conceptualize and (in)validate 'psychological distress' of the patient effectively he/she must, therefore, be both technically skilled and theoretically knowledgable.[4] When working with ethnic minority patients the psychotherapists must also be aware of the 'other' – 'race', culture and ethnicity – parameters which permeate psychotherapy. As 'race', culture and ethnicity transform the ethnographic and cultural icons for ethnic minority communities in socio-political and economic representations, so too will the psychotherapeutic project be influenced by these variables. Through the transference and countertransference communications it becomes possible for the patient's peripheral 'voice' to take centre stage. In 'New Ethnicities', Stewart Hall (1992) attempts to mark this shift from the margins of 'dominant hegemonic discourses' by the recognition that black people 'speak from a particular space, out of a particular history (and) out of a particular experience' (p. 258). However, this shift from the periphery, from the margins, is further complicated by a history that is already waiting (in the space of the therapist) for the ethnic minority patient. In *Black Skin White Masks*, Frantz Fanon (1967) identifies with the construction of this kind of subjectivity when he says that: 'It is not I who make a meaning for myself, but it is the meaning that was already there, pre-existing, waiting for me . . . waiting for that turn of history' (p. 134); to which Bhabha (1994) argues that Fanon is: 'not principally posing the question of political oppression as the violation of human essence, although he lapses into such a lament in his more existential moments . . . [but] Fanon radically questions the formation of both individual and social authority as they come to be developed in the discourse of social sovereignty' (pp. 42–43).

These parameters may indulge significantly in psychotherapy with black patients making un(re)presentable 'psychological distress' easily interpretable or important socio-political frames of the person's self-concept empty and meaningless, for example the emphasis that psychotherapy with ethnic minority patients must take account of slavery, indentureship, colonialism and present-day racism. These experiences are potentially oppressive, promoting conflict and pathology (see Fanon, 1967; Burke, 1986). However, empowered with competent skills, theoretical knowledge and expertise of the 'other', the psychotherapist can enter the narrative of the ethnic minority patient with comfortable ease.

CONCLUSION

When culture is situated within any model of illness representation it begins to interrogate the privileged site of 'internal experience' in psychology. Social, religious and cultural influences, metaphors and complexes have a profound effect on the individual. 'Psychological distress' is then conceptualized and presented in ways that are inclusive of and at the same time removed from these socio-cultural constructs. The models used in therapy are expected to 'heal' the patient at the individual level as well as at the cultural and the social. In the past, the universal models of the transcultural approach with ethnic minority patients advocated a non-Eurocentric way of conducting psychotherapy, but continued to maintain Western categories in diagnosis and interpretations, assuming that they were themselves culture-free. The emphasis on taking account of local meanings of illness patterns, together with a wide range of socially and culturally related behaviours, would be critical in the interpretations that a psychotherapist would make with ethnic minority patients.

Notes

1 A version of this chapter has been published as 'Representation of Subjective Distress in Ethnic Minority Patients: Constructing a Research Agenda', in the journal *Counselling Psychology Quarterly* 13 (2000): 159–174 (www.tandf.co.uk).
2 Ibn Khaldun was an Arab historian and philosopher who explored the 'variety and unity, stability and fluctuation, shifts in power and permanent realities which have organized the Arab world for about a millennium and a half' (Said, 1991, p. 22). Ibn Khaldun offered an understanding of the psycho-social experiences of Bedouin migration from a nomadic existence to an urban sedentary one, linking geographical, social and cultural changes to psychopathology of the person (Ritter, 1948; Said, 1991). In reflecting on the developments following Bedouin migration and the demands for a more self-centred culture, he provided a deeper understanding of the psycho-social experiences of those societies then. His writings, as seen in the excerpt below, clearly illustrate that cultural changes are inevitable in any migration, even one within the same geographical terrain and sharing almost the very same cultural mores as the Arab people in the Middle Ages.

> Corruption of the individual inhabitants is the result of painful and trying efforts to satisfy the needs caused by their (luxury) customs; (the result) of the bad qualities they have acquired in the process of obtaining (those needs); and of the damage the soul suffers after it has obtained them through

acquiring (still) another (bad luxury) quality. Immorality, wrongdoing, insincerity and trickery, for the purposes of making a living in a proper or an improper manner, increase amongst them . . . people are now devoted to lying, gambling, cheating, fraud, theft, perjury and usury.

(cited in Ritter, 1948, pp. 1–44)

Ibn Khaldun in describing such a growing prevalence of jealousy, distrust, self-indulgence and fear of others indicates a natural and rational reaction of the Arab people to the changes in social structure and the failure of the old tribal system to adapt (see Murphy, 1986, p. 7), but he also saw some of these reactions as pathological. Besides the process of social and cultural intervention, it is highly likely that a strong element of capitalist motivation that the Bedouins were exposed to created the psychopathological disturbances to which Ibn Khaldun refers.

3 Littlewood (1990, p. 311) refers to the interest in determining the universality of the Oedipus complex in matrilineal societies. Kakar notes that the Oedipus complex does not work in the same way with Indian patients. He draws this conclusion from his own work as well as from that of Grindrasekhar Bose, the founder of the Indian Psychoanalytic Society. Bose wrote to Freud on 11 April 1929 pointing out that the Oedipus Complex does not work in the same way with Indian patients, referring to the idea of an Oedipus mother being a combined parental image, drawing its origin from Devi, the great Indian goddess. Kakar suggests, 'The real struggle for the Indian male lies between the desire to be male and its opposite, the desire to be female' (Kakar, 1989, p. 129). Some Indian psychotherapists have attempted to integrate South Asian culture and traditions with psychotherapy, namely Satayanand (1972). He 'combined the traditions of psychoanalysis with concepts derived from Hindu mythology and philosophy to develop the techniques of handling primary narcissism' (Bhugra and Bhui, 1998, p. 320). These differences in re-conceptualizing some of the traditional psycho-analytic ideas to meet the cultural and historic diversity of individuals must be seen as a process generally taking place in psychoanalysis and psychotherapy. For example, 'the Oedipus complex is today seen in metaphorical and conceptual rather than literal terms' (Holmes, 1998, p. 231).

4 The technical skill of interpreting was clearly identified and defined by Freud. Freud (1910) indicated that the analyst must strive to 'turn his own unconscious like the receptive organ towards the transmitting unconscious of the patient' which he suggests can create countertransference, a process that the therapist must recognize – 'we have noticed that every analyst's achievement is limited by what his own complexes and resistance permit'.

References

Ahmad, W. I. U. (1996) The Trouble with Culture, in D. Kelleher and S. Hiller (eds), *Researching Cultural Differences in Health*. London: Routledge.

Alladin, W. J. (1993) The Ethnomedical Model as a Conceptual Tool for Counselling in Health Care Decision-Making, *British Journal of Guidance and Counselling* 21: 8–19.

Alladin, W. J. (1999) Models of Counselling and Psychotherapy for a Multiethnic Society, in S. Palmer and P. Laungani (eds), *Counselling in a Multicultural Society*. London: Sage, pp. 90–112.

Asuni, T. (1986) African and Western Psychiatry: A Comparison, in J. L. Cox (ed.), *Transcultural Psychiatry*. London: Croom Helm.

Aveline, M. and Shapiro, D. (eds) (1995) *Research Foundations for Psychotherapy Practice*. Chichester: Wiley.

Barkham, M., Stiles, W. B., Hardy, G. E. and Field, S. D. (1996) The Assimilation Model: Theory, Research and Practical Guidelines, in W. Dryden (ed.), *Research in Counselling and Psychotherapy*. London: Sage.

Bhabha, H. (1986) Signs Taken for Wonders: Questions of Ambivalence and Authority under a Tree Outside Delhi, May 1817, in Henry L. Gates Jr. (ed.), *'Race', Writing and Difference*. Chicago: University of Chicago Press, pp. 163–184.

Bhabha, H. (1994) *The Location of Culture*. London: Routledge.

Bhugra, D. and Bhui, K. (1998) Psychotherapy for Ethnic Minorities: Issues, Context and Practice, *British Journal of Psychotherapy* 14(3): 310–326.

Blaxter, M. (1983) The Causes of Disease: Women Talking, *Social Science and Medicine* 17: 59–69.

Bourdieu, P. (1990) *In Other Words: Essays towards a Reflexive Sociology*, trans. M. Adamson. Cambridge: Polity.

Buhrmann, M. V. (1986) *Living in Two Worlds: Communication between a White Healer and her Black Counterpart*. Chicago: Chiron.

Burke, A. W. (1986) Racism, Prejudice and Mental Health, in J. L. Cox (ed.), *Transcultural Psychiatry*. London: Croom Helm, pp. 139–157.

Calnan, M. (1987) *Health and Illness: The Lay Perspective*. London: Tavistock.

Cross, W. E. Jr. (1971) The Negro-to-Black Conversion Experience: Towards a Psychology of Black Liberation, *Black World* 20: 13–27.

Cross, W. E. Jr., Parham, T. A. and Helms, J. E. (1991) The Stages of Black Identity Development: Nigrescence Models, in R. C. Jones (ed.), *Black Psychology*. Berkeley: University of California Press.

Dryden, W. (ed.) (1996) *Research in Counselling and Psychotherapy*. London: Sage.

Fanon, F. (1967) *Black Skins White Masks*. London: Grove Press.

Fenton, S. and Sadiq, A. (1993) *The Sorrow in my Heart: Sixteen Asian Women Speak about Depression*. London: Commission for Racial Equality.

Fernando, S. (1988) *Race and Culture in Psychiatry*. Kent: Croom Helm.

Freud, S. (1910) The Future Prospect of Psycho-Analytic Therapy, *Standard Edition*, 11, trans. J. Strachey. London: Hogarth Press.

Good, B. J. and Good, M.-J. D. (1982) Towards a Meaning-Centred Analysis of Popular Illness Categories: 'Fright-Illness' and 'Heat Distress' in Iran, in A. J. Marsella and G. M. White (eds), *Cultural Conceptions of Mental Health and Therapy*. Dordrecht: Reidel.

Hall, S. (1992) New Ethnicities, in J. Donald and A. Rattansi (eds), *'Race', Culture and Difference*. Buckingham: Open University Press.

Helms, J. E. (1990) *Black and White Racial Identity: Theory, Research and Practice*. Westport, CT: Greenwood.

Holmes, J. (1998) The Changing Aims of Psychoanalytic Psychotherapy, *International Journal of Psycho-Analysis* 79(2): 227–240.

Ibn Khaldun [1332–1406] (1967–68) *Discours sur l'histoire universelle*, 3 vols, trans. V. Monteil. Paris: Sinbad Press.

Kakar, S. (1989) *Intimate Relations: Exploring Indian Sexuality*. New Delhi: Penguin.

Kemp, S., Morley, S. and Anderson, E. (1999) Coping with Epilepsy: Do Illness Representations Play a Role?, *British Journal of Clinical Psychology* 38(1): 43–58.

Kleinman, A. (1977) Depression, Somatisation and the New 'Cross Cultural Psychiatry', *Social Science and Medicine* 11: 3–10.

Krause, B. (1989) The Sinking Heart: A Punjabi Categorisation of Distress, *Social Science and Medicine* 29: 563–575.

Lau, R. R. and Hartman, K. A. (1983) Common Sense Representations of Common Illness, *Health Psychology* 2: 167–185.

Leventhal, H., Meyer, D. and Nerenz, D. R. (1980) The Common Sense Representation of Illness Danger, in S. Rachman (ed.), *Contributions to Medical Psychology*, vol. 2. New York: Pergamon.

Leventhal, H., Benyamini, Y., Brownlee, S., Diefenbach, M., Leventhal, E. A., Patrick-Miller, L. and Robitaille, C. (1997) Illness Representations: Theoretical Foundations, in K. J. Petrie and J. A. Weinman (eds), *Perceptions of Health and Illness*. London: Harwood Academic Press, pp. 19–45.

Leventhal, H. and Diefenbach, M. (1991) The Active Side of Illness Cognitions, in J. A. Skelton and R. T. Croyle (eds), *Mental Representations in Health and Illness*. New York: Springer-Verlag.

Leventhal, H., Nerenz, D. R. and Steele D. J. (1984) Illness Representations and Coping with Health Threats, in A. Baum, S. E. Taylor and J. E. Singer (eds), *Handbook of Psychology and Health*, vol. 4. Hillsdale, NJ: Erlbaum, pp. 219–252.

Levine, R. M. (1999) Identity and Illness: The Effects of Identity Salience and Frame of Reference on Evaluation of Illness and Injury, *British Journal of Health Psychology* 4: 63–80.

Littlewood, R. (1990) From Categories to Contexts: A Decade of the 'New Cross-Cultural Psychiatry', *British Journal of Psychiatry* 156: 308–327.

Littlewood, R. and Lipsedge, M. (1997) *Aliens and Alienists: Ethnic Minorities and Psychiatry*, 3rd edn. London: Routledge. (originally published 1982).

Moodley, R. (2000) Representation of Subjective Distress in Ethnic Minority Patients: Constructing a Research Agenda, *Counselling Psychology Quarterly* 13: 159–174 (www.tandf.co.uk).

Murphy, H. B. M. (1986) The Historical Development of Transcultural Psychiatry, in J. L. Cox (ed.), *Transcultural Psychiatry*. London: Croom Helm.

Nerenz, D. R. and Leventhal, H. (1983) Self-Regulation Theory in Chronic Illness, in T. G. Burish (ed.), *Coping with Chronic Disease*. London: Academic Press, pp. 13–37.

Pilgrim, D. (1997) *Psychotherapy and Society*. London: Sage.

Rack, P. (1982) *Race, Culture and Mental Disorder*. London: Tavistock Publications.

Ritter, H. (1948) *International Solidarity Groups: A Socio-Psychological Study in Connection with Ibn Khaldun*. Leiden.

Roth, A. and Fonagy, P. (eds) (1996) *What Works For Whom? A Critical Review of Psychotherapy Research*. New York: Guilford.

Said, E. W. (1991) The Greatest Story Never Told, *Independent on Sunday Review*, 24 February, p. 22.

Satayanand, D. (1972) *Dynamic Psychology of the Gita of Hinduism*. New Delhi: Oxford University Press.

Scharloo, M., Kaptein, A. A., Weinman, J., Hazes, J. M., Willems, L. N. A., Bergman, W. and Rooijmans, H. G. M. (1998) Illness Perceptions, Coping and Functioning in Patients with Rheumatoid Arthritis, Chronic Obstructive Pulmonary Disease and Psoriasis, *Journal of Psychosomatic Research* 44(5): 573–585.

Schober, R. and Lacroix, J. M. (1991) Lay Illness Models in the Enlightenment and the 20th Century: Some Historical Lessons, in J. A. Skelton and R. T. Croyle (eds), *Mental Representation in Health and Illness*. New York: Springer.

Stainton-Rogers, W. (1991) *Explaining Health and Illness: An Exploration of Diversity*. London: Harvester Wheatsheaf.

Toukmanian, S. G. and Rennie, D. L. (eds) (1992) *Psychotherapy Process Research: Paradigmatic and Narrative Approach*. Newbury Park, CA: Sage.

Vaughan, M. (1994) Healing and Curing: Issues in the Social History and Anthropology of Medicine in Africa, *Social History of Medicine, Journal of The Society for the Social History of Medicine* 7(2): 283–295.

Chapter 21

A hermeneutic approach to culture and psychotherapy

John Chambers Christopher and Adina J. Smith

Many critics have argued that psychology and the practice of psycho-therapy and counseling have failed to fully address the challenges of working with minority group members, immigrants, and those dwelling in non-Western societies. Concepts, interventions, and measures developed in Western cultures are regularly extended to persons in and from non-Western cultures and research findings are interpreted at face value often resulting in an *imposed etic* and a perpetuation of the socio-political status quo (Christopher, 1999; Pedersen, 1991; Prilleltensky, 1994; Sue and Sue, 1990). Kitayama and Markus (2000) note that, 'cultural influences may be quite pervasive, widespread, and powerful in forming the basis of "being" for ordinary people, and, yet, remain elusive for those researchers who have sought to understand them' (p. 123). Part of the difficulty is that the definitions of culture provided in much of the cross-cultural and multi-cultural literature are often brief and tend to lack substantive value (Cole, 1996; Jahoda, 2000; Ratner, 2000). As Maruyama (1992) contends, psy-chology has not generated the cognitive structures that would allow us to think contextually when we encounter diversity. In addition to needing a comprehensive understanding of the nature of culture and its relationship to the self, psychotherapists must be able to think culturally. Seeley (2000), following Devereaux (1958), maintains that, 'Rather than learning about the stereotypical characteristics of particular cultures, psychotherapists need to become familiar with the general characteristics, categories, and functions of culture per se' (p. 72). Instead of this occurring, Sampson (1993) trenchantly argues that psychology has hastily responded to diversity with what he calls add-on eclectic strategies. Thus, in order to fully address how culture affects psychotherapy, we are faced with two challenges: the first, to define culture in a way that highlights its power and pervasiveness; and the second, to learn to think culturally.

Philosophical hermeneutics provides a nondualistic model of culture and the self. It is also a method for thinking interpretively about cultural meanings and discerning their specific manifestations. Hermeneutics is a framework for thinking about the ways culture permeates every dimension of our clients' world. As a metatheory for psychology, hermeneutics can also deepen our understanding of how we are thoroughly shaped by culture and how much of psychological theory, research, and practice is influenced by individualism, our dominant cultural outlook.

The term hermeneutics derives from the Greek word for interpretation and is related to Hermes, god of communication, who ferried messages between the gods and humans. During the Protestant Reformation, hermeneutics was the theory and method of interpretation and emerged as a means of interpreting the Bible. At the turn of the eighteenth century, Schleiermacher ushered in the contemporary understanding of hermeneutics, when he established a general interpretive methodology for uncovering the original intent of all forms of human communication, not just written texts like the Bible or legal statures (Palmer, 1969; Richardson, Fowers, and Guignon, 1999). This version of hermeneutics currently influences qualitative research methods (Ratner, 1997; Rennie, 1999; Tappan, 1997), theories of epistemology and clinical interpretation in psychodynamic therapies (Barclay, 1992; Gentile, 1998; Spence, 1993), and narrative approaches to psychotherapy (Frank, 1987; Gergen and McNamee, 2000; McNamee, 1996; Schafer, 1993). The most recent turn in hermeneutic thought, *philosophical* or *ontological hermeneutics*, was instigated by Martin Heidegger's work in the 1920s. Philosophical hermeneutics goes beyond methodology to consider the broader ontological questions about human nature that arise when we acknowledge that interpretation is central to human existence. This iteration of hermeneutic thought is highly influential in contemporary philosophy and social theory but is largely unknown within psychology except for a few notable exceptions (Messer, Sass, and Woolfolk, 1988; Richardson *et al.*, 1999; Woolfolk, 1998). We attempt to redress this shortcoming in this chapter by outlining a hermeneutic model of the self and its relationship to culture. We will also consider how the hermeneutic notion of dialogue can provide a framework for engaging with those from different cultural backgrounds.

A HERMENEUTIC VIEW OF CULTURE: WEBS OF SIGNIFICANCE

Geertz (1973) distinguishes, for the sake of analysis, two different but interdependent aspects of culture: world view and ethos. The world view or *weltanschauung* is the more cognitive aspect of culture that describes and defines reality. World views tell us what reality consists of, what it is composed of, how it works. Our world view provides our understanding of causation: why things interact or operate as they do. It establishes forces, entities, objects, levels of existence, and so on. Ethos, in contrast, is the affective, aesthetic and moral component of human existence. As Geertz puts it, 'A people's ethos is the tone, character and quality of their life, its moral and aesthetic style and mood; it is the underlying attitude towards themselves and their world that life reflects' (1973, p. 127).

A central aspect of every culture are the presuppositions pertaining to the nature of human beings. A culture's world view establishes what a person *is*. The world view determines what constitutes a person, what a person's capabilities, resources, characteristics and faculties are. It also defines where the boundaries of the person are. Ethos, in contrast, delineates norms, standards or parameters for desirable ways of functioning and interacting. Ethos guides the assumptions about how a person *ought* to behave, interact, think, and feel. Ethos shapes our presuppositions of how a person should grow, develop, mature. It is ethos that suggests or, at times, dictates what we should do with our capacities and faculties. Together, the world view lays out the nature of the person that will develop while ethos guides the direction that development should take.

The aspect of culture that addresses the nature of the person and psychological issues can be referred to as *folk* or *indigenous psychology* (Bruner, 1990; Heelas and Lock, 1981). Folk psychologies account for such things as motivation, emotion, psychopathology, and the self. Folk psychologies are sometimes explicit and well-developed as with the various Buddhist or Hindu theories about the self. But whether or not they have been explicitly developed, they necessarily exist at a preconscious and implicit level where they inform our moment-to-moment reactions to others and ourselves. We could not function without them. Folk psychologies draw upon both the culture's world view and its ethos.

World view, ethos, and culture more generally, function in Geertz's (1973) view as 'webs of significance' that permeate our social functioning and give meaning and coherence to our daily lives. Culture provides meaning and structure that are not innately available given the almost limitless possibilities afforded by the openness or what Berger and Luckmann (1966) termed the plasticity of our nature. Without the constraints the culture provides, we would live in William James's proverbial 'bloomin', buzzin', confusion'. Cultures are thus collective achievements that orient us to life by establishing a common background framework of understanding between people that enables the social and even the physical world to make sense (Berger and Luckmann, 1966; Geertz, 1973; 1983). Each culture affords some understanding of human nature and what it means to be human. Geertz (1973) sees culture as a universal requirement of living; in his words, we have a 'pervasive orientational necessity' that culture satisfies (p. 363).

To clarify what Geertz means by 'significance' we have found it helpful to consider how Heidegger (1962) uses the word *signification*. According to Heidegger, the most fundamental aspects of our agency, what he called being-in-the-world, are characterized by care, concern, and signification. In other words thoughts, feelings and actions are infused with deep assumptions concerning what is real, important, and valuable. The word care here goes far beyond a sympathetic emotional response. Instead, care refers to what we value, what we attend to in life, what we give our time and energy to, and the aspects of reality that we focus upon. The value and worth of things, from this perspective, are defined by what we actually do, how we spend our time. Culture, then, can be thought of not only as webs of significance but also as webs of care. The particular way in which any culture does express itself, the way we have collectively fashioned and constructed reality, reveals what we care about. Our behavior reflects our values, or better yet, *is* embodied values.

ONTOLOGICAL INDIVIDUALISM: AN IMPEDIMENT TO RECOGNIZING CULTURE'S INFLUENCE

While the dominant cultural outlook in the West is individualism, anthropologists have explored how individualism may be a 'peculiar idea' (Geertz, 1973) within human history. Cross-cultural psychologist Harry Triandis (1989) estimates that individualism is the cultural outlook for only 30 per cent of the world's population. Ontological individualism casts the individual and culture as distinct and separable from each other, making it particularly difficult for us to grasp how we are shaped by culture. In ontological individualism the person is regarded in atomistic terms that render the person metaphysically separate from others, society, and nature (Bellah, Madsen, Sullivan, Swidler, and Tipton, 1985; Dumont, 1986; Gadamer, 1975). Richardson *et al.* (1999) describe this further, 'We tacitly view human beings atomistically as discrete centers of experience and action concatenated in various ways into social groups, struggling to reduce inevitable conflicts with others through negotiations and temporary alliances' (p. 71). Such a self should ideally be 'self-defining' (Taylor, 1975), refusing to rely upon the beliefs, values, and outlooks of others but seizing responsibility for coming to one's own identity. This self is well positioned to freely and rationally treat both itself and the outside world instrumentally, to alter them in desired ways, or, in later permutations of the modern self, to resist social pressure to conform and pursue self-actualization or personal authenticity as it sees fit. Culture, then, can become seen as a potential external threat that can somehow diminish the individual's autonomy or authenticity.

Geertz (1973) offers a powerful example of this underlying individualistic influence when he identifies the 'stratigraphic' concepts of the human being that dominate the social sciences. Like Bronfenbrenner's (1977) ecological model of the person, stratigraphic approaches portray the human being as a set of onion-like concentric circles, each layer of which is complete and irreducible in itself. The innermost circle is biological, which is encircled successively by the psychological, social, and cultural domains. As Geertz puts it:

> Strip off the motley forms of culture and one finds the structural and functional regularities of social organization. Peel these off in turn and one finds the underlying psychological factors – 'basic needs' or what-have-you – that support and make them possible. Peel off psychological factors and one is left with biological foundations – anatomical, physiological, neurological – of the whole edifice of human life.
>
> (p. 37)

The implication is that the psychologist can focus exclusively on the psychological 'circle', leaving the levels of social and cultural organization to sociologists and anthropologists. While these stratigraphic approaches do provide accounts in which culture is addressed, the downside is that culture can become mere extraneous context. Models and theories that take this approach potentially adopt and reinforce the supposition that the individual is ontologically prior to the social; that it somehow makes sense to think of the individual as a biological entity existing independently of society and culture. Geertz (1973) challenges the notion that it is possible to understand the human being stripped of 'the trappings of culture'. In his view, culture permeates human existence so thoroughly that the attempt to separate individuals and culture is incoherent and distorts our understanding of human nature.

A HERMENEUTIC VIEW OF THE PERSON: BEING-IN-THE-WORLD

In the hermeneutic view, individualism is not just one cultural self-interpretation, it is an interpretation that is in error. Heidegger (1962) takes issue with the common notion of ourselves in Western cultures as separate, autonomous, self-motivated agents set over and against a world of discrete objects. He argues that this notion substitutes a derivative form of being that is a cultural achievement for our most basic or 'primordial' way of being. Heidegger described our most primordial self as engaged in the world doing something or 'being-in-the-world' (Heidegger, 1962; cf. Bickhard and Christopher, 1994). In contrast with Descartes, Heidegger (1962) does believe we are most fundamentally, or most of the time, the type of 'I' presupposed in Descartes' *cogito*.

We tend to identify with the 'I', the reflective, conscious, thinking part of us. However, according to hermeneutic thinkers, we are, to use Bruner's (1990) phrase, 'expressions of culture' long before we develop a sense of ourselves as an 'I'. As children we learn patterns of interacting with others and we participate in social practices and institutions. In Heidegger's language we are 'thrown' into cultural practices – actions and behaviors whose significance has largely already been provided by culture. We are born into a social drama whose cadences and rhythms were wholly formed before we arrived, and which shapes and defines us before we are able to recognize ourselves as individuals. In Heidegger's words, 'the Self of everydayness is the "they". The "they" is constituted by the way things have been publicly interpreted' (Heidegger, 1962, p. 296). Through our participation in these social patterns we perpetuate, and at the same time, reinterpret them.

Being-in-the-world is prior to the creation of sharp subject–object boundaries. Heidegger (1962) draws this out through his example of the workshop. Objects in our world are not primarily a collection of *things* that we are set over and against, but more fundamentally, in phenomenological terms, they are extensions of ourselves.

Within our Western world view we tend to think of values and meanings as subjective possessions which we take up and leave behind as they suit us. The ontological assumption is that as beings we are first and foremost physical objects and agents in the world. Culture and values are overlaid onto this presumably more fundamental notion of agency. However, according to Heidegger, 'we do not, so to speak, throw a "signification" over some naked thing which is present-at-hand, we do not stick a value on it' (Heidegger, 1962, p. 190). Heidegger challenges this fact/value split by effectively arguing that the creation of a world that has facts set over and against values actually presupposes a certain notion of the self. Moreover, he argues that this very self that the fact/value dichotomy relies upon can not be ontologically our most fundamental way of being in the world. Instead, for Heidegger we are 'proximally and for the most part' beings that participate in social practices that presuppose particular meanings and values that precede us (Heidegger, 1962, p. 37).

The pervasiveness of culture, indeed its necessity, means that our lives are informed by some set of cultural assumptions about what it means to be a person, and what kind of person it is good to be or become. Heidegger (1962) sees these assumptions as central to the human condition for as he puts it, 'in its very Being, that Being is an *issue* for it' (p. 32).

With cognitive maturation, we can, through the process of reflective abstraction (Bickhard and Christopher, 1994), become conscious of portions of the cultural patterns in which we participate. While we can develop partial, provisional perspectives that allow us to reflect on our culture, we unavoidably take on the meanings implicit in these practices prior to awareness. We are partly constituted by our cultures, which means that it is not possible to fully detach ourselves. Any distance that we get from our culture is always temporary and provisional (Gadamer, 1975). One consequence is that we can best know ourselves 'not by inward-turning and introspection' in the manner of Descartes, 'but by catching sight of ourselves as we are engaged and preoccupied in everyday contexts' (Guignon, 1984, p. 232). Although each individual has a somewhat unique life history and a particular perspective within the culture, nevertheless, the individual's life history unfolds within the possibilities set forth by the shared background meanings that cultures provide. As a result, our own individual uniqueness, according to Taylor (1989), consists largely of variations on important cultural themes and aspirations. And, the very wish to really separate oneself from one's culture is a uniquely modern, individualistic phenomenon.

MULTICULTURALISM AND INTERCULTURAL CONTACT

Cross-cultural interactions entail the intersection of multiple cultures. First, there is the culture of therapy. Every aspect of the therapy process including assessment, diagnosis, treatment goals and objectives, and interventions are influenced by culture. All these aspects of counseling and psychotherapy, in addition to concepts of mental illness and psychological well-being, theories of personality, and both normal and abnormal development, rely on presuppositions about the nature of what the person is and what the good or ideal person should be (Christopher, 1996, 1999, 2001). The situation becomes more complicated when we realize that the values and assumptions underlying professional theory and practice are situated within and exist alongside the cultural values and assumptions manifested in different parts of society. The culture of therapy is influenced by Western culture but is not synonymous with it. It is informed by what Taylor (1989) terms the *moral sources* of Western culture. But psychology reinterprets these moral sources and these reinterpretations in turn influence Western folk psychology. The psychoanalytic notion of defense, for example (which originally had roots in Judeo-Christian beliefs), is now part of American culture. There is thus a dialectical relationship between professional psychology and folk psychology, and there is a dialectical relationship for therapists between their professional theoretical commitments and their cultural orientation as shaped by their own family and socio-economic group. In a sense, all counseling, even when the counselor and client are of the same ethnicity or share other variables of diversity, is cross-cultural. Throw in a client from a widely different culture and it's a real mess. But however messy this situation is, it is inescapable.

Some examples of the complexity of the issues are provided by several Japanese graduate students who completed training in the United States. When we interviewed these students about their training experiences they independently raised questions about cross-cultural applicability of Murray

Bowen's notion of differentiation, which plays an influential role in marriage and family therapy. Bowen defines *differentiation of self* as 'the difference between people in the proportion of life energy prone to be invested and bound in relationships' (Kerr and Bowen, 1988, p. 68). Level of differentiation is passed down through family generations although the degree of emotional separation achieved may vary slightly in family members. A lower level of differentiation indicates that more energy is bound in a relationship such that togetherness needs are stronger and individuality is not as well-developed. In a relationship where two people are not well differentiated, more reactivity, emotionality and anxiety will be present. When a person is more highly differentiated, more of her energy is directed toward her own functioning.

Trying to achieve a higher level of differentiation or more solid (basic) self means increasing one's capacity for emotional detachment or neutrality. More detachment or neutrality depends on changes in thinking. Such changes are reflected in the ability to be in emotional contact with a difficult, emotionally charged problem and not feel compelled to preach about what others 'should' do, not rush in to 'fix' the problem, and not pretend to be detached by emotionally insulating oneself. Improving one's ability to contain these emotionally driven urges is contingent on developing a way of thinking that can counterbalance them (p. 108).

Differentiation is a compelling concept for many therapists. However, it appears to draw upon an individualistic moral vision that possibly limits its potential universal applicability. The Japanese students struggled with the notion of differentiation on a number of levels. One of them, Yoko, stated:

> Originally I was confused about the concept. How can I assert who I am without offending anybody? Is that being selfish almost if I have high sense of differentiation, and say this is what I need, this is what I want you to do, this is my boundaries.

This confusion had a number of important implications for our students. Perhaps most significantly, it raised deep questions for the students about how to live their own lives. Yoko continued:

> I still struggle with being differentiated, like pursuing my own dream and addressing my own needs. I want to stay in the US and pursue counseling but what about my parents? I'm sure my mom will get disappointed if I tell her I chose to stay in this country. But is it selfish to stay in the US? I feel guilty . . . How much is selfish? How much is respecting myself? It's confusing to me. It feels not right for me to just say 'this is my life'.

The perspective Yoko expresses draws attention to a different way of thinking about the person. For this Japanese student the dualistic Western manner of dividing up psychological reality into subjects or objects, self and other, does not capture her folk psychology. She is literally pointing to a different conception of the self. Markus and Kitayama (1991) have called this the *interdependent* construal of the self which they define as 'seeing oneself as part of an encompassing social relationship and recognizing that one's behavior is determined, contingent on, and to a large extent organized by what the actor perceives to be the thoughts, feelings and actions of *others* in the relationship' (p. 227). As an example of an interdependent sense of self, Fajans (1985), in her fieldwork with the Baining in New Guinea, writes, 'the social actor is not a rigidly defined and delimited entity' for 'the boundaries of the individual and the definition of the person are neither permanent nor immutable, but alter and adapt in specific contexts' (p. 381). As Yoko describes it:

> In this country, you have your needs, your dependence, your freedom, and others. Those two components, making me. In Japan there is a middle, a third part. My needs, and others' needs, like my family's needs, and this middle part is like combined. Something like I cannot neglect.

This interdependent sense of self stands in contrast to *independent* construals of the self that are marked by relatively sharper contrasts between self and other. These different notions of what the self is inform any understanding of the demand that different needs have upon oneself. Indeed, in this case they shape the very understanding of whether the needs are mine or another's.

For Yoko, these needs in the middle or third part do not fit neatly into a dualistic framework of 'my' needs or 'their' needs. Failing to recognize this and the legitimacy of the middle, a Western counselor could easily pathologize Yoko's experience and disregard the serious claim that the middle has on her.

One of the implications of different senses of the self is the way they frame our understandings of emotions, as well as how emotions are experienced and expressed. A hub around which the practice of therapy revolves is the stance we should adopt towards our emotional life. In Western cultures, as Taylor (1989) and Foucault (see Dreyfus and Rabinow, 1983) point out, the person is understood to be a being with interiority and depth. Western folk psychologies treat emotions as private and personal things that come from within, often deep within. Americans commonly discuss 'having' emotions, being the owner or possessor of them (cf. MacPherson, 1962). In contrast, much of emotional life in collectivist cultures focuses on other people. People in collectivist cultures are more likely to use external cues (such as the social setting) to interpret their emotional experience, rather than looking within as Westerners do. The focus of emotions is often interpersonal or intersubjective – people share in or participate in emotions, rather than 'having' them in an individualistic sense (Heine, Lehman, Markus, and Kitayama, 1999; Kitayama, Markus, and Kurokawa, 2000). As Mesquita (2001) describes, 'Emotions in collectivist cultures are expected to stress and reproduce the self in relation to others or the self in relation to the world, whereas emotions in individualist cultures are assumed to underline and amplify a bounded, subjective self' (p. 68).

Yoko mentioned struggling with guilt around her desire to be more independent. In Japan she would use the word 'zai-aku-kan' which roughly translates as 'sin', 'bad', and 'feeling'.

> It is a negative emotion. If I did not feel zai-aku-kan for leaving my family to live my own life, it would mean almost as if I did not care about my family at all. Considering all of the things they have done for me (it's called 'onn'), if I did not feel zai-aku-kan for excluding them from making decisions about the course of my life, it could mean I am selfish and I do not value a family bond. . . . If I feel zai-aku-kan, they will know immediately that I care about them, that I'm not being selfish. That they're included in my decision, so I'm connected with them.

Zai-aku-kan seems to carry a different connotation than guilt – it has more an interpersonal quality and function. It seems likely to us that most Western therapists would see her guilt as something negative to be overcome. From a Japanese perspective, however, Yoko's guilt would be appropriate. It is a testament to the fact that her sense of self is interdependent, intertwined with the hopes, aspirations, and desires of her family members. To not feel this sort of guilt would be seen as pathological – a kind of detached and disconnected attitude that would make her almost inhuman. Thus, feeling zai-aku-kan is a sign of virtue, a marker of the good person. From Yoko's standpoint, the worst possible situation would be to make a decision that goes against her family's wishes and then to not feel zai-aku-kan. A therapist working with her, or with clients with similar issues, who attempted to reduce the guilt or help her to differentiate from her family would be failing in an important way to understand her very sense of self. For Japanese clients, working toward integration and connectedness with their relationships and larger social system would be more congruent with their cultural values (Tamura and Lau, 1992).

DIALOGUE

Gadamer's (1975) notion of hermeneutic dialogue provides a framework for thinking about what occurs when cultures clash. Dialogue for Gadamer is the genuine attempt to understand and appreciate another cultural group based on what he termed *a fusion of horizons*. The metaphor of a horizon is used by Gadamer to stress the inherent limitations of human under-standing. Because human knowledge is always interpretive and based on prejudgments or prejudices, it is also always perspectival, partial, and fallible, embedded within a historical community. Our understanding always occurs within a particular horizon. However, this horizon is never fixed. It is continually being formed in our ongoing interaction with our traditions as well as those of others.

The fusion of horizons that Gadamer advocates is not simply a well-intentioned effort to understand the other. It requires the development of a common framework of understanding of the situation in question. To achieve this shared outlook requires us to take the other's perspective seriously and grant it provisional authority to challenge our own views. Often this can be psychologically demanding as it requires us to temporarily bracket our former understanding of what life consists in and what is worth pursuing. However, dialogue does not mean that we need to embrace relativism. Instead, as Taylor (1992) observes, we necessarily come to a transformed set of standards 'that we could not possibly have had at the beginning. We have reached this judgment partly through transforming our standards' (p. 67).

The resolution of these cultural differences and the personal conflicts they engender will clearly not be an easy or straightforward process. However, we believe that recognizing the complexity of what is involved might help to provide some relief for those who are confronting different degrees of acculturative stress or culture shock. To realize that cultural differences often entail very different assumptions about the nature of the self as well as about the nature of the good person and good life can help to normalize the emotional stress that often arises. Through our sensitivity to these issues as therapists and supervisors we might be able to help normalize what can be a traumatizing transition by helping to engender a more compassionate outlook. In effect, we can model to clients and supervisees an attitude of 'Well, who wouldn't feel x when your whole sense of self is at stake'. In our opinion pursuing counseling training in a different culture is one of the most personally challenging tasks conceivable. Not only is learning the subtleties of a second language critical, but trainees must also come face to face with the different moral visions implicit within the culture of counseling. Our Japanese students have attested to how difficult this can be.

Some of the resolution of the issues our students brought to light may occur through a process of renegotiating the meaning of critical terms used in personal evaluation such as selfishness and respect. For Yoko, coming to a working definition of selfishness and respect will be a critical but con-ceivably life-long process. Recognizing it as such and imbuing it with moral meaning instead of just experiencing her struggle as a personal shortcoming may be an essential aspect of finding inner peace. In other words, we are all living in a time of cultural change. Moral visions are being contested in every quarter. For those who are living bi-culturally these contested moral visions are ever salient and they are inescapable. Helping people to realize that this is a concomitant part of globalization and intercultural contact can help to relieve the unnecessary suffering that can come from personalizing these issues.

Yoko described being trapped by her situation, having 'no answer to it'. To some degree American culture and the therapies that uncritically build upon it may lack the resources to help Yoko cope with a situation that does not have readily apparent solutions. The emancipatory thrust of the American ethos emphasizes the elimination of suffering and even freedom from unhappiness, as is promised in much of the popular psychology literature. Some critics have referred to how this cultural outlook can result in a kind of tyranny of happiness (Held, 2002; 2004). Such a one-sided emphasis on emotional satisfaction and happiness tends to neglect, as Frank (1973) thoughtfully commented, other, more traditional, possibly worthwhile values or virtues such as 'the redemptive power of suffering, acceptance of one's lot in life, adherence to tradition, self-restraint and moderation' (p. 7).

In Japan, Yoko described being socialized to tolerate difficult situations, situations where people might feel trapped. Instead of emphasizing liberation from pain and suffering, Japanese culture regards the ability to 'hold the struggle' as a sign of maturity (see also the distinction by Weisz, Rothbaum and Blackburn (1984) between primary and secondary control). In this sense 'bad' feelings aren't bad – they are a part of life. It is learning to live with bad feelings, unmet needs, unwanted constraints, and so on but to do so with poise and dignity that sets off the virtuous or mature person. Yoko poignantly captured the point when she said that in Japan, 'childhood ends early'.

CONCLUSION

In the hermeneutic perspective on culture, moral visions are essential to and inescapable in human living. Hermeneutics emphasizes that individuals are far more thoroughly embedded in and shaped by culture than is ordinarily recognized. If we are not aware that our perspective is limited by the horizon of our own moral visions, the other's outlook and behavior can appear pathological, mistaken, distorted, or even evil to us. It is only through the willingness to have our own cultural 'givens' questioned through dialogue that cultural differences can be bridged and we can avoid being 'culturally encapsulated' (Pedersen, 1991).

Cross-cultural contact offers us one of the best and most profound opportunities to reflect on what we take for granted. Intercultural dialogue will not result in wholesale changes or accommodations in either cultural viewpoint. One's way of life is prior to self-consciousness and it is not easy to alter cherished beliefs and deeply ingrained social practices. However, the mutuality of genuine dialogue can allow an authentic interplay of cultural values that allows participants to reflect on, affirm, and at times, revise their understanding of who and what we are and how we should live. There is great potential for personal and cultural advancement in such endeavors, but we can only find out how much there is to gain by putting our values and assumptions at risk in the play of ideas.

References

Barclay, M. W. (1992) The Utility of Hermeneutic Interpretation in Psychotherapy, *Theoretical & Philosophical Psychology* 12: 103–118.

Bellah, R. N., Madsen, R., Sullivan, W. M., Swidler, A. and Tipton, S. M. (1985) *Habits of the Heart: Individualism and Commitment in American Life*. New York: Harper & Row.

Berger, P. L. and Luckmann, T. (1966) *The Social Construction of Reality*. Garden City, New York: Anchor Books.

Bickhard, M. H. (1994) Rock, Frogs, and the Cartesian Gulf: Toward a Naturalism of Persons, *New Ideas in Psychology* 12: 267–276.

Bickhard, M. H. and Christopher, J. C. (1994) The Influence of Early Experience on Personality Development, *New Ideas in Psychology* 12: 229–252.

Bronfenbrenner, U. (1977) Toward an Experimental Ecology of Human Development, *American Psychologist* 32: 513–531.

Bruner, J. (1990) *Acts of Meaning*. Cambridge, MA: Harvard University Press.

Christopher, J. C. (1996) Counseling's Inescapable Moral Visions, *Journal of Counseling & Development* 75: 17–25.

Christopher, J. C. (1999) Situating Psychological Well-Being: Exploring the Cultural Roots of its Theory and Research, *Journal of Counseling & Development* 77: 141–152.

Christopher, J. C. (2001) Culture and Psychotherapy: Toward a Hermeneutic Approach, *Psychotherapy: Theory, Research, Practice, and Training* 38: 115–128.

Cole, M. (1996) *Cultural Psychology: A Once and Future Discipline*. Cambridge, MA: Harvard University Press.

Devereaux, G. (1958) Cultural Factors in Psychoanalytic Therapy, *Journal of the American Psychoanalytic Association* 1: 629–655.

Dreyfus, H. L. and Rabinow, P. (1983) *Michel Foucault: Beyond Structuralism and Hermeneutics*. Chicago: The University of Chicago Press.

Dumont, L. (1986) *Essays on Individualism: Modern Ideology in Anthropological Perspective*. Chicago: The University of Chicago Press.

Fajans, J. (1985) The Person in Social Context: The Social Character in Baining 'Psychology', in G. M. White, J. Kirkpatrick *et al.* (eds), *Person, Self, and Experience: Exploring Pacific Ethnopsychologies*. Berkeley: University of California Press, pp. 367–397.

Frank, J. D. (1973) *Persuasion and Healing: A Comparative Study of Psychotherapy*. New York: Schocken Books.

Frank, J. D. (1987) Psychotherapy, Rhetoric, and Hermeneutics: Implications for Practice and Research, *Psychotherapy* 24: 293–302.

Gadamer, H.-G. (1975) *Truth and Method*. New York: Crossroad.

Geertz, C. (1973) *The Interpretation of Cultures*. New York: Basic Books.

Geertz, C. (1983) *Local Knowledge: Further Essays in Interpretive Anthropology*. New York: Basic Books.

Gentile, J. (1998) Listening for Deep Structure: Between the A Priori and the Intersubjective, *Contemporary Psychoanalysis* 34: 67–89.

Gergen, K. J. and McNamee, S. (2000) From Disordering Discourse to Transformative Dialogue, in *Constructions of Disorder: Meaning-Making Frameworks for Psychotherapy*. Washington, DC: American Psychological Association, pp. 333–349.

Guignon, C. (1984) Moods in Heidegger's Being and Time, in C. Calhoun and R. C. Solomon (eds), *What is an Emotion?*. New York: Oxford University Press, pp. 230–243.

Heelas, P. and Lock, A. (1981) *Indigenous Psychologies: The Anthropology of the Self*. New York: Academic Press.

Heidegger, M. (1962) *Being and Time*, trans. J. Macquarrie and E. Robinson. New York: Harper & Row.

Heine, S. H., Lehman, D. R., Markus, H. R. and Kitayama, S. (1999) Is there a Universal Need for Positive Self-Regard?, *Psychological Review* 106: 766–794.

Held, B. S. (2002) The Tyranny of the Positive Attitude in America: Observation and Speculation, *Journal of Clinical Psychology* 58: 965–992.

Held, B. S. (2004) The Negative Side of Positive Psychology, *Journal of Humanistic Psychology* 44: 9–46.

Jahoda, G. (2000) *The Shifting Sands of Culture*. Paper presented at the XIV International Congress of the International Association for Cross-Cultural Psychology, Pultusk, Poland, July 2000.

Kerr, M. E. and Bowen, M. (1988) *Family Evaluation*. New York: W. W. Norton.

Kitayama, S. and Markus, H. R. (2000) The Pursuit of Happiness and the Realization of Sympathy: Cultural Patterns of Self, Social Relations, and Well-Being, in *Culture and Subjective Well-Being*. Cambridge, MA: MIT Press, pp. 113–161.

Kitayama, S., Markus, H. R. and Kurokawa, M. (2000) Culture, Emotion, and Well-Being: Good Feelings in Japan and the United States, *Cognition & Emotion* 14: 93–124.

McNamee, S. (1996) Psychotherapy as a Social Construction, in *Constructing Realities: Meaning-Making Perspectives for Psychotherapists*. San Francisco, CA: Jossey-Bass, pp. 115–137.

MacPherson, C. B. (1962) *The Political Theory of Possessive Individualism*. Oxford: Oxford University Press.

Markus, H. R. and Kitayama, S. (1991) Culture and the Self: Implications for Cognition, Emotion, and Motivation, *Psychological Review* 98: 224–253.

Maruyama, M. (1992) *Context and Complexity: Cultivating Contextual Understanding*. New York: Springer-Verlag.

Mesquita, B. (2001) Emotions in Collectivist and Individualist Contexts, *Journal of Personality & Social Psychology* 80: 68–74.

Messer, S. B., Sass, L. A. and Woolfolk, R. L. (1988) *Hermeneutics and Psychological Theory: Interpretive Perspectives on Personality, Psychotherapy, and Psychopathology*. New Brunswick, NJ: Rutgers University Press.

Palmer, R. E. (1969) *Hermeneutics*. Evanston, IL: Northwestern University Press.

Pedersen, P. B. (1991) Multiculturalism as a Generic Approach to Counseling, *Journal of Counseling & Development* 70: 6–12.

Prilleltensky, I. (1994) *The Morals and Politics of Psychology: Psychological Discourse and the Status Quo*. Albany, NY: State University of New York Press.

Ratner, C. (1997) *Cultural Psychology and Qualitative Methodology: Theoretical and Empirical Considerations*. New York, NY: Plenum Press.

Ratner, C. (2000) Outline of a Coherent, Comprehensive Concept of Culture: The Problem of Fragmentary Notions of Culture, *Cross-Cultural Psychology Bulletin* 34: 5–11.

Rennie, D. L. (1999) Qualitative Research: A Matter of Hermeneutics and the Sociology of Knowledge, in M. Kopala and L. A. Suzuki (eds), *Using Qualitative Methods in Psychology*. Thousand Oaks, CA: Sage Publications, pp. 3–13.

Richardson, F. C., Fowers, B. J. and Guignon, C. B. (1999) *Re-envisioning Psychology: Moral Dimensions of Theory and Practice*. San Francisco, CA: Jossey-Bass.

Sampson, E. E. (1993) Identity Politics: Challenges to Psychology's Understanding, *American Psychologist* 48: 1219–1230.

Schafer, R. (1993) Narration in the Psychoanalytic Dialogue, in E. Berman *et al.* (eds), *Essential Papers on Literature and Psychoanalysis*. New York, NY: New York University Press, pp. 341–368.

Seeley, K. M. (2000) *Cultural Psychotherapy*. Northvale, NJ: Jason Aronson.

Spence, D. P. (1993) The Hermeneutic Turn: Soft Science or Loyal Opposition? *Psychoanalytic Dialogues* 3: 1–10.

Sue, D. W. and Sue, D. (1990) *Counseling the Culturally Different: Theory and Practice*. New York: Wiley.

Tamura, T. and Lau, A. (1992) Connectedness versus Separateness: Applicability of Family Therapy to Japanese Families, *Family Process* 31: 319–340.

Tappan, M. B. (1997) Interpretive Psychology: Stories, Circles, and Understanding Lived Experience, *Journal of Social Issues* 53: 645–656.

Taylor, C. (1975) *Hegel*. New York: Cambridge University Press.

Taylor, C. (1989) *Sources of the Self: The Making of the Modern Identity*. Cambridge, MA: Harvard University Press.

Taylor, C. (1992) *The Ethics of Authenticity*. Cambridge, MA: Harvard University Press.

Triandis, H. C. (1989) The Self and Social Behavior in Differing Cultural Contexts, *Psychological Review* 96: 506–520.

Weisz, J. R., Rothbaum, F. M. and Blackburn, T. C. (1984) Standing Out and Standing In: The Psychology of Control in America and Japan, *American Psychologist* 39: 955–969.

Woolfolk, R. L. (1998) *The Cure of Souls: Science, Values, and Psychotherapy*. San Francisco, CA: Jossey-Bass.

Further reading

Campbell, R. L. and Bickhard, M. H. (1986) *Knowing Levels and Developmental Stages*. Basel: S. Karger.

Campbell, R. L. and Christopher, J. C. (1996) *Values and the Self: An Interactivist Foundation for Moral Development*. Paper presented at the Annual Convention of the Association for Moral Education, Ottawa, November 1996.

Postscript

This book has brought together twenty-four well-known international authors to write on issues such as racism in the clinical room, race and countertransference conflicts, spirituality and traditional healing issues, and issues of class, gender and sexual orientations. We were fortunate to be able to work with authors who demonstrated such an in-depth knowledge and understanding of the field. We hope you have enjoyed reading the book as much as we have enjoyed editing it. It has been a challenging, stimulating and rewarding experience.

Index